SALEM WITCH TRIALS

Reader

Also by Frances Hill

A Delusion of Satan: The Full Story of the Salem Witch Trials

Out of Bounds (novel)

A Fatal Delusion (novel)

The SALEM WITCH TRIALS *Reader*

BY FRANCES HILL

DA CAPO PRESS

Hill, Frances, 1943–
The Salem witch trials reader / by Frances Hill.
p. cm.
Includes bibliograpical references and index.
ISBN 0-306-80946-X
1. Witchcraft—Massachusetts—Salem—History—Sources. 2. Trials (Witchcraft)—Massachusetts—Salem. 3. Salem (Mass.)—History—Sources. I. Title.

BF1576.H55 2000
133.4'3'097445—dc21 00-043163

Text Design by Jeff Williams
Set in 10 point Minion by the Perseus Books Group

Published by DaCapo Press
A Member of the Perseus Books Group
http://www.perseusbooksgroup.com

The paper used in this publication meets the requirements of the American National Standard for Permanence of Paper for Printed Library Materials Z39.48-1984.

10 9 8 7 6 5 4 3 2 1

For Daniel Jenkins, with love

Contents

PART III
THE HUNTER AND THE HUNTED, 115

PART IV
THE HISTORIANS, 213

Part V
Fiction, 307

ACKNOWLEDGMENTS

I would like to thank the staff of the Peabody Essex Museum, Salem, Massachusetts, and especially the chief librarian, William la Moy, for all their help, even down to the thoughtful offer of a piece of string weighted at each end for holding open books while taking notes.

My thanks to Richard Trask, archivist at the Danvers Archival Center, Danvers, Massachusetts, for providing me with the photograph of the 1689 covenant of the Church of Christ at Salem Village.

My special gratitude goes to Alison d'Amario, inspired education director of the Salem Witch Museum, Salem, Massachusetts, who has been a rock of support.

My thanks as ever to Leon Arden for reading the manuscript and making many helpful suggestions.

Note: I have modernized the spelling and punctuation of the contemporary records to prevent any chance of confusion; however, I have been careful never to alter the meaning.

The Salem Witch-hunt Death Toll

Persons Hanged for Witchcraft During 1692

JUNE 10	BRIDGET BISHOP
JULY 19	SARAH GOOD
JULY 19	ELIZABETH HOWE
JULY 19	SUSANNAH MARTIN
JULY 19	REBECCA NURSE
JULY 19	SARAH WILDES
AUGUST 19	GEORGE BURROUGHS
AUGUST 19	MARTHA CARRIER
AUGUST 19	GEORGE JACOBS
AUGUST 19	JOHN PROCTOR
AUGUST 19	JOHN WILLARD
SEPTEMBER 19	GILES COREY (pressed to death)
SEPTEMBER 22	MARTHA COREY
SEPTEMBER 22	MARY EASTY
SEPTEMBER 22	ALICE PARKER
SEPTEMBER 22	MARY PARKER
SEPTEMBER 22	ANN PUDEATOR
SEPTEMBER 22	MARGARET SCOTT
SEPTEMBER 22	WILMOT REDD
SEPTEMBER 22	SAMUEL WARDWELL

Persons Accused of Witchcraft Who Died in Jail

MAY 10, 1692	SARAH OBSORNE
JUNE 16, 1692	ROGER TOOTHAKER
DECEMBER 3, 1692	ANN FOSTER
MARCH 10, 1693	LYDIA DUSTIN

An unnamed infant of Sarah Good died prior to July 19, 1692.

INTRODUCTION

The historical significance of the Salem witch trials cannot be overestimated. They were a turning point in the transition from Puritanism, with its values of community, simplicity, and piety, to the new Yankee world of individualism, urbanity, and freedom of conscience. Yet their significance transcends the purely historical. They provide an astonishingly clear and instructive model of the universal and timeless processes by which groups of human beings instigate, justify, and escalate persecution. Precisely because the numbers of people involved in the Salem witch-hunt, and the timescale of events, were on a small scale, the steps are easy to trace by which a few deranged, destructive human beings led ordinary mortals down the dark paths of fear, hatred, and envy to demonize and destroy innocent victims. When those steps are understood, the recurrent persecutions in human history, whether ethnic, religious, political, or superstitious, become less hard to comprehend.

The monster may be Hitler or Slobodan Milosevic. Or Senator Joe McCarthy. Or the mentally disturbed mother of a small child in a day care center in California in 1983. Or Samuel Parris in Salem Village in 1692. Whether operating nationwide or in a tiny community, the disturbed individual's extreme egomania and rage sow the seeds of persecution. These grow quickly in the fertile ground of anxiety and intolerance where particular groups, real or imagined, have already been scapegoated. The majority, who project their own envy, destructiveness, and illicit desires onto those scapegoats, are now encouraged to demonize them further. Soon Nazi party workers, or Serbian politicians and soldiers, or U.S. Senators, or Californian district attorneys and child abuse "experts," or seventeenth century Massachusetts ministers and magistrates, develop agendas that motivate them to push demonization to its ultimate limits. Careers are furthered and nests feathered. People with grievances, formerly powerless, are handed a weapon for settling old scores. As persecution mounts, it becomes risky to oppose it. Those with no other motive but to live quiet lives keep their doubts to themselves. Eventually the rule of law is suspended or perverted so that "just" means can be found to punish or destroy those perceived as the enemy.

The five persecutions I have cited differ vastly in the historical factors that allowed them to happen. The rise of Hitler would not have been possible without

became law

the legacy of Germany's defeat in the First World War. Milosevic's ethnic cleansing took place in the context of the centuries' old conflict in the Balkans. Joe McCarthy's campaign against Communists was created by the Cold War. The accusations of Satanic child sex abuse against seven innocent people in the McMartin case in California, and against other innocents in a rash of subsequent similar cases, emerged from the superstitions of born-again Christians linked with the genuine concerns of social workers about child sex-abuse.

In Salem, the witch-hunt took place against the background of a Puritan theocracy threatened by change, in a population terrified not only of eternal damnation but of the earthly dangers of Indian massacres, recurrent smallpox epidemics, and the loss of the charter from England. It was triggered by the hysteria of a small group of girls in a village rent by bitter local conflicts.

But the steps in all these witch-hunts were in essence the same. To study what happened at Salem is to gain a greater understanding of the human tendency to separate evil from good and project that evil into the enemy, and then to destroy it by destroying the enemy. It is also to gain a greater understanding of how people use persecution to promote their own interests and thereby further promote persecution. Only by the rule of law, proper judicial procedures, and strict rules governing admissible evidence can the dire results of these tendencies be checked.

Thankfully, there is a countertendency that shows itself in due course in all witch-hunts. It is the willingness to recognize human beings as sharing a common humanity and to fight bigotry and injustice even to the extent of endangering one's own life. That countertendency became abundantly evident at Salem, where nineteen people were hanged, and many others risked hanging, for refusing to lie.

The tendency for witch-hunts to start, and continue, is exacerbated by a society or group's insistence on its monopoly of righteousness. The countertendency is promoted by an understanding and acceptance of the fallibility of all human beings, including ourselves.

Part I of this book illustrates the historical background to the witch-hunt. Part II tells its story in the words of some of those who took part. Part III explores the roles of two key participants, Samuel Parris and George Burroughs. Part IV shows how the episode has been represented, and sometimes distorted, by historians, and part V shows how it has fired the imaginations of poets, playwrights, and novelists.

Chronology

1620
The Mayflower lands at Plymouth Rock and the "Pilgrims," Calvinists who have separated from the Church of England, found Plymouth Colony.

1626
Roger Conant establishes Salem as a fishing station and trading post.

1629
A group of Calvinist merchants, landed gentlemen and lawyers, who wish to reform the Anglican Church rather than separate from it, organize the Massachusetts Bay Company. They procure a royal charter that gives title to the lands of, and the right to govern, a region corresponding to most of present-day Massachusetts and New Hampshire.

1630
John Winthrop is elected the first governor and sails to Massachusetts with the vanguard of what is to the "Great Migration," comprising twenty thousand immigrants in twelve years.

1639
The Massachusetts governing body, the General Court, gives the town of Salem the legal right to settle its hinterland as far west as the Ipswich River. The area was at first known as "Salem Farms" and, later, Salem Village.

1672
The men of Salem Village are given permission by the General Court to elect a committee, lay plans for a meetinghouse, and hire a preacher. The Reverend James Bayley arrives in October.

1680
James Bayley leaves Salem Village after bitter disputes. The Reverend George Burroughs is appointed in his place.

1683
After further disputes, George Burroughs leaves for Casco, Maine. His salary has ceased being paid.

1684

The Reverend Deodat Lawson is appointed Salem Village minister. Further strife focuses on whether he should be ordained and form a Salem Village church.

1688

Deodat Lawson leaves Salem Village.

1689

Samuel Parris and family arrive in Salem Village.
November: Salem Village Church is formed and Parris ordained as its minister.

1692

January: Parris's daughter Betty and niece Abigail Williams begin acting strangely and babbling incoherently.

February: Parris's Caribbean Indian slaves, Tituba and John Indian, bake a "witch cake" with the girls' urine to feed to the dog. Other girls in the neighborhood, including Ann Putnam and Elizabeth Hubbard, join Betty Parris and Abigail Williams in having fits. They accuse Tituba, Sarah Good, and Sarah Osborne of bewitching them.

March 1–5: The three accused witches are examined in the Salem Village meetinghouse by magistrates John Hathorne and Jonathan Corwin. Tituba confesses to witchcraft. The three are sent to prison.

March 6–19: The girls accuse Martha Corey, a respectable church member, of bewitching them. It is probably now that Betty Parris is sent to stay with the Stephen Sewall family in Salem Town.

March 19: Deodat Lawson arrives in Salem Village on a visit, probably at the invitation of Thomas Putnam, Ann Putnam's father.

March 21: Martha Corey is examined and sent to prison.

March 21–23: Ann Putnam's mother, Ann, joins the afflicted girls in having fits. They accuse seventy-one-year-old Rebecca Nurse of bewitching them.

March 24: Rebecca Nurse and Sarah Good's four-and-a-half-year-old daughter Dorcas are examined and sent to prison.

April: The accusations, examinations, and imprisonments continue. By the end of the month twenty-three more suspected witches are in jail. These include John and Elizabeth Proctor, Bridget Bishop, Giles Corey, and Mary and Phillip English. Four out of the eleven legal complaints against the accused, leading to their arrests, have been made by Thomas Putnam.

May 4: George Burroughs is arrested and brought back to Salem from Maine, examined and imprisoned.

May 14: Sir William Phipps, the new governor of Massachusetts, and Increase Mather arrive from England with the new provincial charter. By the end of the month at least thirty-nine more people are in jail.

June 2: Sir William appoints a Court of Oyer and Terminer to try the accused witches, with William Stoughton, the deputy governor, as chief judge. Bridget Bishop is tried, convicted of witchcraft and sentenced to death.

June 10: Bridget Bishop is hanged on Gallows Hill. One of the judges, Nathaniel Saltonstall, resigns. Sir William Phipps consults the ministers of Boston, including Increase and Cotton Mather. They write the *Return of the Ministers Consulted,* which advises caution in the witchcraft proceedings but also "speed and vigour." Meanwhile, the arrests and examinations continue, now including accused in Andover, Ipswich, Gloucester, and other outlying areas rather than Salem itself.

June 29: Five more accused witches are tried: Sarah Good, Rebecca Nurse, Susannah Martin, Elizabeth Howe, and Sarah Wildes. Rebecca Nurse is acquitted but the judges ask the jury to reconsider and they find her guilty. Sir William Phipps reprieves her but later withdraws the reprieve. All five are sentenced to death.

July 19: Sarah Good, Rebecca Nurse, Susannah Martin, Elizabeth Howe, and Sarah Wildes are hanged on Gallows Hill.

August 5: George Burroughs, John and Elizabeth Proctor, John Willard, George Jacobs, and Martha Carrier are brought to trial.

August 14: By this time Nurse family members have ceased to take communion in Salem Village Church.

August 19: George Burroughs, John Proctor, John Willard, George Jacobs, and Martha Carrier are hanged. Elizabeth Proctor is spared because she is pregnant.

September 9: Six more are tried and sentenced to death: Martha Corey, Mary Easty, Alice Parker, Ann Pudeator, Dorcas Hoar, and Mary Bradbury.

September 17: Nine more are sentenced to death: Margaret Scott, Wilmot Redd, Samuel Wardwell, Mary Parker, Abigail Falkner, Rebecca Eames, Mary Lacy, Ann Foster, and Abigail Hobbs. The last five are spared, Abigail Falkner because of pregnancy, the others because they confess. Giles Corey refuses to stand trial.

September 19: Giles Corey is pressed to death.

September 22: Martha Corey, Mary Easty, Alice Parker, Mary Parker, Ann Pudeator, Margaret Scott, Wilmot Redd, and Samuel Wardwell are hanged. These are the last hangings.

October: The afflicted girls are sent for by Andover. As a result more than fifty people are accused and many confess. The girls are then sent for by Gloucester. Four women are imprisoned. But the backlash to the witch-hunt has started. The girls have overreached themselves by naming as witches several extremely prominent people, including Lady Phipps, the wife of the governor.

October 3: Increase Mather delivers a sermon (later published as an essay) called *Cases of Conscience Concerning Evil Spirits Personating Men,* which casts serious doubt on the validity of spectral evidence—the girls' visions—and says, "It were better that ten suspected witches should escape, than that one innocent person should be condemned."

October 8: Thomas Brattle, a merchant, mathematician, and astronomer, writes an eloquent letter criticizing the trials and convictions.

October 12: Sir William Phipps forbids further imprisonments for witchcraft.

October 26: The General Court votes for a day of fasting and a convocation of ministers to consider how to proceed "as to the witchcrafts."

October 29: Sir William Phipps formally dissolves the Court of Oyer and Terminer.

November: The afflicted girls are sent for again by Gloucester, but when they have fits are ignored and withdraw.

1693

January 3: A newly formed Superior Court, with William Stoughton as chief judge, sits in Salem to try accused witches. Only three are found guilty. Sir William Phipps reprieves them, along with five others previously sentenced.

January 31: The Superior Court sits at Charlestown. Stoughton learns of the reprieves and walks off the bench.

April 25: The Superior Court sits at Boston. None found guilty.

May: Sir William Phipps orders the release of all accused witches remaining in jail, on payment of their fees.

1697

Samuel Parris is ousted from Salem Village Church and leaves the village.

1706

Ann Putnam makes an apology in Salem Village Church for causing the deaths of innocent people and says it was due to a "great delusion of Satan."

Part I

THE BACKGROUND

The Salem witch-hunt was remarkable not for the numbers hanged and imprisoned but for happening when it did. Thousands had died at the stake or gallows in the European witch-frenzy that lasted from about 1500 to 1650, but, by 1692, the few remaining witch trials in Europe and New England involved only one or two victims and often led to acquittals. In Salem nineteen were hanged, one was pressed to death, and five died in jail, at a time when advances in science and the expansion of trade were undermining superstition everywhere.

The extracts in this section illuminate the background to the witch-hunt. Part I comprises witchcraft texts and Part II excerpts works illustrating the aspects of Puritan society that helped bring about the catastrophe that killed nearly thirty and devastated eastern Massachusetts.

1

WITCHCRAFT

The witch-hunt could never have happened if the supernatural beliefs the Puritans had brought with them from England, rooted in immemorial folklore but redefined and embellished in written works, had not retained their conviction and power right through the seventeenth century.

The first book on witchcraft ever published, *Malleus Maleficarum,* or *Witch Hammer,* written in Latin and printed in 1486, was the work of Dominican monks, with a preface by the Pope. It was hardly favorite Puritan reading, but it had served as a handbook for witch-hunters for 150 years and profoundly influenced attitudes to witchcraft among all denominations throughout Europe and Britain. Without it, the delusion that devil-worshiping witches existed and must be destroyed might not have been as widespread or disastrous.

A Discourse on the Damned Art of Witchcraft, by William Perkins, first published in 1608, was the most important of several English works widely read by New England ministers, if not ordinary people. But English pamphlets written between about 1570 and 1620 describing witchcraft cases, including the one printed below, were devoured by all classes. This is hardly surprising, since the Puritans were allowed no secular books, and these pamphlets make sensational reading.

Despite their popularity, they could not counteract the influence of science and trade as much as the rulers in Boston would have wished, Skepticism was spreading, as was dissatisfaction with the colony's rigid theocracy. In an attempt to halt the trend, Boston ministers took to writing up witchcraft cases themselves. In 1684 Increase Mather published his *Essay for the Recording of Illustrious Providences,* and five years later his son, Cotton Mather, published his *Late Memorable Providences.*

From: James Sprenger and Heinrich Kramer, *Malleus Maleficarum* (1486), translated by Montague Summers, 1928

This is one of the most terrifying and obnoxious books ever written, comparable to Adolf Hitler's *Mein Kampf* or the racist novel *The Turner Diaries.* Full of sexual terror and a merciless hatred of women, its crazed notions about witches and how they should be dealt with are expressed in the complacent style of ideologues who have no comprehension of their own secret motives. Alas, Pope Innocent VIII gave Sprenger and Kramer the chance to put their sick fantasies into practice when he appointed them inquisitors into heresy and witchcraft in North Germany in 1484. He gave his blessing to the *Malleus Maleficarum* in the form of a Papal Bull published as a preface.

The following two short excerpts give a taste of the authors' cruelty, sexual obsessions, and absence of ordinary understanding of human emotions and behavior.

From: part 2, question 1, chapter 7

How, as it were, they [witches] deprive man of his virile member.

In the town of Ratisbon, a certain young man who had an intrigue with a girl, wishing to leave her, lost his member, that is to say, some glamour was cast over it so that he could see or touch nothing but his smooth body. In his worry over this he went to a tavern to drink wine; and after he had sat there for a while he got into conversation with another woman who was there, and told her the cause of his sadness, explaining everything, and demonstrating in his body that it was so. The woman was astute, and asked whether he suspected anyone; and when he named such a one, unfolding the whole matter, she said; "If persuasion is not enough, you must use some violence, to induce her to restore to you your health." So in the evening he watched the way by which the witch was in the habit of going, and finding her, prayed her to restore to him the health of his body. And when she maintained that she was innocent and knew nothing about it, he fell upon her, and winding a towel tightly round her neck, choked her, saying; "Unless you give me back my health, you shall die at my hands." Then she, being unable to cry out, and with her face already swelling and growing black, said: "Let me go, and I will heal you." The young man then relaxed the pressure of the towel, and the witch touched him with her hand between the thighs, saying: "Now you have what you desire." And the young man, as he afterwards said, plainly felt, before he had verified it by looking or touching that his member had been restored to him by the mere touch of the witch.

From: Part 3, question 15

If he wishes to find out whether she [the witch] is endowed with a witch's power of preserving silence, let him take note whether she is able to shed tears when standing in his presence, or when being tortured. For we are taught both by the words of worthy men of old and by our own experience that this is a most certain sign, and it has been found that even if she be urged and exhorted by solemn conjurations to shed tears, if she be a witch she will not be able to weep; although she will assume a tearful aspect and smear her cheeks and eyes with spittle to make it appear that she is weeping; wherefore she must be closely watched by the attendants.

In passing sentence the judge or priest may use some such method as the following in conjuring her to true tears if she be innocent, or in restraining false tears. Let him place his hand on the head of the accused and say: I conjure you by the bitter tears shed on the cross by our Saviour the Lord Jesus Christ for the salvation of the world, and by the burning tears poured in the evening hour over his wounds by the most glorious Virgin Mary, His Mother, and by all the tears which have been shed here in this world by the saints and elect of God, from whose eyes he has now wiped away all tears, that if you be innocent you do now shed tears, but if you be guilty that you shall by no means do so. In the name of the Father, and of the Son, and of the Holy Ghost, Amen.

From: William Perkins, *A Discourse on the Damned Art of Witchcraft, So Far Forth as It Is Revealed in the Scriptures and Manifest by True Experience* (Cambridge, 1608)

This is an altogether more moderate work than the *Malleus Maleficarum*. In England torture was never systematically used to elicit confessions, as it was on the continent, though strong pressure might be applied by keeping prisoners in dreadful conditions, interrogating them repeatedly, and depriving them of sleep.

William Perkins, a Cambridge Puritan preacher, points out the unreliability of popular methods of deciding if a woman was a witch, such as by throwing her into water to see if she would drown. (If she did not drown, she was a witch; if she did drown, she was not. A sadly belated vindication, one might think.) Unlike later Puritan writers, such as Joseph Glanville in England and Increase and Cotton Mather in Massachusetts, Perkins viewed popular superstitions as undermining, rather than bolstering, true religious belief. As the second extract shows, he laid much emphasis on the best "proof" of witchcraft being the confession of the witch. The first extract reveals that Perkins had no doubt that witches were in league with the devil or should be punished by death.

From: chapter 5

What witches be, and of how many sorts.

A witch is a magician, who either by open or secret league, wittingly and willingly, contenteth to use the aid and assistance of the devil, in the working of wonders.

. . . the woman being the weaker sex, is sooner entangled by the devil's illusions with this damnable art, than the man. And in all ages it is found true by experience that the devil hath more easily and oftener prevailed with women, than with men. Hence it was, that the Hebrews of ancient times, used it for a proverb, *The more women, the more witches.* His first temptation in the beginning, was with Eve a woman, and since he pursueth his practice accordingly, as making most for his advantage. For where he findesth easiest entrance, and best entertainment, thither will he oftenest resort.

Secondly, to take away all exception of punishment from any party that shall practice this trade, and to show that weakness cannot exempt the witch from death. For in all reason, if any might allege infirmity, and plead for favour, it were the woman, who is weaker than the man. But the Lord saith, if any person of either sex among his people, be found to have entered covenant with Satan, and become a practiser of sorcery, though it be a woman and the weaker vessel, she shall not escape, she shall not be suffered to live, she must die the death. And though weakness in other cases, may lessen both the crime and the punishment, yet in this it shall take no place.

From: chapter 7

How we may be able in these days to discern and discover a witch.

Now follow the true proofs, and sufficient means of conviction, all which may be reduced to two heads.

The first, is the free and voluntary confession of the crime, made by the party suspected and accused after examination. This hath been thought generally of all men, both divines and lawyers, a proof sufficient. For what needs more witness, or further enquiry, when a man from the touch of his own conscience acknowledgeth the fault.

And yet the patrons and advocates of witches except against it, and object in the manner: That a man or woman may confess against themselves an untruth, being urged thereto either by fear or threatening, or by a desire, upon some grief conceived, to be out of the world; or at least, being in trouble, and persuaded it is the best course to save their lives, and obtain liberty, they may upon simplicity be induced to confess that, which they never did, even against themselves. *Answer:* I say not, that a bare confession is sufficient, but a confession after due examination taken upon pregnant presumptions. For if a man examined, without any ground of presumptions, should openly acknowledge the crime, his act may be justly suspected, as grounded upon by respects; but when proceeding is made against him at the first, upon good probabilities, and hereupon he be drawn to a free confession, that which he hath manifested thereby, cannot but be a truth. Other points of exception urged by them, are of final moment, and may easily be answered out of the grounds before delivered, and therefore I omit them.

Now if the party held in suspicion, be examined, and will not confess, but obstinately persist in denial, as commonly it falleth out; then there is another course to be taken by a second sufficient means of conviction: which is, the testimony of two witnesses, of good and honest report, avouching before the magistrate upon their own knowledge, these two things: Either that the party accused, hath made a league with the devil; or hath done some known practices of witchcraft. And all the arguments that do necessarily prove either of these, being brought by two sufficient witnesses, are of force fully to convice the party suspected. For example.

First, if they can prove that the party suspected, hath invocated and called upon the devil, or desired his help. For this is a branch of that worship, which Satan bindeth his instruments to give unto him, And it is a pregnant proof of a league formerly made between them.

Secondly, if they can give evidence, that the party hath entertained a familiar spirit, and had conference with it, in form or likeness of a mouse, cat or some other visible creature,

Thirdly, if they affirm upon oath, that the suspected person hath done any action or work, which necessarily inferreth a covenant made; as that he hath shewed the face of a man suspected, being absent, in a glass, or used enchantment, or such like feats. In a word, if they both can avouch upon their own proper knowledge, that such a man or woman suspected, have put in practice any other actions of witchcraft, as to have divined of things afore they came to pass, and that peremptorily; to have raised tempests, to have caused the form of a dead man to appear, or the like, standing either in divination or operation, it proveth sufficiently that he or she is a witch.

From: *The Wonderful Discovery of the Witchcrafts of Margaret and Phillip Flower, Daughters of Joan Flower near Beaver Castle: Executed at Lincoln, March 11, 1618* (London, 1619)

This anonymous pamphlet, after a verbose introduction on the wickedness of witches and the folly of doubting their power, proceeds with, "The story follows." Because of archaic terms and occasionally confusing sentence structure, the precise meaning is not always clear though the gist is never in doubt.

It became increasingly common, through the late sixteenth and early seventeenth centuries, for a witch's victims in English witchcraft cases to be children. This trend was to be followed in New England, as shall be seen.

After the Right Honourable Sir Francis Manners succeeded his brother in the earldom of Rutland, and so not only took possession of Beaver Castle, but of all other his demesnes, lordships, tonnes [taxes], manors, lands and revenues appropriate to the same earldom, he proceeded so honourably in the course of his life, as neither displacing tenants, discharging servants, denying the access of the poor, welcoming of strangers, and performing all the duties of a noble lord, that he fastened as it were unto himself the love and good opinion of the country wherein he walked the more cheerfully and remarkable, because his honourable countess marched arm in arm with him in the same race; so that Beaver Castle was a continual palace of entertainment, and a daily reception for all sorts both rich and poor, especially such ancient people as neighboured the same; amongst whom one Joan Flower, with her daughters Margaret and Phillip, were not only relieved [helped] at first from thence, but quickly entertained as chairwomen [regular diners], and Margaret admitted as a continual dweller in the castle, looking both to the poultry abroad and the wash-house within doors: In which life they continued with equal correspondency, till something was discovered [told] to the noble lady, which concerned the misdeamenour of these women. . . . First that Joan Flower the mother was a monstrous malicious woman, full of oaths, curses and imprecations irreligious, and for any thing they saw by her, a plain atheist; besides of late days her very countenance was estranged, her eyes were fiery and hollow, her speech fell and envious, her demeanour strange and exotic, and her conversation sequestered [secretive]; so that the whole course of her life gave great suspicion that she was a notorious witch, yea some of her neighbours dared to affirm that she dealt with familiar spirits, and terrified them all with curses and threatening of revenge, if there were never so little cause of displeasure and unkindness. Concerning Margaret, that she often resorted from the castle to her mother, bringing such provision as they thought was unbefitting for a servant to purloin, and coming at such unseasonable hours, that they could not but conjecture some mischief between them, and that their extraordinary riot and expenses tended both to rob the lady, and to maintain certain debauched and base company. . . . Concerning Phillip, that she was lewdly transported with the love of one Thomas Simpson, who presumed to say, that she had bewitched him; for he had no power to leave, and was as he supposed marvellously altered both in mind and body, since her acquainted company. . . . [The earl] discharged [Joan Flower] from lying any more in the castle, yet gave her forty shillings, a bolster and a mattress of wool; commanding her to go home, until the slackness of her repairing to the castle, as she was wont, did turn her love and liking toward this honourable earl and his family into hate and rancour: whereupon despighted [upset] to be so neglected, and exprobated [reproached] by her neighbours for her daughters' casting out of doors, and other conceived displeasures, she grew past all shame and womanhood, and many times cursed them all that were the cause of this discontentment, and her so loathsome to her former familiar friends and beneficial acquaintance.

When the devil perceived the inficious disposition of this wretch, and that she and her daughters might easily be made instruments to enlarge his kingdom, and be as it were the executioners of his vengeance; not caring whether it lighted upon innocents or no, he came more nearer unto them, and in plain terms to come quickly to the purpose, offered them his service, and that in such a manner, as they might command what they pleased: for he would attend you in such pretty forms of dog, cat or rat, that they should neither be terrified nor anybody else suspicious of the matter. Upon this they agree, and (as it should seem) give away their souls for the service of such spirits, as he had promised them; which filthy conditions were ratified with abominable kisses, and an odious sacrifice of blood, not leaving out certain charms and conjurations with which the devil deceived them, as though nothing could be done without ceremony, and a solemnity of orderly ratification. By this time doth Satan triumph, and goeth away satisfied to have caught such fish in the net of his illusions: By this time are those women devils incarnate, and grow proud again in their cunning and artificial power, to do what mischief they listed: by this time they have learned the manner of incantations, spells and charms: By this they will kill what cattle they list: and under the court of flattery and familiar entertainment, keep hidden the stinging serpent of malice, and a venemous inclination to mischief: by this time is the earl and his family threatened, and must feel the burden of a terrible tempest, which from these women's devilish devices fell upon him, he neither suspecting nor understanding the same: By this time both himself and honourable countess, are many times subject to sickness and extraordinary convulsions, which they taking as gentle corrections from the hand of God, submit with quietness to his mercy, and study nothing more, than to glorify their Creator in heaven, and bear his crosses on earth.

At last, as malice increased in these damnable women: so his family felt the smart of their revenge and inficious disposition, for his eldest son Henry Lord Rosse sickened very strangely, and after a while died: his next named Francis Lord Rosse accordingly, was severly tormented by them: and most barbarously and inhumanely tortured by a strange sickness: not long after the Lady Katherine was set upon by their dangerous and devilish practices, and many times in great danger of life, through extreme maladies and unusual fits, nay (as it should seem, and they afterwards confessed) both the earl and his countess were brought into their snares as they imagined, and indeed determined to keep them from having any more children. Oh unheard of wickedness and mischievous damnation! Notwithstanding all this did the noble earl attend his Majesty, both at Newmarket before Christmas, and at Christmas at Whitehall; bearing the loss of his children most nobly, and little suspecting they had miscarried by witchcraft, or such like intentions of the devil, until it pleased God to discover the villainous practices, of these women, and to command the devil from executing any further vengeance on innocents, but leave them to their shames, and the hands of justice, that they might only be confounded for their villainous practices, but remain as a notorious example to all ages of judgment and fury. Thus were they apprehended about Christmas and carried to Lincoln jail, after due examination, before sufficent justices of the peace, and discreet magistrates, who wondered at their audacious wickedness, but Joan Flower the mother before conviction, (as they say) called for bread and butter, and wished it might never go through if she were guilty of that, whereupon she was examined: so mumbling it in her mouth, never spake more words after, but fell down and died as she was carried to Lincoln jail, with a horrible excruciation of soul and body, and was buried at Ancaster.

When the earl heard of their apprehension he hastened down with his brother Sir George, and sometimes examining them himself, and sometimes sending them to others; at last left them to the trial at law, before the judges of Assize at Lincoln; and so they were convicted of murder and executed accordingly, about the 11 of March, to the terror of all beholders, and example of such dissolute and abominable creatures, and because you shall have both cause to glorify God for this discovery, and occasion to apprehend the strangeness of their lives, and truth of their proceedings: I thought it both meet and convenient to lay open their own examinations and evidences against one another, with such apparent circumstances, as do not only show the cause of their mislike and distasting against the earl and his family; but the manner of their proceedings and revenges, with other particulars belonging to the true and plain discovery of the villainy and witchcraft.

The pamphlet continues with accounts of the examinations of three other, unconnected witches, and then of Phillip and Margaret Flower. Phillip at first accused her sister and mother but pleaded her own innocence. Margaret confessed merely to fetching Henry Rosse's glove for her mother to aid in bewitching him. But in further examinations, presumably after pressure, both sisters confessed to keeping "familiar spirits." They were convicted and hanged.

From: Increase Mather, *An Essay for the Recording of Illustrious Providences* (popularly known as *Remarkable Providences*) (1684), chapter 5: "Preternatural Happenings in New England"

Increase Mather (1639–1723) was one of New England's leading politicians and ministers. He believed that the devastating King Philip's war with the Indians of 1675, and a series of smallpox epidemics, were God's punishments on Massachusetts for declining from the piety and high ideals of its founders. He convened a synod of the clergy in 1680 to affirm the ministers' commitment to those ideals, and four years later published his *Remarkable Providences* with the stated aim of bolstering belief in supernatural occurrences and the "invisible world." The events he describes would today be ascribed to fraud, self-delusion or telekinesis. Though no doubt harrowing for the sufferers, they at times make unintentionally hilarious reading.

Another thing which caused a noise in the country, and wherein Satan had undoubtedly a great influence, was that which happened at Groton. There was a maid in that town (one Elizabeth Knap) who in the month of October, Anno 1671, was taken after a very strange manner, sometimes weeping, sometimes laughing, sometimes roaring hideously, with violent motions and agitations of her body, crying out "money, money," etc. In November following, her tongue for many hours together was drawn like a semicircle up to the roof of her mouth, not to be removed, though some tried with their fingers to do it. Six men were scarce able to hold her in some of her fits, but she would skip about the house yelling and looking with a most frightful aspect. *December* 17. Her tongue was drawn out of her mouth to an extraordinary length; and now a demon began manifestly to speak in her. Many words were uttered wherein are the labial letters, without any motion of her lips, which was a clear demonstration that the voice was not her own. Sometimes words were spoken seeming to proceed out of her throat, when her mouth was shut. Sometimes with her mouth wide open, without the use of any of the organs of speech. The things then uttered by the devil were chiefly railings and revilings of Mr. Willard (who was at that time a worthy and faithful pastor to the church in Groton.) Also the demon belched forth most horrid and nefandous blasphemies, exalting himself above the most High. After this she was taken speechless for some time. One thing more is worthy of remark concerning this miserable creature. She cried out in some of her fits, that a woman, (one of her neighbours) appeared to her, and was the cause of her affliction. The person thus accused was a very sincere, holy woman, who did hereupon with the advice of friends visit the poor wretch; and though she was in one of her fits, having her eyes shut, when the innocent person impeached by her came in; yet could she (so powerful were Satan's operations upon her) declare who was there, and could tell the touch of that woman from any ones else. But the gracious party thus accused and abused by a malicious devil, prayed earnestly with and for the possessed creature; after which she confessed that Satan had deluded her, making her believe evil of her good neighbour without any cause. Nor did she after that complain of any apparition or disturbance from such an one. Yea, she said, that the devil had himself in the likeness and shape of divers tormented her, and then told her it was not he but they that did it.

As there have been several persons vexed with evil spirits, so divers houses have been woefully haunted by them. In the year 1679, the house of William Morse in Newberry in New England, was strangely disquieted by a demon. After those troubles began, he did by the advice of friends write down the particulars of those unusual accidents. And the account which he giveth thereof is as followeth;

On *December* 3, in the night time, he and his wife heard a noise upon the roof of their house, as if sticks and stones had been thrown against it with great violence; whereupon he rose out of his bed, but could see nothing. Locking the doors fast, he returned to bed again. About midnight they heard an hog making a great noise in the house, so that the man rose again, and found a great hog in the house, the door being shut, but upon the opening of the door it ran out.

On *December* 8, in the morning, there were five great stones and bricks by an invisible hand thrown in at the west end of the house while the man's wife was making the bed, the bedstead was lifted up from the floor, and the bedstaff flung out of the window, and a cat was hurled at her; a long staff danced up and down in the chimney; a burnt brick, and a piece of a weatherboard were thrown in at the window: The man at his going to bed put out his lamp, but in the morning found that the saveall of it was taken away, and yet it was unaccountably brought into its former place. On the same day, the long staff but now spoken of, was hanged up by a line, and swung to and fro, the man's wife laid it in the fire, but she could not hold it there, inasmuch as it would forcibly fly out; yet after much ado with joint strength they made it to burn. A shingle flew from the window, though no body near it, many sticks came in at the same place, only one of these was so scragged that it could enter the hole but a little way, whereupon the man pushed it out, a great rail likewise was thrust in at the window, so as to break the glass.

At another time an iron crook that was hanged on a nail violently flew up and down, also a chair flew about, and at last lighted on the table where victuals stood ready for them to eat, and was likely to spoil all, only by a nimble catching they saved some of their meal with the loss of the rest, and the overturning of their table.

People were sometimes barricaded out of doors, when as yet there was nobody to do it: and a chest was removed from place to place, no hand touching it. Their keys being tied together, one was taken from the rest, and the remaining two would fly about making a loud noise by knocking against each other. But the greatest part of this devil's feats were his mischievous ones, wherein indeed he was sometimes antic enough too, and therein the chief sufferers were, the man and his wife, and his grandson. The man especially had his share in these diabolical molestations. For one while they could not eat their suppers quietly, but had the ashes on the hearth before their eyes thrown into their victuals; yea, and upon their heads and clothes, insomuch that they were forced up into their chamber, and yet they had no rest there; for one of the man's shoes being left below, 'twas filled with ashes and coals, and thrown up after them. Their light was beaten out, and they being laid in their bed with their little boy between them, a great stone (from the floor of the loft) weighing above three pounds was thrown upon the man's stomach, and he turning it down upon the floor, it was once more thrown upon him. A box and a board were likewise thrown upon them all. And a bag of hops was taken out of their chest, wherewith they were beaten, till some of the hops were scattered on the floor, where the bag was then laid, and left.

In another evening, when they sat by the fire, the ashes were so whirled at them, that they could neither eat their meat, nor endure the house. A peel [fire shovel] struck the man in the face. An apron hanging by the fire was flung upon it, and singed before they could snatch it off. The man being at prayer with his family, a beesom [broom] gave him a blow on his head behind, and fell down before his face.

On another day, when they were winnowing of barley, some hard dirt was thrown in, hitting the man on the head, and both the man and his wife on the back; and when they had made themselves clean, they essayed to fill their half bushel but the foul corn was in spite of them often cast in amongst the clean, and the man being divers times thus abused was forced to give over what he was about.

On *January* 23 (in particular) the man had an iron pin twice thrown at him, and his inkhorn was taken away from him while he was writing, and when by all his seeking it he could not find it, at last he saw it drop out of the air, down by the fire: a piece of leather was twice thrown at him; and a shoe was laid upon his shoulder, which he catching at, was suddenly rapt from him. An handful of ashes was thrown at his face, and upon his clothes: and the shoe was then clapped upon his head, and upon it he clapped his hand, holding it so fast, that somewhat unseen pulled him with it backward on the floor.

On the next day at night, as they were going to bed, a lost ladder was thrown against the door, and their light put out; and when the man was abed, he was beaten with an heavy pair of leather breeches, and pulled by the hair of his head and beard, pinched and scratched, and his bed-board was taken away from him; yet more in the next night, when the man was likewise abed; his bed-board did rise out of its place, notwithstanding his putting forth all his strength to keep it in; one of his awls (sharp-pointed tools) was brought out of the next room into his bed, and did prick him; the clothes wherewith he hoped to save his head from blows were violently plucked from thence. Within a night or two after, the man and his wife received both of them a blow upon their heads, but it was so dark that they could not see the stone which gave it; the man had his cap pulled off from his head while he sat by the fire.

The night following, they went to bed undressed, because of their late disturbances, and the man, wife, boy, presently felt themselves pricked, and upon search found in the bed a bodkin, a knitting needle, and two sticks picked [pointed] at both ends. He received also a great blow, as on his thigh, so on his face, which fetched blood: and while he was writing a candlestick was twice thrown at him, and a great piece of bark fiercely smote him, and a pail of water turned up without hands. On the 28 of the mentioned month, frozen clods of cow-dung were divers times thrown at the man out of the house in which they were; his wife went to milk the cow, and received a blow on her head, and sitting down at her milking-work had cow-dung divers times thrown into her pail, the man tried to save the milk, by holding a piggin [pail] side-ways under the cow's belly, but the dung would in for all, and the milk was only made fit for hogs. On that night ashes were thrown into the porridge which they had made ready for their supper, so as that they could not eat it; ashes were likewise often thrown into the man's eyes, as he sat by the fire. And an iron hammer flying at him, gave him a great blow on his back; the man's wife going into the cellar for beer, a great iron peel [fire shovel] flew and fell after her through the trap-door of the cellar; and going after-wards on the same errand to the same place, the door shut down upon her, and the table came and lay upon the door, and the man was forced to remove it e're his wife could be released from where she was; on the following day while he was writing, a dish went out of its place, leapt into the pale, and cast water upon the man, his paper, his table, and disappointed his procedure in what he was about; his cap jumped off from his head, and on again, and the pot-lid leaped off from the pot into the kettle on the fire.

February 2. While he and his boy were eating of cheese, the pieces which he cut were wrested from them, but they were afterwards found upon the table under an apron, and a pair of breeches: And also from the fire arose little sticks and ashes, which flying upon the man and his boy, brought them into an uncomfortable pickle; but as for the boy, which the last passage spoke of, there remains much to be said concerning him, and a principal sufferer in these afflictions: For on the 18 of December, he sitting by his grandfather, was hurried into great motions and the man thereupon took him, and made him stand between his legs, but the chair danced up and down, and had like to have cast both man and boy into the fire: and the child was afterwards flung about in such a manner, as that they feared that his brains would have been beaten out; and in the evening he was tossed as afore, and the man tried the project of holding him, but ineffectually. The lad was soon put to bed, and they presently heard an huge noise, and demanded what was the matter? and he answered that his bed-stead leaped up and down: and they (*i.e.* the man and his wife) went up, and at first found all quiet, but before they had bean there long, they saw the board by his bed trembling by him, and the bed-clothes flying off him, the latter they laid on immediately, but they were no sooner on than off; so they took him out of his bed for quietness.

December 29. The boy was violently thrown to and fro, only they carried him to the house of a doctor in the town, and there he was free from disturbances, but returning home at night, his former trouble began, and the man taking him by the hand, they were both of them almost tripped into the fire. They put him to bed, and he was attended with the same iterated loss of his clothes, shaking off his bed-board, and noises, that he had in his last conflict; they took him up, designing to sit by the fire, but the doors clattered, and the chair was thrown at him, wherefore they carried him to the doctor's house, and so for that night all was well. The next morning he came home quiet, but as they were doing somewhat, he cried out that he was pricked on the back, they looked, and found a three-tined fork sticking strangely there; which being carried to the doctor's house, not only the doctor himself said that it was his, but also the doctor's servant affirmed it was seen at home after the boy was gone. The boy's vexations continuing, they left him at the doctor's, where he remained well till awhile after, and then he complained he was pricked, they looked and found an iron spindle sticking below his back; he complained he was pricked still, they looked, and found pins in a paper sticking to his skin; he once more complained of his back, they looked, and found there a long iron, a bowl of a spoon, and a piece of a pansheard. They lay down by him on the bed, with the light burning, but he was twice thrown from them, and the second time thrown quite under the bed; in the morning the bed was tossed about with such a creaking noise, as was heard to the neighbours; in the afternoon their knives were one after another brought, and put into his back, but pulled out by the spectators; only one knife which was missing seemed to the standers by to come out of his mouth: he was bidden to read his book, was taken and thrown about several times, at last hitting the boy's grandmother on the head. Another time he was thrust out of his chair and rolled up and down with outcries, that all things were on fire; yes, he was three times very dangerously thrown into the fire, and preserved by his friends with much ado. The boy also made for a long time together a noise like a dog, and like an hen with her chickens, and could not speak rationally.

Particularly, on *December* 26. He barked like a dog, and clucked like an hen, and after long distraining to speak, said, "There's Powell, I am pinched"; his tongue likewise hung out of his mouth, so as that it could by no means be forced in till his fit was over, and then he said 'twas forced out by Powell. He and the house also after this had rest till the ninth of January: at which time because of his intolerable ravings, and because the child lying between the man and his wife, was pulled out of bed, and knocked so vehemently against the bedstead boards, in a manner very perilous and amazing. In the daytime he was carried away beyond all possibility of their finding him. His grandmother at last saw him creeping on one side, and dragged him in, where he lay miserable lame, but recovering his speech, he said, that he was carried above the doctor's house, and that Powell carried him, and that the said Powell had him into the barn, throwing him against the cart-wheel there, and then thrusting him out at an hole; and accordingly they found some of the remainders of the threshed barley which was on the barn-floor hanging to his clothes.

At another time he fell into a swoon, they forced somewhat refreshing into his mouth, and it was turned out as fast as they put it in; e're long he came to himself, and expressed some willingness to eat, but the meat would forcibly fly out of his mouth; and when he was able to speak, he said Powell would not let him eat: Having found the boy to be best at a neighbour's house, the man carried him to his daughter's, three miles from his own. The boy was growing antic as he was on the journey, but before the end of it he made a grievous hollowing, and when he lighted, he threw a great stone at a maid in the house, and fell on eating of ashes. Being at home afterwards, they had rest awhile, but on the 19 of January in the morning he swooned, and coming to himself, he roared terribly, and did eat ashes, sticks, rugyarn. The morning following, there was such a racket with the boy, that the man and his wife took him to bed to them. A bed-staff was thereupon thrown at them, and a chamber pot with its contents was thrown upon them, and they were severely pinched. The man being about to rise, his clothes were divers times pulled from them, himself thrust out of his bed, and his pillow thrown after him. The lad also would have his clothes plucked off from him in these winter nights, and was woefully dogged with such fruits of devilish spite, till it pleased God to shorten the chain of the wicked demon.

All this while the devil did not use to appear in any visible shape, only they would think they had hold of the hand that sometimes scratched them; but it would give them the slip. And once the man was discernably beaten by a fist, and an hand got hold of his wrist which he saw, but could not catch; and the likeness of a blackamore child did appear from under the rug and blanket, where the man lay, and it would rise up, fall down, nod and slip under the clothes when they endeavoured to clasp it, never speaking anything.

Neither were there many words spoken by Satan all this time, only once having put out their light, they heard a scraping on the boards, and then a piping and drumming on them, which was followed with a voice, singing, "Revenge! Revenge! Sweet is revenge!" And they being well terrified with it, called upon God;

the issue of which was, that suddenly with a mournful note, there were six times over uttered such expressions as, "Alas! Alas! me knock no more! me knock no more!" and now all ceased.

The man does moreover affirm, that a seaman (being a mate of a ship) coming often to visit him, told him that they wronged his wife who suspected her to be guilty of witchcraft; and that the boy (his grandchild) was the cause of this trouble; and that if he would let him have the boy one day, he would warrant him his house should be no more troubled as it had been; to which motion he consented. The mate came the next day betimes, and the boy was with him until night; after which his house he saith was not for some time molested with evil spirits.

Thus far is the relation concerning the demon at William Morse his house in Newberry. The true reason of these strange disturbances is as yet not certainly known: some (as has been hinted) did suspect Morse's wife to be guilty of witchcraft.

From: Cotton Mather, *Memorable Providences, Relating to Witchcrafts and Possessions* (1689), "Witchcrafts and Possessions," "The First Example"

Cotton Mather (1662–1729) spent his life trying to emulate his famous father. It is therefore hardly surprising that this, one of his earliest books, treats the same type of material, with the same aim, as the *Remarkable Providences.* But Cotton's hysterical tone and abusive language toward the witch suspect are very much his own.

The bodily contortions he describes, undergone by the children of the Goodwin family, closely resemble those of a family of children in an English case of 1664, recounted in a pamphlet called *A Trial of Witches Held at Bury St. Edmunds*, by Sir Matthew Hale, published in London in 1682.

Such "fits" were to be the stock-in-trade of the accusing girls in Salem Village in 1692. Human suggestibility, rather than fraud, seems to have started them, though fraud unquestionably played its part later.

Section I. There dwells at this time, in the south part of Boston, a sober and pious man, whose name is John Goodwin, whose trade is that of a mason, and whose wife (to which a good report gives a share with him in all the characters of virtue) has made him the father of six (now living) children. Of these children, all but the eldest, who works with his father at his calling, and the youngest, who lives yet upon the breast of its mother, have laboured under the direful effects of a (no less palpable than) stupendous witchcraft. Indeed that exempted son had also, as was thought, some lighter touches of it, in unaccountable stabs and pains now and then upon him; as indeed every person in the family at some time or other had, except the godly father, and the sucking infant, who never felt any impressions of it. But these four children mentioned, were handled in so sad and strange a manner, as has given matter of discourse and wonder to all the country, and of history not unworthy to be considered by more than all the serious or the curious readers in this New English World.

Sect. II. The four children (whereof the eldest was about thirteen, and the youngest was perhaps about a third part so many years of age) had enjoyed a religious education, and answered it with a very towardly ingenuity [encouraging promise]. They had an observable affection unto divine and sacred things; and those of them that were capable of it, seemed to have such a resentment [awareness] of their eternal concernments as is not altogether usual. Their parents also kept them to a continual employment, which did more than deliver them from the temptations of idleness, and as young as they were, they took a delight in it, it may be as much as they should have done. In a word, such was the whole temper and carriage of the children, that there cannot easily be any thing more unreasonable, than to imagine that a design to dissemble could cause them to fall into any of their odd fits; though there should not have happened [even if these had not happened], as there did, a thousand things, wherein it was perfectly impossible for any dissimulation of theirs to produce what scores of spectators were amazed at.

Sect. III. About midsummer, in the year 1688, the eldest of these children, who is a daughter, saw cause to examine their washerwoman, upon their missing of some linen, which twas feared she had stolen from them; and of what use this linen might be to serve the witchcraft intended, the thief's tempter knows! This laundress was the daughter of an ignorant and a scandalous old woman in the neighbourhood; whose miserable husband before he died, had sometimes complained of her, that she was undoubtedly a witch, and that whenever his head was laid, she would quickly arrive unto the punishments due to such an one. This woman in her daughter's defence bestowed very bad language upon the girl that put her to the question; immediately upon which, the poor child became variously indisposed in her health, and visited with strange fits, beyond those that attend an epilepsy, or a catalepsy, or those that they call the diseases of astonishment.

Sect. IV. It was not long before one of her sisters, and two of her brothers, were seized, in order one after another, with affects [ailments] like those that molested her. Within a few weeks, they were all four tortured everywhere in a manner so very grievous, that it would have broke an heart of stone to have seen their agonies. Skilful physicians were consulted for their help, and particularly our worthy and prudent friend Dr. Thomas Oakes, who found himself so affronted [nonplussed] by the distempers of the children, that he concluded nothing but an hellish witchcraft could be the original [origin] of these maladies. And that which yet more confirmed such apprehension was, that for one good while, the children were tormented just in the same part of their bodies all at the same time together; and though they saw and heard not one another's complaints, though like-wise their pains and sprains were swift like lightning, yet when (suppose) the neck, or the hand, or the back of one was racked, so it was at that instant with t'other too.

Sect. V. The variety of their tortures increased continually; and though about nine or ten at night they always had a release from their miseries, and ate and slept all night for the most part indifferently well, yet in the daytime they were handled with so many sorts of ails, that it would require of us almost as much time to relate them all, as it did of them to endure them. Sometimes they would be deaf, sometimes dumb, and sometimes blind, and often, all this at once. One while [time] their tongues would be drawn down their throats; another while [time] they would be pulled out upon their chins, to a prodigious length. They would have their mouths opened unto such a wideness, that their jaws went out of joint; and anon they would clap together again with a force like that of a strong spring-lock. The same would happen to their shoulder-blades, and their elbows, and hand-wrists, and several of their joints. They would at times lie in a benumbed condition; and be drawn together as those that are tied neck and heels; and presently be stretched out, yea, drawn backwards, to such a degree that it was feared the very skin of their bellies would have cracked. They would make most piteous outcries, that they were cut with knives, and struck with blows that they could not bear. Their necks would be broken, so that their neck-bone would seem dissolved unto them that felt after it; and yet on the sudden, it would become again so stiff that there was no stirring of their heads; yea, their heads would be twisted almost round; and if main force at any time obstructed a dangerous motion which they seemed to be upon, they would roar exceedingly. Thus they lay some weeks most pitiful spectacles; and this while as a further demonstration of witchcraft in these horrid effects, when I went to prayer by one of them, that was very desirous to hear what I said, the child utterly lost her hearing till our prayer was over.

Sect. VI. It was a religious family that these afflictions happened unto; and none but a religious contrivance to obtain relief, would have been welcome to them. Many superstitious proposals were made unto them, by persons that were I know not who, nor what, with arguments fetched from I know not how much necessity and experience; but the distressed parents rejected all such counsels, with a gracious resolution, to oppose devils with no other weapons but prayers and tears, unto Him that has the chaining of them; and to try first whether graces were not the best things to encounter witchcrafts with. Accordingly they requested the four ministers of Boston, with the minister of Charlestown, to keep a day of prayer at their thus haunted house; which they did in the company of some devout people there. Immediately upon this day, the youngest of the four children was delivered, and never felt any trouble as afore. But there was yet a greater effect of these our applications unto our God!

Sect. VII. The report of the calamities of the family for which we were thus concerned, arrived now unto the ears of the magistrates, who presently and prudently applied themselves, with a just vigour, to enquire into the story. The father of the children complained of his neighbour, the suspected ill woman, whose name was Glover; and she being sent for by the justices, gave such a wretched account of herself, that they saw cause to commit her unto the gaoler's custody. Goodwin had no proof that could have done her any hurt; but the hag had not power to deny her interest in the enchantment of the children; and when she was asked, whether she believed there was a God? her answer was too blasphemous and horrible for any pen of mine to mention. An experiment was made, whether she could recite the Lord's Prayer; and it was found, that though clause after clause was most carefully repeated unto her, yet when she said it after them that prompted her, she could not possibly avoid making nonsense of it, with some ridiculous depravations. This experiment I had the curiosity since to see made upon two more, and it had the same event. Upon the commitment of this extraordinary woman, all the children had some present ease; until one (related unto her) accidentally meeting one or two of them, entertained them with her blessing, that is, railing; upon which three of them fell ill again, as they were before.

Sect. VIII. It was not long before the witch thus in the trap, was brought upon her trial; at which, through the efficacy of a charm, I suppose, used upon her, by one or some of her crew, the court could receive answers from her in none but the Irish, which was her native language; although she understood the English very well, and had accustomed her whole family to none but that language in her former conversation; and therefore the communication between the bench and the bar, was now chiefly conveyed by two honest and faithful men that were interpreters. It was long before she could with any direct answers plead unto her indictment; and when she did plead, it was with confession rather than denial of her guilt. Order was given to search the old woman's house, from whence there were brought into the court, several small images, or puppets, or babies, made of rags, and stuffed with goat's hair, and other such ingredients. When these were produced, the vile woman acknowledged, that her way to torment the objects of her malice, was by wetting of her finger with her spittle, and stroking of those little images. The abused children were then present, and the woman still kept stooping and shrinking as one that was almost pressed to death with a mighty weight upon her. But one of the images being brought unto her, immediately she started up after an odd manner, and took it into her hand; but she had no sooner taken it, than one of the children fell into sad fits, before the whole assembly. This the judges had their just apprehensions at; and carefully causing the repetition of the experiment, found again the same event of it. They asked her, whether she had any to stand by her: She replied, she had; and looking very pertly in the air, she added, "No, he's gone." And she then confessed, that she had one, who was her prince, with whom she maintained, I know not what communion. For which cause, the night after, she was heard expostulating with a devil, for his thus deserting her; telling him that because he had served her so basely and falsely, she had confessed all. However, to make all clear, the court appointed five or six physicians one evening to examine her very strictly, whether she were not crazed in her intellectuals, and had not procured to herself by folly and madness the reputation of a witch. Diverse hours did they spend with her; and in all that while no discourse came from her, but what was pertinent and agreeable: particularly, when they asked her, what she thought would become of her soul? She replied "You ask me a very solemn question, and I cannot well tell what to say to it." She owned herself a Roman Catholic; and could recite her Pater Noster in Latin very readily; but there was one clause or two always too hard for her, whereof she said, "She could not repeat it, if she might have all the world." In the upshot, the doctors returned her "compos mentis," and sentence of death was passed upon her.

Matthew Hopkins Witch Finder Generall
My Imps names are
Holt
1 Ilemauzar
2 Pyewackett
Jarmara
Sacke & Sugar
3 Pecke in the Crowne
4 Griezzell Greedigutt
Newes
Vinegar tom

A
DISCOVRSE
OF THE DAM-
NED ART OF WITCH-
CRAFT; SO FARRE FORTH
as it is reuealed in the Scriptures, and
manifest by true expe-
rience.
FRAMED AND DELIVERED
by M. WILLIAM PERKINS, *in his ordi-*
narie course of Preaching, and now published
by THO. PICKERING *Batchelour of*
Diuinitie, and Minister of Fin-
chingfield in Essex.
WHEREVNTO IS ADIOYNED
a twofold Table; one of the order and Heades
of the Treatise; another of the texts of Scripture
explaned, or vindicated from the cor-
rupt interpretation of the
Aduersarie.
PRINTED BY CANTREL LEGGE,
Printer to the Vniuersitie of *Cambridge*.
1608.

A BLOW at
Modern SADDUCISM
In some
Philosophical Considerations
ABOUT
Witchcraft.
And the
Relation of the *Famed Disturbance*
at the House of
M. MOMPESSON.
WITH
REFLECTIONS
ON
Drollery, and *Atheisme*.
The Fourth Edition Corrected and Inlarged.
By *Jos. Glanvill* Fellow of
the *Royal Society*.
LONDON,
Printed by *E. Cotes* for *James Collins* at the
Kings Head in *Westminster-Hall*, 1668.

Page 22, top left. Nightmarish vision of three witches on a broomstick, from the early period of the great European witch hunt. Woodcut from Augsburg, Germany, 1508.

Page 22, top right. Two witches identify their imps (or "familiars") under the gaze of Matthew Hopkins, the self-appointed "witch finder general" who created a witch hunt in the mid-17th century in Suffolk, England. Many New England Puritans came from that region. Frontispiece from the original edition of Hopkins's, *The Discovery of Witches*, 1647.

Page 22, bottom. Top: Witch in a magic circle, invoking her familiars. 17th century woodcut from the anonymous pamphlet, "The Strange and Wonderful History of Old Mother Shipton." Bottom: Three of the witches accused of bewitching the children of Sir Francis Manners, Earl of Rutland, as described in the anonymous pamphlet, "The Wonderful Discovery of the Witchcrafts of Margaret and Phillip Flower."

Above left. Front cover of the original edition of William Perkins's, *A Discourse of the Damned Art of Witchcraft*, 1608.

Above right. Front cover of a later work, also influential in New England, intended to counter skepticism about the supernatural in general and witchcraft in particular.

2

The Massachusetts Bay Colony

As well as their superstitions, the Puritans brought from England their belief in their own unique righteousness. In founding their theocracy, they aimed to form a spearhead of saintliness in the worldwide war against Satan. The sermon given by one of the colony's founders, John Winthrop, onboard the ship the *Arabella* in 1630 to the first band of settlers, gave eloquent voice to these noble but dangerous ideals. It expressed a shining vision whose dark side was merciless intolerance.

Excerpts from the poem *The Day of Doom,* Cotton Mather's *Corderius Americanus*, the *Essex County Court Records,* and George Bishop's *New England Judged* convey various aspects of that intolerance and some of its effects.

"Fear is the enemy of love," said Saint Augustine. To add to the anxieties created by one of the harshest religious creeds the world has known, the colonists lived in terror of the Native Americans. They were seen as agents of the devil if not devils themselves. This belief, and the earthly dangers the Native Americans presented of sudden attack, arson, and massacre, caused reactions such as that described by Robert Roules in his *Deposition to the General Court.* The Indian attack recounted in Mary Rowlandson's *Narrative* helps the modern reader understand those reactions.

In this anxious atmosphere, local conflicts that had simmered for decades became increasingly desperate and vicious. Excerpts from the Salem Village Book of Record show the areas of dispute that fatally divided Salem Village into two opposed factions.

From: John Winthrop, first governor of Massachusetts, concluding section of *The Model of Christian Charity,* a sermon delivered onboard the *Arabella* in 1630, *The Winthrop Papers, vol. 2,* The Massachusetts Historical Society, (1931)

John Winthrop (1588–1649) was governor of the Bay Colony almost continuously from 1630 to 1649. He was a passionate advocate of rigid theocratic rule, giving no quarter to dissenters and opposing any curtailment of the magistrates' authority. The ideals propounded in his famous sermon remain influential, for good and bad, in American society to this day.

The "shipwreck" of the first sentence refers to the destruction of the society he and his fellow colonists hoped to build.

Now the only way to avoid this shipwreck and to provide for our posterity is to follow the counsel of Micah, to do justly, to love mercy, to walk humbly, with our God. For this end, we must be knit together in this work as one man, we must entertain each other in brotherly affection, we must be willing to abridge ourselves of our superfluities, for the supply of others' necessities, we must uphold a familiar commerce together in all meekness, gentleness, patience and liberality, we must delight in each other, make other's conditions our own, rejoice together, mourn together, labour and suffer together, always having before our eyes our commission and community in the work, our community as members of the same body, so shall we keep the unity of the spirit in the bond of peace, the Lord will be our God and delight to dwell among us, as his own people and will command a blessing upon us in all our ways, so that we shall see much more his wisdom, power, goodness and truth than formerly we have been acquainted with, we shall find that the God of Israel is among us, when ten of us shall be able to resist a thousand of our enemies, when he shall make us a praise and glory, that men shall say of succeeding plantations: the Lord make us like that of New England: for we must consider that we shall be as a City upon a Hill, the eyes of all people are upon us; so that if we shall deal falsely with our God in this work we have undertaken and to cause him to withdraw his present help from us, we shall be made a story and a by-word through the world, we shall open the mouths of enemies to speak evil of the ways of God and all professors for God's sake; we shall shame the faces of many of God's worthy servants, and cause their prayers to be turned into curses upon us till we be consumed out of the good land whither we are going: And to shut up this discourse with the exhortation of Moses that faithful servant of the Lord in his last farewell to Israel. Deuteronomy 30, Beloved, there is now set before us life, and good, death and evil in that we are commanded this day to love the Lord our God, and to love one another to walk in his ways and to keep his commandments and his ordinance, and his laws, and the articles of our covenant with him that we may love and be multiplied, and the Lord our God may bless us in the land whither we go to possess it: But if our hearts shall turn away so that we will not obey, but shall be seduced and worship other Gods our pleasures, and profits, and serve them; it is propounded unto us this day, we shall surely perish out of the good land whither we pass over this vast sea to possess it. Therefore let us choose life, that we, and our seed, may live; by obeying to Him, for He is our life, and our prosperity.

From: Kenneth B. Murdock, Michael Wigglesworth, eds., *The Day of Doom, or A Poetical Description of the Great and Last Judgment, with a Short Discourse on Eternity,* (New York, 1929)

This was one of the few books to be found in ordinary Puritan households, along with the Bible and a catechism. It was written sometime in the 1660s. Stanzas 10–22 graphically describe the horrors of judgment day; stanzas 166–181 recount an imaginary dialogue between Christ and the unbaptized infants called before him.

Stanzas 10–22

No heart so bold, but now grows cold
and almost dead with fear:
No eye so dry, but now can cry,
and pour out many a tear,
Earth's potentates and powerful states,
Captains and men of might
Are quite abashed, their courage dashed
at this most dreadful sight.

Mean men lament, great men do rent
their robes, and tear their hair:
They do not spare their flesh to tear
through horrible despair.
Kindreds wail: all hearts do fail:
horror the world doth fill
With weeping eyes, and loud outcries,
yet knows not how to kill.

Some hide themselves in caves and delve
in places underground;

Some rashly leap into the deep,
to 'scape by being drowned:
Some to the rocks (O senseless blocks!)
and woody mountains run,
that there they might this fearful sight,
and dreadful presence shun.

In vain do they to mountains say,
fall on us and us hide
From judges' ire, more hot than fire,
for who may it abide?
No hiding place can from his face
sinners all conceal,
Whose flaming eye hid things doth 'spy
and darkest things reveal.

The judge draws nigh, exalted high
upon a lofty throne,
Amidst the throng of angels strong,
lo, Israel's Holy One!
The excellence of whose presence
and awful Majesty,
Amazeth nature, and every creature,
doth more than terrify.

The mountains smoke, the hills are shook
the Earth is rent and torn,
As if she should be clear dissolved,
or from the centre born,
the sea doth roar, forsakes the shore,
and shrinks away from fear;
The wild beasts flee into the sea,
as soon as he draws near.

Whose glory bright, whose wondrous might
whose power imperial,
So far surpass whatever was
in realms terrestial;
That tongues of men (nor angel's pen)
cannot the same express,
And therefore I must pass it by,
lest speaking should transgress.

Before this throne a trump is blown,
Proclaiming the day of doom:
Forthwith he cries, "Ye dead arise,
and unto judgment come."
No sooner said, but 'tis obeyed,
Sepulchers opened are:
Dead bodies all rise at his call
and's mighty power declare.

Both sea and land, at his command,
their dead at once surrender:
The fire and air constrained are
also their dead to tender.
The mighty word of this great Lord
links body and soul together,
Both of the just, and the unjust,
to part no more for ever.

The same translates, from mortal states
to immortality.
All that survive, and be alive,
'i the twinkling of an eye:
That so they may abide for ay
to endless weal or woe;
Both the rate and reprobate
are made to die no more.

His winged hosts fly through all coasts,
together gathering,
both good and bad, both quick and dead,
and all to judgment bring.
Out of their holes those creeping moles,
that themselves for fear,
by force they take, and quickly make
before the judge appear.

Thus everyone before the throne
of Christ the judge is brought,
Both righteous and impious
that good or ill hath wrought.
A separation, and diff'ring station
by Christ appointed is

(To sinners sad) 'twixt good and bad,
'twixt heirs of woe and bliss.

Stanzas 166–181

Then to the bar, all they drew near
Who died in infancy,
And never had or good or bad
effected pers'nally.
But from the womb unto the tomb
were straightway carried,
(Or at the last e'er they transgressed)
who thus began to plead:

If for our own transgression,
or disobedience,
We here did stand at thy left hand
just were the recompense:
But Adam's *guilt our souls hath spilled,*
his fault is charged on us:
And that alone hath overthrown,
and utterly undone us.

Not we, but he ate of the tree,
whose fruit was interdicted:
Yet on us all of his sad fall,
the punishment's inflicted,
how could we sin that had not been
or how is his sin our
Without consent, which is prevent,
we never had a power?

O great Creator, why was our nature
depraved and forlorn?
Why so defiled, and made so viled
whilst we were yet unborn?
If it be just, and needs we must
transgressors reckoned be,
Thy mercy lord, to us afford,
which sinners hath set free,

Behold we see Adam set free,
and saved from his trespass,
Whose sinful fall hath split us all,
and brought us to this pass.
Canst thou deny us once to try,
or grace to us to tender,
when he finds grace before they face,
that was the chief offender?

Then answered the judge most dread,
God doth such doom forbid,
that men should die eternally
for what they never did,
But what you call old Adam's fall,
and only his trespass,
You call amiss to call it his,
both his and yours it was,

He was designed of all mankind
to be a public head,
A common root, whence all should shoot,
and stood in all their stead,
He stood and fell, did ill or well,
not for himself alone,
but for you all, who now his fall,
and trespass would disown.

If he had stood, then all his brood
had been established
In God's true love never to move,
nor once awry to tread:
Then all his race, my father's grace,
should have enjoyed for ever,
And wicked sprights by subtle sleights
could them have harmed never,

Would you have grieved to have received
through Adam so much good,
As had been your for evermore,
if he at first had stood?
Would you have said, we ne'r obeyed,

nor did thy laws regard;
It ill befits with benefits,
us, Lord, so to reward,

Since then to share in his welfare,
you could have been content,
you may with reason share in his treason,
and in the punishment,
hence you were born in state forlorn,
with natures so depraved:
Death was your due, because that you
had thus yourselves behaved.

You think if we had been as he,
whom God did so betrust,
We to our cost would ne'er have lost
all for a paltry lust,
Had you been made in Adam's stead,
you would like things have wrought,
And so into the self same woe,
yourselves and yours have brought,

I may deny you once to try,
or grace for you to tender,
Though he finds grace before my face,
who was the chief offender;
Else should my grace cease to be grace;
for it should not be free,
If to release whom I should please,
I have no liberty.

If upon one what's due to none
I frankly shall bestow,
And on the rest shall not think best,
compassion skirts to throw,
Whom injure I? will you envy,
and grudge at others weal?
Or me accuse, who do refuse
yourselves to help and heal.

Am I alone of what's my own,
no master or no lord?

O if I am, how can you claim
what I to some afford?
Will you demand grace at my hand,
and challenge what is mine?
Will you teach me whom to set free,
and thus my grace confine?

You sinners are, and such a share
as sinners may expect,
Such you shall have; for I do save
none by my own elect.
Yet to compare your sin with their
who lived a longer time,
I do confess yours is much less,
though every sin's a crime.

A crime it is, therefore in bliss
you may not hope to dwell;
But unto you I shall allow
the easiest room in hell,
The glorious King thus answering,
they cease, and plead no longer:
Their consciences must needs confess
his reasons are the stronger.

Thus all men's pleas the judge with ease
doth answer and confute,
Until that all, both great and small,
are silenced and mute.
Vain hopes are cropped, all mouths are stopped,
sinners have nought to say,
But that 'tis just, and equal most
they should be damned for ay.

From: Cotton Mather, *Corderius Americanus, an Essay upon the Good Education of Children, in a Funeral Sermon upon Mr. Ezekiel Cheever, Master of the Free School in Boston* (Boston, 1708)

This essay was published sixteen years after the Salem witch trials but is included here because it illustrates so well the terror Puritan teaching attempted to instill into the population, even the children.

Children, 'tis your dawning time, it may be your dying time. A child once grew very solid, and was more for his book than for his play, and prayed unto God more than once every day. Being asked the cause, the child said, "Why, I was in the burying place a while ago, and there I saw a grave shorter than myself!" Children, go unto the burying place; There you will see many a grave shorter than yourselves. 'Tis now the computation found, That more than half the children of men die before they come to be seventeen years of age, And what needs any more be said, for your awakening, to learn the Holy Scriptures . . .

Children, you may by your piety, approve yourselves the regenerate children of God, while you are yet children. Cry unto God, My Father! Ah, children; be afraid of going prayer less to bed, lest the devil be your bedfellow. Be afraid of playing on the Lord's Day, lest the devil be your play fellow. Be afraid of telling lies, or speaking wickedly, lest that evil tongue be one day tormented in the flames, where a drop of water to cool the tongue, will be roared for.

From: *Records and Files of the Quarterly Courts of Essex County, Massachusetts, volume I, 1636–1656,* (Salem 1911), court held at Salem, June 27, 1644

Americans today take for granted the freedoms of speech and religious observance guaranteed by the Constitution. It may seem strange that the country's first settlers were not only denied such freedoms but cruelly punished for dissension and breaches of conformity. In the Massachusetts theocracy there was no conceptual distinction between crime, sin, and sheer deviance from the norm. This extract from the records of the Essex County Court shows, within one court session, the range of offences the Puritan theocracy considered punishable by law. Some of them, such as letting one's goat into a neighbor's field or endangering life by shoddy building construction, would be criminal today. But these are vastly outnumbered by acts that we would regard as nobody's business but the individual's. These include challenges to authority, such as criticizing ministers, and sin or misbehavior such as fornication or drunkenness.

Many of the culprits brought before the magistrates were not Puritans who had come from England to practice their religion, but indentured servants (in effect, temporary slaves) and others who had come just to earn a living. These people were forced by law to worship in the Puritan meetinghouses, whatever their private convictions.

The magistrates regarded themselves as inquisitors eliciting confessions and repentance rather than interpreters of a body of law. There was no right of appeal against their judgments or sentences. Even after

1648, when a code called Laws and Liberties of Massachusetts was enacted, the range of punishable offences, and the role of magistrates, scarcely changed.

One of the magistrates at this session of the court was William Hathorne, father of John Hathorne, chief magistrate at the examinations of witches in 1692.

William Burriot fined for suffering his cattle, oxen, cows and hogs to do damage to his neighbors in the North field. Deputy, Thomas Pickton. Witnesses, Samuel Eaborne and Jeffry Massy.

Robert Goodell fined for suffering his goat to go in his neighbor's cornfield.

Alice George of Gloucester to be whipped or fined for railing against Mr. Blynman, "calling him wicked wretch," etc. Witnesses, Thomas Joans and William Meads.

"The old house (in Salem) which once was Mr. Skelton's, being in imminent danger of present falling to the endangering of the lives of children & cattle and others," it was ordered that the house be taken down in ten days. Transcript given to Mr. Browne, and another to be set on the meeting house. Witnesses: Peter Palfrey and Elias Mason.

William Hewes and son John fined 50s. each and to confess "for deriding such as sing in the congregation, terming them fools," and William for saying that Mr. Whiting preached confusedly, and John for charging Mr. Cobbitt with falsehood in his doctrine. Witnesses: Timothy Coop and his wife and William Longley. William Hewes testified that they falsified his words; "as for this woman she is scandalous throughout the plantation."

Hugh Laskin and his wife fined 40s. for hard usage of his late servant in victuals and clothes. Witnesses: Jacob Barney, John Balch, William Kinge, William Dodge and Edmund Grover. Jacob Barney testified that he heard the greater part of his diet was coarse bread and whey; but Goodman Laskin denied it. John Balch acknowledged the sin of not having dealt brotherly with him. Edmund Grover said he had come to their house and said that he had eaten nothing that day. William King said that from the report of his wife concerning coarse bread he inquired of "brother Balch" who said he had dealt with him about clothing and purposed to deal further. The bed and clothing were not as should be and King showed the piece of coarse bread and Goodman Laskin did chide his wife for it. One time the boy did not eat until 11 o'clock. Goodman Balch said the boy was growing thin.

Richard Leech received a pig of John Burrage, servant to Jonathan Porter and himself, and his uncle Jonathan Leech concealed it, not having it cried, until three months later. Witnesses: Jacob Barney. Richard and Jonathan Leech fined 20s. each.

Michaell Lambert of Lynn, drunk. Witnesses: William Bicknoll and Jabez Hackett. Also for giving two contrary testimonies. Witness: Timothy Tomlins. At request of Mr. Nash, confessed that he drank three or four cups of sack.

Mr. Adam Ottley for forging Captain Hawking's name. Witnesses: Mr. Downing and Mr. Hathorne. Respitted until next General Court. To pay Joseph Armetag 8s. per test.

Jonathan Pride of Salem fined for contemning a warrant. Witnesses: Mr. Holgrave and Jonathan Hardy.

Daniel Ray, for trespass of his horses, cows and hogs in North field to his neighbor's damage. Witnesses: Jeferey Masy. Mr. Hathorne and Mr. Downing to fix damages.

Goodman Joseph Redknap for not suffering a child of his to be baptized. His wife to see it done next Lord's day. If her husband object the constable of Lynn to take him to Boston to the prison. Witness: Goodman Evans. The Governor asked, "What is the reason you will not have the child baptized?" Mr Redknap said "he would not trouble ye Court & he is not satisfied in the thing, he himself not being in fellowship. I would not justify myself nor yet condemn myself, he would have no hand in it." The Governor said, "You shall have no hand in it & the child shall be baptized & then there will be no sin of yours." Redknap said, "I would see the mind of God in it," and the Governor asked, "Upon what ground?" Redknap answered, "because it doth not understand the Covenant of the Lord Jesus: & is willing to submit unto the ordinance of the Lord Jesus Christ & of the Court too. I understand the Covenant of Grace is far otherwise than the Jews had." Mr. Hathorne quoted 2 Acts, 38 v. "God is many times in his dispensation beyond our faith."

John Stone of Gloucester fined 50s. for scandalizing [talking scandal about] Mr. Blinman, charging him with false interpretation of the scriptures, etc., and for saying that "if an angel from Heaven should preach the same he would not believe it," and there were others of his mind. Also, for telling James Smith things that tended to the reproach of the doctrine delivered by Mr. Blynman. Witnesses: James Smith, Goodman Stone himself and William Cotten and his wife. William Cotten testified that "Goodman Stone came & sat him down in my house & said, a poor man had starved had it not been for him, & that it would be longer Mr. Blinman of this, & said that Blinman had falsely interpreted scripture, . . . naming 2 places of scripture: in Nehemiah & Ezra."

Alice Williams fined five pounds and whipped for fornication with William Flynt. Mr. Downing, security.

James George, servant to William Cantleburie, to be whipped for often running away from his master, and "the boy" to make up his time at end of service.

John Croxton fined 40s. for refusing to obey the corporal of the watch, Richard More.

Jury of inquest on the servant of Ralph Elwood, who was found dead: Mr. Thomas Gardener, William Lord, Richard Bishop, Thomas Spooner, Mr. Alen Keniston, Thomas Goldthwait, William Waller, James Hynde, Daniel Baxter, John Balie, Thomas Oliver and Phillip Crumwell.

Present: Jonathan Endicott, Gov., Mr. William Hathorne and Mr. Emanuel Downing.

Inventory of estate of widow Wathen brought into court. The two deacons of Salem, Mr. Charles Gott and John Horne, appointed executors. Nathaniel Porter took oath in court.

From: George Bishop, *New England Judged* (London, 1667)

George Bishop was an Englishman who wrote eloquently of the outrages committed on Quakers in Massachusetts. This excerpt tells of the imprisonment, whipping, and banishment not only of Quakers but of Puritans who were kind to Quakers. The chapter follows the tale of Mary Fisher, who traveled safely to Constantinople to preach to the Grand Turk but was clapped in jail the moment she arrived in New England. It precedes an account of the hanging of Mary Dyer and two other Quakers. Bishop writes of "you" and "your meeting" as though addressing the Boston ministers directly.

The year is 1657. Note the part played by William Hathorne, father of the magistrate John Hathorne.

Christopher Holder and John Copeland are the next, who being moved of the Lord to go to Salem, a Town in your Colony, and speaking a few words in your meeting, after the priest had done, was hauled back by the hair of the head, and his mouth violently stopped with a glove and handkerchief thrust thereinto with much fury, by one of your church-members and commissioners, and they both thrust out, and had to a house, and continued there till the next day, and then had to Boston, where ye laid it on with thirty stripes a piece at once, with a knotted whip of three cords, as near as the hang-man could in one place, measuring his ground, and fetching his strokes with the greatest strength and advantage he could, to cut their flesh, and to put them to suffering; the cruelty of which was so great, that a woman seeing it, fell down as dead: Yet it did not end there, for that night, and three days after, your jailor kept them without food or water (lying on the boards, without bed or straw, after so cruel execution) and so close, that none might come to speak with them, so they might have perished, but the Lord preserved them under your merciless cruelty; and when all this would not do, ye kept them nine weeks prisoners without fire, in the cold winter season, and then turned them forth. And the friend of Salem (Samuel Shattock by name) who pulled away the hand of the said church-member's and commissioner, when he thrust the glove and handkerchief into the mouth of Christopher Holder, lest it should have choked him, being not able to behold so barbarous an act, ye sent to Boston (though an inhabitant of Salem, and a man of good repute amongst ye) and there ye kept him prisoner (whom since ye have whipped and banished upon pain of death) as a friend of Quakers (though ye had no law so to do) who only did this friendly act, till he had given in bond of twenty pounds to answer it at the next court, and not to come at any of the people called Quakers at their meetings. And this was the second progress of your house of correction, and the further infliction of your insufficient punishment, which ye laid on without compassion or pity, and yet call it insufficient—the penalty inflicted proving insufficient—say ye, who are thus drunk in blood, and filled with madness, that ye care not what ye do to the innocent, nor what cruelty ye inflict, nor how your rage reacheth up to heaven in causing them to suffer; but being mounted in blood, ye ride on with speed, and no consideration of tenderness or bowels can stop your career, no, not the sad condition of your neighbours (the inhabitants) who had lived long amongst ye, and were partakers of the same distance from their country, and other inconveniencies, and were known to you to be of sober conversations; your eye pitied not, neither did ye spare them; the cry of their oppressions came not into your ears, neither did your hearts relent; but as men given up to a reprobate sense, implacable, unmerciful, without natural affection: So ye proceeded with the inhabitants, as with the strangers, and more cruelly too, neither regarding age nor sex, neither the hoary head, nor him that stoopeth for age; neither child nor old woman; neither infant of days, nor the man of riper years; neither a man and his house, nor a man and his heritage; neither many men and their houses, nor many men and their heritages, wives, children, families, relations, estates, goods, lands, persons, beings; as I shall set in order before you by and by (though therein you are silent) and the righteous judgments of God, who will not spare you for your iniquities and hard-heartedness to the poor; neither will his eye pity you, nor will he spare you; but the reward of your hands shall be given ye, and the fruit of your doings, because ye spared not, neither have had mercy: And this the Lord will fulfil, whose word it is, who is a God of faithfulness and truth: Blessed are all they who put their trust in him.

And here Cassandra Southick and Lawrence her husband (an aged grave couple, inhabitants of Salem, and members of your church) come to be considered; who, because they entertained the two strangers, Christopher Holder and John Copeland, were committed to prison, and sent to Boston (your metropolis of blood) where Lawrence ye released (to be dealt withal by them who reputed him of their congregation) but Cassandra ye kept seven weeks a prisoner, and then fined her forty shillings, for owning a paper written by the strangers, aforesaid, in reference to truth, and the scriptures, which your Governor put to her wherewithal to ensnare her, and to bring her under your law, who had none before, after ye had detained her as aforesaid; and which she owning, (for that she could not deny, unless she had denied the truth) ye fined her, though even that law by which ye fined her, fineth only for heretical papers, which this was not proved to be.

Richard Dowdney was the next who felt your hand, upon whom there being a necessity laid from the Lord, to come from England to you, ye apprehended at Dedham, and brought to Boston, where he never was before, nor in that country, and having given him thirty stripes at once, with such a whip as aforesaid, and laid it on with as much cruelty as the former, and searched for his papers and books, and took from him what ye would (all which in the space of three hours after his coming to town, to the wounding of the hearts of many who heard and saw so innocent a man so inhumanely abused). Ye continued him twenty days a prisoner, and then sent him away with the four former, after ye had threatened him and them with the loss of their ears, if they came, there again, into your jurisdiction; which leads me to the next step of your proceedings, mentioned in your declaration, viz. the cutting off ears was increased (to wit, the penalty) by the loss of the ears of those that offended the second time. The whole runs thus: And the penalty inflicted proving insufficient to restrain their impudent and in solent obstructions, was increased by the loss of the ears of those that offended the second time.

Before I come to the particular execution of this increase of your cruelty, I must necessarily turn aside to show the reader the effect of the former upon the inhabitants, and what it produced as to them, and your proceedings thereupon.

Your violent and bloody proceedings so affected the inhabitants of Salem, and so preached unto them, that divers of them could no longer partake with you, who mingled blood with your sacrifices, but choosing rather peace with God in their consciences, whose witness in them testified against such worships, than to join with you, whatsoever they might therefore suffer, withdrew from your public assemblies, and met together by themselves on the first days of the week, quiet and peaceable in one another's houses, waiting on the Lord.

This separation ye soon observed (for it could not be long hid) and it grieved you sore, and William Hathorne (one of your commissioners) having knowledge thereof, sent forth his warrants to bring all before him, who were taken together the next morning; before whom being brought, he read unto them an old law, made in 1646, to convict them which should absent from their public meetings, after the rate of five shillings a week (now the bishop's was but twelve pence in the days of Queen Elizabeth) with which ye convicted them (a practice never used by Christ nor his apostles, nor by the Jews of old) which yet satisfied him not; but this Captain Hathorne sent for them again, and asked them ensnaring questions, concerning the sufficiency of the light which convinced of sin, and had the clerk of the court to write what they said; which light that convinced of sin, being the light of Christ, which enlighteneth every man that cometh into the world; who saith, "I am the light of the world," and John, "That that is the true light that lighteth every man that cometh into the world; in whom was life, and the light was the light of men." They owning it to be that which it was (as it is) to be minded by all, he sent three of them to you at Boston, viz, the said Lawrence Southick and Cassandra his wife, and Josiah their son (all of a family, to terrify the rest) whom ye sent to your house of correction (as ye call it) and caused to be whipped in the coldest season of the year with cords, as those afore, though two of them were aged people; and having kept them eleven days in prison, and commanded them to work for the jailor, who had families of their own, and business to attend upon, from which ye detained them, and caused them to work for another, under the penalty of your law, as if they were rogues or vagabonds, and such as would not work, nor have regard to their families, but wander up and down to beg and steal, as is the law of England, and as it provides; and then set them at liberty, nothing in a legal way: For, as for the information, the said Hathorne, sent them in a private way (as his manner was) sealed up to your governor, which he produceth not. Nevertheless, with this the said Hathorne was not satisfied, but being filled with cruelty and blood, sent forth his warrants, and caused several of the beasts of the said Lawrence and Josiah to be destrained, to the value of four pounds thirteen shillings, that is to say, for six weeks absence of the said Lawrence and Cassandra, three pounds six shillings, and the rest for Josiah their son, being two young beasts, and a fat hog.

Neither with this was the said Hathorne satisfied, nor with the departure of some out of that jurisdiction, because of your cruelty; but from one Edward Harnet (aged about sixty nine years, and his wife seventy three) and another aged family, he caused thirty seven shillings to be taken, for not coming to your meetings, though they were low in the outward, and had more need to have been ministered unto, than to be taken from.

And William Shattock an inhabitant of Boston, ye committed to your house of correction, and cruelly whipped him at his first entrance, because he was found alone in his own house by your constable, on a first day, where ye kept him to work (which was making of shoes) and the jailor took his labour from his wife and children; which putting him on straits to think what he should do for their sustenance, though he could have well endured the thing as to himself, yet in regard your deputy-governor told his wife (in part of whose house his family then was) that in regard he was poor, and could not pay them five shillings a week, for not coming to your meetings, you would continue him still in prison: He desired to depart your jurisdiction, which to do ye gave him but a very short time. And your said deputy-governor endeavoured to make a separation between him and his wife, persuading her that she should never hear of him more, when he was gone to seek out a place for them in another jurisdiction; and that what William had done, was to be rid of her and her four children, and told her, That if she would disown him, and persuade his children to it (a cursed work) neither she nor her children should want; for two of them he intended to keep himself, his son being (as your said deputy said) fit to keep his sheep, whom he took from the place where William had appointed him to abide, lest the deputy should make a prey of him. And so he had but three days' time to depart your jurisdiction, provide for his family, receive and pay his debts, which he was necessitated to accept, because ye had concluded to keep him still in prison, and to take of his children to be your servants, and to make his wife to do your wills, or perpetually banish him, as he understood by her. Besides, ye committed him, and ordered him to be severely whipped at his first entrance, according to your first law, entitled, A Law concerning Quakers, and there to be kept, and none suffered to converse with him whilst he was in prison. And this is the justice of the Court of the Massachusetts, and the religion of your deputy towards God.

From: *Robert Roules's Signed Deposition to the General Court, July 17th 1677,* The Edward A. Ayer Collection, The Newberry Library, Chicago

This deposition shockingly conveys the fear and hatred of the Indians felt by the ordinary inhabitants of Massachusetts.

I Robert Roules of Marblehead, mariner, aged thirty years or thereabouts, belonging to the catch William and Sarah of Salem, do upon oath say, that Joseph Bovey went out master of the said ketch upon a fishing voyage to the eastern coast. After we had caught, and being about half laden with fish, and riding at an anchor at port La Tour, near cape Sable, and on the easterly side thereof, on the 7th of this instant, July, it being Saturday, purposing here to take in wood and water, and in two days to be again upon our fishing design, but on the Lord's day, being the 8th instant, in the dawning of the day, there came suddenly on board of us a canoe of Indians, in number nine or ten, as near as I could judge, with their arms ready fixed, loaded and cocked. I first discovered them, and dropped down upon deck to save myself from their shot. They immediately fired upon us, and their shot chiefly struck against the windlass, and so did not hurt us. I then called to them, and said "What for you kill Englishmen?" They answered me, "If Englishmen shoot' we kill—if not shoot, we no kill." They then ordered us to come up. By this time they had boarded us, and we were obliged to surrender without conditions. They then proceeded to bind me, and the other four men with me, the master, Capt. Bovey being one. They stripped us, one after the other of all our clothes, only leaving me a greasy shirt and waistcoat, and drawers we used to fish in; our shoes and stockings being in the cabin. They then gave us liberty to sit upon deck, bound as we were all, till about two of the clock in the afternoon. After this they unbound us, and commanded us to sail our vessel towards Penobscot, which we endeavored to do; but the wind shortening, we were forced to come to an anchor again, and lay there till the second day of our capture. In the meantime, they told us they intended to kill all of us, and all the Englishmen, being in number twenty six, including boys, except three. They had taken four other vessels besides ours. On the second day they commanded us and the other ketches to sail together for Penobscot. The Indians had dispersed themselves into all the ketches; there being seventy or eighty of them. As we sailed onward we espied a bark and gave her chase and soon took her, and found it Mr. Watts' vessel. The Indians compelled us to hail him, and he answered us he was from Boston, bound on a fishing voyage. To prevent the murder of him and his men, as soon as we came up with him we told him he was taken, but he thinking it only a joke, laughed at us. The Indians now rose up and told Capt. Watts if he did not strike they were all dead men. All but four of the Indians then went on board him; divided and mixed the Englishmen in the different vessels with themselves; sending master Bovey with one man more of our company, onboard another ketch, and left me as master of the ketch, (they wholly disliking the said Bovey) with an old man, whom I desired. And now being on board with Capt. Watts, the Indians having sent two of their number away, took two of Capt. Watts' men in their place, whereof one was William Buswell.

We had not been thus situated but a short time, when another sail was discovered, and we were commanded to give chase. We did so till it began to grow dusky, and then the Indian Sagamore of our vessel ordered me, who being at the helm, to bear up; but I refused. Thereupon the Sagamore grew angry, and was about to fall upon me, which William Buswell observing, seized him by the throat, and a close scuffle ensued. Buswell however soon tripped up his heels, fell upon him, and kept him down with his knee upon his breast. Meantime, another of my companions in captivity, named Richard Downes, closing with a second Indian, succeeded in getting him down also; and in attempting to throw him overboard, his legs became entangled, which Buswell perceiving, left his man, and seizing upon him too, they quickly threw him into the sea.

While this was going on the other Englishmen were enabled to confine the other Sagamore in the cook room, by shutting down the scuttle upon him. All hands then grasped another Indian and threw him overboard. It was a desperate attempt, but the victory was now certain. The two remaining Indians were Sagamores, one was an old man, the other was a young man. One was fast in the cook room, and the other was glad to surrender to save his life.

We next proceeded to bind the two Indians, and then made all the sail we could to the southward, and on the fifteenth day [Sunday], a little before sundown, we came to an anchor in the harbor of Marblehead.

News had reached this place that we were all killed and many people flocked to the water side to learn who we were and what other news they could, concerning the many vessels that had been taken by the Indians. They hailed us, and then some came on board; and when they saw the Indians, they demanded why we kept them alive and why we had not killed them. We answered them, that we had lost everything, even to our clothes, and thought if we brought them in alive, we might get somewhat by them towards our losses. But this did not satisfy the people, who were angry at the sight of the Indians, and now began to grow clamorous. We told them we should take them on shore and deliver them into the hands of the constable of the town, that they might be answerable to the court at Boston; and so we carried them on shore with their hands bound behind them.

Being on shore, the whole town flocked about them, begining at first to insult them, and soon after, the women surrounded them, drove us by force from them, (we escaping at no little peril,) and laid violent hands upon the captives, some stoning us in the meantime, because we would protect them, others seizing them by the hair, got full possession of them, nor was there any way left by which we could rescue them. Then with stones, billets of wood, and what else they might, they made an end of these Indians. We were kept at such distance that we could not see them till they were dead, and then we found them with their heads off and gone, and their flesh in a manner pulled from their bones. And such was the tumultation these women made, that for my life I could not tell who these women were, or the names of any of them. They cried out and said, if the Indians had been carried to Boston, that would have been the end of it, and they would have been set at liberty; but said they, if there had been forty of the best Indians in the country here, they would have killed them all, though they should be hanged for it. They suffered neither constable nor mandrake, nor any other person to come near them, until they had finished their bloody purpose.

Robert Roules

Taken upon oath this 7th of July, 1677

Edward Rawson, Sec.

From: *A Narrative of the Captivity, Sufferings and Removes of Mrs. Mary Rowlandson* (1682)

This excerpt from Mrs. Rowlandson's famous narrative graphically conveys why the settlers had good reason to be afraid of the Indians, though it should be mentioned that they had largely brought the Indians' wrath on themselves by killing them and stealing their land. Mrs. Rowlandson was taken captive but, in due course, released.

On the tenth of February 1676 came the Indians with great numbers upon Lancaster. Their first coming was about sunrising. Hearing the noise of some guns, we looked out; several houses were burning and the smoke ascending to heaven. There were five persons taken in one house; the father and the mother and a sucking child they knocked on the head; the other two they took and carried away alive. There were two others, who being out of their garrison upon some occasion were set upon; one was knocked on the head, the other escaped. Another there was who running along was shot and wounded and fell down; he begged of them his life, promising them money (as they told me), but they would not hearken to him but knocked him in the head, stripped him naked, and split open his bowels. Another, seeing many of the Indians about his barn, ventured and went out but was quickly shot down. There were three others belonging to the same garrison who were killed; the Indians, getting up upon the roof of the barn, had advantage to shoot down upon them over their fortification. Thus these murderous wretches went on, burning and destroying before them.

At length they came and beset our own house, and quickly it was the dolefullest day that ever mine eyes saw. The house stood upon the edge of a hill. Some of the Indians got behind the hill, others into the barn, and others behind anything that could shelter them; from all which places they shot against the house so that the bullets seemed to fly like hail; and quickly they wounded one man among us, then another, and then a third. About two hours (according to my observation in that amazing time) they had been about the house before they prevailed to fire it (which they did with flax and hemp which they brought out of the barn, and there being no defense about the house, only two flankers at two opposite corners and one of them not finished). They fired it once, and one ventured out and quenched it, but they quickly fired it again and that took.

Now is that dreadful hour come that I have often heard of (in time of war as it was the case of others), but now mine eyes see it. Some in our house were fighting for their lives, others wallowing in their blood, the house on fire over our heads, and the bloody heathen ready to knock us on the head if we stirred out. Now might we hear mothers and children crying out for themselves and one another, "Lord, what shall we do?" Then I took my children (and one of my sisters, hers) to go forth and leave the house, but as soon as we came to the door and appeared, the Indians shot so thick that the bullets rattled against the house as if one had taken an handful of stones and threw them so that we were fain to give back. We had six stout dogs belonging to our garrison, but none of them would stir although another time, if any Indian had come to the door, they were ready to fly upon him and tear him down. The Lord hereby would make us the more to acknowledge His hand and to see that our help is always in Him. But out we must go, the fire increasing and coming along behind us roaring, and the Indians gaping before us with their guns, spears, and hatchets to devour us. No sooner were we out of the house, but my brother-in-law (being before wounded, in defending the house, in or near the throat) fell down dead; whereat the Indians scornfully shouted, halloed, and were presently upon him, stripping off his clothes. The bullets flying thick, one went through my side, and the same (as would seem) through the bowels and hand of my dear child in my arms. One of my elder sister's children, named William, had then his leg broken, which the Indians perceiving, they knocked him on the head. Thus were we butchered by those merciless heathen, standing amazed, with the blood running down to our heels.

My eldest sister being yet in the house and seeing those woeful sights, the infidels hailing mothers one way and children another and some wallowing in their blood, and her elder son telling her that her son William was dead and myself was wounded, she said, "And, Lord, let me die with them." Which was no sooner said, but she was struck with a bullet and fell down dead over the threshold. I hope she is reaping the fruit of her good labors, being faithful to the service of God in her place. In her younger years she lay under much trouble upon spiritual accounts till it pleased God to make that precious scripture take hold of her heart, 2 Corinthians, 12:9, "And he said unto me, my grace is sufficient for thee." More than twenty years after I have heard her tell how sweet and comfortable that place was to her. But to return: the Indians laid hold of us, pulling me one way and the children another, and said, "Come go along with us." I told them they would kill me. They answered, if I were willing to go along with them they would not hurt me.

Oh, the doleful sight that now was to behold at this house! "Come, behold the works of the Lord, what desolation He has made in the earth." Of thirty-seven persons who were in this one house none escaped either present death or a bitter captivity save only one, who might say as he, Job 1:15, "And I only am escaped alone to tell the news." There were twelve killed, some shot, some stabbed with their spears, some knocked down with their hatchets. When we are in prosperity, oh, the little that we think of such dreadful sights, and to see our dear friends and relations lie bleeding out their heart-blood upon the ground! There was one who was chopped into the head with a hatchet and stripped naked, and yet was crawling up and down. It is a solemn sight to see so many Christians lying in their blood, some here and some there, like a company of sheep torn by wolves, all of them stripped naked by a company of hell-hounds, roaring, singing, ranting and insulting, as if they would have torn our very hearts out. Yet the Lord by his almighty power preserved a number of us from death, for there were twenty-four of us taken alive and carried captive.

I had often before this said that if the Indians should come I should choose rather to be killed by them than taken alive, but when it came to the trial, my mind changed; their glittering weapons so daunted my spirit that I chose rather to go along with those (as I may say) ravenous beasts than that moment to end my days. And that I may the better declare what happened to me during that grievous captivity, I shall particularly speak of the several removes we had up and down the wilderness.

From: The Salem Village Book of Record (1672–1697), Danvers Archival Center—First Church Collection, Danvers, Massachusetts

Salem Village, which has since changed its name to Danvers, covered a large, remote area west of Salem Town.

The full story of the Salem Village conflicts that led up to 1692, and continued after it, is complicated. But this excerpt from the Salem Village Book of Record gives some notion of two crucial areas of dispute: the ownership of lands in Topsfield, on the Salem Village and Ipswich borders, and the status of the village minister. The towns of Salem and Ipswich had both regarded the same lands as in their gift, causing bitter ownership disputes, particularly between the Putnam and Nurse families. The question of whether the new minister, Deodat Lawson, should be ordained or merely serve the community as a pastor without the authority to hold communion also reflected deep divisions between the Putnams and others.

The Putnams had been established in Salem Village for three generations and felt threatened by the changes taking place in society and by newcomers such as the Nurses. They were in the forefront of those pressing to form an official Salem Village church. A "church" in the Puritan sense was a gathering of people who had been accepted by an ordained minister as "visible saints", that is, who had proved themselves to the minister's satisfaction as among those chosen by God as destined for heaven.

As is seen here, the ordination issue became so fraught that three magistrates were asked to come from Salem to arbitrate. Their subsequent reference to "uncharitable expressions and uncomely reflections" suggests that civilized interchange had completely broken down. Their remark that the gap in understanding "will let out peace and order and let in confusion and every evil work" proved prophetic. It was unfortunate that the two of them who came back to Salem Village five years later, to sit in judgment on the accused witches, did not reflect on the possible implications of their own words with regard to the causes of the witch-hunt.

Salem Village, this 25th of September, 1686

The inhabitants of this place are desired to meet together at their ordinary place of meeting on Friday the first day of October next, at twelve of the clock, to receive the answer of the selectmen of Salem Town concerning the land which was granted to this Village by the honored General Court in the year 1639 which Topsfield men lay claim to, and to consider what shall be done further in that matter. Also to give answer to a petition of several young men which desire a seat in the west gallery; also to consider what to do about the meetinghouse land that is fenced in. By order of the Committee.

THOMAS PUTNAM, CLERK

The first day of October, 1686

At a general meeting of the inhabitants of Salem Village, it was voted that the young men's petition is granted, and the committee is to order how high they shall set their seat.

The first day of October, 1686

At a general meeting of the inhabitants of Salem Village it was agreed and voted by a general concurrence that whereas some of Salem did make a motion to the General Court in the year 1639 and did obtain a grant from the court of all the lands that did lie between Salem bounds and Ipswich River not formerly granted, for the accommodation of a Village that Salem did intend to plant near said river, and Salem having declared us to be that Village for whom they did obtain the abovesaid grant; and in consideration that Topsfield men do lay claim unto our land granted unto us above, and we being deprived of our just right by them; therefore we do now make choice of our loving friends, *viz.:* Lieutenant Nathaniel Putnam, Captain Jonathan Putnam, Sargeant Nathaniel Ingersoll, and William Sibley, or the major part of them for a committee to transact with Topsfield men about the land abovesaid. And do hereby fully empower them in our name and for our use, for to sue at law any of them that lay claim to our land, or otherwise for to agree with Topsfield Town as they shall see cause, either in court or out of court, or to give discharge to them or any of them; and what our loving friends above named shall do in that case shall be holden good by us as if we ourselves had done it, and the inhabitants to bear their charge.

The first day of October, 1686

At a general meeting of the inhabitants of Salem Village it was agreed and voted by a general concurrence that whereas Joseph Hutchinson of Salem Village did give an acre of land unto the inhabitants of the Farms of Salem or Salem Village, for to set our meetinghouse upon, in the year 1673, and write a deed of gift there of in the Village book of records with his own hand, and doth now refuse to let the Village enjoy the acre of land given as abovesaid, but hath fenced in a great [part] of the land and claimeth the whole acre of land although he did deliver the acre of land by bounds with his own hands; in consideration whereof we do now make choice of our loving friends, *viz.:* Lieutenant Jonathan Walcott, Ensign Thomas Flint, and Thomas Putnam, or the major part of them, for a committee to transact with Joseph Hutchinson about the land aforesaid, and do hereby fully empower them in our name and for our use to sue Joseph Hutchinson at law or otherwise for to settle or to agree with him as they shall think meet, and what our loving friends shall do in the case above named shall be accounted and holden good by us in all respects as if we had done it ourselves, and the inhabitants to bear their charge.

Salem Village, this tenth of December, 1686

The inhabitants of this place are desired to meet together at their ordinary place of meeting on the sixteenth day of this instant month at ten of the clock in the morning to discourse with Mr. Lawson and to agitate amongst ourselves in matters referring to his full settlement with us, also to take order about the transcribing of our book of records. The inhabitants are desired all to come to the meeting, for it is matter of concernment to us all. By order of the Committee.

THOMAS PUTNAM, CLERK

The sixteenth day of December, 1686

At a general meeting of the inhabitants of Salem Village it was agreed and voted by a general concurrence that it was left to the Committee to put it to the vote the next convenient Sabbath day, excepting the next Sabbath day, to know the minds of our inhabitants referring to Mr. Lawson to office in this place.

2. It was agreed and voted by a general concurrence that it was left to the Committee together with Lieutenant Nathaniel Putnam to take care to transcribe our Village book of records according to their best understanding.

Salem Village, this 14th of January, 1687

The inhabitants of this place are desired to take notice that we are informed that Joseph Hutchinson, Job Swinaton, Joseph Porter, and Daniel Andrew do desire that four men may be chosen for to transact with them about their grievances relating to the public affairs of this place, and if they cannot agree among themselves that then they will refer their difference to the honored Major Gedney and John Hathorne Esq and to the reverend elders of the church of Salem; therefore the inhabitants of this place are hereby desired to meet together at their ordinary place of meeting on the seventeenth day of this instant month at one of the clock in the afternoon for to choose four men for the ends above expressed. By order of the Committee.

THOMAS PUTNAM, CLERK

The 17th day of January, 1687

At a public meeting of the inhabitants of Salem Village it was agreed and voted by a general concurrence that we make choice of Captain Jonathan Putnam, Lieutenant Jonathan Walcott, Ensign Thomas Flint, and Corporal Joseph Herrick for to transact with Joseph Hutchinson, Job Swinaton, Joseph Porter, and Daniel Andrew about their grievances relating to the public affairs of this place and if they cannot agree among themselves that then they shall refer their difference to the honored Major Gedney and John Hathorne Esq and to the reverend elders of the Salem Church for a full determination of those differences.

Salem Village, this 16th of February, 1687

The inhabitants of this Village are hereby required in his Majesty's name to meet together at their ordinary place of meeting on the eighteenth day of this instant month at nine o'clock in the morning to hear and to consider of, to receive and embrace, or to refuse, the advice of the honored Major Gedney and John Hathorne and William Brown, Esqrs. and the reverend elders of Salem Church. Also to view what is already transcribed of our Village book of records and to give some direction to the Committee and Lieutenant Nathaniel Putnam about the transcribing of the rest. Also to consider of and make void some votes that have passed amongst us that have been grievous to us for time past or that may be unprofitable to us for time to come. All our inhabitants are desired to come to this meeting, for it is matter of great concernment to us all. By order of the Committee.

THOMAS PUTNAM, CLERK

The eighteenth day of February, 1687

At a general meeting of the inhabitants of Salem Village it was first voted that Captain Jonathan Putnam is chosen moderator for this meeting.

2. It was agreed and voted by a general concurrence that this meeting is adjourned for one hour and a half and removed to Sargeant Nathaniel Ingersoll's house.

3. It was agreed and voted that we make choice of Mr. Joseph Hutchinson, Mr. Joseph Porter, Mr. Daniel Andrew, Captain Jonathan Putnam, Lieutenant Jonathan Walcott, and Thomas Putnam for to view our books of records and to copy out any entries that are therein which they conceive have been grievous to any of us in time past or that may be unprofitable to us for time to come and to bring such entries as they copy out to the inhabitants to the adjournment of this meeting to see which of them they will annul and make void in our book of records.

4. It was agreed and voted by a general concurrence that this meeting is adjourned to the twenty-eighth or last day of this instant month February to ten o'clock in the morning.

At an adjournment of the meeting of the inhabitants of Salem Village from the eighteenth day of February 1687 to the twenty-eighth or last day of the same month, it was first voted that the acceptance of the advice of the honored and reverend gentlemen of Salem should be voted in general and not in parts.

2. It was agreed and voted by a general concurrence that we do accept of and embrace the advice of the honored and reverend gentlemen of Salem sent to us under their hands bearing date the 14th of February, 1687 and order that it shall be entered in our book of records.

3. It was agreed and voted by a general concurrence that all votes that passed amongst us concerning the building of a ministry house are hereby made void and of none effect.

4. It was agreed and voted by a general concurrence that all votes that have passed amongst us about building a kitchen or lean-to to our ministry house are hereby made void and of none effect.

5. It was agreed and voted by a general concurrence that all the votes that passed amongst us on the fifth day of June, 1683, that are entered in our book of records are hereby made void and of none effect, except it be that vote about warning a public meeting.

6. It was voted that Mr. Lawson's salary is regulated as followeth, and this to continue so long as he continues in the work of the ministry amongst us as now he doth.

7. It was agreed and voted by a general concurrence that we, having viewed our new book of records, we do find it already transcribed so far as it is to the full satisfaction of the whole inhabitants, and Mr. Joseph Hutchinson, Mr. Joseph Porter, and Mr. Daniel Andrew, and Captain Jonathan Putnam, Lieutenant Jonathan Walcott, and Thomas Putnam, having had the perusal of it, they approve of all that is transcribed, except one vote, which vote the people see no cause to annul, and they approve also of the leaving out of all that is left out that is not transcribed, and we finding our book of records already transcribed from the beginning of it to the 24th day of May, 1683, though there are some votes left out that passed in Mr. Bayley's days and some votes left out that passed in Mr. Burroughs' days that are not transcribed, which we conceive will be of no great use us for the time to come which we leave to lie in the old book of records as they are and order that all other votes that have passed amongst us from the 24th day of May, 1683, shall be fairly and fully transcribed according to the advice of the honored and reverend gentlemen of Salem, except such votes as are or shall be made void and of none effect.

Letter to John Putnam and Joseph Hutchinson

To Captain John Putnam, Mr. Joseph Hutchinson, etc.
To be communicated to the rest of the inhabitants of Salem Village. Loving brethren, friends, and neighbors: Upon serious consideration of and mature deliberation upon what hath been offered to us about your calling and transacting in order to the settling and ordaining the Reverend Mr. Deodat Lawson, and the grievances offered by some to obstruct and impede that proceeding, our sense of the matter is:

1. That the affair of calling and transacting in order to the settling and ordaining the reverend Mr. Lawson hath not been so inoffensively managed as might have been, at least not in all the parts and passages of it.

2. That the grievances offered by some among you are not in themselves of sufficient weight to obstruct so great a work and that they have not been improved so peaceably and orderly as Christian prudence and self-denial doth direct.

3. To our grief we observe such uncharitable expressions and uncomely reflections tossed to and fro as look like the effects of settled prejudice and resolved animosity, though we are much rather willing to account them the product of weakness than wilfulness. However, we must needs say that come whence they will, they have a tendency to make such a gap as we fear if not timely prevented, will let out peace and order and let in confusion and every evil work.

4. As things drew to a conclusion when you met with us, you did seem on both parts to be under a conviction of the necessity of peace, and there was some promising appearance of mutual condescension, and that for the future you would on all hands study to be quiet, and to that end you desired us to give you such advice as we judged would conduce to the promotion of righteousness, peace and order among you. Thus you have our sense of the matter as to what is past and present, and at your request we shall give you what is with us to direct by way of advice to prevent contention and trouble for the future, that it may not devour forever, and that if the Lord please you may be happier henceforth than to make one another miserable and not make your place uncomfortable to your present and undesirable to any other minister, and the ministry itself in a great measure unprofitable; and that you may not bring impositions on yourselves by convincing all about you that you cannot or will not use your liberty as becomes the gospel, as also in testimony of the care we have of you and our unfeigned desire and endeavour of your peace and welfare.

For these ends we advise you:

1. That you desist at present from urging the ordination of the Reverend Mr. Lawson till your spirits are better quieted and composed.

2. That you encourage him in his ministerial work from time to time by an honest fulfilling of your last agreement with him till such time as he is ordained amongst you unless any juster cause shall appear to the contrary than any yet hath done.

3. That the last agreement about his maintenance be not held binding after the time of his ordination unless that act be again confirmed by full and free consent of the major part of the householders lawfully called together upon sufficient notice of time, place, and end of the meeting; yea, if more than a mere major part should not consent to it, we should be loath to advise our brethren to proceed but rather advise upon that condition that some other way may be propounded as may be acceptable to Mr. Lawson and may be more pleasing to the people, as part money and part as money, or part money and part in pay at common price so as Mr. Lawson be not damaged and the people better pleased; we confiding in Mr. Law-

son's readiness to comply with any proposition that will suit with the condition of his family.

4. We advise all possible care be taken for the future to prevent the grievance objected about the choice of the Committee, though we cannot totally comply with that proposition which pretends a court order for choosing a Committee without your own limits, seeing we find no such order, but a Committee nominated and appointed by the court in case of disagreement among yourselves, two of which three are dead. We advise, therefore, that whilst this contention lasts, one at least of the Town of Salem out of your limits be fairly chosen as one of your Committee, and that the householders have liberty to choose the rest of themselves or otherwise as they please.

5. We advise the old book of records be kept in being and that such votes in it as are offensive to any come to a further consideration in some lawful meeting appointed to that end, that all inconvenient votes may be repealed or regulated to satisfaction, and such repeals and regulations be inserted in the new book of records and all other votes fairly, fully, and impartially transcribed, and for the future that no votes be recorded but in the presence of the assembly that votes them, or at least at the next lawful meeting being again publicly read, which if it be done and the vote read publicly after it is recorded will undoubtedly prevent any reflection for the future upon the book or bookkeeper.

Finally, we think peace cheap if it may be procured by complying with the aforementioned particulars, which are few, fair, and easy, and that they will hardly pass for lovers of peace, truth, and ministry and order in the day of the Lord that shall so lean to their own understanding and will that they shall refuse such easy methods for the obtaining of them. And if peace and agreement amongst you be once comfortably obtained, we advise you with all convenient speed to go on with your intended ordination, and so we shall follow our advice with our prayers. But if our advice be rejected we wish you better and hearts to follow it, and only add if you will unreasonably trouble yourselves we pray you not any further to trouble us. We leave all to the blessing of God the wonderful counsellor and your own serious consideration. Praying you to read and consider the whole and then act as God shall direct you. Farewell.

SALEM, FEBRUARY 14TH, 1687

BARTHOLOMEW GEDNEY, JOHN HATHORNE,
WILLIAM BROWN, JR., JOHN HIGGINSON, NICOLAS NOYES

Part II

The Witch-hunt

The surviving contemporary accounts of the Salem witchcraft episode, by people involved in or close to events, are graphic and detailed. Together with the records of the examinations conducted by John Hathorne and the other magistrates, and the depositions, petitions, formal accusations, and arrest warrants, as well as Samuel Parris's sermons and the material in the Salem Village Book of Record and the Salem Village Church Book of Record, they provide a good picture of what happened in 1692.

In this part of the book, the Salem story is told by means of the personal accounts, arranged so as to provide a continuous narrative. They consist of long excerpts from, or in some cases the whole of, six works: *A Modest Inquiry into the Nature of Witchcraft* by John Hale, *More Wonders of the Invisible World* by Robert Calef, *A Brief and True Narrative of Witchcraft at Salem Village* by Deodat Lawson, the letter of Thomas Brattle, Governor William Phipps's *Letters to the Home Government,* and *The Confession of Ann Putnam.*

One crucial aspect of the witch-hunt is missing from these accounts; that is, the part played by the family of Thomas Putnam, whose daughter Ann was the leader of the accusing girls. However, that aspect will emerge fully from texts in later sections.

Details of the first five works are given here together, instead of one by one as they appear, so as not to interrupt the flow of the narrative.

Because a different calendar from our modern one was in use in 1692, "the latter end of the year 1691", in John Hale's *A Modest Enquiry,* was, in fact, January and February of 1692.

John Hale, *A Modest Enquiry into the Nature of Witchcraft* (Boston, 1702)

The Reverend John Hale (1636–1700), pastor of Beverly, near Salem, was an active participant in the witch hunt until his own wife was accused in October 1692. He wrote this book partly as a defense and partly an apology, in 1697. It was not published till five years later, after his death.

Robert Calef, *More Wonders of the Invisible World* (1700)

Calef (1648–1719), a Boston merchant, finished this book in 1697 but it was not published till three years later, in London, no doubt due to its criticisms of Increase and Cotton Mather. When it arrived in Massachusetts, Increase ordered it burned in the college yard at Harvard. Calef's horror at the cruelty and injustice of the witch trials does not detract from the reliability of his account, which always corresponds with the other narratives and evidence.

Deodat Lawson, *A Brief and True Narrative of Witchcraft at Salem Village* (Boston, 1692)

Lawson, who was born and died in England (dates unknown), was the pastor of Salem Village from 1684–1688. The dispute whether he should be ordained or not led John Hathorne to write prophetically, that if there were no reconciliation, "every evil work" might follow, (see section 1, part 2.) The Putnam family and their associates had desired his ordination, and it was probably they who invited him to Salem Village in April 1692. The sequence of events he describes, from the moment he arrived, when Mary Walcott visited him and showed him teeth marks on her wrist, has every appearance of being carefully orchestrated by the Putnams.

Thomas Brattle, letter (1692)

Brattle (1658–1713) was a wealthy Boston merchant, distinguished mathematician and astronomer, a member of The Royal Society and treasurer of Harvard College. He wrote this letter to an unknown correspondent in October 1692, probably with a view to its being circulated in manuscript and influencing Sir William Phipps, the new governor, and the General Court, on the future of the witch trials.

Governor Phipps, *Letters to the Home Government* (1692–1693)

Sir William Phips (1651–1694) provides an extraordinary example of seventeenth-century upward mobility. The son of a Maine gunsmith, he did not learn to read and write till the age of twenty-two. After working as a shepherd and ship's carpenter, he made his fortune by rescuing treasure from a Spanish galleon, thereby gaining a knighthood. He was taken up by the Mathers, who had him appointed governor to succeed the deposed Sir Edmund Andros.

Sir William's letters make clear his bewilderment—faced with the witchcraft crisis, his initial reliance on the advice of the Mathers and the deputy governor, Sir William Stoughton—and his subsequent fear of being blamed for the injustices perpetrated by the Court of Oyer and Terminer, with the loss of innocent lives.

3

The Guilt of Innocent Blood

From: John Hale, *A Modest Enquiry into the Nature of Witchcraft* (Boston, 1702)

From: chapter 2

In the latter end of the year 1691, Mr. Samuel Parris, pastor of the church in Salem Village, had a daughter of nine [Betty Parris], and a niece of about eleven years of age [Abigail Williams], sadly afflicted of they knew not what distempers; and he made his application to physicians, yet still they grew worse: And at length one physician [Dr. William Griggs] gave his opinion, that they were under an evil hand. This the neighbours quickly took up, and concluded they were bewitched. He had also an Indian manservant, and his wife who afterwards confessed, that without the knowledge of their master or mistress, they had taken some of the afflicted persons' urine, and mixing it with meal had made a cake, and baked it, to find out the witch, as they said. After this, the afflicted persons cried out of the Indian woman, named Tituba, that she did pinch, prick, and grievously torment them, and that they saw her here and there, where nobody else could. Yea, they could tell where she was, and what she did, when out of their human sight. These children were bitten and pinched by invisible agents; their arms, necks, and backs turned this way and that way, and returned back again, so as it was impossible for them to do of themselves, and beyond the power of any epileptic fits, or natural disease to effect. Sometimes they were taken dumb, their mouths stopped, their throats choked, their limbs wracked and tormented so as might move an heart of stone, to sympathize with them, with bowels of compassion for them. I will not enlarge in the description of their cruel sufferings, because they were in all things afflicted as bad as John Goodwin's children at Boston, in the year 1689. So that he that will read Mr. Mather's book of *Memorable Providences,* page 3, etc., may read part of what these children, and afterwards sundry grown persons, suffered by the hand of Satan, at Salem Village, and parts adjacent, *Anno* 1691–2. Yet there was more in these sufferings, than in those at Boston, by pins invisibly stuck into their flesh, pricking with irons. (As in part published in a book printed 1693, *viz. The Wonders of the Invisible World.*) Mr. Parris seeing the distressed condition of his family, desired the presence of some worthy gentlemen of Salem, and some neighbour ministers to consult together at his house; who when they came, and had enquired diligently into the sufferings of the afflicted, concluded they were preternatural, and feared the hand of Satan was in them.

The advice given to Mr. Parris by them was, that he should sit still and wait upon the providence of God to see what time might discover; and to be much in prayer for the discovery of what was yet secret. They also examined Tituba, who confessed the making a cake, as is above mentioned, and said her mistress in her own country was a witch, and had taught her some means to be used for the discovery of a witch and for the prevention of being bewitched, etc. But said that she herself was not a witch.

Soon after this, there were two or three private fasts at the minister's house, one of which was kept by sundry neighbour ministers, and after this, another in public at the Village, and several days afterwards of public humiliation, during these molestations, not only there, but in other congregations for them. And one general fast by order of the General Court, observed throughout the colony to seek the Lord that he would rebuke Satan, and be a light unto his people in this day of darkness.

But I return to the history of these troubles. In a short time after other persons who were of age to be witnesses [Ann Putnam, 12, daughter of Thomas Putnam, and Elizabeth Hubbard, 17, great-niece of Dr. William Griggs], were molested by Satan, and in their fits cried out upon Tituba and Goody Osborn and Sarah Good that they or specters in their shapes did grievously torment them; hereupon some of their village neighbours complained to the magistrates at Salem, desiring they would come and examine the afflicted and accused together; the which they did: the effect of which examination was, that Tituba confessed she was a witch, and that she with the two others accused did torment and bewitch the complainers, and that these with two others whose names she knew not, had their witch meeting together; relating the times when and places where they met, with many other circumstances to be seen at large. Upon this the said Tituba and Osborn and Sarah Good were committed to prison upon suspicion of acting witchcraft. After this the said Tituba was again examined in prison, and owned her first confession in all points, and then was herself afflicted and complained of her fellow witches tormenting of her, for her confession, and accusing them, and being searched by a woman, she was found to have upon her body the marks of the devil's wounding of her.

From: Robert Calef, *More Wonders of the Invisible World* (1700)

From: part 5

The account [Tituba] since gives of it is, that her master did beat her and otherways abuse her, to make her confess and accuse (such as he called) her sister witches, and that whatsoever she said by way of confessing or accusing others, was the effect of such usage; her master refused to pay her [prison] fees, unless she would stand to what she had said.

From: Deodat Lawson, *A Brief and True Narrative of Witchcraft at Salem Village* (Boston, 1692)

On the nineteenth day of March last, I went to Salem Village, and lodged at Nathaniel Ingersoll's near to the minister Mr. Parris' house, and presently after I came into my lodging Captain Walcott's daughter Mary came to Lieutenant Ingersoll's and spake to me, but, suddenly after as she stood by the door, was bitten, so that she cried out of her wrist, and looking on it with a candle, we saw apparently the marks of teeth both upper and lower set, on each side of her wrist.

In the beginning of the evening, I went to give Mr. Parris a visit. When I was there, his kinswoman [niece], Abigail Williams, (about 12 years of age,) had a grievous fit; she was at first hurried with violence to and fro in the room, (though Mrs. Ingersoll endeavoured to hold her,) sometimes making as if she would fly, stretching up her arms as high as she could, and crying "Whish, Whish, Whish!" several times; presently after she said there was Goodwife Nurse and said, "Do you not see her? Why there she stands!" And the said Goodwife offered her the book, but she was resolved she would not take it, saying often, "I won't, I won't, I won't, take it, I do not know what book it is: I am sure it is none of God's book, it is the devil's book, for aught I know." After that, she run to the fire, and begun to throw fire brands, about the house; and run against the back, as if she would run up [the] chimney, and, as they said, she had attempted to go into the fire in other fits.

On Lord's day, the twentieth of March, there were sundry of the afflicted persons at meeting, as, Mrs. Pope, and Goodwife Bibber, Abigail Williams, Mary Walcott, Mercy Lewis [Thomas Putnam's servant], and Doctor Griggs' maid [Elizabeth Hubbard]. There was also at meeting, Goodwife Corey (who was afterward examined on suspicion of being a witch): They had several sore fits, in the time of public worship, which did something interrupt me in my first prayer; being so unusual. After psalm was sung, Abigail Williams said to me, "Now stand up, and name your text": And after it was read, she said, "It is a long text." In the beginning of sermon, Mrs. Pope, a woman afflicted, said to me, "Now there is enough of that." And in the afternoon, Abigail Williams upon my referring to my doctrine said to me, "I know no doctrine you had. If you did name one, I have forgot it."

In sermon time when Goodwife Corey was present in the meetinghouse Abigail Williams called out, "Look where Goodwife Corey sits on the beam suckling her yellow bird betwixt her fingers"! Ann Putnam, another girl afflicted, said there was a yellow bird sat on my hat as it hung on the pin in the pulpit: but those that were by, restrained her from speaking loud about it.

On Monday the 21st of March, the magistrates of Salem appointed to come to examination of Goodwife Corey. And about twelve of the clock, they went into the meetinghouse, which was thronged with spectators: Mr. Noyes [a Salem minister] began with a very pertinent and pathetic prayer; and Goodwife Corey being called to answer to what was alleged against her, she desired to go to prayer, which was much wondered at, in the presence of so many hundred people: The magistrates told her, they would not admit it; they came not there to hear her pray, but to examine her, in what was alleged against her. The worshipful Mr. Hathorne asked her, Why she afflicted those children? She said, she did not afflict them. He asked her, who did then? She said, "I do not know; How should I know?" The number of the afflicted persons were about that time ten, *viz.* four married women, Mrs. Pope, Mrs. Putman, [Ann Putman Senior] wife of Thomas Putnam], Goodwife Bibber, and an ancient woman, named Goodall, three maids, Mary Walcott, Mercy Lewis, at Thomas Putman's, and a maid at Dr. Griggs's [Elizabeth Hubbard]. There were three girls from 9 to 12 years of age, each of them, or thereabouts, *viz.* Elizabeth Parris, Abigail Williams and Ann Putman; these were most of them at Goodwife Corey's examination, and did vehemently accuse her in the assembly of afflicting them, by biting, pinching, strangling, etc. And that they did in their fit see her likeness coming to them, and bringing a book to them, she said, she had no book; they affirmed, she had a yellow bird, that used to suck betwixt her fingers, and being asked about it, if she had any familiar spirit, that attended her, she said, She had no familiarity with any such thing. She was a gospel woman: which title she called her self by; and the afflicted persons told her, ah! She was, a gospel witch. Ann Putman did there affirm, that one day when Lieutenant Fuller was at prayer at her father's house, she saw the shape of Goodwife Corey and she thought Goodwife Nurse praying at the same time to the devil, she was not sure it was Goodwife Nurse. She thought it was; but very sure she saw the shape of Goodwife Corey. The said Corey said, they were poor, distracted children, and no heed to be given to what they said. Mr. Hathorne and Mr. Noyes replied, it was the judgment of all that were present, they were bewitched, and only she, the accused person said, they were distracted. It was observed several times, that if she did but bite her under lip in time of examination the persons afflicted were bitten on their arms and wrists and produced the marks before the magistrates, ministers and others. And being watched for that, if she did but pinch her fingers, or grasp one hand hard in another, they were pinched and produced the marks before the magistrates and spectators. After that, it was observed, that if she did but lean her breast against the seat, in the meetinghouse, (being the bar at which she stood,) they were afflicted. Particularly Mrs. Pope complained of grievous torment in her bowels as if they were torn out. She vehemently accused said Corey as the instrument, and first threw her muff at her; but that flying not home, she got off her shoe, and hit Goodwife Corey on the head with it. After these postures were watched, if said Corey did but stir her feet, they were afflicted in their feet, and stamped fearfully. The afflicted persons asked her why she did not go to the company of witches which were before the meetinghouse mustering? Did she not hear the drum beat? They accused her of having familiarity with the devil, in the time of examination, in the shape of a black man whispering in her ear; they affirmed, that her yellow bird sucked betwixt her fingers in the assembly; and order being given to see if there were any sign, the girl that saw it said, it was too late now; she had removed a pin, and put it on her head; which was found there sticking upright.

They told her, she had covenanted with the devil for ten years, six of them were gone, and four more to come. She was required by the magistrates to answer that question in the catechism, "How many persons be there in the Godhead?" She answered it but oddly, yet was there no great thing to be gathered from it: She denied all that was charged upon her, and said, They could not prove a witch; she was that afternoon committed to Salem Prison; and after she was in custody, she did not so appear to them, and afflict them as before.

On Wednesday the 23 of March, I went to Thomas Putman's, on purpose to see his wife: I found her lying on the bed, having had a sore fit a little before. She spake to me, and said, she was glad to see me; her husband and she both desired me to pray with her, while she was sensible; which I did, though the apparition said, I should not go to prayer. At the first beginning she attended; but after a little time, was taken with a fit: yet continued silent, and seemed to be asleep: when prayer was done, her husband going to her, found her in a fit; he took her off the bed, to set her on his knees; but at first she was so stiff, she could not be bended; but she afterwards set down; but quickly began to strive violently with her arms and legs; she then began to complain of, and as it were to converse personally with, Goodwife Nurse, saying, "Goodwife Nurse! Be gone! Be gone! Be gone! Are you not ashamed, a woman of your profession, to afflict a poor creature so? what hurt did I ever do you in my life! you have but two years to live, and then the devil will torment your soul, for this your name is blotted out of God's book, and it shall never be put in God's book again, be gone for shame, are you not afraid of that which is coming upon you? I know, I know, what will make you afraid; the wrath of an angry God, I am sure that will make you afraid; be gone, do not torment me, I know what you would have (we judged she meant, her soul) but it is out of your reach; it is clothed with the white robes of Christ's righteousness." After this, she seemed to dispute with the apparition about a particular text of scripture. The apparition seemed to deny it, (the woman's eyes being fast closed all this time); she said, She was sure there was such a text; and she would tell it; and then the shape would be gone, for said she, "I am sure you cannot stand before that text!" then she was sorely afflicted; her mouth drawn on one side, and her body strained for about a minute, and then said, "I will tell, I will tell; it is, it is, it is!" three or four times, and then was afflicted to hinder her from telling, at last she broke forth and said, "It is the third chapter of the Revelations." I did something scruple the reading it, and did let my scruple appear, lest Satan should make any superstitious lie to improve the word of the eternal God. However, though not versed in these things, I judged I might do it this once for an experiment. I began to read, and before I had near read through the first verse, she opened her eyes, and was well; this fit continued near half an hour. Her husband and the spectators told me, she had often been so relieved by reading texts that she named, something pertinent to her case; as Isaiah 40. 1, Isaiah 49. 1, Isaiah 50. 1, and several others.

On Thursday the twenty fourth of March, (being in course the lecture day, at the Village,) Goodwife Nurse was brought before the magistrates Mr. Hathorne and Mr. Corwin, about ten of the clock, in the forenoon, to be examined in the meetinghouse; the Reverend Mr. Hale begun with prayer, and the warrant being read, she was required to give answer, Why she afflicted those persons? She pleaded her own innocency with earnestness. Thomas Putman's wife, Abigail Williams and Thomas Putman's daughter accused her that she appeared to them, and afflicted them in their fits: but some of the others said, that they had seen her, but knew not that ever she had hurt them; amongst which was Mary Walcott, who was presently after she had so declared bitten, and cried out of her in the meetinghouse; producing the marks of teeth on her wrist. It was so disposed, that I had not leisure to attend the whole time of examination, but both magistrates and ministers told me, that the things alleged by the afflicted, and defences made by her, were much after the same manner, as the former was. And her motions did produce like effects as to biting, pinching, bruising, tormenting, at their breasts, by her leaning, and when, bended back, were as if their backs was broken. The afflicted persons said, the Black Man whispered to her in the assembly, and therefore she could not hear what the magistrates said unto her. They said also that she did then ride by the meetinghouse, behind the Black Man. Thomas Putman's wife had a grievous fit, in the time of examination, to the very great Impairing of her strength, and wasting of her spirits, insomuch as she could hardly move hand, or foot, when she was carried out. Others also were there grievously afflicted, so that there was once such an hideous screech and noise, (which I heard as I walked, at a little distance from the meetinghouse,) as did amaze me, and some that were within told me the whole assembly was struck with consternation, and they were afraid, that those that sat next to them, were under the influence of witchcraft. This woman also was that day committed to Salem Prison. The magistrates and ministers also did inform me, that they apprehended a child of Sarah Good and examined it, being between 4 and 5 years of age, and as to matter of fact, they did unanimously affirm, that when this child did but cast its eye upon the afflicted persons, they were tormented, and they held her head, and yet so many as her eye could fix upon were afflicted. Which they did several times make careful observation of: the afflicted complained, they had often been bitten by this child, and produced the marks of a small set of teeth, accordingly, this was also committed to Salem Prison; the child looked hale, and well as other children. I saw it at Lieutenant Ingersoll's. After the commitment of Goodwife Nurse, Thomas Putman's wife was much better, and had no violent fits at all from that 24th of March to the 5th of April. Some others also said they had not seen her so frequently appear to them, to hurt them.

On the 25th of March, (as Captain Stephen Sewall, of Salem, did afterwards inform me) Elizabeth Parris had sore fits, at his house, which much troubled himself, and his wife, so as he told me they were almost discouraged. She related, that the great Black Man came to her, and told her, if she would be ruled by him, she should have whatsoever she desired, and go to a Golden City. She relating this to Mrs. Sewall, she told the child, it was the devil, and he was a liar from the beginning, and bid her tell him so, if he came again: which she did accordingly, at the next coming to her, in her fits.

On the 26th of March, Mr. Hathorne, Mr. Corwin, and Mr. Higginson were at the prison keeper's house, to examine the child, and it told them there, it had a little snake that used to suck on the lowest joint of its forefinger; and when they inquired where, pointing to other places, it told them, not there, but there, pointing on the lowest point of forefinger; where they observed a deep red spot, about the bigness of a fleabite, they asked who gave it that snake? whether the great Black Man, it said no, its mother gave it.

The 31 of March there was a public fast kept at Salem on account of these afflicted persons. And Abigail Williams said, that the witches had a sacrament that day at an house in the Village, and that they had red bread and red drink. The first of April, Mercy Lewis, Thomas Putman's maid, in her fit, said, they did eat red bread like man's flesh, and would have had her eat some: but she would not; but turned away her head, and spit at them, and said, "I will not eat, I will not drink, it is blood," etc. She said, "That is not the bread of life, that is not the water of life; Christ gives the bread of life, I will have none of it!" This first of April also Mercy Lewis aforesaid saw in her fit a white man and was with him in a glorious place, which had no candles nor sun, yet was full of light and brightness; where was a great multitude in white glittering robes, and they sung the song in the fifth of Revelation the ninth verse, and the 110 Psalm, and the 149 Psalm; and said with herself, "How long shall I stay here? let me be along with you": She was loath to leave this place, and grieved that she could tarry no longer. This white man hath appeared several times to some of them, and given them notice how long it should be before they had another fit, which was sometimes a day, or day and half, or more or less: it hath fallen out accordingly.

The third of April, the Lord's day, being sacrament day, at the Village, Goodwife Corey upon Mr. Parris's naming his text, John 6, 70, *One of them is a Devil,* the said Goodwife Corey went immediately out of the meetinghouse, and flung the door after her violently, to the amazement of the congregation: She was afterward seen by some in their fits, who said, "O Goodwife Corey, I did not think to see you here!" (and being at their red bread and drink) said to her, "Is this a time to receive the sacrament, you ran away on the Lord's day, and scorned to receive it in the meetinghouse, and, Is this a time to receive it? I wonder at you!" This is the sum of what I either saw myself, or did receive information from persons of undoubted reputation and credit.

From: Robert Calef, *More Wonders of the Invisible World (1700)*

April the 11*th.* By this time the number of the accused and accusers being much increased, was a public examination at Salem, six of the magistrates with several ministers being present; there appeared several who complained against others with hideous clamors and screechings. Goodwife Proctor was brought thither, being accused or cried out against; her husband coming to attend and assist her, as there might be need, the accusers cried out of him also, and that with so much earnestness, that he was committed with his wife. About this time, besides the experiment of the afflicted falling at the sight, etc., they put the accused upon saying the Lord's prayer, which one among them performed, except in that petition, *Deliver us from Evil,* she expressed it thus, *Deliver us from all Evil.* This was looked upon as if she prayed against what she was now justly under, and being put upon it again, and repeating those words, *Hallowed be thy name,* she expressed it, *Hollowed be thy name,* this was counted a depraving the words, as signifying to make void, and so a curse rather than a prayer, upon the whole it was concluded that she also could not say it, etc. Proceeding in this work of examination and commitment, many were sent to prison. As an instance, see the following mittimus:

To their Majesties' goal-keeper in Salem.

You are in their Majesties' names hereby required to take into your care, and safe custody, the bodies of William Hobbes, and Deliverance his wife, Mary Easty, the wife of Isaac Easty, and Sarah Wilde, the wife of John Wilde, all of Topsfield; and Edward Bishop of Salem Village, husbandman, and Sarah his wife, and Mary Black, a negro of Lieutenant Nathaniel Putmans of Salem Village; also Mary English the Wife of Philip English, merchant in Salem; who stand charged with high suspicion of sundry acts of witchcraft, done or committed by them lately upon the bodies of Ann Putman, Mercy Lewis and Abigail Williams, of Salem Village, whereby great hurt and damage hath been done to the bodies of the said persons, according to the complaint of Thomas Putman and John Buxton of Salem Village, exhibited Salem, Apr 21, 1692, appears, whom you are to secure in order to their further Examination. Fail not.

JOHN HATHORNE,
ASSISTANTS
JONATHAN CORWIN,
DATED SALEM, APRIL 22, 1692

To Marshal George Herrick of Salem Essex.

You are in their Majesties' names hereby required to convey the abovenamed to the goal at Salem. Fail not.

JOHN HATHORNE,
ASSISTANTS
JONATHAN CORWIN,
DATED SALEM, APR 22, 1692

The occasion of Bishop's being cried out of was, he being at an examination in Salem, when at the Inn the afflicted Indian [John Indian, husband to Tituba] was very unruly, whom he undertook, and so managed him, that he was very orderly, after which in riding home, in company of him and other accusers, the Indian fell into a fit, and clapping hold with his teeth on the back of the man that rode before him, thereby held himself upon the horse, but said Bishop striking him with his stick, the Indian soon recovered, and promised he would do so no more; to which Bishop replied, that he doubted not, but he could cure them all, with more to the same effect; immediately after he was parted from them, he was cried out of, etc.

May 14, 1692. Sir William Phips arrived with Commission from their Majesties to be Governor, pursuant to the new charter; which he now brought with him; the ancient charter having been vacated by King Charles, and King James (by which they had a power not only to make their own laws; but also to choose their own Governor and officers;) and the country for some years was put under an absolute Commission Government, till the revolution, at which time though more than two thirds of the people were for reassuming their ancient government, (to which they had encouragement by His then Royal Highness's Proclamation) yet some that might have been better employed (in another station) made it their business (by printing, as well as speaking) to their utmost to divert them from such a settlement; and so far prevailed, that for about seven weeks after the revolution, here was not so much as a face of any government; but some few men upon their own nomination would be called a Committee of Safety; but at length the assembly prevailed with those that had been of the government, to promise that they would reassume; and accordingly a proclamation was drawn, but before publishing it, it was underwritten, that they would not have it understood that they did reassume charter government; so that between government and no government, this country remained till Sir William arrived; agents being in this time empowered in England, which no doubt did not all of them act according to the minds or interests of those that empowered them, which is manifest by their not acting jointly in what was done; so that this place is perhaps a single instance (even in the best of reigns) of a charter not restored after so happy a revolution.

This settlement by Sir William Phips, his being come governor, put an end to all disputes of these things, and being arrived, and having read his commission, the first thing he exerted his power in was said to be his giving orders that irons should be put upon those in prison; for though for some time after these were committed, the accusers ceased to cry out of them, yet now the cry against them was renewed, which occasioned such order; and though there was partiality in the executing it (some having taken them off almost as soon as put on) yet the cry of these accusers against such ceased after this order.

May 24. Mrs. Cary of Charlestown, was examined and committed. Her husband Mr. Nathaniel Cary has given account thereof, as also of her escape, to this effect,

> I having heard some days, that my wife was accused of witchcraft, being much disturbed at it, by advice, we went to Salem Village, to see if the afflicted did know her; we arrived there, 24 May, it happened to be a day appointed for examination; accordingly soon after our arrival, Mr. Hathorne and Mr. Corwin, etc., went to the meetinghouse, which was the place appointed for that work, the minister began with prayer, and having taken care to get a convenient place, I observed, that the afflicted were two girls of about ten years old, and about two or three others, of about eighteen. One of the girls talked most, and could discern more than the rest. The prisoners were called in one by one, and as they came in were cried out of, etc. The prisoner was placed about 7 or 8 foot from the justices, and the accusers between the justices and them; the prisoner was ordered to stand right before the justices, with an officer appointed to hold each hand, lest they should therewith afflict them, and the prisoner's eyes must be constantly on the justices; for if they looked on the afflicted, they would either fall into their fits,

or cry out of being hurt by them; after examination of the prisoners, who it was afflicted these girls, etc., they were put upon saying the Lord's prayer, as a trial of their guilt; after the afflicted seemed to be out of their fits, they would look steadfastly on some one person, and frequently not speak; and then the justices said they were struck dumb, and after a little time would speak again; then the justices said to the accusers, "which of you will go and touch the prisoner at the bar?" then the most courageous would adventure, but before they had made three steps would ordinarily fall down as in a fit; the justices ordered that they should be taken up and carried to the prisoner, that she might touch them; and as soon as they were touched by the accused, the justices would say, they are well, before I could discern any alteration; by which I observed that the justices understood the manner of it. Thus far I was only as a spectator, my wife also was there part of the time, but no notice taken of her by the afflicted, except once or twice they came to her and asked her name.

But I having an opportunity to discourse [with] Mr. Hale (with whom I had formerly acquaintance) I took his advice, what I had best to do, and desired of him that I might have an opportunity to speak with her that accused my wife; which he promised should be, I acquainting him that I reposed my trust in him.

Accordingly he came to me after the examination was over, and told me I had now an opportunity to speak with the said accuser, *viz.* Abigail Williams, a girl of 11 or 12 years old; but that we could not be in private at Mr. Parris's house, as he had promised me; we went therefore into the ale house, where an Indian man attended us, who it seems was one of the afflicted: to him we gave some cider, he showed several scars, that seemed as if they had been long there, and showed them as done by witchcraft, and acquainted us that his wife, who also was a slave, was imprisoned for witchcraft. And now instead of one accuser, they all came in, who began to tumble down like swine, and then three women were called in to attend them. We in the room were all at a stand, to see who they would cry out of; but in a short time they cried out, Cary; and immediately after a warrant was sent from the justices to bring my wife before them, who were sitting in a chamber near by, waiting for this.

Being brought before the justices, her chief accusers were two girls; my wife declared to the justices, that she never had any knowledge of them before that day; she was forced to stand with her arms stretched out. I did request that I might hold one of her hands, but it was denied me; then she desired me to wipe the tears from her eyes, and the sweat from her face, which I did; then she desired she might lean herself on me, saying, she should faint.

Justice Hathorne replied, she had strength enough to torment those persons, and she should have strength enough to stand. I speaking something against their cruel proceedings, they commanded me to be silent, or else I should be turned out of the room. The Indian before mentioned, was also brought in, to be one of her accusers; being come in, he now (when before the justices) fell down and tumbled about like a hog, but said nothing. The justices asked the girls, who afflicted the Indian? They answered she (meaning my wife) and now lay upon him; the justices ordered her to touch him, in order to his cure, but her head must be turned another way, lest instead of curing, she should make him worse, by her looking on him, her hand being guided to take hold of his; but the Indian took hold on her hand, and pulled her down on the floor, in a barbarous manner; then his hand was taken off, and her hand put on his, and the cure was quickly wrought. I being extremely troubled at their inhumane dealings, uttered a hasty speech (that God would take vengeance on them, and desired that God would deliver us out of the hands of unmerciful men.) Then her Mittimus was writ. I did with difficulty and charge obtain the liberty of a room, but no beds in it; if there had, could have taken but little rest that night. She was committed to Boston prison; but I obtained a habeas corpus to remove her to Cambridge prison, which is in our County of Middlesex. Having been there one night, next morning the jailer put irons on her legs (having received such a command) the weight of them was about eight pounds; these irons and her other afflictions, soon brought her into convulsion fits, so that I thought she would have died that night. I sent to entreat that the irons might be taken off, but all entreaties were in vain, if it would have saved her life, so that in this condition she must continue. The trials at Salem coming on, I went thither, to see how things were there managed; and finding that the spectre evidence was there received, together with idle, if not malicious stories, against people's lives, I did easily perceive which way the rest would go; for the same evidence that served for one, would serve for all the rest. I acquainted her with her danger; and that if she were carried to Salem to be tried, I feared she would never return. I did my utmost that she might have her trial in our own county, I with several others petitioning the judge for it, and were put in hopes of it; but I soon saw so much, that I understood thereby it was not intended, which put me upon consulting the means of her escape; which through the goodness of God was effected, and she got to Rhode Island, but soon found herself not safe when there, by reason of the pursuit after her; from thence she went to New York, along with some others that had escaped their cruel hands; where we found his Excellency Benjamin Fletcher, Esq., governor, who was very courteous to us. After this some of my goods were seized in a friend's hands, with whom I had left them, and myself imprisoned by the sheriff, and kept in custody half a day, and then dismissed; but to speak of their usage of the prisoners, and their inhumanity shown to them, at the time of their execution, no sober Christian could bear; they had also trials of cruel mockings; which is the more, considering what a people for religion, I mean the profession of it, we have been; those that suffered being many of them church members, and most of them unspotted in their conversation, till their adversary the devil took up this method for accusing them.

PER NATHANIEL CARY

May 31. Captain John Alden was examined at Salem, and committed to Boston prison. The prison keeper seeing such a man committed, of whom he had a good esteem, was after this the more compassionate to those that were in prison on the like account; and did refrain from such hard things to the prisoners, as before he had used. Mr. Alden himself has given account of his examination, in these words.

An account how John Alden, Senior, was dealt with at Salem Village

John Alden Senior, of Boston, in the County of Suffolk, mariner, on the 28th Day of May, 1692, was sent for by the magistrates of Salem, in the County of Essex, upon the accusation of a company of poor distracted, or possessed creatures or witches; and being sent by Mr. Stoughton [lieutenant governor of Massachusetts], arrived there the 31st of May, and appeared at Salem Village, before Mr. Gedney, Mr. Hathorne, and Mr. Corwin.

Those wenches being present, who played their juggling tricks, falling down, crying out, and staring in peoples faces; the magistrates demanded of them several times, who it was of all the people in the room that hurt them? One of these accusers pointed several times at one Captain Hill, there present, but spake nothing; the same accuser had a man standing at her back to hold her up; he stooped down to her ear, then she cried out, Alden, Alden afflicted her; one of the magistrates asked her if she had ever seen Alden, she answered no, he asked her how she knew it was Alden? She said, the man told her so.

Then all were ordered to go down into the street, where a ring was made; and the same accuser cried out, "there stands Alden, a bold fellow with his hat on before the judges, he sells powder and shot to the Indians and French, and lies with the Indian squaws, and has Indian papooses." Then was Alden committed to the marshal's custody, and his sword taken from him; for they said he afflicted them with his sword. After some hours Alden was sent for to the meetinghouse in the

Village before the magistrates; who required Alden to stand upon a chair, to the open view of all the people.

The accusers cried out that Alden did pinch them, then, when he stood upon the chair, in the sight of all the people, a good way distant from them. One of the magistrates bid the marshal to hold open Alden's hands, that he might not pinch those creatures. Alden asked them why they should think, that he should come to that Village to afflict those persons that he never knew or saw before? Mr. Gedney bade Alden confess, and give glory to God; Alden said he hoped he should give glory to God, and hoped he should never gratify the devil; but appealed to all that ever knew him, if they ever suspected him to be such a person, and challenged any one, that could bring in anything upon their own knowledge, that might give suspicion of his being such an one. Mr. Gedney said he had known Alden many years, and had been at sea with him, and always looked upon him to be an honest man, but now he did see cause to alter his judgment: Alden answered, he was sorry for that, but he hoped God would clear up his innocency, that he would recall that judgment again, and added that he hoped that he should with Job maintain his integrity till he died. They bid Alden look upon the accusers, which he did, and then they fell down. Alden asked Mr. Gedney, what reason there could be given, why Alden's looking upon *him* did not strike *him* down as well; but no reason was given that I heard. But the accusers were brought to Alden to touch them, and this touch they said made them well. Alden began to speak of the providence of God in suffering these creatures to accuse innocent persons. Mr. Noyes asked Alden why he would offer to speak of the providence of God. God by his Providence (said Mr. Noyes) governs the world, and keeps it in peace; and so went on with discourse, and stopped Alden's mouth, as to that. Alden told Mr. Gedney, that he could assure him that there was a lying spirit in them, for I can assure you that there is not a word of truth in all these say of me. But Alden was again committed to the marshal, and his mittimus written, which was as follows.

To Mr. John Arnold, Keeper of the Prison in Boston, in the County of Suffolk.

Whereas Captain John Alden of Boston, Mariner, and Sarah Rice, wife of Nicholas Rice of Reading, husbandman, have been this day brought before us, John Hathorne and Jonathan Corwin, Esquires; being accused and suspected of perpetrating divers acts of witchcraft, contrary to the form of the statute, in that case made and provided: These are therefore in their Majesties', King William and Queen Mary's names, to will and require you, to take into your custody, the bodies of the said John Alden, and Sarah Rice, and them safely keep, until they shall thence be delivered by due course of law; as you will answer the contrary at your peril; and this shall be your sufficient warrant. Given under our hands at Salem Village, the 31st of May, in the fourth year of the reign of our sovereign Lord and Lady, William and Mary, now King and Queen over England, etc., Anno Dom. 1692.

JOHN HATHORNE,
JONATHAN CORWIN,
ASSISTANTS

To Boston Alden was carried by a constable, no bail would be taken for him; but was delivered to the prison keeper, where he remained fifteen weeks, and then observing the manner of trials, and evidence then taken, was at length prevailed with to make his escape, and being returned, was bound over to answer at the Superior Court at Boston, the last Tuesday in April, Anno 1693. And was there cleared by proclamation, none appearing against him.

PER JOHN ALDEN

At examination, and at other times, 'twas usual for the accusers to tell of the Black Man, or of a spectre, as being then on the table, etc. The people about would strike with swords, or sticks at those places. One justice broke his cane at this exercise, and sometimes the accusers would say, they struck the spectre, and it is reported several of the accused were hurt and wounded thereby, though at home at the same time.

The justices proceeding in these works of examination, and commitment, to the end of May, there was by that time about a hundred persons imprisoned upon that account.

June 2. A special commission of Oyer and Terminer having been issued out, to Mr. Stoughton, the new lieutenant governor, Major Saltonstall, Major Richards, Major Gedney, Mr. Wait Winthrop, Captain Sewall, and Mr. Sergeant; These (a Quorum of them) sat at Salem this day; where the most that was done this week, was the trial of one [Bridget] Bishop, *alias* Oliver, of Salem; who having long undergone the repute of a witch, occasioned by the accusations of one Samuel Gray; he about 20 years since, having charged her with such crimes, and though upon his deathbed he testified his sorrow and repentance for such accusations, as being wholly groundless; yet the report taken up by his means continued, and she being accused by those afflicted, and upon search a teat, as they call it, being found, she was brought in guilty by the jury; she received her sentence of death, and was executed, June 10, but made not the least confession of any thing relating to witchcraft.

June 15. Several ministers in and near Boston, having been to that end consulted by his Excellency, expressed their minds to this effect, *viz.*

That they were affected with the deplorable state of the afflicted; That they were thankful for the diligent care of the rulers, to detect the abominable witchcrafts, which have been committed in the country, praying for a perfect discovery thereof. But advised to a cautious proceeding, lest many evils ensue, etc. And that tenderness be used towards those accused, relating to matters presumptive and convictive, and also to privacy in examinations, and to consult the books Mr. William Perkins and Mr. Richard Bernard, what tests to make use of in the scrutiny: That presumptions and convictions ought to have better grounds, than the accusers affirming that they see such persons spectres afflicting them: And that the devil may afflict in the shape of good men; and that falling at the sight, and rising at the touch of the accused, is no infallible proof of guilt; That seeing the devil's strength consists in such accusations, our disbelieving them may be a means to put a period to the dreadful calamities; Nevertheless they humbly recommend to the government, the speedy and vigorous prosecution of such as have rendered themselves obnoxious, according to the direction given in the laws of God, and the wholesome statutes of the English nation, for the detection of witchcraft.

This is briefly the substance of what may be seen more at large in *Cases of Conscience.* And one of them since taking occasion to repeat some part of this advice, *Wonders of the Invisible World,* p. 83, declares, (notwithstanding the dissatisfaction of others) that if his said book may conduce to promote thankfulness to God for such executions, he shall rejoice, etc.

The 30*th of June,* the court according to adjournment again sat; five more were tried, *viz.* Sarah Good and Rebecca Nurse, of Salem Village; Susanna Martin of Amsbury; Elizabeth Howe of Ipswich; and Sarah Wildes of Topsfield; these were all condemned that sessions, and were all executed on the 19th of July.

At the trial of Sarah Good, one of the afflicted fell in a fit, and after coming out of it, she cried out of the prisoner, for stabbing her in the breast with a knife, and that she had broken the knife in stabbing of her, accordingly a piece of the blade of a knife was found about her. Immediately information being given to the court, a young man was called, who produced a haft and part of the blade, which the court having viewed and compared, saw it to be the same. And upon inquiry the young man affirmed, that yesterday he happened to break that knife, and that he cast away the upper part, this afflicted person being then present. The young man was dismissed, and she was bidden by the court not to tell lies; and was improved (after as she had been before) to give evidence against the prisoners.

At execution, Mr. Noyes urged Sarah Good to confess, and told her she was a witch, and she knew she was a witch, to which she replied, "you are a liar; I am no more a witch than you are a wizard, and if you take away my life, God will give you blood to drink."

At the trial of Rebecca Nurse, this was remarkable that the jury brought in their verdict not guilty, immediately all the accusers in the court, and suddenly after all the afflicted out of court, made an hideous outcry, to the amazement, not only of the spectators, but the court also seemed strangely surprized; one of the judges expressed himself not satisfied, another of them as he was going off the bench, said they would have her indicted anew. The chief judge said he would not impose upon the jury; but intimated, as if they had not well considered one expression of the prisoners, when she was upon trial, *viz.* That when one Hobbes, who had confessed herself to be a witch, was brought into the court to witness against her, the prisoner turning her head to her, said, "What, do you bring her? she is one of us," or to that effect; this together with the clamours of the accusers, induced the jury to go out again, after their verdict, not guilty. But not agreeing, they came into the court, and she being then at the bar, her words were repeated to her, in order to have had her explanation of them, and she making no reply to them, they found the bill, and brought her in guilty; these words being the inducement to it, as the foreman has signified in writing, as follows.

> *July* 4, 1692. I Thomas Fisk, the subscriber hereof, being one of them that were of the jury the last week at Salem Court, upon the trial of Rebecca Nurse, etc., being desired by some of the relations to give a reason why the jury brought her in guilty, after her verdict not guilty; I do hereby give my reasons to be as follows, *viz.*
>
> When the verdict not guilty was, the honoured court was pleased to object against it, saying to them, that they think they let slip [did not hear] the words, which the prisoner at the bar spake against herself, which were spoken in reply to Goodwife Hobbes and her daughter, who had been faulty in setting their hands to the devil's book, as they have confessed formerly; the words were "What, do these persons give in evidence against me now, they used to come among us." After the honoured court had manifested their dissatisfaction of the verdict, several of the jury declared themselves desirous to go out again, and thereupon the honoured court gave leave; but when we came to consider of the case, I could not tell how to take her words, as an evidence against her, till she had a further opportunity to put her sense upon them, if she would take it; and then going into court, I mentioned the words aforesaid, which by one of the court were affirmed to have been spoken by her, she being then at the bar, but made no reply, nor interpretation of them; whereupon these words were to me a principal evidence against her.
>
> THOMAS FISK

When Goodwife Nurse was informed what use was made of these words, she put in this following declaration into the court.

> These presents do humbly show, to the honoured court and jury, that I being informed, that the jury brought me in guilty, upon my saying that

> Goodwife Hobbes and her daughter were of our company; but I intended no otherways, than as [that] they were prisoners with us, and therefore did then, and yet do judge them not legal evidence against their fellow prisoners. And I being something hard of hearing, and full of grief, none informing me how the court took up my words, and therefore had not opportunity to declare what I intended, when I said they were of our company.
>
> REBECCA NURSE

After her condemnation she was by one of the ministers of Salem excommunicated; yet the governor saw cause to grant a reprieve, which when known (and some say immediately upon granting) the accusers renewed their dismal outcries against her, insomuch that the governor was by some Salem gentleman prevailed with to recall the reprieve, and she was executed with the rest.

The testimonials of her Christian behaviour, both in the course of her life, and at her death, and her extraordinary care in educating her children, and setting them good examples, etc., under the hands of so many, are so numerous, that for brevity they are here omitted.

It was at the trial of these that one of the accusers cried out publicly of Mr. Willard, minister in Boston, as afflicting of her; she was sent out of the court, and it was told about she was mistaken in the person.

August 5. The court again sitting, six more were tried on the same account, *viz.* Mr. George Burroughs, sometime minister of Wells, John Proctor, and Elizabeth Proctor his wife, with John Willard of Salem Village, George Jacobs Senior, of Salem, and Martha Carrier of Andover, these were all brought in guilty and condemned; and were all executed August 19, except Proctor's wife, who pleaded pregnancy.

Mr. Burroughs was carried in a cart with the others, through the streets of Salem to execution; when he was upon the ladder, he made a speech for the clearing of his innocency, with such solemn and serious expressions, as were to the admiration of all present; his prayer (which he concluded by repeating the Lord's prayer,) was so well worded, and uttered with such composedness, and such (at least seeming) fervency of spirit, as was very affecting, and drew tears from many (so that it seemed to some, that the spectators would hinder the execution). The accusers said the Black Man stood and dictated to him; as soon as he was turned off, Mr. Cotton Mather, being mounted upon a horse, addressed himself to the people, partly to declare, that he was no ordained minister, and partly to possess the people of his guilt; saying, that the devil has often been transformed into an angel of light; and this did somewhat appease the people, and the executions went on; when he was cut down, he was dragged by the halter to a hole, or grave, between the rocks, about two foot deep, his shirt and breeches being pulled off, and an old pair of trousers of one executed, put on his lower parts, he was so put in, together with Willard and Carrier, one of his hands and his chin, and a foot of one [of] them being left uncovered.

John Willard had been employed to fetch in several that were accused; but taking dissatisfaction from his being sent, to fetch up some that he had better thoughts of, he declined the service, and presently after he himself was accused of the same crime, and that with such vehemency, that they sent after him to apprehend him; he had made his escape as far as Nashawag, about 40 miles from Salem; yet 'tis said those accusers did then presently tell the exact time, saying, now Willard is taken.

John Proctor and his wife being in prison, the sheriff came to his house and seized all the goods, provisions, and cattle that he could come at, and sold some of the cattle at half price, and killed others, and put them up for the West Indies; threw out the beer out of a barrel, and carried away the barrel; emptied a pot of broth, and took away the pot, and left nothing in the house for the support of the children: No part of the said goods are known to be returned. Proctor earnestly requested Mr. Noyes to pray with and for him, but it was wholly denied, because he would not own himself to be a witch.

During his imprisonment he sent the following letter, in behalf of himself and others.

Salem-Prison, July 23, 1692.
Mr. Mather, Mr. Allen,
Mr. Moody, Mr. Willard, and Mr. Bailey.
Reverend Gentlemen.

The innocency of our case with the enmity of our accusers and our judges, and jury, whom nothing but our innocent blood will serve their turn, having condemned us already before our trials, being so much incensed and engaged against us by the devil, makes us bold to beg and implore your favourable assistance of this our humble petition to his Excellency, that if it be possible our innocent blood may be spared, which undoubtedly otherwise will be shed, if the Lord doth not mercifully step in. The magistrates, ministers, juries, and all the people in general, being so much enraged and incensed against us by the delusion of the devil, which we can term no other, by reason we know in our own consciences, we are all innocent persons. Here are five persons who have lately confessed themselves to be witches, and do accuse some of us, of being along with them at a sacrament, since we were committed into close prison, which we know to be lies. Two of the 5 are (Carrier's sons) young men, who would not confess anything till they tied them neck and heels till the blood was ready to come out of their noses, and 'tis credibly believed and reported this was the occasion of making them confess that they never did, by reason they said one had been a witch a month, and another five weeks, and that their mother had made them so, who has been confined here this nine weeks. My son William Proctor, when he was examined, because he would not confess that he was guilty, when he was innocent, they tied him neck and heels till the blood gushed out at his nose, and would have kept him so 24 hours, if one more merciful than the rest, had not taken pity on him, and caused him to be unbound. These actions are very like the popish cruelties. They have already undone us in our estates, and that will not serve their turns, without our innocent bloods. If it cannot be granted that we can have our trials at Boston, we humbly beg that you would endeavour to have these magistrates changed, and others in their rooms, begging also and beseeching you would be pleased to be here, if not all, some of you at our trials, hoping thereby you may be the means of saving the shedding our innocent bloods, desiring your prayers to the Lord in our behalf, we rest your poor afflicted servants,

JOHN PROCTOR, ETC.

He pleaded very hard at execution, for a little respite of time, saying that he was not fit to die; but it was not granted.

Old Jacobs being condemned, the sheriff and officers came and seized all he had, his wife had her wedding ring taken from her, but with great difficulty obtained it again. She was forced to buy provisions of the sheriff, such as he had taken, towards her own support, which not being sufficient, the neighbours out of charity relieved her.

Margaret Jacobs being one that had confessed her own guilt, and testified against her grandfather Jacobs, Mr. Burroughs, and John Willard, she the day before executions, came to Mr. Burroughs, acknowledging that she had belied them, and begged Mr. Burroughs' forgiveness, who not only forgave her, but also prayed with and for her. She wrote the following letter to her Father.

From the Dungeon in Salem Prison, August 20, 92.
Honoured Father
After my humble duty remembered to you, hoping in the Lord of your good health, as blessed be God I enjoy, though in abundance of affliction, being close confined here in a loathsome dungeon, the Lord look down in mercy upon me, not knowing how soon I shall be put to death, by means of the afflicted persons; my grandfather having suffered already, and all his

estate seized for the King. The reason of my confinement is this, I having, through the magistrates' threatenings, and my own vile and wretched heart, confessed several things contrary to my conscience and knowledge, though to the wounding of my own soul, the Lord pardon me for it, but Oh! the terrors of a wounded conscience who can bear. But blessed be the Lord, he would not let me go on in my sins, but in mercy I hope so my soul would not suffer me to keep it in any longer, but I was forced to confess the truth of all before the magistrates, who would not believe me, but tis their pleasure to put me in here, and God knows how soon I shall be put to death. Dear father, let me beg your prayers to the Lord on my behalf, and send us a joyful and happy meeting in Heaven. My mother poor woman is very crazy [unwell], and remembers her kind love to you, and to Uncle, *viz.* Daniel Andrew. So leaving you to the protection of the Lord, I rest your dutiful daughter,

MARGARET JACOBS.

At the time appointed for her trial, she had an imposthume [illness] in her head, which was her escape.

September 9. Six more, were tried, and received sentence of death, *viz.* Martha Corey of Salem Village, Mary Easty of Topsfield, Alice Parker and Ann Pudeater of Salem, Dorcas Hoar of Beverly, and Mary Bradberry of Salisbury. *September* 16, Giles Corey was pressed to death.

September 17. Nine more received sentence of death, *viz.* Margaret Scot of Rowly, Goodwife Redd of Marblehead, Samuel Wardwell, and Mary Parker of Andover, also Abigail Faulkner of Andover, who pleaded pregnancy, Rebecca Eames of Boxford, Mary Lacy, and Ann Foster of Andover, and Abigail Hobbs of Topsfield. Of these eight were executed, *September* 22, *viz.* Martha Corey, Mary Easty, Alice Parker, Ann Pudeater, Margaret Scot, Willmet Redd, Samuel Wardwell, and Mary Parker.

Giles Corey pleaded not guilty to his indictment, but would not put himself upon trial by the jury (they having cleared none upon trial) and knowing there would be the same witnesses against him, rather chose to undergo what death they would put him to. In pressing his tongue being pressed out of his mouth, the sheriff with his cane forced it in again, when he was dying. He was the first in New England, that was ever pressed to death.

The cart going up the hill with these eight to execution, was for some time at a set; the afflicted and others said, that the devil hindered it, etc.

Martha Corey, wife to Giles Corey, protesting her innocency, concluded her life with an eminent prayer upon the ladder.

Wardwell having formerly confessed himself guilty, and after denied it, was soon brought upon his trial; his former confession and spectre testimony was all that appeared against him. At execution while he was speaking to the people, protesting his innocency, the executioner being at the same time smoking tobacco, the smoke coming in his face, interrupted his discourse, those accusers said, the devil hindered him with smoke.

Mary Easty, sister also to Rebecca Nurse, when she took her last farewell of her husband, children and friends, was, as is reported by them present, as serious, religious, distinct, and affectionate as could well be expressed, drawing tears from the eyes of almost all present. It seems besides the testimony of the accusers and confessors, another proof, as it was counted, appeared against her, it having been usual to search the accused for teats; upon some parts of her body, not here to be named, was found an excrescence, which they called a teat. Before her death she put up the following petition:

> To the honorable judge and bench now sitting in judicature in Salem and the reverend ministers, humbly showeth, that whereas your humble poor petitioner being condemned to die, doth humbly beg of you, to take it into your judicious and pious consideration, that your poor and humble petitioner knowing my own innocency (blessed be the Lord for it) and seeing plainly the wiles and subtlety of my accusers, by myself, cannot but judge charitably of others, that are going the same way with myself, if the Lord step not mightily in. I was confined a whole month on the same account that I am now condemned for, and then cleared by the afflicted persons, as some of your honours know, and in two days time I was cried out upon by them, and have been confined, and now am condemned to die. The Lord above knows my innocency then, and likewise doth now, as at the great day will be known to men and angels. I petition to your honours not for my own life, for I know I must die, and my appointed time is set; but the Lord he knows it is, if it be possible, that no more innocent blood be shed, which undoubtedly cannot be avoided in the way and course you go in. I question not, but your honours do to the utmost of your powers, in the discovery and detecting of witchcraft and witches, and would not be guilty of innocent blood for the world; but by my own innocency I know you are in the wrong way. The Lord in his infinite mercy direct you in this great work, if it be his blessed will, that innocent blood be not shed; I would humbly beg of you, that your honours would be pleased to examine some of those confessing witches, I being confident there are several of them have belied themselves and others, as will appear, if not in this world, I am sure in the world to come, whither I am going; and I question not, but yourselves will see an al-

teration in these things: They say, myself and others have made a league with the devil, we cannot confess. I know and the Lord he knows (as will shortly appear) they belie me, and so I question not but they do others; the Lord alone, who is the searcher of all hearts, knows that as I shall answer it at the tribunal seat, that I know not the least thing of witchcraft, therefore I cannot, I durst not belie my own soul. I beg your honours not to deny this my humble petition, from a poor dying innocent person, and I question not but the Lord will give a blessing to your endeavours.

MARY EASTY.

After execution Mr. Noyes turning him to the bodies, said, what a sad thing it is to see eight firebrands of hell hanging there.

In October 1692, One of Wenham complained of Mrs. Hale, whose husband, the minister of Beverly, had been very forward in these prosecutions, but being fully satisfied of his wife's sincere Christianity, caused him to alter his judgment; for it was come to a stated controversy, among the New England divines, whether the devil could afflict in a good man's shape; it seems nothing else could convince him: yet when it came so near to himself, he was soon convinced that the devil might so afflict. Which same reason did afterwards prevail with many others; and much influenced to the succeeding change at trials.

October 7. (Edward Bishop and his wife having made their escape out of prison). This day Mr. Corwin the sheriff, came and seized his goods, and cattle and had it not been for his second son (who borrowed ten pound and gave it him) they had been wholly lost, the receipt follows; but it seems they must be content with such a receipt as he would give them.

Received this 7th day of October 1692, of Samuel Bishop of the Town of Salem, of the County of Essex, in New England, Cordwainer, in full satisfaction, a valuable sum of money, for the goods and chattels of Edward Bishop, Senior, of the Town and County aforesaid, husbandman; which goods and chattels being seized, for that the said Edward Bishop, and Sarah his wife, having been committed for witchcraft and felony, have made their escape; and their goods and chattles were forfeited unto their Majesties, and now being in possession of the said Samuel Bishop: and in behalf of their Majesties, I do hereby discharge the said goods and chattles, the day and year above written, as witness my hand,

GEORGE CORWIN, *SHERIFF.*

But before this the said Bishop's eldest Son, having married into that family of the Putmans who were chief prosecutors in this business; he holding a cow to be branded lest it should be seized, and having a push or boil upon his thigh, with his straining it broke; this is that that was pretended to be burned with the said brand; and is one of the bones thrown to the dogmatical to pick, in *Wonders of the Invisible World,* P. 143. the other, of a corner of a sheet, pretended to be taken from a spectre, it is known that it was provided the day before, by that afflicted person, and the third bone of a spindle is almost as easily provided, as the piece of the knife; so that Apollo needs not herein be consulted, etc.

Mr. Philip English and his wife having made their escape out of prison, Mr. Corwin the Sheriff seized his estate, to the value of about fifteen hundred pound, which was wholly lost to him, except about three hundred pound value, (which was afterward restored.)

After Goodwife Hoar was condemned, her estate was seized, and was also bought again for eight pound.

George Jacobs, son to old Jacobs, being accused, he fled, then the officers came to his house, his wife was a woman crazy in her senses and had been so several years. She it seems had been also accused; there were in the house with her only four small children, and one of them sucked, her eldest daughter being in prison; the officer persuaded her out of the house, to go along with him, telling her she should speedily return, the children ran a great way after her crying.

When she came where the afflicted were, being asked, they said they did not know her, at length one said, don't you know Jacobs the old witch, and then they cried out of her, and fell down in their fits; she was sent to prison, and lay there ten months, the neighbours of pity took care of the children to preserve them from perishing.

About this time a new scene was begun, one Joseph Ballard of Andover, whose wife was ill (and after died of a fever) sent to Salem for some of those accusers, to tell him who afflicted his wife; others did the like: Horse and man were sent from several places to fetch those accusers who had the spectral sight, that they might thereby tell who afflicted those that were any ways ill.

When these came into any place where such were, usually they fell into a fit; after which being asked who it was that afflicted the person, they would, for the most part, name one whom they said sat on the head, and another that sat on the lower parts of the afflicted. Soon after Ballard's sending (as above) more than fifty of the people of Andover were complained of, for afflicting their neighbours. Here it was that many accused themselves, of riding upon poles through the air; Many parents believing their children to be witches, and many husbands their wives, etc. When these accusers came to the house of any upon such account, it was ordinary for other young people to be taken in fits, and to have the same spectral sight.

Mr. Dudley Bradstreet, a justice of peace in Andover, having granted out warrants against, and committed thirty or forty to prisons, for the supposed witchcrafts, at length saw cause to forbear granting out any more warrants. Soon after which he and his wife were cried out of, himself was (by them) said to have killed nine persons by witchcraft, and found it his safest course to make his escape.

A dog being afflicted at Salem Village, those that had the spectral sight being sent for, they accused Mr. John Bradstreet (brother to the Justice) that he afflicted the said dog, and now rid upon him: He made his escape into Pescattequa Government [New Hampshire], and the dog was put to death, and was all of the afflicted that suffered death.

At Andover, the afflicted complained of a dog, as afflicting of them, and would fall into their fits at the dog's looking upon them; the dog was put to death.

A worthy gentleman of Boston, being about this time accused by those at Andover, he sent by some particular friends a writ to arrest those accusers in a thousand pound action for defamation, with instructions to them, to inform themselves of the certainty of the proof, in doing which their business was perceived, and from thence forward the accusations at Andover generally ceased.

In October some of these accusers were sent for to Gloucester, and occasioned four women to be sent to prison, but Salem prison being so full it could receive no more, two were sent to Ipswich prison. In November they were sent for again by Lieutenant Stephens, who was told that a sister of his was bewitched; in their way passing over Ipswich Bridge, they met with an old woman, and instantly fell into their fits: But by this time the validity of such accusations being much questioned, they found not that encouragement they had done elsewhere, and soon withdrew.

These accusers swore that they saw three persons sitting upon Lieutenant Stephens's sister till she died; yet bond was accepted for those three.

And now nineteen persons having been hanged, and one pressed to death, and eight more condemned, in all twenty and eight, of which above a third part were members of some of the churches in New England, and more than half of them of a good conversation in general, and not one cleared; about fifty having confessed themselves to be witches, of which not one executed; above an hundred and fifty in prison, and above two hundred more accused; the special commission of Oyer and Terminer comes to a period, which has no other foundation than the governor's commission, and had proceeded in the manner of swearing witnesses, *viz.* By holding up the hand, (and by receiving evidences in writing) according to the ancient usage of this country; as also having their indictments in English. In the trials, when any were indicted for afflicting, pining, and wasting the bodies of particular persons by witchcraft; it was usual to hear evidence of matter foreign, and of perhaps twenty or thirty years' standing, about oversetting carts, the death of cattle, unkindness to relations, or unexpected accidents befalling after some quarrel. Whether this was admitted by the law of England, or by what other law, wants to be determined; the executions seemed mixed, in pressing to death for not pleading, which most agrees with the laws of England, and sentencing women to be hanged for witchcraft, according to the former practice of this country, and not by burning, as is said to have been the law of England. And though the confessing witches were many; yet not one of them that confessed their own guilt, and abode by their confession were put to death.

Here followeth what account some of those miserable creatures give of their confession under their own hands.

> We whose names are under written, inhabitants of Andover, when as that horrible and tremendous judgment beginning at Salem Village, in the Year 1692, (by some) called witchcraft, first breaking forth at Mr. Parris's house, several young persons being seemingly afflicted, did accuse several persons for afflicting them, and many there believing it so to be; we being informed that if a person were sick, that the afflicted persons could tell, what or who was the cause of that sickness. Joseph Ballard of Andover (his wife being sick at the same time) he either from himself, or by the advice of others, fetched two of the persons called the afflicted persons, from Salem Village to Andover. Which was the beginning of that dreadful calamity that befel us in Andover. And the authority in Andover, believing the said accusations to be true, sent for the said persons to come together, to the meetinghouse in Andover (the afflicted persons being there.) After Mr. Barnard had been at prayer, we were blindfolded, and our hands were laid upon the afflicted persons, they being in their fits, and falling into their fits at our coming into their presence (as they said) and some led us and laid our hands upon them, and then they said they were well, and that we were guilty of afflicting of them; whereupon we were all seized as prisoners, by a warrant from the justice of the peace, and forthwith carried to Salem. And by reason of that sudden surprisal, we knowing ourselves altogether innocent of that crime, we were all exceedingly astonished and amazed, and consternated and affrighted even out of our reason; and our nearest and dearest relations, seeing us in that dreadful condition, and knowing our great danger, apprehending that there was no other way to save our lives, as the case was then circumstantiated, but by our confessing ourselves to be such and such persons, as the afflicted represented us to be, they out of tender love and pity persuaded us to confess what we did confess. And indeed that confession, that is said we made, was no other than what was suggested to us by some gentlemen; they telling us, that we were witches, and they knew it, and we

knew it, and they knew that we knew it, which made us think that it was so; and our understanding, our reason, and our faculties almost gone, we were not capable of judging our condition; as also the hard measures they used with us, rendered us incapable of making our defence; but said anything and everything which they desired, and most of what we said, was but in effect a consenting to what they said. Sometime after when we were better composed, they telling of us what we had confessed, we did profess that we were innocent, and ignorant of such things. And we hearing that Samuel Wardwell had renounced his confession, and quickly after condemned and executed, some of us were told that we were going after Wardwell.

MARY OSGOOD, MARY TILER, DELIVERANCE DANE,
ABIGAIL BARKER, SARAH WILSON, HANNAH TILER.

It may here be further added concerning those that did confess, that besides that powerful argument, of life (and freedom from hardships and irons not only promised, but also performed to all that owned their guilt), there are numerous instances, too many to be here inserted, of the tedious examinations before private persons, many hours together; they all that time urging them to confess (and taking turns to persuade them) till the accused were wearied out by being forced to stand so long, or for want of sleep, etc. and so brought to give an assent to what they said; they then asking them, Were you at such a witchmeeting, or have you signed the devil's book, etc. upon their replying, yes, the whole was drawn into form as their confession.

But that which did mightily further such confessions, was their nearest and dearest relations urging them to it. These seeing no other way of escape for them, thought it the best advice that could be given; hence it was that the husbands of some, by counsel often urging, and utmost earnestness, and children upon their knees entreating, have at length prevailed with them, to say they were guilty.

From: Thomas Brattle, letter (1692)

October 8, 1692.

Reverend Sir,

Your's I received the other day, and am very ready to serve you to my utmost. I should be very loath to bring myself into any snare by my freedom with you, and therefore hope that you will put the best construction on what I write, and secure me from such as would interpret my lines otherwise than they are designed. Obedience to lawful authority I evermore accounted a great duty; and willingly I would not practise any thing that might thwart and contradict such a principle. Too many are ready to despise dominions, and speak evil of dignities; and I am sure the mischiefs, which arise from a factious and rebellious spirit, are very sad and notorious; insomuch that I would sooner bite my fingers' ends than willingly cast dirt on authority, or any way offer reproach to it: Far, therefore, be it from me, to have anything to do with those men your letter mentions, whom you acknowledge to be men of a factious spirit, and never more in their element than when they are declaiming against men in public place, and contriving methods that tend to the disturbance of the common peace. I never accounted it a credit to my cause, to have the good liking of such men. *My son!* (says Solomon) *fear thou the Lord and the King, and meddle not with them that are given to change.* Prov. xxiv. 21. However, Sir, I never thought judges infallible; but reckoned that they, as well as private men, might err; and that when they were guilty of erring, standers by, who possibly had not half their judgment, might, notwithstanding, be able to detect and behold their errors. And furthermore, when errors of that nature are thus detected and observed, I never thought it an interfering with dutifullness and subjection for one man to communicate his thoughts to another thereabout; and with modesty and due reverence to debate the premised failings; at least, when errors are fundamental, and palpably pervert the great end of authority and government: for as to circumstantial errors, I must confess my principle is, that it is the duty of a good subject to cover with his silence a multitude of them. But I shall no longer detain you with my preface, but pass to some things you look for, and whether you expect such freedom from me, yea or no, yet shall you find, that I am very open to communicate my thoughts unto you, and in plain terms to tell you what my opinion is of the Salem proceedings.

First, as to the method which the Salem justices do take in their examinations, it is truly this: A warrant being issued out to apprehend the persons that are charged and complained of by the afflicted children, (as they are called); said persons are brought before the justices, (the afflicted being present.) The justices ask the apprehended why they afflict those poor children; to which the apprehended answer, they do not afflict them. The justices order the apprehended to look upon the said children, which accordingly they do; and at the time of that look, (I dare not say by that look, as the Salem gentlemen do) the afflicted are cast into a fit. The apprehended are then blinded, and ordered to touch the afflicted; and at that touch, though not by the touch, (as above) the afflicted ordinarily do come out of their fits. The afflicted persons then declare and affirm, that the apprehended have afflicted them; upon which the apprehended persons, though of never so good repute, are forthwith committed to prison, on suspicion for witchcraft. One of the Salem justices was pleased to tell Mr. Alden, (when upon his examination) that truly he had been acquainted with him these many years; and had always accounted him a good man; but indeed now he should be obliged to change his opinion. This, there are more than one or two did hear, and are ready to swear to, if not in so many words, yet as to its natural and plain meaning. He saw reason to change his opinion of Mr. Alden, because that at the time he touched the poor child, the poor child came out of her fit. I suppose his honour never made the experiment, whether there was not as much virtue in his own hand, as there was in Mr. Alden's, to cure by a touch. I know a man that will venture two to one with any Salemite whatever, that let the matter be duly managed, and the afflicted person shall come out of her fit upon the touch of the most religious hand in Salem. It is worthily noted by some, that at some times the afflicted will not presently come out of their fits upon the touch of the suspected; and then, forsooth, they are ordered by the justices to grasp hard, harder yet, etc. insomuch that at length the afflicted come out of their fits; and the reason is very good, because that a touch of any hand, and process of time, will work the cure; infallibly they will do it, as experience teaches.

I cannot but condemn this method of the justices, of making this touch of the hand a rule to discover witchcraft; because I am fully persuaded that it is sorcery, and a superstitious method, and that which we have no rule for, either from reason or religion. The Salem justices, at least some of them, do assert, that the cure of the afflicted persons is a natural effect of this touch; and they are so well instructed in the Cartesian philosophy, and in the doctrine of *effluvia,* that they undertake to give a demonstration how this touch does cure the afflicted persons; and the account they give of it is this; that by this touch, the venemous and malignant particles, that were ejected from the eye, do, by this means, return to the body whence they came, and so leave the afflicted persons pure and whole. I must confess to you, that I am no small admirer of the Cartesian philosophy; but yet I have not so learned it. Certainly this is a strain that it will by no means allow of.

I would fain know of these Salem gentlemen, but as yet could never know, how it comes about, that if these apprehended persons are witches, and, by a look of the eye, do cast the afflicted into their fits by poisoning them, how it comes about, I say, that, by a look of their eye, they do not cast others into fits, and poison others by their looks; and in particular, tender, fearful women, who often are beheld by them, and as likely as any in the whole world to receive an ill impression from them. This Salem philosophy, some men may call the new philosophy; but I think it rather deserves the name of Salem superstition and sorcery, and it is not fit to be named in a land of such light as New England is. I think the matter might be better solved another way; but I shall not make any attempt that way, further than to say, that these afflicted children, (as they are called,) do hold correspondence with the devil, even in the esteem and account of the Salem gentlemen for when the Black Man, *i.e.* (say these gentlemen,) the devil, does appear to them, they ask him many questions, and accordingly give information to the inquirer; and if this is not holding correspondence with the devil, and something worse, I know not what is.

But furthermore, I would fain know of these Salem justices what need there is of further proof and evidence to convict and condemn these apprehended persons, than this look and touch, if so be they are so certain that this falling down and arising up, when there is a look and a touch, are natural effects of the said look and touch, and so a perfect demonstration and proof of witchcraft in those persons. What can the jury or judges desire more, to convict any man of witchcraft, than a plain demonstration, that the said man is a witch? Now if this look and touch, circumstanced as before, be a plain demonstration, (as their philosophy teaches,) what need they seek for further evidences, when, after all, it can be but a demonstration?

But let this pass with the Salem gentlemen for never so plain and natural a demonstration; yet certain is it, that the reasonable part of the world, when acquainted herewith, will laugh at the demonstration, and conclude that the said Salem gentlemen are actually possessed, at least, with ignorance and folly.

I most admire [marvel] that Mr. Nicholas Noyes, the Reverend teacher at Salem, who was educated at the school of knowledge, and is certainly a learned, a charitable, and a good man, though all the devils in hell, and all the possessed girls in Salem, should say to the contrary; at him, (I say,) I do most admire [marvel]; that he should cry up the above mentioned philosophy after the manner that he does. I can assure you, that I can bring you more than two, or twice two, (very credible persons) that will affirm, that they have heard him vindicate the above mentioned demonstration as very reasonable.

Secondly, with respect to the confessors, (as they are improperly called,) or such as confess themselves to be witches, (the second thing you inquire into in your letter), there are now about fifty of them in prison; many of which I have again and again seen and heard; and I cannot but tell you, that my faith is strong concerning them, that they are deluded, imposed upon, and under the influence of some evil spirit; and therefore unfit to be evidences either against themselves, or any one else. I now speak of one sort of them, and of others afterward.

These confessors, (as they are called,) do very often contradict themselves, as inconsistently as is usual for any crazed, distempered person to do. This the Salem gentlemen do see and take notice of; and even the judges themselves have, at some times, taken these confessors in flat lies, or contradictions, even in the courts; by reason of which, one would have thought, that the judges would have frowned upon the said confessors, discarded them, and not minded one tittle of any thing that they said; but instead thereof, (as sure as we are men,) the judges vindicate these confessors, and salve their contradictions, by proclaiming, that the devil takes away their memory, and imposes upon their brain. If this reflects anywhere, I am very sorry for it: I can but assure you, that, upon the word of an honest man, it is truth, and that I can bring you many credible persons to witness it, who have been eye and ear witnesses to these things.

These confessors then, at least some of them, even in the judges' own account, are under the influence of the devil; and the brain of these confessors is imposed upon by the devil, even in the judges' account. But now, if, in the judges' account, these confessors are under the influence of the devil, and their brains are affected and imposed upon by the devil, so that they are not their own men, why then should these judges, or any other men, make such account of, and set so much by, the words of these confessors, as they do? In short, I argue thus:

If the devil does actually take away the memory of them at some times, certainly the devil, at other times, may very reasonably be thought to affect their fancies, and to represent false ideas to their imagination. But now, if it be thus granted, that the devil is able to represent false ideas (to speak vulgarly) to the imaginations of the confessors, what man of sense will regard the confessions, or any of the words, of these confessors?

The great cry of many of our neighbours now is, What, will you not believe the confessors? Will you not believe men and women who confess that they have signed to the devil's book? that they were baptized by the devil; and that they were at the mock-sacrament once and again? What! will you not believe that this is witchcraft, and that such and such men are witches, although the confessors do own and assert it?

Thus, I say, many of our good neighbours do argue; but methinks they might soon be convinced that there is nothing at all in all these their arguings, if they would but duly consider of the premises.

In the meantime, I think we must rest satisfied in it, and be thankful to God for it, that all men are not thus bereft of their senses; but that we have here and there considerate and thinking men, who will not thus be imposed upon, and abused, by the subtle endeavours of the crafty one.

In the next place, I proceed to the form of their inditements, and the trials thereupon.

The inditement runs for sorcery and witchcraft, acted upon the body of such an one, (say M. Warren), at such a particular time, (say April 14, '92,) and at divers other times before and after, whereby the said M. W. is wasted and consumed, pined, etc.

Now for the proof of the said sorcery and witchcraft, the prisoner at the bar pleading not guilty.

1. The afflicted persons are brought into court; and after much patience and pains taken with them, do take their oaths, that the prisoner at the bar did afflict

them: And here I think it very observable, that often, when the afflicted do mean and intend only the appearance and shape of such an one, (say G. Proctor) yet they positively swear that G. Proctor did afflict them; and they have been allowed so to do; as though there was no real difference between G. Proctor and the shape of G. Proctor. This, methinks, may readily prove a stumbling block to the jury, lead them into a very fundamental error, and occasion innocent blood, yea the innocentest blood imaginable, to be in great danger. Whom it belongs unto, to be eyes unto the blind, and to remove such stumbling blocks, I know full well; and yet you, and every one else, do know as well as I who do not.

2. The confessors do declare what they know of the said prisoner; and some of the confessors are allowed to give their oaths; a thing which I believe was never heard of in this world; that such as confess themselves to be witches, to have renounced God and Christ, and all that is sacred, should yet be allowed and ordered to swear by the name of the great God! This indeed seemeth to me to be a gross taking of God's name in vain. I know the Salem gentlemen do say, that there is hopes that the said confessors have repented; I shall only say, that if they have repented, it is well for themselves; but if they have not, it is very ill for you know who. But then,

3. Whoever can be an evidence against the prisoner at the bar is ordered to come into court; and here it scarce ever fails but that evidences, of one nature and another, are brought in, though, I think, all of them altogether alien to the matter of inditement; for they none of them do respect witchcraft upon the bodies of the afflicted, which is the alone matter of charge in the inditement.

4. They are searched by a jury; and as to some of them, the jury brought in, that on such or such a place there was a preternatural excrescence. And I wonder what person there is, whether man or woman, of whom it cannot be said but that, in some part of their body or other, there is a preternatural excrescence. The term is a very general and inclusive term.

Some of the Salem gentlemen are very forward to censure and condemn the poor prisoner at the bar, because he sheds no tears: but such betray great ignorance in the nature of passion, and as great heedlessness as to common passages of a man's life. Some there are who never shed tears; others there are that ordinarily shed tears upon light occasions, and yet for their lives cannot shed a tear when the deepest sorrow is upon their hearts; and who is there that knows not these things? Who knows not that an ecstasy of joy will sometimes fetch tears, when as the quite contrary passion will shut them close up? Why then should any be so silly and foolish as to take an argument from this appearance? But this is by the by. In short, the prisoner at the bar is indited for sorcery and witchcraft acted upon the bodes of the afflicted. Now, for the proof of this, I reckon that the only pertinent evidences brought in are the evidences of the said afflicted.

It is true, that over and above the evidences of the afflicted persons, there are many evidences brought in, against the prisoner at the bar; either that he was at a witch meeting, or that he performed things which could not be done by an ordinary natural power; or that she sold butter to a sailor, which proving bad at sea, and the seamen exclaiming against her, she appeared, and soon after there was a storm, or the like. But what if there were ten thousand evidences of this nature; how do they prove the matter of inditement! And if they do not reach the matter of inditement, then I think it is clear, that the prisoner at the bar is brought in guilty, and condemned, merely from the evidences of the afflicted persons.

The Salem gentlemen will by no means allow, that any are brought in guilty, and condemned, by virtue of spectre evidence, (as it is called,) *i. e.* the evidence of these afflicted persons, who are said to have spectral eyes; but whether it is not purely by virtue of these spectre evidences, that these persons are found guilty, (considering what before has been said,) I leave you, and any man of sense, to judge and determine. When any man is indited for murdering the person of A. B. and all the direct evidence be, that the said man pistolled the shadow of the said A. B. though there be never so many evidences that the said person murdered C. D., E. F. and ten more persons, yet all this will not amount to a legal proof, that he murdered A. B.; and upon that inditement, the person cannot be legally brought in guilty of the said inditement; it must be upon this supposition, that the evidence of a man's pistolling the shadow of A. B. is a legal evidence to prove that the said man did murder the person of A. B. Now no man will be so much out of his wits as to make this a legal evidence; and yet this seems to be our case; and how to apply it is very easy and obvious.

As to the late executions, I shall only tell you, that in the opinion of many unprejudiced, considerate and considerable spectators, some of the condemned went out of the world not only with as great protestations, but also with as good shows of innocency, as men could do.

They protested their innocency as in the presence of the great God, whom forthwith they were to appear before: they wished, and declared their wish, that their blood might be the last innocent blood shed upon that account. With great affection [emotion] they entreated Mr. Cotton Mather to pray with them: they prayed that God would discover what witchcrafts were among us; they forgave their accusers; they spake without reflection on jury and judges, for bringing them in guilty, and condemning them: they prayed earnestly for pardon for all other sins, and for an interest in the precious blood of our dear Redeemer; and seemed to be very sincere, upright, and sensible of their circumstances on all accounts; especially Proctor and Willard, whose whole management of themselves, from the goal to the gallows, and whilst at the gallows, was very affecting and melting to the hearts of some considerable spectators, whom I could mention to you:—but they are executed, and so I leave them.

Many things I cannot but admire and wonder at, an account of which I shall here send you. And

1. I do admire that some particular persons, and particularly Mrs. Thatcher of Boston, should be much complained of by the afflicted persons, and yet that the justices should never issue out their warrants to apprehend them, when as upon the same account they issue out their warrants for the apprehending and imprisoning many others.

This occasions much discourse and many hot words, and is a very great scandal and stumbling block to many good people; certainly distributive justice should have its course, without respect to persons; and although the said Mrs. Thatcher be mother in law to Mr. Corwin, who is one of the justices and judges, yet if justice and conscience do oblige them to apprehend others on the account of the afflicted their complaints, I cannot see how, without injustice and violence to conscience, Mrs. Thatcher can escape, when it is well known how much she is, and has been, complained of.

2. I cannot but admire that Mr. Hezekiah Usher (whom we all think innocent,) should yet be apprehended on this account, and ordered to prison, by a mittimus under Mr. Lynde's hand, and yet that he should be suffered, for above a fortnight, to be in a private house; and after that, to quit the house, the town, and the province, and yet that authority should not take effectual notice of it. Methinks that same justice, that actually imprisoned others, and refused bail for them on any terms, should not be satisfied without actually imprisoning Mr. Usher and refusing bail for him, when his case is known to be the very same with the case of those others.

If he may be suffered to go away, why may not others? If others may not be suffered to go, how in justice can he be allowed herein?

3. If our justices do think that Mrs. Cary, Mr. English and his wife, Mr. Alden and others, were capital offenders, and justly imprisoned on a capital account, I do admire that the said justices should hear of their escape from prison, and where they are gone and entertained, and yet not send forthwith to the said places, for the surrendering of them, that justice might be done them. In other capital cases this has been practised; why then is it not practised in this case, if really judged to be so heinous as is made for?

4. I cannot but admire [marvel], that any should go with their distempered friends and relations to the afflicted children, to know what their distempered friends ail; whether they are not bewitched; who it is that afflicts them, and the like. It is true, I know no reason why these afflicted may not be consulted as well

as any other, if so be that it was only their natural and ordinary knowledge that was had recourse to: but it is not on this notion that these afflicted children are sought unto; but as they have a supernatural knowledge; a knowledge which they obtain by their holding correspondence with spectres or evil spirits, as they themselves grant. This consulting of these afflicted children, as abovesaid, seems to me to be a very gross evil, a real abomination, not fit to be known in New England and yet is a thing practised, not only by Tom and John—I mean the ruder and more ignorant sort—but by many who profess high, and pass among us for some of the better sort. This is that which aggravates the evil, and makes it heinous and tremendous; and yet this is not the worst of it, for, as sure as I now write to you, even some of our civil leaders, and spiritual teachers, who, (I think,) should punish and preach down such sorcery and wickedness, do yet allow of, encourage, yea, and practise this very abomination.

I know there are several worthy gentlemen in Salem, who account this practise as an abomination, have trembled to see the methods of this nature which others have used, and have declared themselves to think the practise to be very evil and corrupt; but all avails little with the abettors of the said practice.

A person from Boston, of no small note, carried up his child to Salem, (near 20 miles,) on purpose that he might consult the afflicted about his child; which accordingly he did; and the afflicted told him, that his child was afflicted by Mrs. Cary and Mrs. Obinson. The man returned to Boston, and went forthwith to the justices for a warrant to seize the said Obinson, (the said Cary being out of the way); but the Boston justices saw reason to deny a warrant. The Rev. Mr. Increase Mather of Boston, took occasion severely to reprove the said man; asking him whether there was not a God in Boston, that he should go to the devil in Salem for advice; warning him very seriously against such naughty practices; which, I hope, proved to the conviction and good of the said person; if not, his blood will be upon his own head.

This consulting of these afflicted children, about their sick, was the unhappy beginning of the unhappy troubles at poor Andover: Horse and man were sent up to Salem Village, from the said Andover, for some of the said afflicted; and more than one or two of them were carried down to see Ballard's wife, and to tell who it was that did afflict her. I understand that the said Ballard took advice before he took this method; but what pity was it, that he should meet with, and hearken to such bad counsellors? Poor Andover does now rue the day that ever the said afflicted went among them; they lament their folly, and are an object of great pity and commiseration. Captain Bradstreet and Mr. Stevens are complained of by the afflicted, have left the town, and do abscond. Deacon Fry's wife, Captain Osgood's wife, and some others, remarkably pious and good people in repute, are apprehended and imprisoned; and that that is more admirable [astonishing], the forementioned women are become a kind of confessors, being first brought thereto by the urgings and arguings of their good husbands, who, having taken up that corrupt and highly pernicious opinion, that whoever were accused by the afflicted, were guilty, did break charity with their dear wives, upon their being accused, and urge them to confess their guilt; which so far prevailed with them as to make them say, they were afraid of their being in the snare of the devil; and which, through the rude and barbarous methods* that were afterwards used at Salem, issued in somewhat plainer degrees of confession, and was attended with imprisonment. The good deacon and captain are now sensible of the error they were in; do grieve and mourn bitterly, that they should break their charity with their wives, and urge them to confess themselves witches. They now see and acknowledge their rashness and uncharitableness, and are very fit objects for the pity and prayers of every good Christian. Now I am writing concerning Andover, I cannot omit the opportunity of sending you this information; that whereas there is a report spread abroad the country, how that they were much addicted to sorcery in the said town, and that there were forty men in it that could raise the devil as well as any astrologer, and the like; after the best search that I can make into it, it proves a mere slander, and a very unrighteous imputation.

The Reverend elders of the said place were much surprised upon their hearing of the said report, and faithfully made inquiry about it; but the whole of naughtiness, that they could discover and find out, was only this, that two or three girls had foolishly made use of the sieve and scissors [method of fortune telling], as children have done in other towns. This method of the girls I do not justify in any measure; but yet I think it very hard and unreasonable, that a town should lie under the blemish and scandal of sorceries and conjuration, merely for the inconsiderate practices of two or three girls in the said town.

5. I cannot but admire that the justices, whom I think to be well-meaning men, should so far give ear to the devil, as merely upon his authority to issue out their warrants, and apprehend people. Liberty was evermore accounted the great privilege of an Englishman; but certainly, if the devil will be heard against us, and his testimony taken, to the seizing and apprehending of us, our liberty vanishes, and we are fools if we boast of our liberty. Now, that the justices have thus far given ear to the devil, I think may be mathematically demonstrated to any man of common sense: And for the demonstration and proof hereof, I desire, only, that these two things may be duly considered, *viz.*

---

*You may possibly think that my terms are too severe; but should I tell you what a kind of blade was employed in bringing these women to their confession; what methods from damnation were taken; with what violence urged; how unseasonably they were kept up; what buzzings and chuckings of the hand were used, and the like, I am sure that you would call them, (as I do), rude and barbarous methods.

1. That several persons have been apprehended purely upon the complaints of these afflicted, to whom the afflicted were perfect strangers, and had not the least knowledge of imaginable, before they were apprehended.

2. That the afflicted do own and assert, and the justices do grant, that the devil does inform and tell the afflicted the names of those persons that are thus unknown unto them. Now these two things being duly considered, I think it will appear evident to any one, that the devil's information is the fundamental testimony that is gone upon in the apprehending of the aforesaid people.

If I believe such or such an assertion as comes immediately from the Minister of God in the pulpit, because it is the word of the everliving God, I build my faith on God's testimony: and if I practise upon it, this my practice is properly built on the word of God: even so in the case before us.

If I believe the afflicted persons as informed by the devil, and act thereupon, this my act may properly be said to be grounded upon the testimony or information of the devil, And now, if things are thus, I think it ought to be for a lamentation to you and me, and all such as would be accounted good Christians.

If any should see the force of this argument, and upon it say, (as I heard a wise and good judge once propose,) that they know not but that God almighty, or a good spirit, does give this information to these afflicted persons; I make answer thereto, and say, that it is most certain that it is neither almighty God, nor yet any good spirit, that gives this information; and my reason is good, because God is a God of truth; and the good spirits will not lie; whereas these informations have several times proved false, when the accused were brought before the afflicted.

6. I cannot but admire [marvel] that these afflicted persons should be so much countenanced and encouraged in their accusations as they are: I often think of the Groton woman [Elizabeth Knapp], that was afflicted, an account of which we have in print, and is a most certain truth, not to be doubted of. I shall only say, that there was as much ground, in the hour of it, to countenance the said Groton woman, and to apprehend and imprison, on her accusations, as there is now to countenance these afflicted persons, and to apprehend and imprison on their accusations. But furthermore, it is worthy of our deepest consideration, that in the conclusion, (after multitudes have been imprisoned, and many have been put to death,) these afflicted persons should own that all was a mere fancy and delusion of the devil's, as the Groton woman did own and acknowledge with respect to herself; if, I say, in after times, this be acknowledged by them, how can the justices, judges, or any else concerned in these matters, look back upon these things without the greatest of sorrow and grief imaginable? I confess to you, it makes me tremble when I seriously consider of this thing. I have heard that the chief judge [William Stoughton] has expressed himself very hardly of the accused woman at Groton, as though he believed her to be a witch to this day; but by such as knew

the said woman, this is judged a very uncharitable opinion of the said judge, and I do not understand that any are proselyted thereto.

Reverend Sir, these things I cannot but admire and wonder at. Now, if so be it is the effect of my dullness that I thus admire, I hope you will pity, not censure me: but if, on the contrary, these things are just matter of admiration, I know that you will join with me in expressing your admiration hereat.

The chief judge is very zealous in these proceedings, and says, he is very clear as to all that hath as yet been acted by this court, and, as far as ever I could perceive, is very impatient in hearing any thing that looks another way. I very highly honour and reverence the wisdom and integrity of the said judge, and hope that this matter shall not diminish my veneration for his honour; however, I cannot but say, my great fear is, that wisdom and counsel are withheld from his honour as to this matter, which yet I look upon not so much as a judgment to his honour as to this poor land.

But although the chief judge, and some of the other judges, be very zealous in these proceedings, yet this you may take for a truth, that there are several about the Bay, men for understanding, judgment, and piety, inferior to few, (if any,) in New England that do utterly condemn the said proceedings, and do freely deliver their judgment in the case to be this, *viz.* that these methods will utterly ruin and undo poor New England. I shall nominate some of these to you, *viz.* The honourable Simon Bradstreet, Esq. (our late governor); the honourable Thomas Danforth, Esq. (our late deputy governor); the Reverend Mr. Increase Mather, and the Reverend Mr. Samuel Willard. Major N. Saltonstall, Esq. who was one of the judges, has left the court, and is very much dissatisfied with the proceedings of it. Excepting Mr. Hale, Mr. Noyes, and Mr. Parris, the Reverend elders, almost throughout the whole country, are very much dissatisfied. Several of the late justices, *viz.* Thomas Graves, Esq. N. Byfield, Esq. Francis Foxcroft, Esq. are much dissatisfied; also several of the present justices; and in particular, some of the Boston justices, were resolved rather to throw up their commissions than be active in disturbing the liberty of their Majesties' subjects, merely on the accusations of these afflicted, possessed children.

Finally; the principal gentlemen in Boston, and thereabout, are generally agreed that irregular and dangerous methods have been taken as to these matters.

Sir, I would not willingly lead you into any error, and therefore would desire you to note,

1. That when I call these afflicted "the afflicted children," I would not be understood as though I meant, that all that are afflicted are *children:* there are several young men and women that are afflicted, as well as children: but this term has most prevailed among us, because of the younger sort that were first afflicted, and therefore I make use of it.

2. That when I speak of the Salem gentlemen, I would not be understood as though I meant every individual gentleman in Salem; nor yet as though I meant, that there were no men but in Salem that run upon these notions: some term they must have, and this seems not improper, because in Salem this sort of gentlemen does most abound.

3. That other justices in the country, besides the Salem justices, have issued out their warrants, and imprisoned, on the accusations of the afflicted as aforesaid; and therefore, when I speak of the Salem justices, I do not mean them exclusively.

4. That as to the above mentioned judges, that are commissionated for this court at Salem, five of them do belong to Suffolk county; four of which five do belong to Boston; and therefore I see no reason why Boston should talk of Salem, as though their own judges had had no hand in these proceedings at Salem.

Nineteen persons have now been executed, and one pressed to death for a mute: seven more are condemned; two of which are reprieved, because they pretend [claim] their being with child; one, *viz.* Mrs. Bradbury of Salisbury, from the intercession of some friends; and two or three more, because they are confessors.

The court is adjourned to the first Tuesday in November, then to be kept at Salem; between this and then will be [the] great assembly [of the General Court] and this matter will be a peculiar matter of their agitation. I think it is a matter of earnest supplication and prayer to almighty God, that he would afford his gracious presence to the said assembly, and direct them aright in this weighty matter. Our hopes are here; and if, at this juncture, God does not graciously appear for us, I think we may conclude that New England is undone and undone.

I am very sensible, that it is irksome and disagreeable to go back, when a man's doing so is an implication that he has been walking in a wrong path: however, nothing is more honourable than, upon due conviction, to retract and undo, (so far as may be,) what has been amiss and irregular.

I would hope that, in the conclusion, both the judges and justices will see and acknowledge that such were their best friends and advisers as dissuaded from the methods which they have taken, though hitherto they have been angry with them, and apt to speak very hardly of them.

I cannot but highly applaud, and think it our duty to be very thankful, for the endeavours of several elders, whose lips, (I think,) should preserve knowledge, and whose counsel should, I think, have been more regarded, in a case of this nature, than as yet it has been: in particular, I cannot but think very honourably of the endeavours of a reverend person in Boston, whose good affection to his country in general, and spiritual relation to three of the judges in particular, has made him very solicitous and industrious in this matter; and I am fully persuaded, that had his notions and proposals been hearkened to, and followed, when these troubles were in their birth, in an ordinary way, they would never have grown unto that height which now they have. He has as yet met with little but unkindness, abuse, and reproach from many men; but I trust that, in after times, his wisdom and service will find a more universal acknowledgment; and if not, his reward is with the Lord.

Two or three things I should have hinted to you before, but they slipped my thoughts in their proper place.

Many of these afflicted persons, who have scores of strange fits in a day, yet in the intervals of time are hale and hearty, robust and lusty, as though nothing had afflicted them. I remember that when the chief judge gave the first jury their charge, he told them, that they were not to mind whether the bodies of the said afflicted were really pined and consumed, as was expressed in the inditement; but whether the said afflicted did not suffer from the accused such afflictions as naturally *tended* to their being pined and consumed, wasted, etc. This, (said he,) is a pining and consuming in the sense of the law. I add not.

Furthermore: These afflicted persons do say, and often have declared it, that they can see spectres when their eyes are shut, as well as when they are open. This one thing I evermore accounted as very observable, and that which might serve as a good key to unlock the nature of these mysterious troubles, if duly improved by us. Can they see spectres when their eyes are shut? I am sure they lie, at least speak falsely, if they say so; for the thing, in nature, is an utter impossibility. It is true, they may strongly fancy, or have things represented to their imagination, when their eyes are shut; and I think this is all which ought to be allowed to these blind, nonsensical girls; and if our officers and courts have apprehended, imprisoned, condemned, and executed our guiltless neighbours, certainly our error is great, and we shall rue it in the conclusion. There are two or three other things that I have observed in and by these afflicted persons, which make me strongly suspect that the devil imposes upon their brains, and deludes their fancy and imagination; and that the devil's book (which they say has been offered them) is a mere fancy of theirs, and no reality: That the witches' meeting, the devil's baptism, and mock sacraments, which they oft speak of, are nothing else but the effect of their fancy, depraved and deluded by the devil, and not a reality to be regarded or minded by any wise man. And whereas the confessors have owned and asserted the said meetings, the said baptism, and mock sacrament, (which the Salem gentlemen and some others, make much account of) I am very apt to think, that, did you know the circumstances of the said confessors, you would not be swayed thereby, any otherwise than to be confirmed, that all is perfect devilism, and an hellish design to ruin and destroy this poor land: For whereas there are of the said confessors 55 in number, some of them are known to be distracted, crazed women, something of which you may see by a petition lately offered to the chief judge, a copy whereof I may now send you [account by the six Andover women]; others of them denied their guilt, and maintained their innocency for above eighteen hours, after most violent, distracting, and draggooning methods had been used with them, to make them confess. Such methods they were, that more than one of the said confessors did since tell many, with tears in their eyes, that they thought their very lives would have gone out of their bodies; and wished that they might have been cast into the lowest dungeon, rather than be tortured with such repeated buzzings and chuckings and unreasonable urgings as they were treated withal.

They soon recanted their confessions, acknowledging, with sorrow and grief, that it was an hour of great temptation with them; and I am very apt to think, that as for five or six of the said confessors, if they are not very good Christian women, it will be no easy matter to find so many good Christian women in New England. But, finally, as to about thirty of these fifty-five confessors, they are possessed (I reckon) with the devil, and afflicted as the children are, and therefore not fit to be regarded as to anything they say of themselves or others. And whereas the Salem gentlemen do say that these confessors made their confessions before they were afflicted, it is absolutely contrary to universal experience, as far as ever I could understand. It is true, that some of these have made their confession before they had their falling, tumbling fits, but yet not absolutely before they had any fits and marks of possession, for (as the Salem gentlemen know full well) when these persons were about first confessing, their mouths would be stopped, and their throats affected, as though there was danger of strangling, and afterward (it is true) came their tumbling fits. So that, I say, the confessions of these persons were in the beginning of their fits, and not truly before their fits, as the Salem gentlemen would make us believe.

Thus, (Sir,) I have given you as full a narrative of these matters as readily occurs to my mind, and I think every word of it is matter of fact; the several glosses and descants where-upon, by way of reasoning, I refer to your judgment, whether to approve or disapprove.

What will be the issue of these troubles, God only knows; I am afraid that ages will not wear off that reproach and those stains which these things will leave behind them upon our land. I pray God pity us, humble us, forgive us, and appear mercifully for us in this our mount of distress: Herewith I conclude, and subscribe myself,

Reverend Sir, your real friend and humble servant,

T. B.

From: Governor Phipps's *Letters to the Home Government* (1692–1693)

When I first arrived I found this province miserably harrassed with a most horrible witchcraft or possession of devils which had broke in upon several towns, some scores of poor people were taken with preternatural torments, some scalded with brimstone, some had pins stuck in their flesh, others hurried into the fire and water and some dragged out of their houses and carried over the tops of trees and hills for many miles together; it hath been represented to me much like that of Sweden about thirty years ago, and there were many committed to prison upon suspicion of witchcraft before my arrival. The loud cries and clamours of the friends of the afflicted people with the advice of the deputy governor and many others prevailed with me to give a commission of Oyer and Terminer for discovering what witchcraft might be at the bottom or whether it were not a possession. The chief judge in this commission was the deputy governor and the rest were persons of the best prudence and figure that could then be pitched upon. When the court came to sit at Salem in the County of Essex they convicted more than twenty persons of being guilty of witchcraft, some of the convicted were such as confessed their guilt, the court as I understand began their proceedings with the accusations of the afflicted and then went upon other human evidences to strengthen that. I was almost the whole time of the proceeding abroad in the service of their majesties in the eastern part of the country and depended upon the judgement of the court as to a right method of proceeding in cases of witchcraft but when I came home I found many persons in a strange ferment of dissatisfaction which was increased by some hot spirits that blew up the flame, but on enquiring into the matter I found that the devil had taken upon him the name and shape of several persons who were doubtless innocent and to my certain knowledge of good reputation, for which cause I have now forbidden the committing of any more that shall be accused without unavoidable necessity, and those that have been committed I would shelter from any proceedings against them wherein there may be the least suspicion of any wrong to be done unto the innocent. I would also wait for any particular directions or commands if their Majesties please to give me any for the fuller ordering this perplexed affair. I have also put a stop to the printing of any discourses one way or other, that may increase the needless disputes of people upon this occasion, because I saw a likelihood of kindling an inextinguishable flame if I should admit any public and open contests and I have grieved to see that some who should have done their Majesties and this province better service have so far taken council of passion as to desire the precipitancy of these matters. These things have been improved by some [as] to give me many interruptions in their Majesties' service and in truth none of my vexations have been greater than this, than that their Majesties' service has been hereby unhappily clogged, and the persons who have made so ill improvement of these matters here are seeking to turn it all upon me, but I hereby declare that as soon as I came from fighting against their Majesties' enemies and understood what danger some of their innocent subjects might be exposed to, if the evidence of the afflicted persons only did prevail either to the committing or trying any of them, I did before any application was made unto me about it put a stop to the proceedings of the court and they are now stopped till their Majesties' pleasure be known. Sir I beg pardon for giving you all this trouble, the reason is because I know my enemies are seeking to turn it all upon me and I take this liberty because I depend upon your friendship, and desire you will please to give a true understanding of the matter if anything of this kind be urged or made use of against me. Because the justness of my proceeding herein will be a sufficient defence. Sir

I am with all imaginable respect
Your most humble Servant,

WILLIAM PHIPPS

Dated at Boston
the 12th of October 1692.

Memorandum

That my Lord President be pleased to acquaint his Majesty in Council with the account received from New England from Sir William Phips the Governor there touching proceedings against several persons for witchcraft as appears by the governor's letter concerning those matters.

Boston in New England February 21st, 1693

May it please your Lordship,

By the captain of the *Samuell and Henry* I gave an account that at my arrival here I found the prisons full of people committed upon suspicion of witchcraft and that continual complaints were made to me that many persons were grievously tormented by witches and that they cried out upon several persons by name, as the cause of their torments. The number of these complaints increasing every day, by advice of the lieutenant governor and the council I gave a commission of Oyer and Terminer to try the suspected witches and at that time the generality of the people represented the matter to me as real witchcraft and gave very strange instances of the same. The first in commission was the lieutenant governor and the rest persons of the best prudence and figure that could then be pitched upon and I depended upon the court for a right method of proceeding in cases of witchcraft. At that time I went to command the army at the eastern part of the province, for the French and Indians had made an attack upon some of our frontier towns. I continued there for some time but when I returned I found people much dissatisfied at the proceedings of the court, for about twenty persons were condemned and executed of which number some were thought by many persons to be innocent. The court still proceeded in the same method of trying them, which was by the evidence of the afflicted persons who when they were brought into the court as soon as the suspected witches looked upon them instantly fell to the ground in strange agonies and grievous torments, but when touched by them upon the arm or some other part of their flesh they immediately revived and came to themselves, upon which they made oath that the prisoner at the bar did afflict them and that they saw their shape or spectre come from their bodies which put them to such pains and torments: When I enquired into the matter I was informed by the judges that they begin with this, but had human testimony against such as were condemned and undoubted proof of their being witches, but at length I found that the devil did take upon him the shape of innocent persons and some were accused of whose innocency I was well assured and many considerable persons of unblameable life and conversation were cried out upon as witches and wizards. The deputy governor notwithstanding persisted vigorously in the same method, to the great dissatisfaction and disturbance of the people, until I put an end to the court and stopped the proceedings, which I did because I saw many innocent persons might otherwise perish and at that time I thought it my duty to give an account thereof that their Majesties pleasure might be signified, hoping that for the better ordering thereof the judges learned in the law in England might give such rules and directions as have been practised in England for proceedings in so difficult and so nice a point. When I put an end to the Court there were at least fifty persons in prison in great misery by reason of the extreme cold and their poverty, most of them having only spectre evidence against them, and their mittimusses being defective, I caused some of them to be let out upon bail and put the judges upon considering of a way to relieve others and prevent them from perishing in prison, upon which some of them were convinced and acknowledged that their former proceedings were too violent and not grounded upon a right foundation but that if they might sit again, they would proceed after another method, and whereas Mr. Increase Mather and several other divines did give it as their judgment that the devil might afflict in the shape of an innocent person and that the look and the touch of the suspected persons was not sufficient proof against them, these things had not the same stress laid upon them as before, and upon this consideration I permitted a special Superior Court to be held at Salem in the County of Essex on the third day of January, the lieutenant governor being chief judge. Their method of proceeding being altered, all that were brought to trial to the number of fifty-two, were cleared saving three, and I was informed by the King's Attorney General that some of the cleared and the condemned were under the same circumstances or that there was the same reason to clear the three condemned as the rest according to his judgment. The deputy governor signed a warrant for their speedy execution and also of five others who were condemned at the former Court of Oyer and Terminer, but considering how the matter had been managed I sent a reprieve whereby the execution was stopped until their Majesties' pleasure be signified and declared. The lieutenant governor upon this occasion was enraged and filled with passionate anger and refused to sit upon the bench in a Superior Court then held at Charlestown, and indeed hath from the beginning hurried on these matters with great precipitancy and by his warrant hath caused the estates, goods and chattles of the executed to be seized and disposed of without my knowledge or consent. The stop put to the first method of proceedings hath dissipated the black cloud that threatened this province with destruction; for whereas this delusion of the devil did spread and its dismal effects touched the lives and estates of many of their Majesties' subjects and the reputation of some of the principal persons here, and indeed unhappily clogged and interrupted their Majesties' affairs which hath been a great vexation to me, I have no new complaints but peoples' minds before divided and distracted by differing opinions concerning this matter are now well composed.

I am
Your Lordships' most faithful
humble servant

William Phips

To the Rt. Honourable
the Earl of Nottingham
at Whitehall
London
Received May 24, 93
abt. witches

From: Robert Calef, *More Wonders of the Invisible World*

January 3. By virtue of an Act of the General Court, the first Superior Court was held at Salem, for the County of Essex. The Judges appointed were Mr. William Stoughton (the lieutenant governor), Thomas Danforth, John Richards, Wait

Winthrop, and Samuel Sewall, Esquires. Where Ignoramus[no basis for prosecution] was found upon the several bills of indictment against thirty, and *Billa Vera* [a true bill] against twenty six more; of all these three only were found guilty by the jury upon trial, two of which were (as appears by their behaviour) the most senseless and ignorant creatures that could be found; besides which it does not appear what came in against those more than against the rest that were acquitted.

The third was the wife of Wardwell, who was one of the twenty executed, and it seems they had both confessed themselves guilty; but he retracting his said confession, was tried and executed; it is supposed that this woman fearing her husband's fate, was not so stiff in her denials of her former confession, such as it was. These three received sentence of death.

At these trials some of the jury made inquiry of the court, what account they ought to make of the spectre evidence? and received for Answer "as much as of chips in wort."

January 31, 1693. The Superior Court began at Charlestown, for the County of Middlesex, Mr. Stoughton, Mr. Danforth, Mr. Winthorp, and Mr. Sewall, judges, where several had Ignoramus returned upon their Bills of Indictment, and *Billa Vera* upon others.

In the time the court sat, word was brought in, that a reprieve was sent to Salem, and had prevented the execution of seven of those that were there condemned, which so moved the chief judge, that he said to this effect, "We were in a way to have cleared the land of these, etc., who it is obstructs the course of justice I know not; the Lord be merciful to the country," and so went off the bench, and came no more that court: The most remarkable of the trials, was of Sarah Daston, she was a woman of about 70 or 80 years of age. To usher in her trial, a report went before, that if there were a witch in the world she was one, as having been so accounted of, for 20 or 30 years; which drew many people from Boston, etc., to hear her trial. There were a multitude of witnesses produced against her; but what testimony they gave in seemed wholly foreign, as of accidents, illness, etc., befalling them, or theirs after some quarrel; what these testified was much of it of actions said to be done 20 years before that time. The spectre evidence was not made use of in these trials, so that the jury soon brought her in not guilty; her daughter and granddaughter, and the rest that were then tried, were also acquitted. After she was cleared Judge Danforth admonished her in these words, "Woman, woman, repent, there are shrewd things come in against you"; she was remanded to prison for her fees, and there in a short time expired. One of Boston that had been at the trial of Daston, being the same evening in company with one of the judges in a public place, acquainted him that some that had been both at the trials at Salem and at this at Charlestown, had asserted that there was more evidence against the said Daston than against any at Salem, to which the said judge conceeded, saying, That it was so. It was replied by that person, that he dare give it under his hand, that there was not enough come in against her to bear a just reproof.

April 25, 1693. The first Superior Court was held at Boston, for the County of Suffolk, the judges were the lieutenant governor, Mr. Danforth, Mr. Richards and Mr. Sewall, Esquires.

Where (besides the acquitting Mr. John Alden by proclamation) the most remarkable was, what related to Mary Watkins, who had been a servant, and lived about seven miles from Boston, having formerly accused her mistress of witchcraft, and was supposed to be distracted, she was threatened if she persisted in such accusations to be punished; this with the necessary care to recover her health, had that good effect, that she not only had her health restored, but also wholly acquitted her mistress of any such crimes, and continued in health till the return of the year, and then again falling into melancholy humours she was found strangling herself; her life being hereby prolonged, she immediately accused herself of being a witch; was carried before a magistrate and committed. At this court a fill of indictment was brought to the grand jury against her, and her confession upon her examination given in as evidence, but these not wholly satisfied herewith, sent for her, who gave such account of herself, that they (after they had returned into the court to ask some questions) twelve of them agreed to find Ignoramus, but the court was pleased to send them out again, who again at coming in returned it as before.

She was continued for some time in prison, etc., and at length was sold to Virginia. About this time the prisoners in all the prisons were released.

To omit here the mentioning of several wenches in Boston, etc., who pretended to be afflicted, and accused several, the ministers often visiting them, and praying with them, concerning whose affliction narratives are in being in manuscript. Not only these, but the generality of those accusers may have since convinced the ministers by their vicious courses that they might err in extending too much charity to them.

The conclusion of the whole in the Massachusetts Colony was, Sir William Phips, Governor, being called home, before he went he pardoned such as had been condemned, for which they gave about 30 shillings each to the King's Attorney.

In August 1697, the Superior Court sat at Hartford, in the Colony of Connecticut, where one Mistress Benom was tried for witchcraft. She had been accused by some children that pretended to the spectral sight; they searched her several times for teats; they tried the experiment of casting her into the water, and after this she was excommunicated by the minister of Wallinsford. Upon her trial nothing material appearing against her, save spectre evidence, she was acquitted, as also her daughter, a girl of twelve or thirteen years old, who had been likewise accused; but upon renewed complaints against them, they both fled into New York Government.

Before this the Government issued forth the following Proclamation.

By the Honourable the Lieutenant Governor, Council and Assembly of his Majesties Province of the Massachusetts Bay, in General Court Assembled.

Whereas the anger of God is not yet turned away, but his hand is still stretched out against his people in manifold judgments, particularly in drawing out to such a length the troubles of Europe, by a perplexing war; and more especially, respecting ourselves in this province, in that God is pleased still to go on in diminishing our substance, cutting short our harvest, blasting our most promising undertakings more ways than one, unsettling of us, and by his more immediate hand, snatching away many out of our embraces, by sudden and violent deaths, even at this time when the sword is devouring so many both at home and abroad, and that after many days of public and solemn addressing of him, and although considering the many sins prevailing in the midst of us, we cannot but wonder at the patience and mercy moderating these rebukes; yet we cannot but also fear that there is something still wanting to accompany our supplications. And doubtless there are some particular sins, which God is angry with our Israel for, that have not been duly seen and resented by us, about which God expects to be sought, if ever he turn again our captivity.

Wherefore it is commanded and appointed, that Thursday the fourteenth of January next be observed as a day of prayer, with fasting throughout this province, strictly forbidding all servile labour thereon; that so all God's people may offer up fervent supplications unto him, for the preservation, and prosperity of his Majesty's Royal Person and Government, and success to attend his affairs both at home and abroad; that all iniquity may be put away which hath stirred God's holy jealousy against this land; that he would show us what we know not, and help us wherein we have done amiss to do so no more; and especially that whatever mistakes on either hand have been fallen into, either by the body of this people, or any orders of men, referring to the late tragedy, raised among us by Satan and his instruments, through the awful judgment of God, he would humble us therefore and pardon all the errors of his servants and people, that desire to love his name and be atoned to his land; that he would remove the rod of the wicked from off the lot of the righteous; that he would bring the American heathen, and cause them to hear and obey his voice.

Given at Boston, Decemb. 17, 1696, in the 8th year of his Majesty's reign

ISAAC ADDINGTON, SECRETARY

Upon the day of the fast in the full Assembly, at the South Meetinghouse in Boston, one of the honourable judges, who had sat in judicature in Salem, delivered in a paper, and while it was in reading stood up, But the copy being not to be obtained at present, it can only be reported by memory to this effect, *viz.* It was to desire the prayers of God's people for him and his, and that God having visited his family, etc., he was apprehensive that he might have fallen into some errors in the matters at Salem, and pray that the guilt of such miscarriages may not be imputed either to the country in general, or to him or his family in particular.

Some that had been of several juries, have given forth a paper, signed with their own hands in these words.

We whose names are under written, being in the year 1692 called to serve as jurors, in court at Salem, on trial of many, who were by some suspected guilty of doing acts of witchcraft upon the bodies of sundry persons:

We confess that we our selves were not capable to understand, nor able to withstand the mysterious delusions of the powers of darkness, and prince of the air; but were for want of knowledge in ourselves, and better information from others, prevailed with to take up with such evidence against the accused, as on further consideration, and better information, we justly fear was insufficient for the touching the lives of any, Deut, 17. 6, whereby we fear we have been instrumental with others, though ignorantly and unwittingly, to bring upon ourselves, and this people of the Lord, the guilt of innocent blood; which sin the Lord saith in Scripture, he would not pardon, 2 Kings 24. 4, that is we suppose in regard of his temporal judgments. We do therefore hereby signify to all in general (and to the surviving sufferers in especial) our deep sense of, and sorrow for our errors, in acting on such evidence to the condemning of any person.

And do hereby declare that we justly fear that we were sadly deluded and mistaken, for which we are much disquieted and distressed in our minds; and do therefore humbly beg forgiveness, first of God for Christ's sake for this our error; And pray that God would not impute the guilt of it to ourselves, nor others; and we also pray that we may be considered candidly, and aright by the living sufferers as being then under the power of a strong and general delusion, utterly unacquainted with, and not experienced in matters of that nature.

We do heartily ask forgiveness of you all, whom we have justly offended, and do declare according to our present minds, we would none of us do such things again on such grounds for the whole world; praying you to accept of this in way of satisfaction for our offence; and that you would bless the inheritance of the Lord, that he may be entreated for the land.

Foreman, THOMAS FISK,	THOMAS PERLY, *Senior*
WILLIAM FISK	JOHN PEBODY,

JOHN BATCHELER, THOMAS PERKINS,
THOMAS FISK, *Junior* SAMUEL SAYER,
JOHN DANE, ANDREW ELLIOTT,
JOSEPH EVELITH, HENRY HERRICK, *Senior*

From: *The Confession of Ann Putnam, (1706)*

Ann Putnam was the leader of the "afflicted children," who called out the names of supposed "witches." She was particularly active in accusing Rebecca Nurse, the seventy-year-old church member hanged on July 19, 1692. The daughter of Thomas and Ann Putnam, she was twelve at the time of the witch-hunt and twenty-four when she made this confession. It was read out by Joseph Green, the pastor who had replaced Samuel Parris in 1697. As the Reverend Green read her words, Ann stood before the congregation, which included many members of the Nurse family. She died thirteen years later, never having married.

I desire to be humbled before God for that sad and humbling providence that befell my father's family in the year about '92;

that I, then being in my childhood, should, by such a providence of God, be made an instrument for the accusing of several persons of a grievous crime, whereby their lives were taken away from them, whom now I have just grounds and good reason to believe they were innocent persons; and that it was a great delusion of Satan that deceived me in that sad time, whereby I justly fear I have been instrumental, with others, though ignorantly and unwittingly, to bring upon myself and this land the guilt of innocent blood; though what was said or done by me against any person I can truly and uprightly say, before God and man, I did it not out of any anger, malice, or ill-will to any person, for I had no such thing against one of them; but what I did was ignorantly, being deluded by Satan. And particularly, as I was a chief instrument of accusing of Goodwife Nurse and her two sisters, I desire to lie in the dust, and to be humbled for it, in that I was a cause, with others, of so sad a calamity to them and their families; for which cause I desire to lie in the dust, and earnestly beg forgiveness of God, and from all those unto whom I have given just cause of sorrow and offence, whose relations were taken away or accused.

anne putnam

This confession was read before the congregation, together with her relation, Aug. 25, 1706; and she acknowledged it.

J. GREEN, *PASTOR*

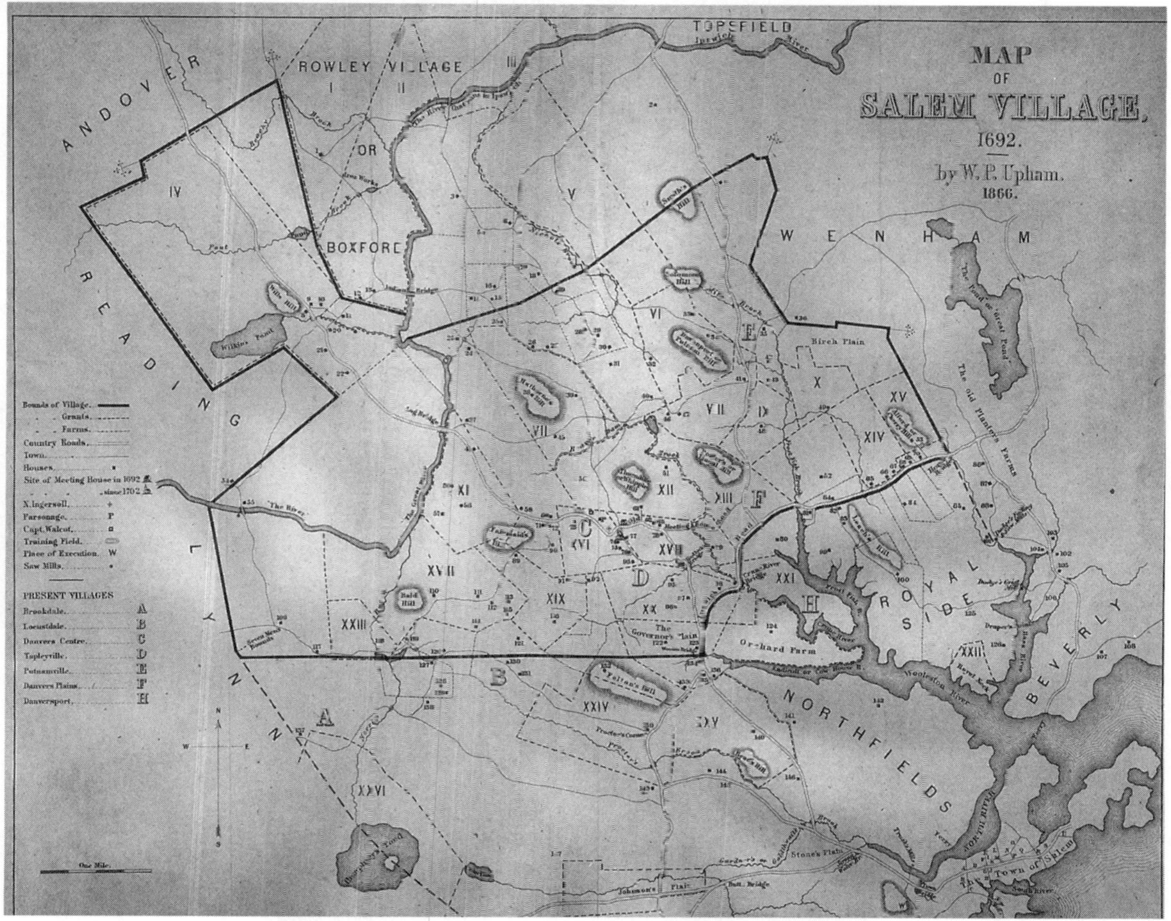

Salem Village as it was in 1692, showing some of the key locations in the witch trials, such as the meeting house and parsonage. In 1752 the Village changed its name to Danvers. Salem Town can be found in the map's bottom right hand corner. Courtesy, Peabody Essex Museum, Salem, Mass.

Top left. Cotton Mather, grandson of two of Massachusetts' first religious leaders and son of Increase Mather, minister and politician, was influential in creating the witch hunt and driving it on. Courtesy, Peabody Essex Museum, Salem, Mass.

Page 111, top left. Samuel Parris (the pastor of Salem Village in 1692), in whose house the witch hunt began, with his daughter and niece accusing the family's Indian slave and others of bewitching them. Courtesy, Massachusetts Historical Society.

Page 111, top right. The covenant of the Salem Village church, formed by Samuel Parris in November 1689. Eleven of the signatures bear the surname Putnam. From the Salem Village Church Book of Record. Courtesy, Danvers Archival Center, Danvers, Mass.

Page 111, bottom. Pages from Samuel Parris's sermon notebook, showing part of the sermon he preached on March 27, 1692, which helped drive on the witch hunt. Courtesy, Connecticut Historical Society, Hartford, Connecticut.

Bottom left. A Puritan minister prays over a young New England woman afflicted by witchcraft.

We resolve uprightly to study what is our duty, & to make it our greif, & reckon it our shame, wherein soever we find our selves to come short in the discharge of it, & for par-don thereof ~~to betake~~ humbly to betake our selves to the Blood of the Everlasting Covenant.

And that we may keep this covenant, & all the branches of it inviolable for ever, being sensible that we can do nothing of our selves,

We humbly implore the help & grace of our Mediator may be sufficient for us: Beseeching that whilst we are working out our own salvation, with fear & trembling, He would graciously work in us both to will, & to do. And that he being the great Shepherd of our souls would lead us into the paths of Righteousness, for his own Names sake. And at length receive us all into the Inheritance of the saints in Light.

1. Samuel Parris Pastor.	The women which embodyed with us are by their severall Names as followeth viz:
2. Nathaniell Putnam	1. Eliz: (wife to Sam:) Parris
3. John putnam	2. Rebek: (wife to John) Putman.
4. Henry Wilkins 79.	3. Anna (wife to Bray) Wilkins.
5. Joshua Rea	
6. Nathaniel Ingersoll	4. Sarah (wife to Joshuah) Rea.
7.	
8. peter Clayes	5. Hannah (wife to Jno (jun:)) Putman.
9. Thomas putnam	6. Sarah (wife to Benj:) Putman
10. John Putnam Jun	7. Sarah Putman.
11. Edward [illegible]	8. ~~Deliverance Walcott~~
12. Jonathan putnam	9. Parris ~~Delivy~~ (wife to William) Way.
13. Benjamin putnam	10. mary (wife to Sam:) Abbie.
14. Ezekiel Cheever	
Henry Wilkins	
15. Benj. Wilkins	
16. william way	
17. [illegible]	
~~18.~~	

Illi quorum nominibus hoc signum praefigitur [illegible]

Christ knows how many Devils there are (147)

27. Mar. 169½ Sacrament day.

Occasioned by dreadfull Witchcraft broke out here a few weeks past, & one member of this church, & another of Salem upon publick examination by civil Authority vehemently suspected for [illegible] it committed

6. John. 70.

Have not I chosen you twelve, & one of you is a Devil. This chap: consist of 3. principal parts.

1. Part consists of a declaration of Christs miraculous feeding of 5000. with 5. loaves & 2. small fishes. 1—15. v.
2. Part treats of Christs miraculous walking upon the Sea. 15—22. v.
3. Last part consists of Christs Sermon to the Capernaites 22. v. ad finem concerning the Heavenly or truly vivifical Bread. This part consists of sundry particles. viz.

1. The occasion of this sermon. 22. 23. 24. 25. v.
2. The Sermon it self. 26—59. v.
3. Last: The event of this sermon. 59. ad finem Now this event consists of

1. The offence of many 59. v &c.
2. A Reprehension of their error from whence this their offence arose: in which Reprehension he shows them that it was not the eating of his flesh carnally but spiritually that he spake of. 61 &c.
3. Christs complaint of the incredulity of many 64. 65. v.
4. An other event which was worse than the former, namely the total departure of several of his disciples from him. 66. v. Whereupon Note

1 Our Lord takes occasion to ask his Disciples whither they also would depart him. 67. v.
2. Peter in the name of the rest answers by confessing ~~both~~ the excellency both of Christs Doctrine & his Person. 68. 69. v.
3. Last: This confession Christ so approves of, that

in his Churches, & who they are. (148)

in the mean while he doth admonish them, that there is an Hypocrite among them, a Devil among them. 70. 71. verses. Have not I chosen you 12. & one of you is a Devil. i.e. I have chosen 12. of you to familiarity with me, to be my Apostles, & for all one of you is a Devil.

Doctr: Our Lord Jesus Christ knows how many Devils there are in his Church, & who they are.

1. There are Devils as well as Saints in Christs Church.
2. Christ knows how many of these Devils there are.
3. Last: Christ knows who these Devils are.

1. Prop: There are Devils as well as Saints in the Church of Christ: Here 3 things may be spoken to

1. Show you what is meant here by Devils
2. That there are such Devils in the Church
3. Last: That there are also true Saints in such Churches

1. What is meant here by Devils. One of you is a Devil. By Devil is ordinarily meant any wicked Angel or Spirit. Sometimes it is put for the Prince or head of the evil spirits, or fallen Angels. Sometimes it is used for vile & wicked persons, the worst of such, who for their villany & impiety do most resemble Devils & wicked Spirits. Thus Christ in our text calls Judas a Devil, for his great likeness to the Devil. One of you is a Devil i.e. a Devil for quality & disposition: not a Devil for Nature, for he was a man &c but a Devil for likeness & operation. 8. Joh. 38. 41 44. Ye are of your Father the Devil

2. There are such Devils in the Church. Not only sinners but notorious sinners; sinners more like to the Devil than others. So here in Christs little Church. Text This also Christ teacheth us in the Parable of the Tares 13. Matth. 38. where Christ tells us that such are the children of the wicked one. i.e. of the Devil.

Reason: Because Hypocrites are the very worst of men

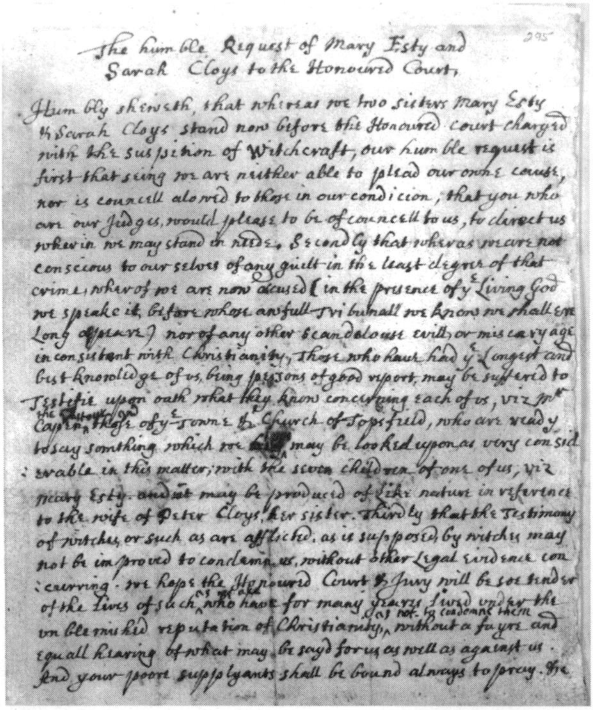

295

The humble Request of Mary Esty and
Sarah Cloys to the Honoured Court,

Humbly sheweth, that whereas we two sisters Mary Esty
& Sarah Cloys stand now before the Honoured court charged
with the suspition of Witchcraft, our humble request is
first that seing we are neither able to plead our owne cause,
nor is councell alowed to those in our condicion; that you who
are our Judges, would please to be of councell to us, to directt us
wherein we may stand in neede. Secondly that whereas we are not
conscious to our selves of any guilt in the least degree of that
crime, wherof we are now accused (in the presence of ye Living God
we speake it, before whose awfull Tribunall we know we shall ere
Long appeare) nor of any other scandalouse evill, or miscaryage
inconsistant with Christianity, Those who have had ye Longest and
best knowledge of us, being persons of good report, may be suffered to
Testifie upon oath what they know concerning each of us, viz Mr
Capen the minister of ye towne & the Church of Topsfield, who are ready
to say something which we hope may be looked upon as very consid
:erable in this matter; with the seven children of one of us, viz
Mary Esty: and it may be produced of like nature in reference
to the wife of Peter Cloys her sister. Thirdly that the Testimony
of witches, or such as are afflicted, as is supposed, by witches may
not be improved to condemn us, without other Legal evidence con
:curring. we hope the Honoured Court & Jury will be soe tender
of the Lives of such as we are who have for many years lived under the
unblemished reputation of Christianity, as not to condemne them without a fayre and
equall hearing of what may be sayd for us as well as against us.
And your poore supplyants shall be bound always to pray &c

Part of the petition from prison by Mary Easty and Sarah Cloyes, sisters of Rebecca Nurse, asserting their innocence of witchcraft and pleading for a fair trial. Courtesy, Peabody Essex Museum, Salem, Mass.

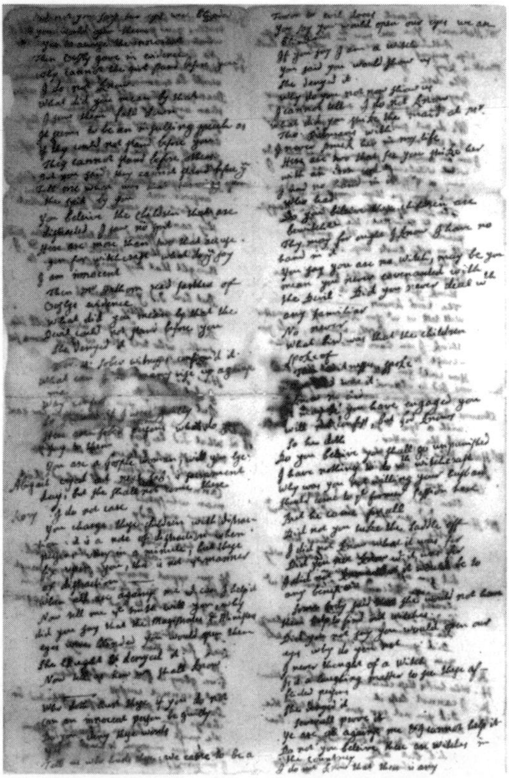

Part of the examination for witchcraft (in the Salem Village meeting house on March 21, 1692) of Martha Corey, the first church member to be accused. The questioning was conducted by John Hathorne and Jonathan Corwin and taken down by Samuel Parris. Courtesy, Peabody Essex Museum, Salem, Mass.

The Rebecca Nurse house in Salem Village, now Danvers, where the seventy-year-old accused witch lived with her husband, children, and grandchildren. The house and land are still today much as they were and are open to visitors. Photo, Leon Arden.

The bed from which the ailing Rebecca Nurse was dragged to her examination for witchcraft, and then to prison, on March 24, 1692. Photo, Leon Arden.

Beadle's Tavern, Salem, where some of the later examinations for witchcraft were conducted. It no longer stands.

Part III

THE HUNTER AND THE HUNTED

The parallels in the lives of Samuel Parris and George Burroughs are startling, given their opposite roles in the witch-hunt. They were born in London within a few years of each other and both traveled early to the New World, studied at Harvard and became Salem Village ministers.

But when they met for the first time, Parris was a witch-hunter, Burroughs a witch. Looked at more closely, their lives show deep divergences that reveal deeply different characters. Parris failed at everything he did, blamed others, and often tried to retrieve the situation by litigation, bullying, and worse. Burroughs excelled as a scholar and athlete and was greatly admired as a pastor and town leader in the outposts of Casco and Wells where, when Indian attacks drove others to flee, he stayed behind and fought. The two men's styles as Puritan ministers were totally opposed. Parris was self-important and inflexible, demanding golden candlesticks for the altar and adhering to outdated rules about baptisms, Burroughs preached to Anglicans as well as Puritans and was never ordained.

The differences in the men's characters determined their fates. Parris's fear and anger, paranoia and rigidity, drove him to induce and abet accusations of witchcraft and whip up fear and anger in others. Burroughs's qualities of generosity, flexibility, and tolerance made him a pariah, in a society governed by frightened fanaticism, and brought him to the gallows.

There is no evidence that, in 1692, Parris was personally gunning for Burroughs. But there is a great deal of evidence that his close allies, the Putnam family, went to more trouble to bring down their ex-minister than any other of their enemies.

4

Samuel Parris (1653–1720)

Parris's first recorded setback in life was to drop out of Harvard. It set a trend of bold beginnings leading to failure. In 1673 he moved to Barbados, trying unsuccessfully to make a going concern of the sugar plantation left him by his father. Back in Boston, he set up as a businessman but by 1688 his modest income had dwindled almost to nothing and he made a career switch to the ministry. This was not as bizarre as it seems to us today since Harvard was considered a training ground for pastors and Parris had for some years taken an interest in ecclesiastical matters. Still, he must by that time have felt he lacked options. Yet the job at Salem Village, a backwater with a history of conflict between pastor and parishioners, may not have been quite what he had hoped for. After receiving the offer, he dallied for months, then embarked on detailed negotiations about pay and conditions. One of his demands was that his flock should provide him with firewood. Unfortunately the conclusions reached on this issue, and others, were never put into writing and there were later differences of view about what had been agreed.

Once Parris and his family were installed, he began still more negotiations, this time for the ownership of the ministry house. Such a demand was unheard of. The pastor's house normally remained the property of the village or town. But Thomas Putnam and his family were desperate to form a Salem Village church and, to make this possible, Parris had to be ordained. The Putnams broke a legally binding agreement of 1681, and all precedents, to give him what he asked for. This incensed those in the community who had opposed Deodat Lawson's ordination and now had small enthusiasm for Parris's. They included, among others, Joseph Hutchinson, Joseph Porter, and Daniel

Andrew. By his insensitivity, poor judgment, and greed, Parris greatly deepened Salem Village's bitter divisions.

By the end of 1691, his enemies were in the ascendant in village affairs and his salary, and even job, were at risk. He had every motive to drive on a witch-hunt that the faction that supported him could use for their own ends. When he did so, he must have told himself that he was doing God's work. Whether he always believed himself, when he woke at four in the morning, we cannot know; it seems unlikely. In all his lengthy entries in the Salem Village Church Book of Record, now in the Danvers Archival Center, and the fifty-two surviving sermons in his Sermon Notebook, and in The Connecticut Historical Society in Hartford, he never betrays a moment's self-doubt.

From: Charles W. Upham, *Salem Witchcraft* (April 1689)

Note the differences on the firewood issue between the demands below and the description of the meeting of June 18 that follows. With no final written agreement, the later divergence of view as to what had been settled could never be resolved. As is seen in the third extract, by October Parris had had his way over the ownership of the house.

Samuel Parris's response to the offer from Salem villagers of £60 per annum, one-third in money, the rest in corn and other provisions

First, when money shall be more plenteous, the money part to be paid me shall accordingly be increased. Second, though corn or like provisions should arise to a higher price than you have set, yet, for my own family use, I shall have what is needful at the price now stated, and so if it fall lower. Third, the whole sixty pounds to be only from our inhabitants that are dwelling in our bounds, proportionable to what lands they have within the same. Fourth, no provision to be brought in without first asking whether needed, and myself to make choice of what, unless the person is unable to pay in any sort but one. Fifth, firewood to be given in yearly, freely. Sixth, two men to be chosen yearly to see that due payments be made. Seventh, contributions each sabbath in papers; and only such as are in papers, and dwelling within our bounds, to be accounted a part of the sixty pounds. Eighth, as God shall please to bless the place so as to be able to rise higher than the sixty pounds, that then a proportionable increase be made. If God shall please, for our sins, to diminish the substance of said place, I will endeavor accordingly to bear such losses, by proportionable abatements of such as shall reasonably desire it.

From: Salem Village Book of Record

Record of meeting of June 18, 1689

At the same meeting—the 18th of June, 1689—it was agreed and voted by general concurrence, that, for Mr. Parris, his encouragement and settlement in the work of the ministry amongst us, we will give him sixty six pounds for his yearly salary,—one-third paid in money, the other two-third parts for provisions, &c.; and Mr. Parris to find himself firewood, and Mr. Parris to keep the ministry-house in good repair; and that Mr. Parris shall also have the use of the ministry-pasture, and the inhabitants to keep the fence in repair; and that we will keep up our contributions, and our inhabitants to put their money in papers, and this to continue so long as Mr. Parris continues in the work of the ministry amongst us, and all productions to be good and merchantable. And, if it please God to bless the inhabitants, we shall be willing to give more; and to expect, that if God shall diminish the estates of the people, that then Mr. Parris do abate of his salary according to proportion."

Record of Salem Village meeting, 10th of October, 1689

It was agreed and voted that the vote in our book of records of 1681, that lays as some say an entailment upon our ministry house and land, is hereby made void and of no effect; one man only dissenting.

2. It was voted and agreed by a general concurrence that we will give to Mr. Parris our ministry house and barn and two acres of land next adjoining to the house, and that Mr. Parris take office upon him amongst us and live and die in the work of the ministry amongst us.

And if Mr. Parris or his heirs do sell the house and land, that the people may have the first refusal of it, giving as much as other men will.

3. There was chosen to lay out the land and make a conveyance of the house and land and to make the conveyance in the name and in the behalf of the inhabitants unto Mr. Parris and his heirs, *viz.:* Lieutenant Nathaniel Putnam, Captain John Putnam, Captain Jonathan Walcott, and Ensign Thomas Flint, and Lieutenant Nathaniel Ingersoll.

From: *More Wonders of the Invisible World*

Par 5: "An Impartial Account of the Most Memorable Matters of Fact, Touching the Supposed Witchcraft in New England."

Robert Calef lays the blame for the witch-hunt squarely on the making over to Parris of the ministry house.

Mr. Parris had been some years a minister in Salem Village, when this sad calamity (as a deluge) overflowed them, spreading itself far and near: He was a gentleman of liberal education, and not meeting with any great encouragement, or advantage in merchandizing, to which for some time he applied himself, betook himself to the work of the ministry; this village being then vacant, he met with so much encouragement, as to settle in that capacity among them.

After he had been there about two years, he obtained a grant from a part of the town, that the house and land he occupied, and which had been alotted by the whole people to the ministry, should be and remain to him, etc. as his own estate in fee simple. This occasioned great divisions both between the inhabitants themselves, and between a considerable part of them and their said minister, which divisions were but as a beginning or præludium to what immediately followed.

It was the latter end of February 1692, when divers young persons belonging to Mr. Parris's family, and one or more of the neighbourhood, began to act, after a strange and unusual manner, *viz.* as by getting into holes, and creeping under chairs and stools, and to use sundry odd postures and antic gestures, uttering foolish, ridiculous speeches, which neither they themselves nor any others could make sense of; the physicians that were called could assign no reason for this; but it seems one of them, having recourse to the old shift, told them he was afraid they were bewitched; upon such suggestions, they that were concerned applied themselves to fasting and prayer, which was attended not only in their own private families, but with calling in the help of others.

From: Salem Village Book of Record

Record of Salem Village meeting, October 16, 1691

By October 1691, the balance of power had swung in favor of the anti-Parris faction.

At a general meeting of the inhabitants of Salem Village the 16th of October, 1691, there was chosen for a Committee for the year ensuing:

Francis Nurse, Joseph Porter, Joseph Hutchinson, Daniel Andrew, and Joseph Putnam.

The 16th of this instant October, 1691, the inhabitants being met together according to the warrant; it being then voted whether there should be instructions given to the Committee then chosen in order to making a rate for payment of Parris' salary: it was voted on the negative.

The inhabitants of this Village are desired to meet at their ordinary places of meeting on the 1st day of December, 1691, at 10 of the clock in the morning to consider by what means the inhabitants were convened together on the 18th of June, 1689 (then there was a Committee chosen and a yearly salary stated to Mr.

Parris that day, but no warrant appearing in the book for it), and to consider of a vote in the book on the 10th of October, 1689, where in our right in the ministry house and land seems to be impaired and made void; also to consider about our ministry house and 2 acres of land given to Mr. Parris, and a committee chosen to make conveyances to Mr. Parris in the name of the inhabitants; and to consider about Mr. Parris's maintenance for this year—whether by voluntary contributions or by subscription.

JOSEPH PORTER, DANIEL ANDREW, FRANCIS NURSE,
JOSEPH HUTCHINSON, JOSEPH PUTNAM

November 1689 to October 1696, as kept by the Reverend Samuel Parris

Samuel Parris takes up the story in his own words. Sometimes he refers to himself in the first person, sometimes the third.

2 Nov. 1691

After sunset, about seventeen of the brethren met; to whom, after prayer, I spoke to this effect: Brethren, I have not much to trouble you with now; but you know what committee, the last town-meeting here, were chosen; and what they have done, or intend to do; it may be, better than I. But, you see, I have hardly any wood to burn. I need say no more, but leave the matter to your serious and godly consideration.

In fine, after some discourse to and fro, the church voted that Captain Putnam and the two deacons should go, as messengers from the church, to the committee, to desire them to make a rate for the minister, and to take care of necessary supplies for him; and that said messengers should make their return to the church the next tenth day, an hour before sunset, at the minister's house, where they would expect it.*

10 Nov. 1691

The messengers abovesaid came with their return, as appointed; which was, that the committee did not see good to take notice of their message, without they had some letter to show under the church's and pastor's hand. But, at this last church-

*[*Marginal note in Mr. Parris's hand:* "The town-meeting about or at 16 October last (elected):
Joseph Porter
Joseph Hutchinson
Joseph Putnam
Daniel Andrew
Francis Nurse"]

meeting, besides the three messengers, but three other brethren did appear,—namely, brother Thomas Putnam, Thomas Wilkins, and Peter Prescot,—which slight and neglect of other brethren did not a little trouble me, as I expressed myself. But I told these brethren I expected the church should be more mindful of me than other people, and their way was plain before them, &c.

Sab:, 15 Nov. 1691

The church were desired to meet at brother Nathaniel Putnam's, the next 18th instant, at twelve o'clock, to spend some time in prayer, and seeking God's presence with us, the next Lord's Day, at his table, as has been usual with us, some time before the sacrament.

18 Nov. 1691

After some time spent, as above said, at this church-meeting, the pastor desired the brethren to stay, for as much as he had somewhat to offer to them, which was to this purpose; *viz.:* Brethren, several church-meetings have been occasionally warned, and sometimes the appearance of the brethren is but small to what it might be expected, and particularly the case mentioned 10th instant. I told them I did not desire to warn meetings unnecessarily, and, therefore, when I did, I prayed them they would regularly attend them.

Furthermore, I told them I had scarce wood enough to burn till tomorrow, and prayed that some care might be taken. In fine, after discourses passed, these following votes were made unanimously, namely:—

1. That it was needful that complaint should be made to the next honoured County Court, to sit at Salem, the next third day of the week, against the neglects of the present committee.
2. That the said complaint should be drawn up, which was immediately done by one of the brethren, and consented to.
3. That our brethren, Nathaniel Putnam, Thomas Putnam, and Thomas Wilkins, should sign said complaint in behalf of the church.
4. Last, That our brethren, Captain John Putnam and the two deacons, should be improved to present the said complaint to the said Court.

In the meantime, the pastor desired the brethren that care might be taken that he might not be destitute of wood.

After this last entry, there was nothing more about the complaint to the court, or even about firewood. The next entry is on March 27, 1692. It is

Samuel Parris's account of the witchcraft outbreak. At this point Tituba, Sarah Good, Sarah Osborne, Rebecca Nurse, and Martha Corey were in prison. Parris strenuously lays as much blame as possible for the outbreak on an unfortunate church member called Mary Sibley, who asked John Indian to bake a "witch cake." But that same day, on which Parris lamented that "the devil hath been raised amongst us," he preached a sermon driving on the witch-hunt. It hammered home the opinions that church members may be witches and that the devil cannot masquerade as an innocent person. The intention was to allay doubts that there might have been a mistake in the arrest of Rebecca Nurse and Martha Corey. While Parris was speaking, Rebecca Nurse's sister, Sarah Cloyse, walked out of the meetinghouse, slamming the door.

27 March, Sab. 1692, Sacrament day

After the common auditory was dismissed, and before the church communion at the Lord's Table, the following testimony against the error of our sister, Mary Sibley, who had given direction to my Indian man in an unwarrantable way to find out witches, was read by the pastor.

It is altogether undeniable, that our great and blessed God, for wise and holy ends, hath suffered many persons in several families of this little village, to be grievously vexed, and tortured in body, and to be deeply tempted, to the endangering of the destruction of their souls; and all these amazing feats (well known to many of us) to be done by witchcraft and diabolical operations.

It is also well known, that when these calamities first began, which was in my own family, the affliction was several weeks before such hellish operations, as witchcraft, was suspected. Nay, it never brake forth to any considerable light, until diabolical means were used, by the making of a cake by my Indian man, who had his direction from this our sister, Mary Sibley; since which apparitions have been plenty, and exceeding much mischief hath followed. But by this means (it seems) the devil hath been raised amongst us, and his rage is vehement and terrible, and when he shall be silenced, the Lord only knows.

But now that this our sister should be instrumental to such distress, is a great grief to myself, and our godly, honored, and reverend neighbours, who have had the knowledge of it. Nevertheless, I do truly hope, and believe, that this our sister doth truly fear the Lord, and am well satisfied from her, that what she did, she did it ignorantly, from what she had heard of this nature

> from other ignorant, or worse, persons. Yet we are in duty bound to protest against such actions, as being indeed a going to the devil for help against the devil; we having no such directions from nature, or God's word, it must, therefore be, and is, accounted by godly Protestants, who write or speak of such matters, as diabolical, and therefore, call this our sister to deep humiliation for what she has done; and all of us to be watchful against Satan's wiles and devices.
>
> Therefore, as we in duty, as a church of Christ, are deeply bound to protest against it, as most directly contrary to the gospel, yet inasmuch, as this our sister did it in ignorance, as she professeth, and we believe, we can continue in our holy fellowship, upon her serious promise of future better advisedness and caution, and acknowledging, that she is indeed sorrowful for her rashness herein.

Brethren, if this be your mind, that this iniquity be thus borne witness against, manifest it by your usual sign of lifting up your hands.

The brethren voted generally, or universally: None made any exceptions.

Sister Sibley, if you are convinced that you herein did sinfully, and are sorry for it; let us hear it from your own mouth. She did manifest to satisfaction her error and grief for it.

Brethren, if herein you have received satisfaction, testify it by lifting up of your hands.

A general vote passed: No exception made.

Note. 25 March, 1692. I discoursed said sister in my study about the grand error above said, and also, then read to her what I had written as above to read to the church, and said sister Sibley assented to the same with tears and sorrowful confession.

From: Samuel Parris's Sermon Notebook

27 March 1692, *Sacrament Day*

Occasioned by dreadful witchcraft broke out here a few weeks past, & one member of this church, & another of Salem, upon public examination by civil authority, vehemently suspected for she-witches, & upon it committed.

6. John. 70

Have not I chosen you twelve, & one of you is a devil.

This chapter consists of *3* principal parts.

Part 1 consists of a declaration of Christ's miraculous feeding of 5000 with 5 Loaves & 2 small fishes. *1–15. v.*

Part 2 treats of Christ's miraculous walking upon the Sea. *15–22. v.*

Last part consists of Christ's sermon to the Capernaites *22. v.* ad finem concerning the heavenly or truly vivifical bread. This part consists of sundry particles. viz.

1. The occasion of this sermon. *22. 23. 24. 25. v.*

2. The Sermon itself. *26–59. v.*

3. Last: The event of this Sermon. *59.* ad finem. Now this event consists of

1. The offence of many *59. v. &c.*

2. A reprehension of their error from whence this their offence arose: in which reprehension he shows them that it was not the eating of his flesh carnally but spiritually that he spake of. *61 &c.*

3. Christ's complaint of the incredulity of many *64. 65. v.*

4. Another event which was worse than the former, namely the total departure of several of his disciples from him. *66. v.* Whereupon Note

1. Our Lord takes occasion to ask his disciples whether they also would desert him. *67. v.*

2. Peter in the name of the rest answers by confessing the excellency both of Christ's doctrine & his person. *68. 69. v.*

3. Last: This confession Christ so approves of, that in the meanwhile he doth admonish them, that there is an hypocrite among them, a devil among them *70. 71. verses.* Have not I chosen you 12 & one of you is a devil. i.e. I have chosen 12 of you to familiarity with me, to be my apostles, & for all one of you is a devil.

Doctrine: Our Lord Jesus Christ knows how many devils there are in his church, & who they are.

1. There are devils as well as saints in Christ's church.

2. Christ knows how many of these devils there are.

3. Last: Christ Knows who these devils are.

1. Proposition: There are devils as well as saints in the church of Christ: Here 3 things may be spoken to.

1. Show you what is meant here by devils.

2. That there are such devils in the church.

3. Last: That there are also true saints in such churches.

1. What is meant here by devils. One of you is a devil.

Answer. By devil is ordinarily meant any wicked angel or spirit: Sometimes it is put for the prince or head of the evil spirits, or fallen angels. Sometimes it is used for vile & wicked persons, the worst of such, who for their villainy & impiety do most resemble devils & wicked spirits. Thus Christ in our text calls Judas a devil, for his great likeness to the devil. One of you is a devil i.e. a devil for quality & disposition: not a devil for nature, for he was a man &c but a devil for likeness & operation. *8. Joh. 38. 41 44.* Ye are of your Father the Devil

2. There are such devils in the church: Not only sinners but notorious sinners; sinners more like to the devil than others. So here in Christ's little church. Text.

This also Christ teacheth us in the parable of the tares. *13. Matth. 38.* Where Christ tells us that such are the children of the wicked one. i.e. of the Devil.

Reason: Because hypocrites are the very worst of men. Corruptio optimi est pessima. Hypocrites are the sons & heirs of the devil, the free-holders of hell, whereas other sinners are but tenants. When Satan repossesseth a Soul he becomes more vile & sinful. *11. Luke. 24. 25. 26.* As the goaler lays load of iron on him that hath escaped. None are worse than those that have been good, & are naught: & might be good, but will be naught.

3. Last: There are also true saints in the church. The church consists of good; & bad: as a garden that has weeds as well as flowers: & as a field that has wheat as well as tares. Hence the gospel is compared to a net that taketh good & bad. *13. Matt. 47. 48. 49. 50.* Here are good men to be found, yea the very best; & here are bad men to be found, yea the very worst: Such as shall have the highest seat in glory; & such also as shall be cast into the lowest & fiercest flames of misery. Saints & devils. Like Jeremiah's basket of figs. *24. Jer. 1–4.*

2. Proposition: Christ knows how many of these devils there are in his churches. As in our text there was one among the twelve. And so in our churches God knows how many devils there are: whither 1, 2, 3 or. 4 in 12. How many devils, how many saints. He that knows whom he has chosen. *13. John. 18.* he also knows who they are that have not chosen him, but prefer farms & merchandize above him, & above his ordinances. *2. Tim. 4. 10*

3. Proposition: Last: Christ knows who these devils are. There is one among you, says Christ to the twelve: Well who is that? Why, it is Judas. Why, so Christ knows how many devils among us: whether one or ten, or 20, & also who they are: He knows us perfectly; & he knows those of us that are in the church, that we are either saints or devils; true believers, or hypocrites & dissembling Judases that would sell Christ & his kingdom to gratify a lust. We do not think we are such. *2 Reg. 8. 12. 13.*

1. Use. Let none then build their hopes of salvation merely upon this, that they are church-members. This you & I may be, & yet devils for all that. *8. Matth. 11. 12.* Many shall come from the east and west, & shall sit down &c. And however we may pass here a true difference shall be made shortly &c.

2. Use. Let none then be stumbled at religion because too often there are devils found among the saints. You see here was a true church, sincere converts, & sound believers, & yet here was a devil among them.

3. Use. Terror to hypocrites, who profess much love to Christ, but indeed are in league with their lusts, which they prefer above Christ. Oh remember that you are devils in Christ's account. Christ is lightly esteemed of you, & you are vilely accounted of by Christ. Oh if there be any such among us, forbear to come this day to the Lord's table, lest Satan enter more powerfully into you. Lest, whilst the

bread be between your teeth, the wrath of the Lord come pouring down upon you. *78. Ps. 30. 31.*

4. Use. Exhort in two branches.

1. To be deeply humbled for the appearances of devils among our churches. If the Church of Corinth were called to mourn because of one incestuous person among them. *1 Cor. 5 initio,* how much more may New England churches mourn that such as work witchcraft, or are vehemently suspected so to do should be found among them.

2. To be much in prayer that God would deliver our churches from devils. That God would not suffer devils in the guise of saints to associate with us. One sinner destroys much good; how much more one devil. Pray we also that not one true saint may suffer as a devil, either in name, or body. The devil would represent the best saints as devils if he could, but it is not easy to imagine that his power is of such extent, to the hazard of the church.

5. Use. Last: Examine we our selves well, what we are: what we church-members are: We are either saints, or devils, the scripture gives us no medium. The apostle tells us we are to examine ourselves. *2 Cor. 13. 5.* Oh it is a dreadful thing to be a devil, & yet to sit down at the Lord's table. *1 Cor. 10. 21.* Such incur the hottest of God's wrath, as follows. *22. v.* Now if we would not be devils we must give ourselves wholly up to Christ: & not suffer the predominancy of one lust, & particularly that lust of covetousness, which is made so light of, & which so sadly prevails in these perilous times: why this one lust made Judas a devil. *12. Joh. 6. 26. Matth. 15.* And no doubt it has made more devils than one. For a little pelf, men sell Christ to his enemies, & their souls to the devil. But there are certain sins that make us devils, see that we be not such

1. A liar or plunderer. *8. Joh. 44.*
2. A slanderer or an accuser of the godly
3. A tempter to sin
4. An opposer of godliness, as Elymas. *13. Acts. 8 & c.*
5. Envious persons as witches
6. A drunkard *1. Sam. 1. 15. 16.*
7. Last. A proud person. Finis Textûs.

None ought, nor is it possible that any should, maintain communion with Christ, & yet keep up fellowship with devils.

From: Salem Village Church Book of Record

Parris's next entry in the church record book is not until August 14. This is hardly surprising, given how busy he was with recording examinations of suspected witches, visiting people committed to prison to urge them to confess, and testifying at trials. By the time of this next entry, the first hangings had occurred. Parris's question as to why Samuel Nurse and his wife, John Tarbell and his wife, and Peter Cloyes, have been absenting themselves from his church services, almost beggars belief. They were, respectively, Rebecca Nurse's son and daughter-in-law, son-in-law and daughter, and brother-in-law. Rebecca had been hanged in July. It also seems extraordinary, at first sight, that the Nurse family avoided answering Parris's question for months. But presumably they were afraid. They finally spoke their minds when the witch-hunt came to an end.

The entry of September 11 describes the excommunication of Martha Corey. On that same day, Parris preached another of his incendiary sermons.

Sabbath-day, 14 Aug. 1692

The church was stayed after the congregation was dismissed, and the pastor spoke to the church after this manner:

Brethren, you may all have taken notice that several sacrament days past, our brother Peter Cloyes, and Samuel Nurse and his wife, and John Tarbell and his wife have absented from Communion with us at the Lord's table, yea have very rarely (except our brother Samuel Nurse) have been with us in common public worship. Now it is needful that the church send some persons to them to know the reason of their absence. Therefore if you be so minded, express yourselves.

None objected: but a general or universal vote after some discourse passed that brother Nathaniel Putman and the two deacons should join with the pastor to discourse with the said absenters about it.

31st August [1692]

Brother Tarbell proves sick, unmeet for discourse. Brother Cloyes hard to be found at home, being often with his wife in prison at Ipswich for witchcraft, and brother Nurse and sometimes his wife attends our public meeting, and he the sacrament.

11 Sept. 1692

Upon all which, we choose to wait further.

11 September, Lord's day

Sister Martha Corey, taken into the church 27th April 1690, was after examination upon suspicion of witchcraft, 21 March, 1692, committed to prison for that fact, and was condemned to the gallows for the same yesterday: and was this day in public by a general consent voted to be excommunicated out of the church; and Lieutenant Nathaniel Putman, and the two deacons chosen to signify to her with the pastor the mind of the church herein. Accordingly this 14 September 1692 the aforesaid brethren went with the pastor to her in Salem prison, whom we found very obdurate, justifying herself and condemning all that had done anything to her just discovery or condemnation. Whereupon after a little discourse (for her imperiousness would not suffer much) and after prayer (which she was willing to decline) the dreadful sentence of excommunication was pronounced against her.

From: Samuel Parris's Sermon Notebook

11. Sept. *1692.* After the condemnation of 6 witches at a court at Salem, one of the witches viz. Martha Corey in full communion with our church.

17. Rev. 14.

These shall make war with the Lamb, & the Lamb shall overcome them: For he is the Lord of Lords, & King of Kings; And they that are with him, are called, & chosen, & faithful.

In these words 2 things are observable.

1. A war prophesied of.

2. The victory that this war shall issue in.

1. Here is mention made of a war. These shall make war &c

Now in all wars are two parties. And so here

1. Here is the offending party. Namely these, viz: Anti-christ (the spiritual whore) & all her assistants, instruments of Satan, & instigated by that dragon to this war. *13. Rev. 1.2.* Namely by sorceries & witchcrafts (plentiful among the Papacy) doing lying wonders whereby multitudes were deluded

2. Here is the offended party viz. the Lamb & his followers. Text. With these they make war.

2. Here is the victory, & the reason of the victory.

1. The victory. Devils, & idolaters will make war with the Lamb, & his followers. But who shall have the victory? Why the Lamb (i.e. Christ) & his followers. Text

2. Here is the reason of it, & that is twofold

1. And main reason is taken from the Lamb (Christ) for he is Lord, of Lords &c

2. Reason is taken from the saints 3 victorial properties

1. They are chosen

2. They are called.

3. Last: They are faithful: of all which hereafter.

1. Doctrine. The devil & his instruments will be making war with the Lamb & his followers as long as they can.

2. Doctrine. The Lamb & his followers shall overcome the devil & his instruments in this war against them.

1. Doctrine. The devil, & his instruments, will be making war, as long as they can, with the Lamb & his followers. Here are 2 things in this doctrine. Namely.

1. The devil & his instruments will be warring against Christ & his followers.

2. This war will be as long as they can. It will not be for ever. There will be a time when they shall war no longer.

1. The devil & his instruments will be warring against Christ & his followers. Text. These shall make war with the Lamb. *11. Chap. 2.* The beast shall make war against them. *12. Ch. 7. 17.* War in heaven: The dragon fought and his angels. *13. Chap. 7.* It was given to him to make war with the saints. &c. *19. Ch. 19.*

We may farther confirm this point by instances & reasons

1. For instances. We find the devil assaulting the Lamb as soon as he was born to the end of his days. As we see in his instrument Herod. *2. Matth. 7 &c.* And afterwards by his manifold temptations of Christ in the wilderness *4. Matt.* And afterwards by his stirring up the chief of the Jews to kill Christ. *26. Matth. 3. 4.* And to help forward that murder the devil puts it into the heart of one of Christ's disciples to betray him. *13. Joh. 2.* And after all though the Lamb be killed, but yet liveth for ever, & no advantage got by the devil by the murder of Christ, why now he seeks to destroy his church: And for this end influenceth bloody Saul to lay all waste. *8. Acts. 3. 9. Ch. 1. 2.* But now when the Lamb had conquered this bloody instrument, & of a Saul, made him Paul, a preacher of righteousness, why now the devil as much opposeth Paul. *13. Acts. 4.* &c. Yea the scripture is full of such instances. Church history abounds also with evidences of this truth. Yea & in our days, how industrious & vigorous is the bloody French monarch, & his confederates against Christ & his interest? Yea, & in our Land (in this, & some neighbouring places) how many, what multitudes, of witches & wizards has the devil instigated with utmost violence to attempt the overthrow of religion?

2. The reason, & that in a word is from the enmity of the devil & his instruments to religion. *13. Acts. 10.* Thou child of the devil, thou enemy of all righteousness. Now the seed of the devil will do the works of the devil. *8. Joh. 44.* Ye are of your father the devil, & the lusts of your father ye will do &c. Satan (says one Trapp in loco) is called the God of this world, because as God at first did but

speak the word & it was done: So if the Devil do but hold up his finger, give the least hint of his mind, his servants & slaves will obey.

3. This war shall be as long as they can. It shall not be for ever, & always. Here

1. Sometimes the devil looseth his volunteers in war. The lawful captive, the captives of the mighty, are sometimes delivered. *49. Isa. 24. 25.* We have an instance in bloody Saul. *9. Acts. 3. &c.*

2. Sometimes the devil is chained up; so that he cannot head & form an army, as otherwise he would against the saints. *20. Rev. 1.2.3.*

3. Last: After this life the saints shall no more be troubled with war from devils & their instruments. The city of Heaven, provided for the saints, is well-walled, & well-gated, & well-guarded, so that no devils nor their instruments shall enter therein. *21. Rev. 10. &c.*

1. Use. It may serve to reprove such as seem to be amazed at the war the devil has raised amongst us by wizards, & witches against the Lamb & his followers that they altogether deny it. If ever there were witches, men & women in covenant with the devil, here are multitudes in New England. Nor is it so strange a thing there should be such: no nor that some church members should be such. The Jews after the return of their captivity, woefully degenerated even unto the horrible sin of sorcery & witchcraft. *3. Mal. 5.* Pious Bishop Hall saith, The devil's prevalency in this age is most clear in the marvellous number of witches abounding in all places. Now hundereds (says he) are discovered in one shire; & if fame deceive us not, in a village of 14 houses in the north, are found so many of this damned brood. Heretofore only barbarous deserts had them, but now the civilest & religious parts are frequently pestered with them: Heretofore some silly ignorant old women, &c. & but now we have known those of both sexes, who professed much knowledge, holiness, & devotion, drawn into this damnable practice. Baxter's *Apparitions & Witches,* pag. 122.

Also the same M. Baxter speaks of a woman who pretended to have the holy Ghost, & had a gift of prayer, & did many wonders, proved to be a witch. p. *123.*

2. Use. We may see here who they are that war against the Lamb, & his followers. Why they are devils, or devils' instruments. Here are but 2 parties in the world, the Lamb & his followers, & the dragon & his followers: & these are contrary one to the other. Well now they that are against the Lamb, against the peace & prosperity of Zion, the interest of Christ: They are for the devil. Here are no newters. Every one is on one side or the other.

3. Use. It calls us all (especially those that would be accounted followers of the Lamb) to mourn that the devil has had so many assistants from amongst us, especially that he should find, or make such in our churches. If so be churches are deeply to mourn the dishonour done to Christ & religion, by fornicators among them. *1. Cor. 5. 1. &c.* how much more, when witches & wizards are amongst them.

4. Use. It may show us the vileness of our natures, & that we should be ever praying that we be not left to our own lusts: for then we shall by & by fall in with devils, & with the dragon make war with the Lamb & his followers.

From: Salem Village Church Book of Record

Parris again takes up the story of the plea to the court regarding a rate, or tax, for his salary. Soon after this, the strange tale continues, of the "dissenting," "dissatisfied," or "displeased" brethren, as Parris variously calls them. (Anyone would be displeased, one would think, by their innocent mother's being hanged.) The record is in effect Parris's diary, recounting each skirmish in the running battles dominating his life. It reveals with great clarity his astonishing lack of comprehension of other people's feelings. The first entry, for 26 Dec., reproduces a petition on Paris's behalf from his supporters.

At a church-meeting at Salem Village 26 Dec. 1692 warned the Lord's day before, the following humble petition was unanimously voted, *viz.:*

Petition of Salem Village Church to the Court of Common Pleas

To the Honored Court of Common Pleas to be held at Salem, 27 Dec. 1692

The humble petition of the church abovesaid humbly showeth, that whereas among the other laws passed by the Great and General Court of their Majesties' Province of the Massachusetts Bay in New England, some of them bear particular respects to the maintenance of religion; and whereas our village, as to some of its inhabitants in special, hath indispensible need of support by such wholesome acts, several among us for several years having made no payment to our Reverend Pastor, and other some as little as they pleased; and some have been chosen to the service of making rates, who have refused (though urged by this church) to make any, insomuch that the first of January next, one year and half is passed, and no rate made.

Besides the former rates in great part uncollected: Nay, no reparation of the very meeting-house has for a great while been regarded, so that by reason of broken windows, stopped-up, some of them, by boards or otherwise, and others wide open, it is sometimes so cold that it makes it uncomfortable, and sometimes so dark that it is almost unuseful. Besides the neglect of our Ministry-land fences, and the great and long disquietments of a few, who in this hour of sore tribulation and temptation have drawn away others who heretofore could not by any means join with them; by reason whereof we have no meetings to relieve our minister; or, if any, several well-affected persons absent themselves because they cannot bear the jars amongst us, by which means others to our great disquietment and injury obtain casting vote; besides many other things too tedious to trouble your Honors with at present.

All which considered, we pray your command of Mr. Joseph Porter, Joseph Hutchinson Senior, Joseph Putnam, Daniel Andrews, and Francis Nurse to appear personally before your Honors (or rather with submission before a committee appointed and fully empowered to settle all differences by your Honors, which we conceive most suitable to this tedious affair) and to give in their reason, if they have any, why the last year which expired the 1st July, last, was suffered to elapse, and their committee-ship to die totally without making any just rate, in such manifest contempt of that Law entitled *An Act for Collecting the Arrears of Town and County Rates* passed at the session 8 June.

The grant of this our necessitous petition, as it will be exceeding joyful to our small church, and many other [of] our religious neighbors, so particularly to your Honors' deputed and humble petitioners,

NATHANIEL PUTNAM
JOHN PUTNAM
JONATHAN WALCOTT

The aforesaid petition was voted the day aforesaid by the church abovesaid to be presented as abovesaid by Lieutenant Nathaniel Putnam, Captain John Putnam, and Captain Jonathan Walcott.

WITNESS US,
NATHANIEL INGERSOL
EDWARD PUTNAM
DEACONS

Note: The petition abovesaid was granted and the honored Court of Quarter Sessions adjourned to this Village to sit 17 Jan. next ensuing to hear and determine the matter.

12 Jan: 1693

At a church-meeting regularly warned the last Sabbath was chosen by a unanimous vote of the present brethren: Lieutenant Nathaniel Putnam, Captain John Putnam, the two deacons, Captain Jonathan Walcott, and Ensign Thomas Flint as principal agents in behalf of the church to negotiate in the affairs respecting the abovesaid petition, before the honoured Court, adjourned as aforesaid.

15 Jan. Sab: 1693

After the sacrament it was fully if not unanimously voted that hereafter, our sacraments shall be the first Lord's Day in each month, partly for better remembrance of such as may not always be warned of it, and partly and more especially for the more easy of getting of bread which then at Salem is provided on purpose for sundry other churches, and we are to begin the 1st March next, if God please.

Action of the court on the petition of the Salem Village Church

At a general sessions of the peace holden at Salem for the County of Essex, by adjournment, 17 Jan. 1693.

> Essex Ss. In answer to the petition of the church at Salem Village relating to the ministry: This court having fully examined the case and heard the pleas and allegations of the parties concerned, do find that the committee for the year 1691 hath wholly neglected their duty, in not raising their minister's maintenance for that year, which was settled upon him by the inhabitants of said village; and the committee for this present year 1692 have also neglected their duty relating thereunto; and also to this court utterly refused to attend their duty in that respect, and several of the principal inhabitants having prayed this court to appoint a meeting requiring the inhabitants to make a choice of a committee that will attend that service, alleging that otherwise they cannot lawfully be convened together.
>
> This court do order that Constable John Putnam of Salem, do warn and give notice unto the inhabitants of said village that they convene together at the usual place of meeting on Wednesday next, being the 25th of this instant January, at ten of the clock in the morning, to make choice of a committee according to the power given them by the General Court at their first settlement.

25 Jan. [1693]

At a meeting of the inhabitants by the order of the Court abovesaid, Joseph Pope, Joseph Holten, Jr., John Tarbell, Thomas Preston, and James Smith, were chosen committee-men.

Sabbath, 5 February 1693

In the evening the church was stayed, and upon discourse the pastor and the two deacons and brother Nathaniel Putman, and brother John Putman Jnr., and brother Bray Wilkins, were chosen by a general vote of the brotherhood to discourse with brother Samuel Nurse, and brother John Tarbell about their withdrawing of late from the Lord's table and public worship of God among us.

7 Feb. 1693

The abovesaid brethren, chosen for debate with the abovementioned brethren, met about one o'clock at the pastor's house; and after prayer the pastor applied himself to the said three dissenting brethren, telling them that we were appointed by the church to inquire into the grounds of their declining religious communion with us of late. After some pause they each one, one after another, desired further time to consider of our demands. The pastor replied, You know, brethren, of your dissent and doubtless you cannot be to seek of the reasons of it. But after some words more, some of us looking upon such pleas needless, others being willing to concede to them, it was concluded, that they should meet us again the 16 instant and then give in their reasons; and also if they saw good to bring their dissenting wives with them, or to leave them to another season, as they pleased: with this proviso, that they may acquaint the pastor timely of it, that he may acquaint the church therewith, that so we may be commissioned to treat with them also, for as yet we were only sent to the brethren, and not to the sisters.

Ten days later the "displeased brethren" cautiously went on the attack. They claimed they had grievances of their own but had been gathering advice from "neighbouring elders" as to how to proceed. But, on February 7, Parris belatedly reveals, Jonathan Tarbell had told him privately that he considered him guilty of idolatry and lying in court. By "idolatry" Tarbell meant making idols of the afflicted girls by asking them for information on supernatural matters. He suggested Parris must have been lying because he could not possibly have known, as he swore he did, that the reason the afflicted girls were "knocked down" was because the accused looked at them or the reason they came out of their fits was because the accused touched them. (The curing of fits by a witch's touch, called the "touch test," was used extensively in the witch trials.) Tarbell also said that, were it not for Parris, his mother Rebecca Nurse would still be alive. He accused the minister of being "the great prosecutor."

Samuel Nurse said the same things as John Tarbell. So, the next day, did Peter Cloyes. And thus the wrangling continued, with the "displeased brethren" trying to find some way out of the mire and Parris obstructing them at every turn, even accusing them of libel.

16 Feb. 1693

According to the aforesaid concession we, the abovesaid, met again at the pastor's house to receive answer from the dissenting brethren abovesaid as to the reasons of their dissent; when they gave in a paper containing the matter following, *viz.:*

Whereas we, Thomas Wilkins, and John Tarbell, and Samuel Nurse, having a long time gone under the burden of great grievances by reason of some unwarrantable actings of Mr. Parris, as we esteem them, and were proceeding in an orderly way to obtain satisfaction from him, and had taken some steps thereunto, according to the advice of some neighbouring elders. But obstructive to our proceeding therein, Mr. Parris and some brethren of the church are appointed by the church to demand a reason of us of our withdrawing from communion. The regularity of which, the proceeding, we do not understand, because in this case we esteem ourselves to be the plaintiffs, and parties offended, and in an orderly way seeking satisfaction, though hitherto denied.

"Our answer to the church is that we esteem ourselves hereby prevented in our duty, which we account a grievance, seeing we were first in prosecution of the rule of our Lord Jesus Christ laid down in Matthew 18, 15–16. Wherefore, if the church please to give us the liberty and freedom of attending our duty, as according to rule bound, possibly then further trouble may be prevented; or otherwise the case will unnecessarily and regularly come before them. But if they deny us this request, we shall as in duty bound give the reasons of our proceeding to the church, or any others, when orderly demanded.

The paper abovesaid was read to us by Samuel Nurse, but they were altogether unwilling to leave it with us; but at length they were prevailed with to let us take a copy of it. I gave it to Deacon Putman who desired a copy of it, and from his copy I wrote as abovesaid. These displeased brethren were told that they did ill to reflect upon the church, who, as also the pastor, was ignorant of their methods; and also that they should first have spoken with the pastor himself before they went to consult with neighbouring elders. But to this last, they pleaded ignorance. So we gave way to their request of proceeding orderly.

The 7 Feb. last before the brethren appointed by the church came, the abovesaid three brethren, Tarbell, Samuel Nurse, and Thomas Wilkins came to my house desiring speech with me; so I took them singly into my study except Thomas Wilkins, for the other two each of them, taken up so much time, *viz.* one an hour at least, and the other more, that before time could be allowed for the other, the appointed brethren came.

Jonathan Tarbell said he thought I was guilty of idolatry, in asking the afflicted persons who they saw upon other afflicted persons. He thought it was agoing to the God of Ekron. Nor did he understand how my oath was safe in court that such and such, by such and such, were knocked down by their looks, and raised up by their touches. And had it not been for me his mother Nurse might have been still living, and so freed from execution; that I had been the great prosecutor, and that others wise and learned who had been as forward as myself were sorry for what they had done, and saw their error, and till I did so too, he could not join. His brother Samuel Nurse, for about an hour's time has the same objections.

I answered them that I did not see yet sufficient grounds to vary my opinion, which was confirmed by known and ancient experience frequent in such cases &c. But however in matters of debate, they must give me my opinion, as I would not now quarrel them for theirs &c.

The 8 Feb: brother Peter Cloyes came from Boston to me with the very same objections, whom I answered after the like manner.

Some short time after this the abovesaid four displeased brethren came again desiring to speak with me, and Brother William Way along with them.

I told them I would go up to my study, asking which would go first: so brother Cloyes came up first, bringing brother Way and Thomas Wilkins with him, as witness to his demand of satisfaction to what he lately objected. I told him there was but one brother, there should be two, Thomas Wilkins was in this case Peter Cloyes, and Peter Cloyes, Thomas Wilkins; and so I told the rest, when I saw what they aimed at, and advised them to take (according to rule) some other brother or brethren besides brother Way, or else I could not hear them, in the way they aimed at. But they would urge that this was enough, and one was sufficient; I answered that Christ's rule was for two or three: so they departed.

27 March 1693

At night brother Cloyes, and brother Tarbell abovesaid came to my house together with Mr. Joseph Hutchinson, Snr., and Mr. Joseph Putman and a little after William Osburne of Salem (which three last, it seems, came for witnesses, as brother Cloyes owned the 20 April following) and they gave me a paper not subscribed by any person, but a cut in the place of subscription, where two or three names might be written. The contents of which paper was as followeth, *viz.:*

> To our pastor and minister, Mr. Samuel Parris of Salem Village, and to some others of the plantation.
>
> We whose names are underwritten, being deeply sensible that those uncomfortable differences that are amongst us, are very dishonourable to God and a scandal to religion, and very uncomfortable to ourselves, and an ill example to those that may come after us. And by our maintaining and upholding differences amongst us, we do but gratify the devil, that grand adversary of our souls. For the removal of which we have thought meet to proffer our present thoughts to your serious consideration, hoping that

there may be such methods propounded as may be for the settling and confirming peace and unity amongst us both at the present and for the future. And our desires are that such a foundation may be laid for peace and truth that the gates of hell may not prevail against it. And in order thereunto Solomon adviseth to counsel. And our desires are that a council of elders may be mutually chosen to hear all our grievances between Mr. Parris and us, and to determine where the blameable cause is. And we hope that their wisdom and prudence may direct us to such a method, as may be for our comfort, for both present and future."

When I had read it, I asked them who this paper came from. They answered, all the plantation, or a great many of them at least. I demanded why, then, did none subscribe it: They said, all in good time. So I put it in my pocket. They demanded an answer to it: I told them I would consider of it.

28 March 1693

The abovesaid brethren, together with said Hutchinson, came again at night for an answer to the abovesaid paper: I told them I had not considered of it yet.

14 April 1693

Our displeased brethren, Jonathan Tarbell, Samuel Nurse, and Thomas Wilkins came again, bringing with them said Hutchinson and Francis Nurse. After a little while I went down from my study to them: asking them if they would speak with me. They said yes, they came to discourse about the paper (abovesaid) they had brought to me. I told them I had no time to talk. I was this day to preach to a private meeting. Nor was I willing to discourse with them alone: but appoint time and place I would meet with them. So we agreed after our next lecture to meet at brother Nathaniel Putman's.

20 April 1693

After lecture, myself, Captain Putnam, Ensign Flint, and the two deacons, met the four displeased brethren abovesaid at Lieutenant Nathaniel Putnam's abovesaid, where we found together with them, and for them, said Mr. Hutchinson and Mr. Israel Porter. After a little while, I told them, to gratify them, I was come to hear what they had to offer. They demanded an answer to the paper abovesaid. Whereupon I plucked it out of my pocket, and read it openly. They owned that to be the paper. I asked them what they called it: they being to seek of a name for it. I told them I looked upon it as a libel. Then they produced a like paper subscribed by said brethren, and divers more to the number of forty and two names, but all seemed to be one and the same hand. I desired the original paper. They said they knew not where it was. Then it was asked whether those men wrote their own names. It was answered, yes, or they were written by their order. Then I desired them to subscribe this paper with the hands to it, testifying that no name was there, but such as had consulted thereto. But none would yield to this. Then I told them we must know what we do: had I to do with displeased people, or displeased brethren? They answered, they came as brethren. Then I told them, none but brethren should have been present. They said they had been with me already; and I refused to give them satisfaction. I answered, I did not understand their drift, and therefore did not discourse them, as I would have done had I apprehended they came to reason as such as had taken offence. And when they came the second time, they brought but one brother, *viz.* William Way, and took others of themselves.

Lieutenant Putnam told them it was not too late yet; now there were several of the brethren [here], and they might take any two of them, and discourse with the pastor. No, they said they had done it already. Thus much time was spent till just night; and myself and other brethren upon going home, the four displeased brethren agreed to meet me tomorrow morning about an hour after sunrise, with the two deacons and Brother William Way and Brother Aaron Way, to discourse the matter; to which I readily assented.

21 April 1693

This morning we met as abovesaid at Deacon Ingersoll's. After a little while, I began with prayer. Then brother Nurse read a large scroll of about fifteen articles, as reasons why they withdrew communion from us. Seven of them I think, were reasons of absenting from public worship with us, and the other eight, I think, causes of separation from my ministry. I desired to see them, but was denied for a great while; at length I had liberty to read them myself, upon the promise of returning them to them. After all, I demanded them, or a copy of them. But they would not consent thereto: nor to the desire of the other four indifferent brethren, though we urged it by argument. But the dissenters said, no: They had told me, and that was enough; and they desired me to call the church, and then I should have it.

Sab: 30 Apr. 1693

After public worship was ended, the church was stayed, to whom the pastor spoke to this effect: Brethren, you know some of our brethren have for a time withdrawn from us. I do not understand their methods. They desire to speak with the church: if you gratify them herein, I recommend their motion to you. After a little discourse it was voted that the church meet 18 May next, after Lecture, at the pastor's house, and in the meantime brother Benjamin Putnam and brother Sam Sibley to acquaint brother Nurse and brother Tarbell tomorrow (brother Cloyes being at Boston, where he has lived these many months; so that we sent not to him, supposing the abovesaid his kinsmen would); and brother Benjamin Wilkins and brother Aaron Wey to acquaint their neighbor Thomas Wilkins tomorrow also; so that all of them may have timely notice.

18 May 1693

At a church-meeting appointed as abovesaid at the pastor's, twenty brethren (besides the pastor and the abovesaid displeased brethren, *viz.* three of them, *viz.* Jonathan Tarbell, Thomas Wilkins and Samuel Nurse) being present. After prayer the pastor applied himself to the three abovesaid brethren, saying to this effect: brethren, you desired the church to give you a meeting, now they are here and I have you to acquaint them with your reason for desiring of it.

They answered it was to tell their charge against Mr. Parris, and now they had witnesses to prove it. After much agitation Brother Nathaniel Putnam was by vote of the church chosen to put to vote which was needful. And it being put to vote whether they apprehended the said brethren had proceeded regularly according to 18 Matthew and so whether the church could now hear it, it was passed negatively by a general or universal vote, excepting the said three dissenting brethren. Also by a like vote it passed in the affirmative that the church would hear the said dissatisfied brethren upon their bringing the case to them according to Christ's rules.

Note: that the general deportment of the said three displeased brethren was at this meeting exceeding unchristian, both to minister and the other brethren; very inreverend towards him, and as rough towards them to the great grief of many, if not the whole church. Nor did they stick to affirm that the church could not judge the case, was not capable of it. Being asked, why then did they desire the church to come together? they replied that they might tell the church, and so bring it to council; which was the point they aimed at and abundantly insisted upon. The church made return, that they would be ready for a council in a regular way. The said three brethren being asked whether they were offended with any of the brethren besides the pastor? they replied, they did not come to tell that now; that was not their present business. Being asked by the pastor himself, whether they there were all one and equal in their offence with him? they answered, yes. The pastor then replied that he would not then have them hereafter meet with him together, but each of them singly; for when they came the very first time he did not understand this drift, and therefore did not debate with them, and the case required arguing. Samuel Nurse replied he did not care to come to the house, nor to discourse me alone.

13 October 1693

I received a letter from the Reverend Mr. Jonathan Higginson directed to myself and brethren of this church. The sum whereof was to advise us to join with the complainants in calling a council of neighbouring churches, not excepting against any on either side. Which letter, he writes, was occasioned from another letter from Mr. Willard in the name of the elders of Boston, directed to himself, Mr. Noyes, and Mr. Hale, to desire him to persuade us so to do. Communicated the same letter this day to sundry of the brethren at a private meeting at Deacon Ingersoll's.

14 October, 1693

I received a letter from the Rev. Mr. Hale and Mr. Noyes, directed to myself and church, of the same tenor, for substance, with the abovesaid of Mr. Higginson's, only herein were several conditions upon which a council should be chosen, omitted in that.

Sab: 15 October 1693

I stayed the church at night, telling them of the 2 abovesaid letters; we appointed a meeting the 10th instant at the pastor's house to read and debate upon them, at three o'clock afternoon.

19 October 1693

A very stormy day, wind and rain, so that but 12 brethren besides myself were present. After prayer, we read and debated the abovesaid 2 letters, and some of the petitions of the complainants to the General Court and several remote churches.

We voted unanimously that we concurred with the advice abovesaid to call a council in an orderly way, and therefore chose brother Bray Wilkins and brother Peter Prescot to go to Brother Thomas Wilkins with our desire that he would meet the church the 23d instant at 2 o'clock afternoon at Deacon Ingersoll's house in order to join with them in calling a council, according to our late advice from some neighboring elders: And brother Nathaniel Putnam and brother Joshua Rea and brother Nathaniel Ingersoll to go likewise tomorrow with the like message to brother Jonathan Tarbell, brother Samuel Nurse and brother Peter Cloyes (if in the Village). And also voted that we the concording brethren meet at the same place at the hour of eleven, and that the brethren have notice of the same the next Lord's day.

Sab: 22 October 1693

The church was stayed in the afternoon and the brethren told by the pastor that the last sixth day we wanted several of them, and supposed that the great storm hindered some of them. But those of us present had consulted the abovesaid letters from neighboring Elders sent to us with advice: upon which we had gone to the dissenting brethren to meet us tomorrow, and desired all come that possibly then could, as agreed 19 instant.

At Deacon Ingersoll's. 23 October 1693

The church (i.e., brethren) met as above agreed, and again there being about 20 brethren the abovesaid letters from Mr. Higginson, Mr. Hale and Mr. Noyes were read, and the counsel therein given us by all approved, *viz.:* to join in calling a council with our dissenting brethren upon these orderly conditions (as abovesaid given) *viz.:* 1. That the case be stated which we go to council for, as 15 Acts 2. 2. That the dissenting brethren give in their charge under their hands and have known which persons they are dissatisfied with, according to 15 Acts 2 and 25–27. 3. That we will likewise give in our charge against them which we would bring to council against them, as we expect of them, under our hands. 4. That as they shall have from us, so we will have from them the particular witnesses to each particular charge. 5. That we agree how the charges of the council shall be borne.

Almost 3 o'clock the dissenting brethren came, and after much debate (they desiring to bring up others which we had not sent for and they had brought with them) we gave way that they should bring up such of them as were in full communion with other churches. So they brought up Mr. Israel Porter. Then I told them we were met in order to call a council, and we desired to know that we should call a council about.

They said their offence was against Mr. Parris and not the church, and offered to read a paper as matter for the council. But we answered that we would not hear it unless they would leave it with us after it was read, or a copy of it, that we might consider of it; And we would deal the like by them, give them our charge under our hands. They replied they would never do so: each of them expressing their unwillingness to this: and withal said they would have a council whether we would or not; and thus they parted, after we had much urged as abovesaid.

To the Reverends Mr. John Higginson Hale and Mr. Nicholas Noyes, ministers of the churches in Salem and Beverly

Reverend and much honored Sirs:

This day and 19th instant also (at church-meetings purposely warned) we deliberately read your advice to us, and debated upon it, concluding with a universal concurrence the scheme following, *viz.:* We do in the first place very acceptably receive your counsel. And as we conceive, we have not hitherto been obstructive to the orderly calling of a council, for help in, and if it might be, healing of our ill-circumstanced case; so we hope we shall not for the future. We are glad to hear our dissenters have promised the Bay worthies a compliance with the motion of mutual and orderly choosing of a council. If they do so, we shall be in a fair way (by the merciful smiles of God) to some needful issue. We are conscious to ourselves of standing upon nothing but what is exceeding requisite, *viz.* matter and order; in which, had we been conceded to before, we presume a union (if possible) had been attained, or a council called in to our help thereto, long ago. It is not a little our frequent and daily grief to consider what amazing confused noises (by the by) we hear go of us. The reports, reporters, and upon what grounds received, we are to seek of. We might groan out some things before men, but we will content ourselves (at present) to sigh them out before the Lord. Our troubles (particularly our minister's) right and left, as far as we know in the circumstances of them, have hitherto been unparalleled; and for Zion's sake we pray they ever may.

Since the abovesaid the dissenting brethren met us (upon appointment the 19 instant, being sent for by us to meet in order to counsel) but refused (as soon as [they] came, and long afterwards) to discourse with the church unless they might be permitted to intrude others not of the church upon us; which we for a time argued against. At length we gave place (still declaring against its irregularity) that they should be suffered to bring up, of such as they had brought with them, such as stood in full communion with other churches. After this they would bring in no charge or accusation against any, otherwise than by reading of what they had prepared, unless we would first consent to the actual choosing of a council: which we, quoting 15 Acts 2 and 25, could not consent unto; unless besides reading of their paper (whatever it was) they would leave it with us, or a copy of it. On the other hand, we offering them the like, to give in our charges against them under our hands, which we would have a hearing of by the said council. But all was rejected, and so near sunset broke up to no purpose. Thus in haste, leaving you to the all-good God, to whom we desire you earnestly and constantly to recommend our persons and bewildered case, we remain, worthy Sirs, yours truly in him who is love and truth,

SAMUEL PARRIS WITH CONSENT OF THE BRETHREN OF THE CHURCH SALEM VILLAGE, 23 OCTOBER 1693

Sab: 5 Nov. 1693

At night, by vote of the church, brother Ingersoll and brother Benjamin Putnam were chosen to go tomorrow to brother Nurse and brother Tarbell with this message: that they meet us the 13 instant at 10 o'clock at the pastor's house, farther to discourse of, and also to have communicated to them, the late advice we spoke of last time from our neighboring elders, in order to calling in of council, if we cannot issue amongst ourselves; and to leave with said Tarbell and Nurse the said message to be communicated to brother Cloyes if he be not too remote. And by same vote the like message was sent to brother Thomas Wilkins by his father and brother Aaron Wey.

13 Nov. 1693

Almost 1 o'clock at noon after the church had been long together, 3 of the abovesaid dissenting brethren came, *viz.:* Peter Cloyes, Samuel Nurse and John Tarbell, to whom after prayer, and caution from the pastor of observing order and meetness, he read the advice of the Reverend Mr. Higginson and of the Reverend Mr. Hale and Mr. Noyes to the church, with the places of Scripture quoted by them; and then desired and long urged an account of their accusations, subscribed by them according to said advice. But after all we could obtain none, they saying the church had refused it already, and ([illegible] to their old irregular proceedings) they would read them now before the church (but not leave them) in case they might be suffered to bring in with them some members of other churches as witnesses, whom they had brought near at hand for that purpose. To which the church answered that it would not give way to such innovations. The upshot was a paper they brought in, signed by said Cloyes, Nurse and Tarbell, dated this day, in way of petition for themselves and neighbors, as follows:

> The humble petition and request of us under-named, though unworthy for ourselves and the rest of our neighbors, who being greatly grieved and much oppressed (unto our Reverend Pastor and the rest of our brethren in the church of Salem Village) humbly showeth, that whereas you have been pleased to give us some encouragement of a discourse this day in order to an accommodation of supposed but unhappy differences; and praying that it may be effectual, we offer if you please that a council of indifferent persons be indifferently chosen: Or that we agree together for a council chosen by the General Court; who may have full power to hear and determine all differences, real and imaginable, which hath arisen amongst us; which if obtained, then we do promise to give unto you our pastor the particulars of our grievances, in writing, thirty days before the said council shall meet, to

consider thereof. Provided that you our said pastor and the rest of our brethren will give us an answer in writing six days before said meeting.

THIS 13 NOV. 1693
PETER CLOYES
SAMUEL NURSE
JOHN TARBELL

When we had this paper, we asked them whether this was all that they would now come to. They said yes. Then brother Cloyes being in haste to be gone, we told them we would consider of it, and give them some answer hereafter to it; and desired them to stay a little and hear what the church had to say against them. So the pastor read a charge against them containing above thirty articles, and so dismissed them.

Samuel Parris inserted the following document later in the record, under the entry for February 7, 1695, when it was again read aloud at another meeting of the dissenting brethren. It is placed here so that it will be clear what Samuel Nurse and the rest found themselves faced with, even at this stage. Parris' record book continues afterwards with a letter.

Sundry objections which we have against our dissenting brethren, and were read to them (at least the heads) 13 Nov., 1693, as matters we would offer to a council, *viz.:*

1. Their precipitant, schismatical and total withdrawing from the church (yea, and congregation) so as at once to renounce all religious communion, without giving the least reason for their so doing. See Daniel 2: 15, Proverbs 25: 8. By which means (1) the church suffers: (a) defamation abroad; (b) reproach and grief at home; (2) the separatists become guilty: (a) of general breach of covenant; Neh. 10: all, Jude 19, Hebrew 10: 25; (b) of evil example.
2. Their refusing to give the church messengers (sent to them on purpose 7 Feb. 1692/93) any reason for their withdrawing; most absurdly desiring time for answer, directly contrary to the laws of Christ: I Pet. 3: 15. And to this end (as we then suspected, and now has proved too true), *viz.:* that they might consult with such others amongst us as have frequently evidenced themselves to be obstructive to church-settlement, as these brethren themselves have heretofore abundantly professed; and yet now are their only companions: see II Corinthians 6: 14 etc., I Corinthians 9: 6.

3. When they came to the church members the next time, *viz.* 16 February 1693 (which time was at their desire granted to them for their answer), instead of lovingly speaking their minds, they read a dateless paper reflecting upon church and elders, for calling them to account; and yet refused to leave said paper, and were exceeding hardly prevailed with to let us take a copy of it.
4. Their bringing 27 March following, together with 3 other men not in full communion, and one of them a stranger to our village, a factious and seditious libel to the pastor, consisting of confused calumnies or reflections on said minister and others of the plantation (we know not whom, because not particularly named therein).
5. Their impetuous pursuit of the minister at his house the night following for an answer to said libel, to his great disquietment.
6. Their (with 2 others not in full communion) restless pursuit of the minister again 14 Apr. 1693 for answer to said libel.
7. Their reading a general and ambiguous charge 21 April 1693 against the minister (if not others of the church) before 4 more Brethren mutually agreed on by them; and the minister to hear their difference in order to bring it to the church, and yet refusing to leave said charge, or to suffer any of us (though much urged thereto by us) to take a copy, and so to debate of them—though this meeting was appointed for that end. See Eph. 5: 21, Phil. 2: 3.
8. Their peremptory withstanding the whole brotherhood's council (met on purpose at their desire 18 May 1693) to bring the matter orderly before them; only insisting on it with great heat that immediately their charge might be read, and witnesses heard, before the church had any knowledge of the matter, contrary to I Timothy 5: 19. Yea, loudly and fiercely before the whole brotherhood clamoring against the church that she would not hear them, whereas the church had, both in their presence and audience, but just before passed a vote that she would hear them in case they brought the matter before them according to Christ's rules.
9. Their publishing under their own hands, in diverse places of the country, sundry obloquies against church and elders, whilst still the persons so besmeared are denied cognizance of the surmised crimes, either wholly or too much. See Proverbs 25: 9 and 10: 12–18.
10. Their ensnaring several themselves (or joining with such as did so) to subscribe a petition to his Excellency and General Court, scandalizing the church and minister as unpeaceable with their neighbors. Whereas several whose names are there and who subscribed do utterly disown

any such speech or intention. See II Samuel 15: 6–11, Romans 16: 17–18, Psalms 101: 5.

11. Their gross dissimulation in their letter to the church at Malden dated 11 Sept. 1693 (and, as we supposed, to other churches they then sent to for a council) wherein they do fallaciously disown the abovesaid petition to his Excellency, notwithstanding all their own 11 names are subscribed thereunto: see Psalms 12: 2, Jeremiah 9: 4–5.
12. Their sending abroad petitions to highest court and churches with names subscribed, unknown to some of the persons whose names they bear, as some of us have been informed by said pretended subscribers.
13. Their frequent soliciting others themselves (or confederating with such as did so) to subscribe such like petitioners. See Acts 14: 2, Proverbs 16: 28–30.
14. Their gross mistake in their letter to the church at Malden 11 September '93, wherein they profess so much dissatisfaction with the doctrine, practice and ministerial administration of their pastor, for above a year before the date of said letter; as that they were forced to withdraw from all public worship for more than 12 months before said letter. Whereas it is most notorious that they were in no wise wanting as to a profession of much respects to their said pastor, all along before—yea, and a considerable while after—the breaking forth of the late horrid witchcraft. And some of them did communicate in September 1692 and after; and one of them had a child baptized 30 October 1692.
15. Their withdrawing their purses (as well as their persons) from upholding the Lord's table and ministry.
16. Their great contempt of the church, as oft as hitherto (*viz.* 13 November '93) they have been with them: (1) In unchristian fastness to such as have treated them mildly, though officers and aged; (2) In constant refusing lovingly and brotherly to debate matters unless a council were first chosen, or in some irregular way; (3) In frequent threatening us with a council whether we would or not; (4) In imposing upon the church others not of our church society, as witnesses (they said) of what was spoken on both hands. Whereby (1) They openly charged the whole church as a nest of deceivers; (2) They bring unheard-of innovations into the house of God; (3) They scandalize the church to all that hear of such a protest: I Corinthians 6: 5; (4) They declare themselves void of all charity to the whole church, etc.
17. In fine, to add no more: by all that has been said, their extremely disturbing the peace of this church and many other good people amongst us, sadly exposing all unto ruin. Gal 5: 15, Matthew 12: 25.

Sab: 26 Nov. 1693

To our beloved brethren, Peter Cloyes, Samuel Nurse and Jonathan Tarbell. When you were with us last, *viz.* 13 instant, at our sending for, to hear and pursue the advice from the Reverend Mr. Higginson, Mr. Hale and Mr. Noyes, sent to us at the request of the Reverend elders at Boston, you knew that the utmost which you would come up to then was at last to leave a paper with us, subscribed with each of your names. To which upon consideration of it (as we then promised) we now return answer, *viz.:*

That we find said paper far other than we hoped for, and altogether alien (or strange) from the said advice, which no sooner came to our hands but had acceptance with us; and since that, we are informed, is well approved by the reverend elders at Boston, who on your behalf, and as your sureties, occasioned it. So that to say no more (though we might enlarge upon it) we cannot at all take up with your offer therein; but hereby manifest to you that we still stand to said advice. So exhorting you to study the things which made for peace (Romans 14: 19). And therefore that you seriously weigh those texts: II Samuel 2: 26, Proverbs 16: 32, Matthew 6: 12 and 18: 21–22, . . . 4: 26–27, Galatians 5: 9, James 3: 13 to the end. And that you have a care of destroying the Church of God. II Corinthians. . . . Always praying for your best good, we subscribe your . . . and affectionate brethren:

Salem Village, 26 Nov. 1693

The same day the abovesaid answer was voted by the brethren: Deacon Ingersol and brother Jonathan Putnam [were] voted to carry it. But the 27th day brother Joshua Rea came to me with Deacon Ingersoll, telling me brother Jonathan could not go this day, so I made said brother Rea join with said Deacon in the message, both which two-mentioned brethren carried it.

Salem, June 14, 1694

We whose names are underwritten, being desired by some persons of Salem Village to meet together and try if we could give any direction how the said differences there may be healed, and having heard the particulars which the dissatisfied Brethren and neighbors have drawn up on matters they would present to a council, and also signifying their averseness to apply themselves to the church there for an accommodation, and considering the sad effects likely to follow on the continuance of this fire of contention, would suggest to the reverend and beloved the pastor and brethren of the church at the village that they join with their dissatisfied brethren and neighbors in calling of a council of six churches, indifferently chosen by your and their consent, mutually agreed on. Provided that they and you consent that the said council be acknowledged to hear and determine according to the mind of Christ upon matters in difference which they shall fairly represent to you and you to them, in writing before the council be called, of all matters proper for an ecclesiastical council; and that you agree how the charges of said council shall be borne before the council be called. We beseech you to study those things which make for peace and edification, Eph. 4: 1–3.

JOHN HIGGINSON
JAMES ALLEN
JOHN HALE
JOSEPH GERRISH
SAMUEL WILLARD
SAMUEL CHEEVER
NICHOLAS NOYES
(consents to this advice with this proviso: that he be not chosen one of the council)

Sab: 17 June 1694

The above advice was in the evening communicated by the pastor to the church, and the 21 instant a church-meeting at 2 o'clock appointed farther to discourse of it.

21 June 1694

At the meeting before appointed, several things were discoursed of and left unto farther consideration. As: (1) The church's compliance with the abovesaid advice; (2) That the charges be borne by such as are so eager for a council, (3) That the brethren following, *viz.:* Lieutenant and Captain Putnam, Bray Wilkins, with the two deacons assist the pastor at meetings, when and where he shall appoint, to negotiate in affairs appertaining to matters abovesaid, that the whole church may not be oppressed otherwise with multitudes of meetings, nor called together but as necessity requires. And at such private meetings any brother may come (he by inquiry knowing when and where they are) and all are desired at such times to meet who can give any personal help for greater expedition. These things were discoursed and left to farther consideration but not voted.

29 June

At a usual church-meeting (before the sacrament) towards evening, we again discoursed of the 7 Ministers' advice abovesaid, but concluded upon nothing—most if not all of the brethren present—being rather farther off from approbation of said advice than before: Nor indeed were some of us willing to come to determination till we had first by solemn fasting and prayer sought unto God for his guidance. And therefore the 4 July next was appointed for that purpose.

July 5, 1694

At a church fast at Lieutenant Putnam's (the text being on Psalms 5: 8, last part) where were 20 Brethren present, in the evening it was voted (after as much reasonings to and fro as time would allow) that the seven ministers' advice dated June 14 last (as abovesaid) should be read publicly before all the congregation the next Lord's day, and then that the thirteenth instant July should be published as a day, wherein at two o'clock in the afternoon, we would meet at the meeting-house, openly to hear all dissatisfactions that should be brought by any of the inhabitants of this village, in order to a council, according to said advice: And that our brethren William and Aaron Way be desired and are hereby appointed to acquaint our dissatisfied brother Thomas Wilkins with this our agreement, both for himself the said Thomas Wilkins, and also the brethren dissatisfied with him. And that the church (and such neighbors as are in amity with them, if they please) meet the same thirteenth instant at 12 o'clock at noon at Deacon Ingersoll's.

Note: That this vote abovesaid was not approved by all; several could not concur with it. I also propounded that some messengers should be sent with notice of said vote to some of the dissatisfied neighbors in behalf of all of them. But this could not be assented to: one and all (I think) did dislike it and gave reasons for their dislike of it.

Sabbath July 8, 1694

The above agreement was published by the pastor.

July 13, 1694

We met in public as above appointed but came to no agreement: the dissenters refusing to give in any charge unless we would first engage to choose a council.

September 20, 1694. Received the following letter:

To the Reverend and beloved the elders and brethren of the church at Salem Village:

Being informed that the advice offered to yourselves and signed by us with one other elder is not accepted by you for calling of a council in your case and that you interpret the meaning of some general and ambiguous expressions in that writing contrary to our unanimous declared sense at the time of our subscribing. We whose names are underwritten find it to be our duty to express our minds more plainly and particularly, that we may be the more clearly understood without mistake, *viz.:* Our advice is that you join with your unsatisfied brethren and neighbors for calling a council of six churches, not excepting against any that are chosen on either side; and that after you have agreed on the place and time of the council's meeting, and how the charges shall be borne, we say after this is done, we advise that the unsatisfied brethren and neighbors do give into Mr. Parris a true copy of those two papers of grievance which were showed to us, at least 20 days before the time of the council's meeting. And because we fear that longer delays will be of dangerous consequences to you in diverse respects, we pray you so to agree, that you may have a council before winter. Consider what we have said, and the Lord give you understanding in all things.

Sept. 10, '94
Subscribed to the Reverend Mr. Parris,
the pastor, and the brethren of the church at Salem Village
JOHN HIGGINSON
JAMES ALLEN
SAMUEL WILLARD
SAMUEL CHEEVER
JOSEPH GERRISH

The same day at a public and general meeting the following offers were given to our dissenters, being before prepared:

We have long discoursed of a council, and look upon yourselves as the only bar to it, because you refuse to give in to us the matters you would bring to a council. But that we may not contend forever, we rather concede that a council shall be chosen this moment, we choosing four churches and you three; and that you give us immediately your dissatisfactions signed under your hands; and only such things be brought in as are proper for an ecclesiastical council; and if we find among your matters such as are improper for such a council, you shall withdraw the same before the session of said council: otherwise the said council to fall [illegible].

Voted this 29 Sept. 1694 by twenty brethren present besides the pastor, Samuel Parris.

To our dissenting Brethren and neighbors.

2 Nov. At a church-meeting at Deacon Ingersoll's—15 Brethren besides the pastor being present. It was debated whether it was not high time to call our 3 dissenting Brethren to give us in the grounds of their withdrawing from us. And after some discourse it was concluded and voted by a universal vote that the next

Lord's day in public it should be put to vote of all the brethren whether they thought meet that the next Lord's day after, brother Jonathan Tarbell should be desired and required in public to bring in his reasons etc.

Sab: 4 Nov. 1694

After sermon in the afternoon, it was propounded to the brethren, whether the church ought not to inquire again of our dissenting brethren after the reason of their dissent. Nothing appearing from any against it, it was put to vote, and carried in the affirmative (by all, as far as I know, except brother Joshua Rea), that Brother Jonathan Tarbell should the next Lord's day, appear and give in his reasons in public; the contrary being propounded, if any had aught to object against it. But no dissent was manifested; and so brother Nathaniel Putnam and Deacon Ingersoll were desired to give this message from the church to said brother Tarbell.

Sab: 11 Nov. 1694

Before the evening blessing was pronounced, brother Tarbell was openly called again and again; but, he not appearing, application was made to the abovesaid church's messengers for his answer: whereupon said brother Putnam reported that said brother Tarbell told him he did not know how to come to us on a Lord's day, but desired rather that he might make his appearance some week-day. Whereupon the congregation was dismissed with the blessing; and the church stayed, and, by a full vote renewed their call of said brother Tarbell to appear the next Lord's day for the ends abovesaid; and Deacon Putnam and brother Jonathan Putnam were desired to be its messengers to said dissenting brother.

Sab: 18 Nov. 1694

The said brother came in the afternoon; and after sermon, he was asked the reasons for his withdrawing. Whereupon he produced a paper which he was urged to deliver to the pastor to communicate to the church; but he refused it, asking who was the church's mouth. To which when he was answered, "The pastor," he replied, Not in this case, because his offence was with him. The pastor demanded whether he had offence against any of the church besides the pastor. He answered, "No." So at length we suffered a non-member, Mr. Joseph Hutchinson, to read it. After which the pastor read openly before the whole congregation his overtures for peace and reconciliation. After which said Tarbell, seemingly (at least) much affected, said that if half so much had been said formerly, it had never come to this. But he added that others also were dissatisfied besides him self: and therefore he desired opportunity that they might come also, which was immediately granted; *viz.*, the 26 instant, at 2 o'clock.

26 Nov. 1694

At the public meeting above appointed at the meeting-house, after the pastor had first sought the grace of God with us in prayer, he then summed up to the church and congregation (among which were several strangers) the occasion of our present assembling, as is hinted the last meeting. Then seeing, together with brother Tarbell, two more of our dissenting brethren, *viz.*, Samuel Nurse and Thomas Wilkins (who had, to suit their designs, placed themselves in a seat conveniently together), the church immediately, to save farther sending for them, voted that said brother Wilkins and brother Nurse should now, together with brothers Tarbell, give their reasons of withdrawing from the church. Then the pastor applied himself to all these three dissenters, pressing the church's desire upon them. So they produced a paper, which they much opposed the coming into the pastor's hands and his reading of, but at length they yielded to it. Whilst the paper was reading, brothers Nurse looked upon another (which he said was the original): and after it was read throughout, he said it was the same with what he had. Their paper was as followeth:—

> The reasons why we withdraw from communion with the church of Salem Village, both as to hearing the word preached, and from partaking with them at the Lord's table, are as followeth:—
>
> 1. Why we attend not on public prayer and preaching the word, these are, (1) The distracting and disturbing tumults and noises made by the persons under diabolical power and delusions, preventing sometimes our hearing and understanding and profiting of the word preached; we having, after many trials and experiences, found no redress in this case, accounted ourselves under a necessity to go where we might hear the word in quiet. (2) The apprehensions of danger of ourselves being accused as the devil's instruments to molest and afflict the persons complaining, we seeing those whom we had reason to esteem better than ourselves thus accused, blemished, and of their lives bereaved, forseeing this evil, thought it our prudence to withdraw. (3) We found so frequent and positive preaching up some principles and practices by Mr. Parris, referring to the trouble then among us and upon us; therefore thought it our most safe and peaceable way to withdraw.

The reasons why we hold not communion with them at the Lord's table are, first, we esteem ourselves justly aggrieved and offended with the officer who doth administer, for the reasons following:

1. From his declared and published principles, referring to our molestation from the invisible world, differing from the opinion of the generality of the orthodox ministers of the whole country.
2. His easy and strong faith and belief of the affirmations and accusations made by those they call the afflicted.
3. His laying aside that grace which above all, we are required to put on; namely, charity towards his neighbors, and especially towards those of his church, when there is no apparent reason for the contrary.
4. His approving and practising unwarrantable and ungrounded methods for discovering what he was desirous to know referring to the bewitched or possessed persons, as in bringing some to others, and by and from them pretending to inform himself and others who were the devil's instruments to afflict the sick and pained.
5. His unsafe and unaccountable oath, given by him against sundry of the accused.
6. His not rendering to the world so fair, if true, an account of what he wrote on examination of the afflicted.
7. Sundry unsafe, if sound, points of doctrine delivered in his preaching, which we esteem not warrantable, if Christian.
8. His persisting in these principles and justifying his practices, not rendering any satisfaction to us when regularly desired, but rather farther offending and dissatisfying ourselves.

JOHN TARBELL
THOMAS WILKINS
SAMUEL NURSE

When the pastor had read these charges, he asked the dissenters above mentioned whether they were offended with none in the church besides himself. They replied that they articled against none else. Then the officer asked them if they withdrew from communion upon account of none in the church besides himself. They answered that they withdrew only on my account. Then I read them my "Meditations for Peace," mentioned 18 instant; *viz.:*—

For as much as it is the undoubted duty of all Christians to pursue peace (Psalms 24: 14) even unto a reaching of it, if it be possible (Romans 12: 18, 19); and whereas, through the righteous, sovereign and awful providence of God, the Grand Enemy of all Christian peace has of late, been most tremendously let loose in divers places hereabouts, and more especially amongst our sinful selves, not only to interrupt that partial peace which we did sometimes enjoy, but also, through his wiles and temptations and our weaknesses and corruptions, to make wider breaches, and raise more bitter animosities between too many of us, of one mind for a time, and afterwards of differing apprehensions, and, at last are but in the dark,—upon serious thoughts of all or most of all, and after many prayers, I have been moved to present to you (my beloved flock) the following particulars, in way of contribution towards regaining of Christian concord (if so be we are not altogether unappeasable, irreconcilable, and so destitute of that good spirit which is first pure, then peaceable, gentle, easy to be entreated, James 3: 17); *viz.*,

1. In that the Lord ordered the late horrid calamity (which afterwards, plague-like, spread in many other places) to break out first in my family, I cannot but look upon as a very sore rebuke, and humbling providence, both to myself and mine, and desire so we may improve it.
2. In that also in my family were some of both parties, *viz.*, accusers and accused, I look also as an aggravation of the rebuke, as an addition of wormwood to the gall.
3. In that means were used in my family (though totally unknown to me or mine, excepts servants, till afterwards) to raise spirits and create apparitions in a no better than diabolical way, I do also look upon as a farther rebuke of divine providence. And by all, I do humbly own this day before the Lord and his people, that God has been righteously spitting in my face (Numbers 12: 14). And I desire to lie low under all this reproach, and to lay my hand upon my mouth.
4. As to the management of those mysteries, as far as concerns myself, I am very desirous (upon farther light) to own any errors I have therein fallen into and can come to a discerning of.

In the meanwhile, I do acknowledge, upon after considerations, that, were the same troubles again (which the Lord of his rich mercy forever prevent), I should not agree with my former apprehensions in all points; as, for instance,

I question not but God sometimes suffers the devil (as of late) to afflict in the shape of not only innocent but pious persons, or so to delude the senses of the afflicted that they strongly conceive their hurt is from such persons, when indeed it is not.

The improving [i.e., use] of one afflicted to inquire by who afflicts the others, I fear may be and has been unlawfully used, to Satan's great advantage.

As to my writing, it was put upon me by authority; and therein have I been very careful to avoid the wrongoing of any.*

As to my oath, I never meant it, nor do I know how it can be otherwise construed, than as vulgarly and [by] everyone understood; yea and upon inquiry it may be found so worded also.

As to any passage in preaching or prayer, in that sore hour of distress and darkness, I always intended but due justice on each hand and that not according to man, but God (who knows all things most perfectly), however, through weakness or sore exercise, I might sometimes, yea and possibly sundry times, unadvisedly expressed myself.

As to several that have confessed against themselves, they being wholly strangers to me but yet of good account with better men than myself, to whom also they are well known, I do not pass so much as a secret condemnation upon them; but rather, seeing God has so amazingly lengthened out Satan's chain in this most formidable outrage, I much more incline to side with the opinion of those that have grounds to hope better of them.

As to all that have unduly suffered in these matters (either in their persons or relations) through the clouds of human weakness, and Satan's wiles and sophistry, I do truly sympathise with them; taking it for granted that such as drew themselves clear of this great transgression, or that have sufficient grounds so to look upon their dear friends, have hereby been under those sore trials and temptations, that not an ordinary measure of true grace would be sufficient to prevent a bewraying of remaining corruption.

I am very much in the mind and abundantly persuaded that God (for holy ends, though for what in particular, is best known to himself) has suffered the evil angels to delude us on both hands, but how far on the one side or the other is much above me to say. And, if we cannot reconcile till we come to a full discerning of these things, I fear we shall never come to agreement, or, at soonest not in this world. Therefore:

In fine, the matter being so dark and perplexed as that there is no present appearance that all God's servants should be altogether of one mind, in all circumstances touching the same, I do most heartily, fervently, and humbly beseech pardon of the merciful God through the blood of Christ, of all my mistakes and trespasses in so weighty a matter; and also all your forgiveness of every offence in this or other affairs, wherein you see or conceive I have

---

*[*Here occurs a marginal note in Mr. Parris's handwriting:* "(a) Added by the desire of the Council, this following paragraph; *viz.*, Nevertheless, I fear that in and through the throng of many things written by me, in the late confusions, there has not been a due exactness always used; and, as I now see the inconveniency of my writing so much on those difficult occasions, so I would lament every error of such writings.—Apr. 3, 1695. *Idem.* S.P."]

erred and offended; professing, in the presence of the Almighty God that what I have done has been, as for substance, as I apprehended was duty,—however through weakness, ignorance, &c., I may have been mistaken; I also, through grace, promising each of you the like of me. And so again, I beg, entreat, and beseech you, that Satan, the devil, the roaring lion, the old dragon, the enemy of all righteousness, may no longer be served by us, by our envy and strifes (where every evil work prevails whilst these bear sway, Isaiah 3: 14–16); but that all from this day forward, may be covered with the mantel of love, and we may on all hands forgive each other heartily, sincerely, and thoroughly, as we do hope and pray that God, for Christ's sake, would forgive each of ourselves (Matthew 28: 21 *ad. fine;* Col. 3: 12, 13). Put on therefore, as the elect of God, holy and beloved, bowels of mercies, kindness, humbleness of mind, meekness, long-suffering, forbearing one another, and forgiving one another. If any man have a quarrel against any, even as Christ forgave you so also do ye (Eph. 4: 31, 32). Let all bitterness and wrath and anger and clamor and evil-speaking be put away from you, with all malice; and be ye kind to one another, tenderhearted, forgiving one another, even as God, for Christ's sake, hath forgiven you.

AMEN. AMEN.
SAMUEL PARRIS
29 NOV., 1694

After I had read these overtures abovesaid, I desired the brethren to declare themselves whether they remained still dissatisfied. Brother Tarbell answered that they desired to consider of it, and to have a copy of what I had read. I replied that then they must subscribe their reasons (abovementioned) for as yet they were anonymous: so at length, with no little difficulty, I purchased the subscription of their charges by my abovesaid overtures, which I gave, subscribed with my name, to them to consider of; and so the meeting broke up.

Note that, during this agitation with our dissenting brethren, they entertained frequent whisperings with comers and goers to them and from them; particularly Daniel Andrews, and Thomas Preston from Mr. Israel Porter, and Joseph Hutchinson, &c.

Nov. 30, 1694

Brother Nurse and brother Tarbell (bringing with them Joseph Putnam and Thomas Preston) towards night came to my house, where they found the two deacons and several other brethren; *viz.*, Thomas Putnam, Jonathan Putnam, Jnr., Benjamin Wilkins, and Ezekial Cheever, besides Lieutenant Jonathan Walcott and brother Tarbell said they came to answer my paper which they had now considered of, and their answer was this; *viz.*, that they remained dissatisfied, and desired that the church would call a council, according to the advice we had lately from the ministers.

Sab: Dec. 2, 1694

I publicly reported the abovesaid answer of the dissenting brethren, and then desired the church to stay after the dismission of the congregation; and then we appointed a church- meeting at Deacon Putnam's for farther agitation the 6 instant.

Dec. 6, 1694

At the meeting above concluded upon, we agreed that the church (excepting the pastor, who was even quite tired out, and also because he thought they might be more free in his absence) would meet the 20 instant with the dissenting brethren at Deacon Ingersoll's to discourse with them about their reasons of withdrawing.

Jan. 21, 1694/95

At a meeting at Captain Putnam's of several of the principals of the church, we concluded that at our next church-meeting we would propound a fresh tender both to our dissenting brethren and neighbors for a council.

Sab: 27 Jan. 1694/95

Received into full communion with the church:

38. Mary (wife to John) Wheldon, and baptized. *An. Aetat* 37

The church was stayed after the congregation was dismissed, and desired to meet the 31st instant at the pastor's house in order to prepare another offer of a council to our dissenters, both brethren and neighbors.

Jan. 31, 1694/95

At a full meeting of the church as above appointed, it was universally voted that the next Lord's day public notice would be given for a public meeting at the meeting house the 7 Feb. next, at 2 of the clock, to prosecute the ministers' advice for a council, dated 14 June last. And our brethren William Way and Jonathan Wilkins be desired this evening to declare this our purpose to brother Thomas

Wilkins in behalf of the rest of the dissenting brethren. We also concluded that the third Tuesday in March next would be as convenient a time as we could pitch upon for the meeting of said council.

Sabbath 3 Feb. 1695

After the afternoon sermon was ended the pastor published the above-mentioned agreement of the church, and desired that all would bring in at that day the matter which they had to offer to a council.

Feb. 7 1695

The church met as above appointed in public, when after prayer, and the occasion of this meeting being hinted, the ministers' advice to us dated 14 June last was again publicly read. And the dissenting neighbors then present were desired to bring in such matters as they desired a council for. This was much urged, but to no purpose. They pleading that the explanation of said advice dated 10 September last and sent to us, was that a council should be first chosen, and then the matters for calling a council should be given in. We answered that we would stand to the advice of 14 June which they themselves had been the procurers of. And therefore desired them only to give in the things they would offer to a council—let them be what they would—and we would join with them, they nominating any 3 churches (excepting Ipswich and those six churches whose elders had already been concerned so as to give advice as before hinted, [i.e.,] only upon hearing of the dissenters, without our church's privity records) and we would immediately before the half-hour was out vote then for them, and then ourselves elect 3 other churches. But none would take up with this notion. Then we told our dissenting brethren, seeing the neighbors had nothing they would offer to us for calling a council, [that] inasmuch as we had lately received their reasons for withdrawing from us, we would also give in to them the charges we had against them, to tender unto a council; which accordingly we did after we had first read them openly and publicly—*viz.,* as followeth:

> Samuel Parris here inserts the list of seventeen grievances first composed and read aloud to a meeting of the dissenting brethren in November 1693.

As soon as the public reading of these articles was ended, brother Thomas Wilkins in a scoffing and contemptuous way said openly: This is a large epistle. Yet our brethren accepted not neither of this offer. So that seeing [that] though there had been by some a loud and long cry for a council, and yet now a declining of it when in so fair a way (as we conceive) tendered, we were forced to break up, it being even sunset; only first we told them, if they saw not good to join with us in a council, we intended to call one ourselves—to be held the third Tuesday in the next month. After we were withdrawn to Deacon Ingersoll's, the brethren Samuel Nurse, and a while after Thomas Wilkins, came to us, desiring time to consider of our offer. We replied that we were even spent and tired out with the multitude of meetings which they had occasioned us; nevertheless we were willing to gratify them in anything we might; and so appointed another church-meeting for their sakes at Lieutenant Putnam's house at 1 a'clock the 12 instant.

Feb. 12, 1695

The church met again, as last agreed upon, and, after a while, our dissenting brethren, Thomas Wilkins, Samuel Nurse, and Jonathan Tarbell, came also.

After our constant way of begging the presence of God with us, we desired our dissenting brethren to acquaint us whether they would accept of our last proposals, which they desired this day to consider of. They answered that they were willing to drop the six churches from whose elders we had had the advice abovesaid, dated 14 June last, but they were not free to exclude Ipswich. This they stuck unto long, and then desired that they might withdraw a little to confer among themselves about it, which was granted.

But they quickly returned, as resolved for Ipswich as before. We desired them to nominate the three churches they would have sent to, and, after much debate, they did, *viz.*, Rowley, Salisbury, and Ipswich. Whereupon we voted, by a full consent, Rowley and Salisbury churches for a part of the council, and desired them to nominate a third church. But still they insisted on Ipswich, which we told them they were openly informed [at] the last meeting that we had excepted against. Then they were told that we would immediately choose three other churches to join with the two before nominated and voted, if they saw not good to nominate any more, or else we would choose two other churches to join with the aforesaid two, if they pleased.

They answered they would be willing to that, if Ipswich might be one of them. Then it was asked them if a dismission to some other orthodox church, where they might better please themselves, would content them. Brother Tarbell answered, Aye, if we could find a way to remove their livings, too.

Then it was propounded whether we could not unite amongst ourselves. The particular answer hereunto I remember not, but (I think) such hints were given by them as if it were impossible.

Thus much time being gone, it being well towards sunset, and we concluding that it was necessary that we should do something ourselves, if they would not (as the elders had heretofore desired) accept of our joining with them, we dismissed them and, by a general agreement amongst ourselves, read and voted letters to the churches at North Boston, Weymouth, Malden, and Rowley, for their help in a council, as followeth:

> To the Reverend. elders of the church in North Boston, to be communicated to the church.
> Salem Village, 12 Feb. '95
> Reverend, Honored, and Beloved:
>
> Grace, mercy and peace from God our Father, through our Lord Jesus Christ to you be multiplied. It hath justly pleased the Lord, in his awful and holy providence, for many months past, sorely to exercise us, his poor and unworthy people, with the fires of strife, division, etc. We have not been wholly wanting, according to our poor ability, as to the use of means for the quenching of the same. But by all obtaining no prospect thereof, we have in the next place, and for a long time together, done what we could to work at making an orderly way for the calling-in of more fit and meet help than our own. Upon [illegible] whereof, our earnest and humble request unto yourselves is, that you would please to send your elders and messengers to meet here, at the minister's house (with other churches now sent to for the same cause) in way of council, the 19 day of the next month, at ten of the clock. So praying for all fullness of spiritual blessing upon you, and most affectionately entreating the like of you for ourselves, we rest, Sirs, your unworthy brethren,
>
> SAMUEL PARRIS, PASTOR
> IN THE NAME OF THE CHURCH

Letters of the like tenor were also wrote to the churches at Rowley and Malden and Weymouth.

Mar. 1, 1695

At a usual church-meeting (at brother Cheever's house) before the sacrament, after the praying, preaching, etc. was ended, our brethren the messengers to the churches before-mentioned made report to us of the answers thereto made by the several reverend elders thereof. By which we understood that the reverend elders in the Bay accounted it advisable that we should add to the 4 churches which we had already sent unto, the other two churches in Boston, *viz.:* the old church and the third church; and also that the said council might be deferred till the first Wednesday in April next. The thing being somewhat debated of, we quickly assented to that advice or motion. And accordingly shortly after dispatched letters and a messenger to said churches, for that end. And deferred the time as above desired for a fortnight longer.

April 3 and 4, 1695

Five of the six churches before mentioned sent messengers and elders: The church of Malden only was absent, occasioned by sickness of the wife of the reverend elder thereof, who it's said had death very near approaching to her. The third day in public they examined matters, having in the first place had this church's question propounded to them, *viz.:*

> To the reverend and honored elders and messengers of the several churches now sitting in council at Salem Village, Apr. 3, 1695
>
> Our gracious God having inclined your hearts to undertake a difficult service for his interest here, which we take thankful notice of; the great request which we have now to lay before you is, that you would by the help and from the word of our common Lord endeavor to rescue us out of the distresses now upon us, with an answer to the ensuing question, which is the case upon which we have desired counsel, *viz.:*
>
> Inasmuch as the church in this place hath labored under much difficulty, through the dissatisfactions of certain brethren upon the late grievous troubles among us, by which others also have been influenced; and our pastor hath made public offers toward the satisfaction of all concerned: hence our question is, *viz.:*
>
> What advice is to be given, or what may there yet remain, for the comfortable composure of our unhappy differences?

The 4th April in public they read and gave in the following advice, as the result of the said council:

The elders and messengers of the churches—met in council at Salem Village, April 3, 1695, to consider and determine what is to be done for the composure of the present unhappy differences in that place—after solemn invocation of God in Christ for his direction, do unanimously declare and advise as followeth:

We judge that, albeit in the late and the dark time of the confusions, wherein Satan had obtained a more than ordinary liberty to be sifting of this plantation, there were sundry unwarrantable and uncomfortable steps taken by Mr. Samuel Parris, the pastor of the church in Salem Village, then under the hurrying distractions of amazing afflictions, yet the said Mr. Parris, by the good hand of God brought unto a better sense of things, hath so fully expressed it, that a Christian charity may and should receive satisfaction therewith.

Inasmuch as divers Christian brethren in the church of Salem Village have been offended at Mr. Parris for his conduct in the time of the difficulties and calamities which have distressed them, we now advise them charitably to accept the satisfaction which he hath tendered in his Christian acknowledgments of the errors therein committed; yea, to endeavor, as far as 'tis possible, the fullest reconciliation of their minds unto communion with him, in the whole exercise of his ministry, and with the rest of the church (Matthew 6:12–14; Luke 17:3, James 5:16).

Considering the extreme trials and troubles which the dissatisfied brethren in the church of Salem Village have undergone in the day of sore temptation which hath been upon them, we cannot but advise the church to treat them with bowels of much compassion, instead of all more critical or rigorous proceedings against them, for the infirmities discovered by them in such an heart-breaking day. And if, after a patient waiting for it, the said brethren cannot so far overcome the uneasiness of their spirits, in the remembrance of the disasters that have happened, as to sit under his ministry, we advise the church, with all tenderness, to grant them a dismission unto any other society of the faithful whereunto they may desire to be dismissed (Galatians 6:1, 2; Psalms 103:13, 14; Job 19:21).

Mr. Parris having, as we understand, with much fidelity and integrity acquitted himself in the main course of his ministry since he hath been pastor to the church in Salem Village, about his first call whereunto, we look upon all contestations now to be both unreasonable and unseasonable; and our Lord having made him a blessing unto the souls of not a few, both old and young, in this place, we advise that he be accordingly respected, honored, and supported, with all the regards that are due to a faithful minister of the gospel (I Thess. 5:12, 13; I Timothy 5:17).

Having observed that there is in Salem Village a spirit full of contentions and animosities, too sadly verifying the blemish which hath heretofore lain upon them, and that some complaints brought against Mr. Parris have been either causeless and groundless, or unduly aggravated, we do, in the name and fear of the Lord, solemnly warn them to consider, whether, if they continue to devour one another, it will not be bitterness in the latter end; and beware lest the Lord be provoked thereby, utterly to deprive them of those which they should account their precious and pleasant things, and abandon them to all the desolations of a people that sin away the mercies of the gospel (James 3:16; Galatians 5:15; II Samuel 2:26; Isaiah 5:4–6; Matthew 21:43).

If the distempers in Salem Village should be (which God forbid!) so incurable, that Mr. Parris, after all, find that he cannot, with any comfort and service, continue in his present station, his removal from thence will not expose him unto any hard character with us, nor we hope, with the rest of the people of God among whom we live (Matthew 10:14; Acts 22:18).

All which advice we follow with our prayers that the God of peace would bruise Satan under our feet. Now, the Lord of peace himself give you peace always by all means.

INCREASE MATHER, MODERATOR

JOSEPH BRIDGHAM	EPHRAIM HUNT
SAMUEL CHECKLEY	NATHANIEL WILLIAMS
WILLIAM TORREY	SAMUEL PHILLIPS
JOSEPH BOYNTON	JAMES ALLEN
RICH'D MIDDLECOT	SAMUEL TORREY
JOHN WALLEY	SAMUEL WILLARD
JEREMIAH DUMMER	EDWARD PAYSON
NEHEMIAH JEWET	COTTON MATHER

To Mr. Samuel Parris, pastor, and the brethren of the church in Salem Village.

Much Respected:

Since that some of us did, in council with other worthy persons met at your desire to consider your difficult affairs, offer you such advice as we judged most according to the mind of God and for the good of your whole plantation: we have had that represented unto us which very much confirms the apprehensions wherewith the last article of that advice was given. We have received an instrument, signed by several score of persons concerned in your Village. Of which there seem to be six men and eleven women, communicants in the church; twenty-nine men householders, five men freeholders, seventeen young men, and sixteen other women—more than four score in all—wherein they express their despair of Mr. Parris's continuing with comfort or profit in the work of the ministry among you. And it is our own just fear, that such implacable offences be arisen, as do render Mr. Parris's removal necessary.

We cannot but think that so considerable a number of souls, as by the invincible temptations and prejudices which have happened among you, will probably be otherwise driven from joining with you in supporting the means of common edification, does call for you to consider what course may be most likely to maintain the kingdom of the Lord Jesus Christ, now threatened through your divisions to be taken from you.

But we think your best friends can't put you into any such course without your consenting that Mr. Parris do come away from his present station. And then your uniting, as far as you can, in calling another minister, and forgiving and forgetting all former grievances.

As for Mr. Parris, you know what care hath been taken to preserve his capacity of being further serviceable in other churches of Christ; and we have now particularly before us a probability of an opportunity, if he please to accept it, of doing elsewhere that service for which we do, with grief, see the door so far shut up among yourselves. 'Tis with all tenderness and affection, and not without utmost concern for his and your prosperity, that we lay these things before you; and recommending you to the mercy of the Lord, subscribe ourselves

Cambridge, May 6, 1695

Your servants in him,

To the Reverend Mr. Samuel Parris, pastor of the church in Salem Village. To be communicated unto the church.

INCREASE MATHER
CHARLES MORTON
MICHAEL WIGGLESWORTH
SAMUEL WILLARD
JABEZ FOX
JAMES SHERMAN
COTTON MATHER
NEHEMIAH WALTER
JONATHAN PIERPONT

The instrument mentioned by the abovesaid elders is as follows, *viz.:*

To the reverend elders of the churches at Boston, with other elders and brethren of other churches late of a council at Salem Village:

We whose names are under-subscribed are bold once more to trouble you with our humble proposals. That whereas there have been long and uncomfortable differences among us, chiefly relating to Mr. Parris; and we have, as we apprehend, attended all probable means for a composure of our troubles; and whereas we had hopes of an happy issue, by your endeavors among us, but now are utterly frustrated of our expectations; and that instead of uniting, our rent is made worse and our breach made wider. We humbly query, whether yourselves being straitened of time might not admit such satisfactory liberty of debating the whole case of our controversy, whereby yourselves had not so long an opportunity of understanding the case, nor the offended so much reason to be satisfied in your advice. We therefore humbly propose:

1. That if yourselves please to take the trouble with patience once more to hear the whole case, and give full liberty of proving and defending what may be charged on either hand, leaving it to yourselves to appoint both time and place;
2. Or that you will more plainly advise Mr. Parris, the case being so circumstanced that he cannot with comfort or profit to himself or others abide in the work of the ministry among us, to cease his labors and seek to dispose of himself elsewhere, as God in his providence may direct; and yourselves would please to help us in advising such a choice wherein we may be more unanimous—which we hope would tend to a composure of our differences;
3. Or that we may without offence take the liberty of calling some other approved minister of the gospel to preach the word of God to us and ours, and that we may not be denied our proportionable privilege in our public disbursements in the place.

So leaving the whole case with the Lord and yourselves, we subscribe our names.

Joseph Porter
Joseph Rea
Samuel Porter
Jonathan Tarbell
Jonathan Preston
Thomas Wilkins
Nathaniel Porter
Thomas Fuller
enjamin Swinnerton
Samuel Nurse

Joseph Holton
Rebecca Preston
Job Swinnerton
Sarah Andrew
Francis Nurse
Ruth Osborn
Joseph Porter
Elizabeth Rea
Joseph Hutchinson
Mary Braybrook

Jonathan Buxton
Joseph Herrick
Joseph Buxton
Mary Smith
Thomas Preston
Daniel Andrew
Elizabeth Putnam
Jonathan Ingersoll
Sarah Needom
Ely Porter
Abigail Flint
Samuel Nurse
Mary Holton
Samuel Byshop
Elizabeth Flint
Jonathan Byshop
Elizabeth Kettel
David Byshop
Mary Herrick
Mary Tarbell
William Buckley
Mary Nurse
William Byshop
Mary Raiment
Thomas Raimen
Edward Byshop
Isaac Needom
Samuel Upton
William Upton
Jonathan Holtin
Jonathan Flint
William Buckley

Daniel Andrew
Bethia Martin
Joseph Swinnerton
William Porter
Joanna Nickols
Jonathan Buxton
Sarah Holton
Alexandra Osburn
Lydia Hutchinson
Joseph Holton
Sarah Buckley
Joseph Rea
Esther Swinnerton
Henry Kenney
Mary Swinnerton
Thomas Wilkins
Hanah Wilkins
Jonathan Martin
Joseph Hutchinson
Samuel Braybrook
Abraham Smith
Elizabeth Porter
Joseph Pope
Elizabeth Swinnerton
tWidow Holt
Joseph Putnam
Joseph Flint
Benjamin Porter
William Small
James Kittel
Israel Porter
Jasper Swinnerton

The following paper (in answer to the aforesaid instrument, and classical letter from Cambridge) was brought by Deacon Putnam and several other of our brethren to the elders assembled at Boston at Mr. Willard's, May 29, 1695, being the day of election, after dinner—where was present the body of elders belonging to this province. *Viz.:*

Salem Village May 20, 1695
To the Reverend Mr. Increase Mather and other reverend elders which lately met at Cambridge:

Whereas by a letter from yourselves dated May 6, 1695, wherein you put us upon consideration how to maintain the religion of our Lord Jesus Christ threatened to be taken from us: we are not insensible of such threatenings; and for prevention hereof, we whose names are hereunto-subscribed are sensible that the removing of Mr. Parris from his present station will not unite us in calling another minister. For we are sensible that the removing of Mr. Parris will not [in] any way be for the upholding of the kingdom of God amongst us. For we have had three ministers removed already, and by every removal our differences have been rather aggravated. Therefore we justly fear that the removing of the fourth may rather prove the ruining of the interests of Christ amongst us, and leave us as sheep without a shepherd. Therefore we desire that Mr. Parris may continue in his present station.

JANE WILKINS
JONATHAN WALCOTT
SARAH WILKINS
THOMAS FLINT
MARY FULLER
JONATHAN WALCOTT SNR.
RUTH WILKINS
BENJAMIN HUTCHINSON
ELIZABETHWILKINS
JONATHAN DALE
MARY RICHARDS
WILLIAM ALLIN
SARAH MORALL
JONATHAN PUTNAM [III]
HANNAH STACY
JONATHAN WHELDON
SUSAN FULLER
JONATHAN WALCOTT, JNR.
SARAH GOODALE
ISAAC GOODALE JNR.
MARY WALCOTT
THOMAS HAINES
MARY GOODALE
GEORGE INGERSOLL
ELIZABETH GOODALE
BENJAMIN STACY
MARY HUTCHINSON
SARAH PUTNAM
ROBERT MORALL
ELIZABETH ALLIN

BRAY WILKINS
ANNA WILKINS
NATHANIEL PUTNAM
REBEKKA PUTNAM
JONATHAN PUTNAM,
RACHEL GRIGGS
WILLIAM GRIGGS
HANNAH INGERSOLL
NATHANIELINGERSOLL
HANNAH PUTNAM
HENRY WILKINS
PRISCILLA WILKINS
THOMAS PUTNAM
RUTH FULLER
BENJAMIN WILKINS
MARY PUTNAM
THOMAS FULLER, JUN.
MARY WAY
EDWARD PUTNAM
LIDIA PUTNAM
AARON WAY
ABAGAIL WALCOTT
JONATHAN PUTNAM
MARY SIBLY
ABRAHAM WALCOTT
ELIZABETH FLINT
SAMUEL WILKINS, JNR.
PRISCILLA WALCOTT
PERCIS WAY
JONATHAN FULLER

SAMUEL ABBY	SARAH PUTNAM
MARY GOODALE	ZECHARIAH GOODALE, JUN.
GEORGE FLINT	ABAGAIL CHEEVER
HANNAH PUTNAM	JONATHAN HUTCHINSON
SAMUEL SIBLY	ELIZABETH PRESCOT
ABAGAIL LAIN	HENRY HOLTON
BENJAMIN PUTNAM	HANNAH PUTNAM
ELIZABETH DALE	WILLIAM WAY
FRANCIS ELIOTT	MARY WHELDON
SUSAN BYSHOP	JOSEPH GOODALE
JAMES PUTNAM	DELIVERANCE WALCOTT
RUTH REA	JONATHAN HADLOCK
EZEKIAL CHEEVER	SARAH FULLER
ABIGAIL ELIOT	HENRY BROWN
PETER PRESCOT	ABAGAIL HOLTON
JANE HUTCHINSON	ELIAZAR PUTNAM
JONATHAN PUTNAM, JUN.	MARY DARLIN
JONATHAN REA	JOSEPH WHIPPLE
SARAH HADLOCK	SAMUEL LANE
JONATHAN WILKINS	SARAH PRINCE
JOSEPH PRINCE	HANNAH BROWN
JAMES PRINCE	EDWARD BYSHOP
ZECHARIAH GOODALE, SEN.	

June 3, 1695

The brethren being met as abovesaid appointed, the pastor acquainted them that here were two messengers from Suffield who were looking out for a minister, and by the direction of some elders in Boston made application to myself who was willing to go with them if the brethren pleased; and in my absence for a few months, they might try if they could (with others who now dissented) to unite in some other minister. But after several hours debate, both with the brethren and some other Christian neighbors, they all declared an averseness to my motion. Whereupon thanking them for their professed love to me, I told them I was not free to go without their consent; and seeing they would not let me go, I pressed them to keep me, and make much of me.

Salem Village, June 3, 1695
Reverend Sirs:

We cannot fault the intendment of our brethren, Seargent David Winchill and Corporal Victory Sikes, messengers from Suffield, sent by yourselves to obtain the ministry of our pastor, if we were so minded as to part with him. But upon a meeting together this day both of the church and others (warned yesterday, being Lord's day) to concert that affair, do hereby signify, at the desire of abovesaid Suffield messengers, that with unanimous agreement—not one excepted (save the four known dissenters)—we are resolved, God helping, against such a separation during our ability to prevent it; and our pastor, though otherwise inclined, yet is unwilling to leave so many of his flock as testify so strong affection toward him. So earnestly requesting the constant help of your prayers, and as much otherwise as you can, we rest, worthy and much-esteemed Sirs,

TO THE REVEREND MR. INCREASE MATHER AND
MR. COTTON MATHER, IN BOSTON
YOUR NEEDY BRETHREN, SAMUEL PARRIS, PASTOR
IN THE NAME OF THE CHURCH AND OTHER CHRISTIAN NEIGHBORS

Oct. 5, 1695

Brother Cloyes came to me desiring a letter of dismission of himself and wife from our church to the church of Marlborough.

Lord's day—Oct. 6, 1695

After the sacrament the abovesaid Brother Cloyes's request was propounded to the brethren, and his dismission together with his wife as desired was voted by the major part.

Salem Village, Oct. 8, 1695
To the Reverend and much-esteemed the pastor and beloved brethren of the Church at Marlborough in New England:

Whereas our Brother Peter Cloyes, for himself and wife (our sister) Sarah Cloyes, hath desired dismission unto yourselves, unto whom by divine providence they are (as we are informed) now become near neighbors: the same request being the last Lord's day propounded to the church here was readily consented unto. So begging all fullness of blessings upon yourselves through our Lord Jesus, and most earnestly requesting the help of your constant and fervent prayers for us,

TO THE REVD. MR.—BRINSMEED,
PASTOR TO THE CHURCH AT
MARLBOROUGH
YOUR NEEDY BRETHREN, SAMUEL PARRIS, PASTOR
IN THE NAME OF THE CHURCH

Oct. 9 1695

I sealed and left the abovesaid letter for brother Cloyes at his cousin Tarbell's, as he desired.

Oct. 10 1695

Brother Cloyes brought me back the letter abovesaid, saying it was a letter of recommendation and not of dismission that he desired.

April 9, 1696

At a church-meeting at brother Thomas Putnam's house, warned at the last sacrament, voted that our brethren John Putnam Snr. and Nathaniel Putnam and Deacon Putnam and John Putnam Jnr. be appointed to meet as many of the dissenters when Colonel Gedney of Salem shall appoint himself being Moderator, to treat in order to an amicable issue. And I acquainted the church that I intended to hold my station not after my year was up, etc.

Salem Village, Apr. 13, 1696
Colonel Gedney:

Sir, upon a motion from yourself sent [by] Captain Putnam and Deacon Putnam to this church, that we would chose and send some brethren to treat with as many of our dissenters (yourself being moderator) in order to an amicable issue for the future, upon condition that I would surcease my min isterial station here. The same being agitated at a church-meeting the ninth instant, the abovesaid Captain and Deacon, together with Lieutenant Putnam and his son John, were accordingly made choice of to meet—when and where you shall appoint for that purpose: Myself, then and now, promising full purpose to attend the same, if I possibly can and have timely notice. I am unwilling to hinder the good of the place, and if my remove may be beneficial, let the church be provided for, and myself be fairly dealt with in payment of all my dues, I shall readily gratify those who are so earnest for my giving way.

To the Honored Bartholomew
Gedney, Esq. in Salem
These per Deacon Putnam
Your servant, Samuel Parris

April 20th, 1696

At a church-meeting at Deacon Ingersoll's (warned yesterday, being Lord's day): Voted (upon a motion sent to us from the Honored Colonel Gedney of Salem, who was willing to advocate between the two parties in this Village) that our brethren Lieutenant Nathaniel Putnam, Captain John Putman, Jonathan Putman, and Benjamin Putman, together with our pastor, be fully empowered to discourse, conclude, and agree with as many of our dissenting brethren and neighbors, who likewise shall be fully empowered by the rest of their party, in writing under their hands, to agree and conclude on their part according to the tenor of the following propositions. (All of whom so chosen on both parts are to choose artibrators to determine, if need be, the second proposition.) *Viz.:*

1. That the pastor's disbursements on the ministry land and buildings shall be duly re-paid by the inhabitants, each his proportion.
2. That as to said pastor's arrears for maintenance, we do engage to pay the whole thereof to him, or what shall be awarded by four men, each party choosing two to hear and determine what thereof shall be paid. And if those four so chosen agree not among themselves, then the same four to choose a fifth. And what shall be awarded by any three of those five so elected, shall be made good and paid by all the inhabitants, each his proportion, according as he shall be found to have fallen short of paying his part thereof.
3. That all persons, both of church and other inhabitants, shall attend the directions of our law in calling and settling some able, pious, and orthodox minister in the place, and procuring him to enter and engage himself therein.
4. That upon the fair and full performance of all the abovesaid propositions, our pastor then to attend the providence of God in removing, or to acquit his ministerial station amongst us.

An extract of the abovesaid premises was the same day sent to Colonel Gedney, per Benjamin Putnam.

Parris wrote no more in the church record book, except for a last entry about letters of dismission for two church members. However, he remained in Salem Village for another year. The legal records show that he fought hard for as much financial compensation as he could get. Eventually, in July 1697, the matter went to a final arbitration before Wait Winthrop, Elisha Cooke, and Samuel Sewall. There follows the petition from John Tarbell, Samuel Nurse, Joseph Putnam, and Daniel

Andrew, to the arbitrators, then comes the account of the meeting that finally settled the dispute, and lastly Parris's long-awaited letter of resignation, in the form of the abandonment of his claim to the minister's house.

Petition of John Tarbell, Samuel Nurse, Joseph Putnam, and Daniel Andrew

To the Honorable Wait Winthrop, Elisha Cook, and Samuel Sewall, Esquires, arbitrators, indifferently chosen, between Mr. Samuel Parris and the inhabitants of Salem Village.

The remonstrances of several aggrieved persons in the said Village, with further reasons why they conceive they ought not to hear Mr. Parris, nor to own him as a minister of the gospel, nor to contribute any support to him as such for several years past, humbly offered as fit for consideration.

We humbly conceive that, having, in April, 1693, given our reasons why we could not join with Mr. Parris in prayer, preaching, or sacrament, if these reasons are found sufficient for our withdrawing (and we cannot yet find but they are), then we conceive ourselves virtually discharged, not only in conscience, but also in law, which requires maintenance to be given to such as are orthodox and blameless; and said Mr. Parris having been teaching such dangerous errors, and preached such scandalous immoralities, as ought to discharge any (though ever so gifted otherways) from the work of the ministry, particularly in his oath against the lives of several, wherein he swears that the prisoners with their looks knock down those pretended sufferers. We humbly conceive that he that swears to more than he is certain of, is equally guilty of perjury with him that swears to what is false. And though they did fall at such a time, yet it could not be known that they did it, much less could they be certain of it; yet did swear positively against the lives of such as he could not have any knowledge but they might be innocent.

His believing the devil's accusations, and readily departing from all charity to persons, though of blameless and godly lives, upon such suggestions; his promoting such accusations; as also his partiality therein in stifling the accusations of some, and, at the same time, vigilantly promoting others,—as we conceive, are just causes for our refusal, &c.

That Mr. Parris's going to Mary Walcott or Abigail Williams, and directing others to them, to know who afflicted the people in their illnesses,—we understand this to be a dealing with them that have a familiar spirit, and an implicit denying the providence of God, who alone, as we believe, can send afflictions, or cause devils to afflict any: this we also conceive sufficient to justify such refusal.

That Mr. Parris, by these practices and principles, has been the beginner and procurer of the sorest afflictions, not to this village only, but to this whole country, that did ever befall them.

We, the subscribers, in behalf of ourselves, and of several others of the same mind with us (touching these things), having some of us had our relations by these practices taken off by an untimely death; others have been imprisoned and suffered in our persons, reputations, and estates,—submit the whole to your honors' decision, to determine whether we are or ought to be any ways obliged to honor, respect, and support such an instrument of our miseries; praying God to guide your honors to act herein as may be for his glory, and the future settlement of our village in amity and unity.

JOHN TARBELL,
SAMUEL NURSE,
JOSEPH PUTNAM,
DANIEL ANDREW,
ATTORNEYS FOR THE PEOPLE OF THE VILLAGE

Boston, July 21, 1697

Vote of Salem-Village Inhabitants, September 14, 1697

At a general meeting of the inhabitants of Salem Village the 14th of September, 1697, it was agreed and voted that the committee in being shall raise a rate of seventy nine pounds, nine shillings and six pence money upon the whole inhabitants of this Village, and shall also gather the same and pay it to Lieutenant Nathaniel Putnam; Daniel Andrew, Senior; Joseph Herrick, Senior; Thomas Putnam; and Joseph Putnam, or either of them, that so they or either of them may pay the same to Mr. Samuel Parris, his heirs or assigns, according to the award, decree, and determination of the honourable Wait Winthrop, Elisha Cooke, and Samuel Sewall, Esqrs., arbitrators between Mr. Samuel Parris and the inhabitants of this village.

At a general meeting of the inhabitants of Salem Village, the 14th of September, 1697, it was agreed and voted that Lieutenant Nathaniel Putnam; Daniel Andrew; Joseph Herrick, Senior; Thomas Putnam; and Joseph Putnam, or the major part of them, are hereby chosen and empowered to be collectors, with as full power as ever any of our committees have, to collect and gather in all the averages of Mr. Parris's rates, and to pay the same to Mr. Samuel Parris, his heirs or assigns, according to the award, decree, and determination of the honourable Wait Winthrop, Elisha Cooke, and Samuel

Sewall, Esqrs., arbitrators between Mr. Samuel Parris and the inhabitants of this Village.

Deed: Samuel Parris to the Salem-Village Trustees [September 24, 1697]

Know all men by these presents, that I, Samuel Parris, late of Salem in the County of Essex in the Province of Massachusetts Bay in New England, clerk, for divers good causes and considerations me thereunto moving, but more especially for and in consideration that, whereas Nathaniel Putnam, Daniel Andrew, Joseph Herrick, Thomas Putnam, and Joseph Putnam, all of Salem aforesaid, for and in behalf of the inhabitants of Salem Village, did agree with myself to leave all controversies, matters, and things whatsoever depending betwixt said Village and myself unto the final determination of Wait Winthrop, Elisha Cooke, and Samuel Sewall, Esqrs, of Boston, being arbitrators mutually chosen betwixt the said inhabitants and myself, and whereas, also, among other things contained in the award of the said arbitrators, given under their hands and seals the thirtieth day of August, 1697, they did award and determine that I, the said Parris, should give unto the said Nathaniel Putnam, Daniel Andrew, Joseph Herrick, Thomas Putnam, and Joseph Putnam, for and in behalf of the inhabitants of said Village, a deed or instrument of release, in writing under my hand and seal, duly executed and acknowledged, of all right, interest, title, pretention, claim and demand of, in, or unto the messuage or tenement known by the name of the ministry house and land in said Village, and dependencies thereof, or to any part or parcel of the same, and to the copper in the lean-to of said house, know ye therefore, that for the consideration aforesaid, I, the said Samuel Parris, do for myself, my heirs, executors, and administrators remiss, release, and surrender and forever quit claim to the said tenement situated in Salem Village, as also unto all of the land purchased by said Village of Joseph Holton of Salem, with all the dependencies thereto belonging, called or known by the name of the ministry house and land, as also to the copper hung or set up in the lean-to of said house. . . .

SAMUEL PARRIS

During that last year in Salem Village, Samuel Parris's wife died. In the autumn of 1697 he went to the remote outpost of Stow where, in November, the inhabitants (a mere twenty-eight families) offered him a job. He demanded more pay than they were offering and, almost incredibly, the ownership of the minister's house! They agreed to the first but wisely not to the second.

It has been claimed that the chief signs of what is called "antisocial personality disorder" are absence of guilt and shame and an inability to learn from experience. Parris was, to use another word for the condition, a sociopath. The sufferer appears rational and can live a life in society, often supporting a family and holding down a job, but lacks empathy, that is, insight into, and concern for, other people's feelings and needs. In other words, for all his preaching about good and evil, saints and devils. Parris lacked a conscience.

His *Meditations for Peace* shows he knew how to put on a conciliatory front if he had to. But he achieved nothing by this exercise in the long run. Sociopaths are good at using wiles and charm to extricate themselves from immediate danger but cannot plan for the future since their lack of empathy leads to extremely poor judgment.

After a year at Stow, Parris demanded yet more money, including five pounds for firewood! The inhabitants refused. By this time he had married a well-to-do widow, Dorothy Noyes, and was in a position to quit. However, the couple soon had four children and money became tight again. Parris tried his hand at retailing, speculating, farming, and teaching, with, as always, small success. He died leaving small debts to nearly thirty people. Buried in Sudbury, Massachusetts, where he had spent his last years, he was given no obituaries and no epitaph.

We do not know if Abigail Williams, Parris's daughter Betty and other children by Elizabeth accompanied him to Stow. We do know Betty married, in 1710. Abigail may be the unfortunate afflicted girl about whom John Hale wrote in *A Modest Enquiry,* "And she was afterward followed with diabolical molestations to her death; and so died a single person."

5

George Burroughs (1650–1692)

After graduating from Harvard in 1670, George Burroughs returned to Roxbury, Massachusetts, where he had lived since his mother had brought him as a small boy from Virginia. He was born in England but the family soon emigrated. In 1673 he married his first wife, Hannah, and, in 1674, found employment as a minister in Casco, an outpost in Maine. Its inhabitants included Anglicans as well as Puritans and had submitted to the rule of Massachusetts only for the sake of extra defense against the Indians. However, the Boston rulers felt threatened by the religious tolerance in the area and were remiss in providing the protection they had promised. They had no love for George Burroughs, who ministered to all faiths, was never ordained, and failed even to have his own children baptized (except the first). In August 1676 an all-out Indian assault left more than thirty of Casco's settlers either captured or killed. George Burroughs escaped, in due course reaching Salisbury, Massachusetts.

Letter from Bryan Pendleton to Governor Leverett of Massachusetts, August 13, 1676

Honored Governor together with the Council

I am sorry my pen must be the messenger of so great a tragedy. On the 11th of this instant, we heard of many killed of our neighbors in Falmouth, or Casco Bay, and on the 12th instant, Mr. Josselyn sent me [a] brief letter written from under the hand of Mr. Burroughs the minister. He gives an account of thirty two killed and carried away by the Indians. Himself escaped to an island—but I hope Black Point men have fetched him off by this time—ten men, six women, sixteen children. Anthony and Thomas Brackett, Mr. Munjoy his son only are named.

BRYAN PENDLETON
WINTER HARBOR AT NIGHT THE 13TH OF AUGUST 1676

Burroughs spent four years in Salisbury. From there he went as minister to Salem Village, about twenty-five miles to the south. Since the parsonage needed repairs, he and his family stayed for nine months with John and Rebecca Putnam. In 1681, Burroughs's wife died. The minister had to borrow money for the funeral and used a credit arrangement with Putnam, whereby his debts would be set against his salary. By 1683 this last was no longer being paid. Burroughs left the village, having accepted the offer of a post back in Casco, now rebuilt. The Putnams took his sudden departure very badly. On May 2, Burroughs returned to the village for a meeting at which his debts to Putnam were to be measured against what the village owed him, and all accounts settled. At that meeting, Putnam had Burroughs arrested for debt.

There follow three accounts of the incident, by witnesses, in the form of depositions to the court. Burroughs's cool-headed, even witty response to his arrest, saying that he had no goods but "there was his body," may have rubbed salt in the Putnams' wound. They may have been reminded that Burroughs was a Harvard graduate and gentleman while they were mere farmers.

Depositions to the County Court, in the case of Lieutenant John Putnam versus Mr. George Burroughs, June, 1683

Deposition by Nathaniel Ingersoll and Samuel Silby

Action of debt for two gallons of canary wine, and cloth, etc., brought of Mr. Gedney on John Putnam's account, for the funeral of Mrs. Burroughs. We, whose names are underwritten, testify and say, that at a public meeting of the people of Salem Farms [Village], April 24, 1683, we heard a letter read, which letter was sent from the court. After the said letter was read, Mr. Burroughs came in. After the said Burroughs had been a while in, he asked "whether they took up with the advice of the court, given in the letter, or whether they rejected it." The moderator made answer, "Yes, we take up with it;" and not a man contradicted it to any of our hearing. After this was passed, was a discourse of settling accounts between the said Burroughs and the inhabitants, and issuing things in peace, and parting in love, as they came together in love. Further, we say that the second, third, and fourth days of the following week were agreed upon by Mr. Burroughs and the people to be the days for every man to come in and to reckon with the said Burroughs; and so they adjourned the meeting to the last of the aforesaid three days, in the afternoon, then to make up the whole account in public.

We further testify and say, that, May the second, 1683, Mr. Burroughs and the inhabitants met at the meeting-house to make up accounts in public, according to their agreement the meeting before; and, just as the said Burroughs began to give in his accounts, the marshal came in, and, after a while, went up to John Putnam, Snr., and whispered to him, and said Putnam said to him, "You know what you have to do: do your office." Then the marshal came to Mr. Burroughs, and said, "Sir, I have a writing to read to you." Then he read the attachment, and demanded goods. Mr. Burroughs answered, "that he had no goods to show, and that he was now reckoning with the inhabitants, for we know not yet who is in debt, but there was his body." As we were ready to go out of the meeting-house, Mr. Burroughs said, "Well, what will you do with me?" Then the marshall went to John Putnam, Snr., and said to him, "What shall I do?" The said Putnam replied, "You know your business." And then the said Putnam went to his brother, Thomas Putnam, and pulled him by the coat; and they went out of the house together, and presently came in again. Then said John Putnam, "Marshall, take your prisoner, and have him up to the ordinary,—that is a public house,—and secure him till the morning."

NATHANIEL INGERSOLL, AGED ABOUT FIFTY
SAMUEL SIBLEY, AGED ABOUT TWENTY-FOUR

To the first of these, I, John Putnam, Jr., testify, being at the meeting.

The Testimony of Thomas Haynes, aged thirty-two years or thereabouts

Testifieth and saith, that, at a meeting of the inhabitants of Salem Farms, May the second, 1683, after the marshall had read John Putnam's attachment to Mr. Burroughs, then Mr. Burroughs asked Putnam "what money it was he attached him for." John Putnam answered, "For five pounds and odd money at Shippen's at Boston, and for thirteen shillings at his father Gedney's, and for twenty-four shillings at Mrs. Darby's;" that then Nathaniel Ingersoll stood up, and said, "Lieutenant, I wonder that you attach Mr. Burroughs for the money at Darby's and your father Gedney's, when, to my knowledge, you and Mr. Burroughs have reckoned and balanced accounts two or three times since, as you say, it was due, and you never made any mention of it when you reckoned with Mr. Burroughs." John Putnam answered, "It is true, and I own it." Samuel Sibley, aged twenty-four years or thereabouts, testifieth to all above written.

The Testimony of Nathaniel Ingersoll

Testifieth, that I heard Mr. Burroughs ask Lieutenant John Putnam to give him a bill to Mr. Shippen. The said Putnam asked the said Burroughs how much he would take up at Mr. Shippen's. Mr. Burroughs said it might be five pounds; but, after the said Burroughs had considered a little, he said to the said Putnam, "It may be it might come to more:" therefore he would have him give him a bill to the value of five or six pounds,—when Putnam answered, it was all one to him. Then the said Putnam went and writ it, and read it to Mr. Burroughs, and said to him that it should go for part of the £33. 6s. 8d. for which he had given a bill to him in behalf of the inhabitants. I, Hannah Ingersoll, aged forty-six years or thereabouts, testify the same.

The marshal released Burroughs on bail. Later, the case was withdrawn. The Putnams had been thoroughly humiliated by the failure of their ploy to land the minister in jail.

Return of the marshall to the court

I have attached the body of George Burroughs he tendered to me,—for he said he had no pay,—and taken bonds to the value of fourteen pounds money, and read this to him.

Per me, Henry Skerry, Marshall.

We whose names are underwritten do bind ourselves jointly and severally to Henry Skerry, Marshall of Salem, our heirs, executors, and administrators, in the sum of fourteen pounds money, that George Burroughs shall appear at the next court at Salem, to answer to Lieutenant John Putnam, according to the summons of this attachment, and to abide the order of the court therein, and not to depart without license; as witness our hands this 2nd of May, 1683.

GEORGE BURROUGHS
NATHANIEL INGERSOLL
JOHN BUXTON
THOMAS HAYNES
SAMUEL SIBLEY
WILLIAM SIBLEY
WILLIAM IRELAND, JR.

During his time in Salem Village, Burroughs had married Sarah Ruck, the daughter of the prosperous Ruck family of Salem and young widow of William Hathorne, John Hathorne's brother. There is reason to believe that the Ruck and Hathorne families disapproved of the marriage. It could also have inspired envy on the part of the Putnams, since Sarah was rich and well connected. (Though she seems not to have had access to her money during her marriage.) When George, with Sarah and his three daughters by his first wife, arrived in Casco, the town officials asked him if he would swap most of the 200 acres of land he owned for less valuable property. He replied that they were welcome to the 150 acres they asked for, without need to give other land in exchange.

Over the next nine years Burroughs and Sarah had four sons. In 1689 Indian attacks began again and the settlements north of Casco were abandoned. On September 21 Casco itself was attacked. The Massachusetts authorities had for once sent reinforcements and their leader, Major Benjamin Church, wrote of Burroughs, "As for the minister of this place. I am well satisfied with him, he being present with us yesterday in the fight." Burroughs was the only minister left in Casco and the only one of two left in Maine. In 1690, with another attack imminent, he took his children to the town of Wells, which was better defended. His wife Sarah had recently died. Casco was destroyed and Wells too was in danger. Burroughs was one of the signers (varying in number between six and nine) of the following letters to the Council in Boston, pleading for help.

Letters from George Burroughs and also signed by eight other people to the Governor's Council in Boston, dated, respectively, July 21, 1691, September 28, 1691 and January 27, 1692

July 21, 1691

We being the front of all the eastern part of the country, remotely situated, for strength weak, and the enemy beating upon us, we can think of no other but we are fair for ruin, and humbly conceive your honors are sensible of it. . . . The thirteenth of June last the enemy killed and drove away upwards of 100 head of cattle, besides sheep and horses; some of our corn is lost, and more in great hazard, we therefore, distressed, make our humble address to your honors for men, with provision and ammunition for the strengthening of our town . . . also that there may be a magazine in the province that supplies may be near, whereby time will be redeemed, soldiers encouraged and opportunity improved against the enemy; also that there be an effectual care taken, that the inhabitants of this province may not quit their places without liberty first obtained from legal authority; thus encouraging ourselves with the hopes that your honors will timely answer us herein, that so we and the rest of this poor province in great hazard, may yet stand, which may be to the honor of God, the interest of his majesty, and of the country, we rest, your honored humble servants.

September 28, 1691

Whereas it hath pleased God (both formerly and now) to let loose the heathen upon us by holding us off from our improvements, keeping us in close garrison, and daily lying in wait to take any that go forth, whereby we are brought very low. . . . The corn raised in the town is [not] judged enough to keep the inhabitants themselves one half year, and our stocks of cattle and swine are very much diminished. We therefore humbly request your honors to continue soldiers among us and appoint a commander over them, and what number shall be judged meet to remain with us for winter, that provisions, corn and clothing suitable for them be seasonably sent, also one hogshead of salt, all ours being spent; also [the] present supply in what was sent before is almost gone. We had a youth seventeen years of age last Saturday carried away, who went (not above gunshot) from Lieutenant Storer's garrison to fetch a little, wood in his arms. We have desired our loving friends, Captain John Littlefield and ensign John Hill, to present this to your honors, who can give a further account of our condition.

January 27, 1692

We doubt not but your honors (before now) have received the sorrowful tidings of the death and captivity of above an hundred persons at York, of the burning of houses, the killing and wounding of cattle, sheep, and horses Jan 25th by the Indians, in number one hundred, or supposed to be there-about, both by those of the town who saw them, and by a captive youth who made his escape from them, as the beholding of the pillars of smoke, the raging of the merciless flames, the insults of the heathen enemy, shooting, hacking (not having regard to the earnest supplication of men, women or children, with sharp cries and bitter tears in most humble manner) and dragging away others (and none to help) is most affecting the heart. . . . God is still manifesting his displeasure against this land, he who formerly hath set his hand to help us, doth even write bitter things against us. The course of God's most sweet and rich promises, and gracious providences may justly be interrupted by the sins of his people. We desire humbly (in the first place) to make address to God (the God of all grace and mercy) and nextly to your honors who cannot but be sensible of the low condition and eminent danger we are in. We therefore humbly entreat your honors to consider us, and take some speedy course for our standing, that there may be not only a sufficient strength to help garrison, and defend the town, but also to issue out upon, and pursue the enemy, to their discouragement, if not destruction; that there may be also a full supply, for having spent so long upon our own provision we are brought very short. If some such course be not taken we must of necessity draw off; and if it must come to that, we entreat your honours' assistance. This day two Indians came into Wells with a flag of truce and said; if the English will come to Saccadehoc (in a fortnight's time, three weeks as the outside) they may redeem their captives. The Lord sit in counsel with your honors; the Lord set his eyes upon us for good, and build us, and not pull us down, and plant us, and not pluck us up, are the hearty prayers of your honor's most humble servants.

In May 1692 Jonathan Partridge, field marshal of Maine, arrived in Wells with a little band of soldiers. George Burroughs must have thought these were the vanguard of the longed-for reinforcements. Instead, they had come to arrest him.

A series of documents shows the working out of the plot, hatched by Thomas Putnam and his brothers and followed through with the help of Jonathan Walcott, the afflicted girls, the magistrates, several members of the Ruck family, the deputy governor of Massachusetts, and others, to have Burroughs hanged. The first is a tantalizing letter from Thomas Putnam to John Hathorne and Jonathan Corwin, which can only refer to Ann Putnam's visions of Burroughs and his wives. The next is the formal complaint to the magistrate from Thomas Putnam and Jonathan Walcott. Then comes a letter from one Elisha Hutchinson, saying he has received an order to apprehend Burroughs from the governor and Council. It would no doubt have been William Stoughton, the deputy governor, who issued that order. There follows the arrest warrant, the minutes of Burroughs's examination—by William Stoughton, John Hathorne, Samuel Sewall, and Jonathan Corwin—the indictments, the summonses, and the account of the physical examination and the depositions. The first five of these last testify to Burroughs's supposedly supernatural strength. All they prove is that Burroughs had a reputation for athleticism, which he himself probably encouraged. The next two depositions testify to his supposedly magical powers. Then comes Ann Putnam's blood-curdling account of her visions of Burroughs's dead wives. It is chilling to think that a twelve-year-old girl was made to produce such stuff. The depositions of Mercy Lewis, Sarah Bibber, Elizabeth Hubbard, Susannah Sheldon, and Mary Walcott are similar, adding personal touches. Mercy Lewis, who had been taken in by Burroughs when her parents were murdered by Indians in Casco, claimed that he offered her a book to sign that he said had been in his study but that she had never actually seen there. She claimed Burroughs took her to a mountaintop and promised her all the kingdoms of the earth. Like all the girls, she knew her New Testament.

How many grains of truth about Burroughs's character—such as harsh treatment of his wives—there may be in these and other depositions, we cannot know. All that is clear is that the Putnams had pulled out all the stops to get him hanged.

Letter of Thomas Putnam to John Hathorne and Jonathan Corwin

Salem Village, this 21st of April, 1692

Much honored:

After most humble and hearty thanks presented to your honors for the great care and pains you have already taken for us, for which we are never able to make you recompense (and we believe you do not expect it of us; therefore a full reward will be given you of the Lord God of Israel, whose cause and interest you have espoused and we trust this shall add to your crown of glory in the day of the Lord Jesus); and we, beholding continually the tremendous words of divine providence—not only every day but every hour—though it is our duty to inform your Honors of what we conceive you have not heard, which are high and dreadful: of a wheel within a wheel, at which our ears do tingle.

Humbly craving continually your prayers and help in this distressed case, so praying almighty God continually to prepare you, that you may be a terror to evil-doers and a praise to them that do well, we remain yours to serve in what we are able.

THOMAS PUTNAM

Complaint, letter, arrest warrant, examination, deposition, and indictments to the Court of Oyer and Terminer, regarding George Burroughs

Complaint v. George Burroughs, Lydia Dustin, Susannah Martin, Dorcas Hoar, Sarah Morey, and Phillip English
Salem, April 30 1692

There being complaint this day made before us by Captain Jonathan Walcott and Sergeant Thomas Putnam of Salem Village, on behalf of their Majesties, for themselves, and also for several of their neighbours against George Burroughs, minister in Wells in the province of Maine, Lydia Dusting in Reading, widow, Susanah Martin of Amesbury, widow, Dorcas Hoar of Beverly, widow, and Sarah Murrell of Beverly, and Phillip English of Salem, merchant, for high suspicion of sundry acts of witchcraft done or committed by them upon the bodies of Mary Walcott, Mercy Lewis, Abigail Williams, Ann Putnam and Elizabeth Hubbard and Susannah Sheldon, viz, upon some or all of them, of Salem Village or Farms, whereby great hurt and damage [has] been done to the bodies of said persons above named, therefore crave justice.

SIGNED BY BOTH THE COMPLAINERS
JONATHAN WALCOTT
THOMAS PUTNAM
ABOVESAID

The abovesaid Complaint was exhibited before us this 30th April 1692
JOHN HATHORNE
JONATHAN CORWIN
ASSISTANTS

Letter of Elisha Hutchinson

Portsmouth, May 2. 1692
Gentlemen,

I received an order from the Governor & Council to apprehend Mr. George Burroughs, at present preacher at Wells, to be sent to Salem, there to be examined, being suspected to have confederacy with the devil in oppressing sundry persons about your town of Salem. Accordingly I have sent him by John Partridge, marshal of this province, except [unless] he meet with any other authority that will commit him to some other officer to be conveyed as above, he pleading it will be to his damage to go so far, I am

YOUR HUMBLE SERVANT
ELISHA HUTCHINSON

Arrest warrant

To Jonathan Partridge, Field M arshal,

You are required in their Majesties' names to aprehend the body of Mr. George Burroughs, at present preacher at Wells in the province of Maine, & convey him with all speed to Salem before the magistrates there, to be examined, he being suspected for a confederacy with the devil in oppressing of sundry about Salem as they relate. I having received particular order from the Governor & Council of their Majesties' Colony of Massachussetts, for the same, you may not fail herein,

DATED IN PORTSMOUTH IN THE PROVINCE OF NEW HAMPSHIRE
APRIL 30TH 1692
ELISHA HUTCHINSON MAJOR

By virtue of this warrant I apprehended said George Burroughs and have brought him to Salem and delivered him to the authority there this fourth day of May 1692

JOHN PARTRIDGE, FIELD MARSHAL OF THE
PROVINCE OF NEW HAMPSHIRE AND MAINE

Minutes of examination of George Burroughs

The examination of George Burroughs. 9. May. 1692

William Stoughton
John Hathorne
Honoured Samuel Sewall
Jonathan Corwin, Esqs

Being asked when he partook of the Lord's supper, he being (as he said) in full communion at Roxbury, he answered it was so long since, he could not tell: yet he owned he was at meeting one Sabbath at Boston part of the day, & the other at Charlestown part of a Sabbath when that sacrament happened to be at both, yet did not partake of either. He denied that his house at Casco was haunted, yet he owned there were toads. He denied that he made his wife swear, that she should not write to her father Ruck without his approbation of her letter to her father. He owned that none of his children, but the eldest was baptized. The abovesaid was in private, none of the bewitched being present. At his entry into the room, many, if not all, of the bewitched, were grievously tortured.

Susannah Sheldon testified that Burroughs' two wives appeared in their winding sheets, & said that man killed them.

He was bid to look upon Susannah Sheldon

He looked back & knocked down all, or most, of the afflicted who stood behind him.

Mercy Lewis' deposition going to be read, & he looked upon her & she fell into a dreadful & tedious fit.

MARY WALCOTT
ELIZABETH HUBBARD

Testimony going to be read & they all fell into fits.

SUSANNAH SHELDON
ANN PUTNAM JUNIOR

Affirmed each of them that he brought the book & would have them write.

Being asked what he thought of these things, he answered it was an amazing & humbling providence, but he understood nothing of it & he said, some of you may observe, that, when they begin to name my name, they cannot name it.

ANN PUTNAM JUNIOR
SUSANNAH SHELDON

Testified that his 2 wives & 2 children did accuse him.

The bewitched were so tortured that authority ordered them to be taken away, some of them.

Sarah Bibber testified that he had hurt her, though she had not seen him personally before, as [far as] she knew.

ABIGAIL HOBBS
DELIVERANCE HOBBS
ELIZA KEYSER

Testimony read.

CAPTAIN WILLARD
JONATHAN BROWN
JONATHAN WHELDON

Testimony about his great strength & the gun.

Captain Putnam testified about the gun.

Captain Wormwood testified about the gun & the molasses. He denied that, about the molasses. About the gun, he said he took it before the lock and rested it upon his breast.

John Brown testified about a barrel of cider.

He denied that his family was affrighted by a white calf in his house.

Captain Putnam testified that he made his wife enter into a covenant, 11 May 1692.

Abigail Hobbs, in prison, affirmed that George Burroughs in his shape appeared to her, & urged her to set her hand to the book, which she did, & afterwards in his own person he acknowledged to her, that he had made her set her hand to the book.

The original minutes (of which the above is a true copy) is in the possession of I. F. Andrews Esq. & was found among Judge Hathorne's papers.

AUG. 8. 1843
I B CURWEN

Indictment no 1.

Anno Regis et Reginae Willim et
Mariae nunc: Angliae &c Quarto

Essex ss. The jurors for our Sovereign Lord and Lady the King and Queen presents that George Burroughs, late of Falmouth within the province of the Massachussets Bay in New England, clerk, the ninth day of May, in the fourth year of the reign of our Sovereign Lord and Lady William and Mary, by the Grace of God, of England, Scotland, France and Ireland, King and Queen, defenders of the faith etc., divers other days and times as well before as after, certain detestable arts called witchcraft & sorceries, wickedly and feloniously hath used, practiced & exercised, at and within the township of Salem in the county of Essex & aforesaid, in, upon & against one Elizabeth Hubbard of Salem in the County of Essex, single woman—by which said wicked arts the said Elizabeth Hubbard, the ninth day of May—in the fourth year abovesaid and divers other days and times as well before as after, was and is tortured, afflicted, pined, consumed, wasted and tormented, also for sundry other acts of witchcrafts by said George Burroughs, committed and done against the peace of our Sovereign Lord & Lady, the King & Queen, their crown and dignity, and against the form of the statute in that case made & Provided:

WITNESSES
ELIZABETH HUBBARD
MARY WALCOTT
ANN PUTNAM

Indictment no 2.

Anno Regis et Reginae Willim et Mariae nunc: Angliae &c Quarto

Essex ss. The jurors for our Sovereign Lord and Lady, the King and Queen, presents that George Burroughs, late of Falmouth in the province of the Massachussets Bay in New England—clerk—The ninth day of May in the fourth year of the reign of our Sovereign Lord and Lady William and Mary, by the Grace of God, of England, Scotland, France and Ireland, King and Queen, defenders of the faith etc., and divers other days and times, as well before as after certain detestable arts called witchcrafts and sorceries, wickedly and feloniously, hath used, practised and exercised at and within the township of Salem in the county of Essex aforesaid in, upon, and against one Mercy Lewis of Salem Village in the county of Essex in New England—by which wicked arts the said Mercy Lewis—the ninth day of May—in the fourth year aforesaid and divers other days and times as well before as after was and is tortured, afflicted, pined, consumed, wasted and tormented: against the peace of our Sovereign Lord and Lady, the King. and Queen, and against the form of the statute in that case made and Provided.

WITNESSES
MERCY LEWIS
MARY WALCOTT
ELIZABETH HUBBARD
ANN PUTNAM

Indictment no 3.

Anno Regis et Reginae Willm et Mariae nunc: Anglia etc.
Quarto

Essex ss. The jurors for our Sovereign Lord and Lady, the King & Queen, presents that George Burroughs, late of Falmouth within the province of the Massachussets Bay in New England, clerk, the ninth day of May in the fourth year of the reign of our Sovereign Lord & Lady William and Mary, by the Grace of God, of England, Scotland, France and Ireland, King and Queen, defenders of the faith &c, divers other days and times, as well before, as after certain detestable arts called witchcrafts & sorceries, wickedly and feloniously hath used, practised & exercised at and within the town of Salem, in the county aforesaid, in, upon and against one Ann Putnam of Salem Village, single woman—by which said wicked arts the said Ann Putnam, the ninth day of May in the fourth year abovesaid and divers other days and times as well before as after, was and is tortured, afflicted, pined, consumed, wasted and is tormented, also for sundry other acts of witchcrafts by said George Burroughs committed and done against the peace of our sovereign Lord and Lady, the King and Queen, their crown & dignity and against the form of the statute in that case made and provided:

WITNESSES
ANN PUTNAM
MARY WALCOTT
ELIZABETH HUBBARD
MARY WARREN

Indictment no 4.

Anno Regis et Reginae Willim et Mariae nunc Angliae &c Quarto

Essex ss. The jurors for our Sovereign Lord and Lady, the King and Queen, presents that George Burroughs, late of Falmouth in the province of the Massachussets Bay in New England, clerk—the ninth day of May in the fourth year of the reign of Our Sovereign Lord and Lady William and Mary, by the Grace of God, of England, Scotland, France and Ireland, King and Queen, defenders of the faith and divers other days and times, as well before, as after, certain detestable arts called witchcrafts, and sorceries, wickedly, and feloniously, hath used, practised & exercised at and within the township of Salem in the county of Essex aforesaid, in, upon and against one Mary Walcott of Salem Village in the county of Essex, single woman—by which said wicked arts the said Mary Walcott, the ninth day of May in the fourth year abovesaid and divers other days and times as well before as after was and is tortured, afflicted, pined, consumed, wasted and tormented against the peace of our Sovereign Lord and Lady, the King and Queen, and against the form of the statute in that case made and provided:

WITNESSES
MARY WALCOTT
SARAH BIBBER JURAT
MERCY LEWIS
ANN PUTNAM
ELIZABETH HUBBARD

Summons for Jonathan, Elizabeth, Thomas and Samuel Ruck

William & Mary, by the Grace of God, of England, Scotland, France & Ireland, King & Queen, defenders of the faith &tc.

Mr. Jonathan Ruck, Mrs. Elizabeth Ruck, Mr. Thomas Ruck & Samuel Ruck

To

Captain William Worwood

Greeting.

We command you all excuses set apart, to be and personally appear at the present Court of Oyer & Terminer held at Salem, there to testify the truth to the best of your knowledge on certain indictments exhibited against Mr. George Burroughs: hereof fail not, dated in Salem August 5th 1692, & in the fourth years of our reign,

STEPHEN SEWALL, CLERK

August 5th. The persons above named, were all, every [one] of them, summoned to appear as above, by me, Joseph Neale, Constable in Salem.

Summons for James Greenslit

William & Mary, by the Grace of God, of England, Scotland, France and Ireland, King, defender of the faith, etc

To James Greenslit
Greeting.

We command you, all excuses set apart, to be & personally appear at the next Court of Oyer & Terminer held at Salem, on the first Tuesday in August next, there to testify the truth on certain indictments to be exhibited against George Burroughs, & not depart the court without license or leave of said court, hereof fail not, on penalty of one hundred pounds money to be levied on your goods chattels etc.

DATED IN SALEM JULY 26TH 1692
TO THE SHERIFF OF ESSEX
STEPHEN SEWALL, CLERK

July 26th 1692, I have summoned the within named James Greenslit according to this within subpoena, to give in his evidence at the time and place within mentioned by me,

GEORGE HERRICK, DEPUTY SHERIFF

Account of physical examinations of George Burroughs and George Jacobs, Jr.

We whose names are underwritten, having received an order from the sheriff for to search the bodies of George Burroughs and George Jacobs, we find nothing upon the body of the abovesaid Burroughs but what is natural; but upon the body of George Jacobs we find 3 teats which according to the best of our judgements we think is not natural, for we run a pin through 2 of them and he was not sensible of it: one of them being within his mouth upon the inside of his right shoulderblade and a 3rd upon his right hip.

ED. WELD SWORN — TOM FLINT JURAT
WILL GILL SWORN — TOM WEST SWORN
ZEB HILL JURAT — SAM MORGAN SWORN
JOHN BARE JURAT
JURYMEN'S RETURN ABOUT JACOBS & BURROUGHS

Deposition of Samuel Webber v. George Burroughs

Samuel Webber, aged about 36 yeares, testifieth and saith that about seven or eight years ago I lived at Casco Bay and George Burroughs was then minister there, and having heard much of the great strength of him, said Burroughs, he coming to our house, we were in discourse about the same and he then told me that he had put his fingers into the bung of a barrel of molasses and lifted it up, and carried it round him and set it down again.

SALEM AUGUST 2ND 1692
SAMUEL WEBBER, JURAT IN CURIA

Deposition of Thomas Greenslit v. George Burroughs

Province of the Massachussets Bay in New England

The deposition of Thomas Greenslit aged about forty years testifieth

Essex ss. That about the breaking out of this last Indian war, being at the house of Captain Scottow's at Black Point, he saw Mr George Burroughs lift and hold out a gun of six foot barrel or thereabouts, putting the forefinger of his right hand into the muzzle of said gun and so held it out at arms end only with that finger, and further this deponent testifieth that at the same time he saw the said Burroughs take up a full barrel of molasses with but two fingers of one of his hands in the bung & carry it from the stage head to the door at the end of the stage without letting it down, & that Richard Hunniwell & John Greenslit & some other persons that are since dead were then present.

Salem September 15th 1692, Thomas Greenslit appeared before their Majesties' justices of Oyer & Terminer in open court & made oath that the above-mentioned particulars & every part of them were true attested.

STEPHEN SEWALL, CLERK

Deposition of Simon Willard and William Wormall v. George Burroughs

The deposition of Simon Willard, aged about forty two years, saith: I being at the house of Mr Robert Lawrence at Falmouth in Casco Bay, in September 1689, said Mr Lawrence was commending Mr. George Burroughs his strength, saying that we none of us could do what he could do, for, said he, Mr Burroughs can hold out this gun with one hand. Mr. Burroughs, being there, said, I held my hand here behind the lock: and took it up: and held it out. I said deponent saw Mr Burroughs put his hand on the gun to show us how he held it and where he held his hand: and saying, there he held his hand when he held said gun out: but I saw him not hold it out then: said gun was about or near seven foot barrel: and very heavy: then tried to hold out said gun with both hands: but could not do it long enough to take sight,

SIMON WILLARD, JURAT IN CURIA

Simon Willard owned to the jury of inquest that the above written evidence is the truth. August 3:1692 (William Wormall v. George Burroughs)

Captain William Wormall sworn to the above & that he saw him raise it from the ground, himself.

JURAT IN CURIA

Deposition of Simon Willard v. George Burroughs

The deposition of Simon Willard, aged about 42 years, saith, I being at Saco in the year 1689, some in Captain Ed Searjeant's garrison was speaking of Mr. George Burroughs, his great strength, saying he could take a barrel of molasses out of a canoe or boat alone: and that he could take it in his hands or arms out of the canoe or boat and carry it and set it on the shore: and Mr. Burroughs being there, said that he had carried one barrel of molasses or cider out of a canoe that had like to have done him a displeasure: said Mr. Burroughs intimated as if [that] he did not want strength to do it but the disadvantage of the shore was such that, his foot slipping in the sand, he had like to have strained his leg.

SIMON WILLARD

Simon Willard owned to the jury of Inquest, that the above written evidence is the truth.

JURAT IN CURIA

Deposition of Mary Webber v. George Burroughs

Mary Webber, widow, aged about 53 years, testifieth and saith that she living at Casco Bay about six, or seven years ago, when George Burroughs was minister at said place, and living a near neighbour to said Burroughs, was well acquainted with his wife which was daughter to Mr. John Ruck of Salem. She hath heard her tell much of her husband's unkindness to her and that she dare not write to her father to acquaint [him] how it was with her, and so desired me to write to her father that he would be pleased to send for her and told me she had been much affrighted, and that something in the night made a noise in the chamber where she lay as if one went about the chamber, and she calling up the negro to come to her, the negro not coming, said that she could not come, something stopped her, then her husband being called he came up. Something jumped down from between the chimney & the side of the house and run down the stairs and said Burroughs followed it down, and the negro then said it was something like a white calf: another time lying with her husband, something came into the house and stood by her bedside and breathed on her, and she being much affrighted at it, would have awakened her husband but could not for a considerable time, but as soon as he did awake it went away, but this I heard her say and know nothing of it myself otherwise, except by common report of others also concerning such things.

SALEM AUGUST 2ND 1692
MARY WEBBER

Deposition of Hannah Harris v. George Burroughs

The deposition of Hannah Harris, aged twenty-seven years or thereabouts, testifieth and saith that she lived at the house of George Burroughs at Falmouth & the abovesaid Hannah Harries many times hath taken notice that when she hath had any discorse with the abovesaid Burroughs' wife when the abovesaid Burroughs was from home that upon his return he hath often scolded his wife and told her that he knew what they said when he was abroad, and further said that upon a time when his wife had lain in, not above one week, that he fell out with his wife and kept her by discource at the door till she fell sick in the place, and grew worse at night, so that the abovesaid Hannah Harris was afraid she would die and thay called in their neighbours, and the abovesaid Burroughs' daughter told one of the women, that was there, the cause of her mother's illness, and the abovesaid Burroughs chid his daughter for telling, and the abovesaid Burroughs came to the abovesaid Hannah Harries and told her, if that his wife did otherwise than well, she should not tell of it, and the abovesaid Hannah Harries told him that she would not be confined to any such things.

JURAT IN CURIA

Deposition of Ann Putnam, Jnr. v. George Burroughs

The deposition of Ann Putnam, who testifieth and saith that on 20th of April 1692 at evening she saw the apparition of a minister at which she was greviously affrighted and cried out, oh dreadful, dreadful, here is a minister come, what, are ministers witches too? whence come you and what is your name for I will complain of you, though you be a minister, if you be a wizard; and immediately I was tortured by him, being racked and almost choked by him, and he tempted me to write in his book which I refused with loud outcries and said I would not write in his book, though he tore me all to pieces, but told him that it was a dreadful thing that he which was a minister, that should teach children to fear God, should come to persuade poor creatures to give their souls to the devil: Oh, dreadful! Tell me your name that I may know who you are: then again he tortured me & urged me to write in his book: which I refused: and then presently he told me that his name was George Burroughs and that he had had three wives: and that he had bewitched the two first of them to death: and that he killed Mistress Lawson because she was so unwilling to go from the village and also killed Mr Lawson's child because he went to the eastward with Sir Edmond and preached so to the soldiers and that he had bewitched a great many soldiers to death at the eastward, when Sir Edmond was there, and that he had made Abigail Hobbs a witch and several witches more: and he has continued ever since; by times tempting me to write in his book and grievously torturing me, by beating, pinching and almost choking me several times a day, and he also told me that he was above a witch for he was a conjurer.

JURAT IN CURIA

Deposition of Thomas Putnam, Peter Prescott, Robert Morrell & Ezekiel Cheever v. George Burroughs

We whose names are underwritten being present with Ann Putnam at the time abovementioned heard her declare what is abovewritten what she said she saw and heard from the apparition of Mr. George Burroughs: and also beheld her tortures: and perceive her hellish temptations by her loud outcries, I will not, I will not write, though you torment [me] all [the] days of my life, and being conversant with her ever since have seen her tortured and complaining that Mr. Burroughs hurt her and tempts her to write in his book.

THOMAS PUTNAM
PETER PRESCOTT
ROBERT MORRELL

Ann Putnam declared her above written evidence to be the truth before the Jury of Inquest: August 3: 1692: upon her oath. Ezekiel Cheever made oath to the latter part of this paper.

JURAT IN CURIA

Deposition of Ann Putnam, Jnr. v. George Burroughs

The deposition of Ann Putnam who testifieth and saith that on the 5th of May 1692 at evening I saw the apparition of Mr. George Burroughs who greviously tortured me and urged me to write in his book, which I refused, then he told me that his two first wives would appear to me presently and tell me a great many lies but I should not beleve them: then immediately appeared to me the form of two women in winding sheets and napkins about their heads: at which I was greatly affrighted: and they turned their faces towards Mr. Burroughs and looked very red and angry and told him that he had been a cruel man to them and that their blood did cry for vengance against him: and also told him that they should be clothed with white robes in heaven, when he should be cast into hell: and immediately he vanished away: and as soon as he was gone the two women turned their faces towards me and looked as pale as a white wall: and told me that they were Mr. Burroughs' two first wives and that he had murdered them: and one told me that she was his first wife and he stabbed her under the left arm and put a piece of sealing wax on the wound and she pulled aside the winding sheet and showed me the place and also told me that she was in the house [that] Mr. Parris now lives in when it was done, and the other told me that Mr. Burroughs and that wife, which he hath now killed in the vessel as she was coming to see her friends, because they would have one another: and they both charged me that I should tell these things to the magistrates before Mr. Burroughs' face and if he did not own them they did not know but that they should appear there: this morning also Mistress Lawson and her daughter Ann appeared to me whom I knew: and told me that Mr. Burroughs murdered them: this morning also appeared to me another woman in a winding sheet and told me that she was Goodman Fuller's first wife and Mr. Burroughs killed her because there was some difference between her husband and him: also on the 9th May during the time of his examination he did most grievously torment and afflict Mary Walcott, Mercy Lewis, Elizabeth Hubburd and Abigail Williams by pinching, pricking and choking them.

JURAT IN CURIA

Deposition of Edward Putnam and Thomas Putnam v. George Burroughs

We whose names are underwritten being present with Ann Putnam at the times abovementioned, saw her tortured and heard her refuse to write in the book also heard her declare what is above written: what she said she saw and heard from the apparition of Mr. George Burroughs and from those which acc[used him] for murdering of them.

EDWARD PUTNAM
THOMAS PUTNAM

Ann Putnam owned this her testimony to be the truth upon her oath before the jurors of Inquest this 3rd day of August 92.

Deposition of Sarah Bibber v. George Burroughs

The deposition of Sarah Bibber who testifieth and saith that on the 9th day of May 1692, as I was agoing to Salem Village I saw the apparition of a little man like a minister with a black coat on and he pinched me by the arm and bid me go along with him but I told him I would not but when I came to the village saw there Mr. George Burroughs, which I never saw before, and then I knew that it was his apparition which I had seen in the morning and he tortured me several times while he was in examination. Also during the time of his examination I saw Mr. George Burroughs or his appearance most grievously torment and afflict Mary Walcott, Mercy Lewis, Elizabeth Hubbard, Ann Putnam and Abigail Williams by pinching, twisting & almost choking them to death. Also several times since Mr. George Burroughs or his appearance has most grievously tormented me with variety of tortures and I believe in my heart that Mr. George Burroughs is a dreadful wizard and that he has most grievously tormented me and the above mentioned persons by his acts of witchcraft.

Sarah Bibber declared to the jury of inquest that the above written evidence is the truth: August 3 1692, the which she owned on her oath.

JURAT IN CURIA

Deposition of Mercy Lewis v. George Burroughs

The deposition of Mercy Lewis who testifieth and saith that one the 7th of May 1692 at evening I saw the apparition of Mr. George Burroughs whom I very well knew, which did grievously torture me and urged me to write in his book and then he brought to me a new-fashioned book which he did not use to bring, and told me I might write in that book, for that was a book that was in his study when I lived with them, but I told him I did not believe him for I had been often in his study but I never saw that book there: but he told me that he had several books in his study which I never saw in his study and he could raise the devil: and now had bewitched Mr. Shepherd's daughter, and I asked him how he could go to bewitch her now he was kept at Salem: and he told me that the devil was his servant and he sent him in his shape to do it, then he again tortured me most dreadfully and threatened to kill me for he said I should not witness against him, also he told me that he had made Abigail Hobbs a witch and several more, then again he did most dreadfully torture me as if he would have racked me all to pieces and urged me to write in his book or else he would kill me but I told him I hoped my life was not in the power of his hand and that I would not write though he did kill me: the next night he told me I should not see his two wives if he could help it because I should not witness against him. This 9th May Mr. Burroughs carried me up to an exceeding high mountain and showed me all the kingdoms of the earth and told me that he would give them all to me if I would write in his book and if I would not he would throw me down and break my neck: but I told him they were none of his to give and I would not write if he threw me down on 100 pitchforks: also on the 9th May being the time of his examination Mr. George Burroughs did most dreadfully torment me: and also several times since.

Mercy Lewis upon her oath did own this her testimony to be the truth before the jurors for Inquest: August 3 92.

Deposition of Thomas Putnam and Edward Putnam v. George Burroughs

We whose names are underwritten being present heard Mercy Lewis declare what is above written, what she said she saw and heard from the apparition of Mr George Burroughs, and also beheld her torture which we cannot express for sometimes we were ready to fear that every joint of her body was ready to be displaced: also we perceived her hellish temptations by her loud outcries, "Mr. Burroughs, I will not write in your book though you do kill me."

THOMAS PUTNAM
EDWARD PUTNAM
JURAT IN CURIA

Deposition of Elizabeth Hubbard v. George Burroughs

May 9 1692.

Elizabeth Hubbard aged about 17 years saith that the last second day, at night, there appeared a little black bearded man to me in blackish apparel. I asked him his name & he told me his name was Borroughs. Then he took a book out of his pocket & opened it & bid me set my hand to it. I told him I would not: the lines in this book was red as blood; then he pinched me twice & went away: The next morning he appeared to me again and told me he was above a wizard, for he was a conjuror, and so went away but since that he hath appeared to me every day & night very often and urged me very much to set my hand to his book: and to run away telling me if I would do so I should be well & that I should need fear nobody: & withall tormented me several ways every time he came except that time he told me he was a conjuror: This night he asked me very much to set my hand to his book or else he said he would kill me; withal torturing me very much by biting and pinching, squeezing my body and running pins into me. Also on the 9th May 1692, being the time of his examination, Mr. George Burroughs or his appearence did most grievously afflict and torment the bodies of Mary Walcott, Mercy Lewis, Ann Putnam and Abigail Williams for if he did but look upon them he would strike them down or almost choke them to death. Also several times since he has most dreadfully afflicted and tormented me with variety of torments and I believe in my heart that Mr. George Burroughs is a dreadful wizard and that he has often tormented me and also the abovenamed persons by his acts of witchcraft.

JURAT IN CURIA

Elizabeth Hubbard declared the above written evidence to be the truth upon her oath, that she had taken. This she owned before the Jury of inquest: August 3 1692.

Susannah Sheldon v. George Burroughs

The complaint of Susannah Sheldon against Mr. Burroughs, which brought a book to me and told me if I would not set my hand to it he would tear me to pieces. I told him I would not, then he told me he would starve me to death, then the next morning he told me he could not starve me to death but he would choke me, that my vittals should do me but little good. Then he told me his name was Burroughs which had preached at the village. The last night he came to me and asked me whether I would go to the village tomorrow to witness against him. I asked him if he was examined then. He told he was, then I told him I would go. Then he told me he would kill me before morning. Then he appeared to me at the house of Nathaniel Ingersoll and told me he had been the death of three children at the eastward and had killed two of his wives. The first he smothered and the second he choked, and killed two of his own children.

Deposition of Benjamin Hutchinson v. George Burroughs

Benjamin Hutchinson said that on the 21st April 92 Abigail Williams said that there was a little black minister that lived at Casco Bay, he told me so, and said that he had killed 3 wives, two for himself and one for Mr. Lawson and that he had made nine witches in this place and said that he could hold out the heaviest gun that is in Casco Bay with one hand which no man can case hold out with both hands. This is about 11 o clock and I ask her whereabout this little man stood, said she just where the cartwheel went along. I had a 3 grained iron fork in my hand and I threw it where she said he stood and she presently fell in a little fit and when it was over, said she, you have torn his coat for I heard it tear. Whereabouts? said I. One side, said she.

Then we come into the house of Lieutenant Ingersoll and I went into the great room and Abigail come in and said, there he stands, I said where, and presently drew my rapier but he immediately was gone as she said. Then said she, there is a gray cat. Then I said, whereabouts doth she stand? There said she, there. Then I struck with my rapier, then she fell in a fit, and when it was over, she said, you killed her and immediately Sarah Good came and carried her away. This was about 12 o clock. The same day after lecture in the said Ingersoll's chamber Abigail Williams, Mary Walcott, said that Goody Hobbs of Topsfield bit Mary Walcott by the foot, then both falling into a fit, as soon as it was over, the said William Hobbs and his wife go both of them along the table; the said Hutchinson took his rapier, stabbed Goody Hobbs on the side as Abigail Williams & Mary Walcott said: the said Abigail & Mary said the room was full of them, then the said Hutchinson & Ely Putnam stabbed with their rapiers at a ventor, then said Mary & Abigail, you have killed a great black woman of Stoningtown and an Indian that comes with her for the floor is all covered with blood. Then the said Mary and Abigail looked out of door & said they saw a great company of them on a hill & there was three of them lay dead, the black woman & the indian, & one more that they knew not.

This being about 4 o clock in the after noon.

Deposition of Abigail Hobbs and Mary Warren v. George Burroughs et al.

1st June 1692

Abigail Hobbs then confessed before John Hathorne & Jonathan Corwin Esqrs that at the general meeting of the witches in the field near Mr Parris's house she saw Mr George Burroughs, Sarah Good, Sarah Osborne, Bridget Bishop, also Oliver, & Giles Corey, two or three nights ago. Mr Burroughs came & sat at the window & told her he would terribly afflict her for saying so much against him & then pinched her. Deliverance Hobbs then saw said Burroughs & he would have tempted her to set her hand to the book & almost shook her to pieces because she would not do it.

Mary Warren testifieth that when she was in prison in Salem about a fortnight agone Mr George Burroughs, Goody Nurse, Goody Proctor, Goody Parker, Goody Pudeator, Abigail Soames, Goodman Proctor, Goody Darling & others unknown came to this deponent & Mr Burroughs had a trumpet & sounded it, & they would have had this deponent to have gone up with them to a feast at Mr Parris' & Goody Nurse & Goody Proctor told her this deponent they were deacons & would have had her eat some of their sweet bread & wine & she asking them what wine that was one of them said it was blood & better than our wine, but this deponent refused to eat or drink with them, & they then dreadfully afflicted her at that time.

SWORN THE FIRST OF JUNE 1692
JOHN HATHORNE
JONATHAN CORWIN
ASSISTANTS

Memorandum. That at the time of the taking of this deposition Goody Nurse appeared in the room & afflicted the deponents Mary & Deliverance Hobbs as they attested, & also almost choked Abigail Hobbs, as also testified, & Mr English then run a pin into Mary's hand as she attested.

Deposition of Mary Warren v. George Burroughs, John Alden, Martha Corey, and Ann Pudeator

The testimony of Mary Warren, aged twenty years or thereabouts, testifieth and saith that sometime in July last Mr. Burroughs pinched me very much and choked me almost to death: and I saw and heard him sound a trumpet and immediately I saw several come to him, as namely, Captain Alden, Mister Corey and Goody Pudeater and several others, and they urged me to go along with them to their sacramental meeting, and Mr. Burroughs brought to me bread to eat and wine to drink, which I refusing he did most grievously torment me, urging me vehemently to write in his book: also I have seen Mr George Burroughs or his appearence most grievously tormenting Mary Walcott and Ann Putnam and I verily believe in my heart that Mr. George Burroughs is a dreadful wizard and that he has several times tormented me and the aforesaid persons by his acts of witchcraft.

Mary Warren declared upon her oath to the Jury of Inquest that the above written evidence is the truth. August 3, 1692.

Deposition of Mary Walcott v. George Burroughs

The deposition of Mary Walcott, aged about 17 years, who testifieth and saith that on the later end of April 1692 Mr. George Burroughs or his appearence came to me, whom I formerly well knew: and he did immediately most grievously torment me by biting, pinching and almost choking me, urging me to write in his book: which, I refusing, he did again most grievously torment me and told me if I would but touch his book I should be well, but I told him I would not for all the world and then he threatened to kill me and said I should never witness against him: but he continued torturing and tempting me till the 8 May: and then he told me he would have killed his first wife and child when his wife was in travail but he kept her in the kitchen till he gave her her death's wound. But he charged me in the name of his God I should not tell of it: but immediately there appeared to me Mr. Burroughs' two first wives in their winding sheets, whom I formerly well knew, and told me that Mr. Burroughs had murdered them and that their blood did cry for vengance against him: also on the 9th May, being the day of his examination, he did most grievously torment me during the time of his examination, for if he did but look on me he would strike me down or almost choke me: also during his examination I saw Mr. George Burroughs or his appearence most grievously torment Mercy Lewis, Elizabeth Hubbard, Abigail Williams and Ann Putnam, and I believe in my heart that Mr. George Burroughs is a dreadful wizard and that he had often afflicted and tormented me and the aforementioned persons by his acts of witchcraft.

Mary Walcott declared this writing to be a true evidence to the jury of inquest August 3 1692 upon the oath she has taken.

JURAT IN CURIA

Deposition of Thomas Putnam and Edward Putnam v. George Burroughs

The deposition of Thomas Putnam aged 40 years, and Edward Putnam aged 38 years, who testifieth and saith that we, having been conversant with several of the afflicted persons, as Mary Walcott, Mercy Lewis, Elizabeth Hubbard, we have seen them most dreadfully tormented, and we have seen dreadful marks in their flesh which they said Mr. Burroughs did make by hurting them: but on 9th May 1692, the day of the examination of Mr. George Burroughs, the aforesaid persons were most dreadfully tormented during the time of his examination, as if they would have been torn all to pieces or all their bones put out of joint, and with such tortures as no tongue can express, also several times since we have seen the aforesaid afflicted persons most dreadfully tormented and grievously complaining of Mr. Burroughs for hurting them, and we believe that Mr. George Burroughs the prisoner at the bar has several times afflicted and tormented the aforesaid persons by acts of witchcraft.

THOMAS PUTNAM
JURAT IN CURIA

Deposition of John Putnam, Sr. and Rebecca Putnam v. George Burroughs

The deposition of John Putnam & Rebecca his wife testifieth and saith that in the year 1680 Mr Burroughs lived in our house nine months, there being a great difference betwixt said Burroughs & his wife, the difference was so great that they did desire us, the deponents, to come into their room to hear their difference. The controvercy that was betwixt them was that the aforesaid Burroughs did require his wife to give him a written covenant under her hand and seal that she would never reveal his secrets. Our answer was that they had once made a covenant before God and men, which covenant we did conceive did bind each other to keep their lawful secrets, and further saith that all the time that said Burroughs did live at our house he was a very sharp man to his wife, notwithstanding to our observation she was a very good and dutiful wife to him.

JURAT IN CURIA

Deposition of Elizar Keyser v. George Burroughs

Elizar Keyser, aged about forty five years, saith that on Thursday last past, being the fifth day of this instant month of May, I was at the house of Thomas Beadles in Salem, and Captain Daniel King being there also, at the same time, and in the same room, said Captain Daniel King asked me whether I would not go up, and see Mr. Burroughs and discourse with him. He being then in one of the chambers in said house. I told him it did not belong to me, and I was not willing to meddle or make with it. Then said King said, are you not a Christian, if you are a Christian go see him and discourse with him, but I told him I did believe it did not belong to such as I was to discourse him, he being a learned man. Then said King said, I believe he is a child of God, a choice child of God, and that God would clear up his innocency; so I told him my opinion or fear was, that he was, the chief of all the persons accused for witchcraft or the ringleader of them all, and told him also that I believed if he was such an one, his master, meaning the devil, had told him before now, what I said of him. And said King seeming to me to be in a passion, I did afterwards forbear. The same evening after these words, being alone in one room of my house, and no candle or light being in the said room, the same afternoon, I having occasion to be at the said Beadles' house and in the chamber where Mr. George Burroughs kept, I observed that said Burroughs did steadfastly fix his eyes upon me, the same evening being in my own house, in a room without any light, I did see very strange things appear in the chimney, I suppose a dozen of them, which seemed to me to be something like jelly that used to be in the water and quaver with a strange motion, and then quickly disappeared, soon after which I did see a light up in the chimney about the bigness of my hand, something about the bar which quivered & shaked and seemed to have a motion upward upon which I called the maid, and she looking up into the chimney saw the same, and my wife looking up could not see anything, so I did and do very certainly consider it was some diabolical apparition.

JURAT IN CURIA BY MR. KEYSER,
SWORN ALSO BY ELIZABETH WARDWELL
AS TO THE LAST NIGHT

Memorandum in case of George Burroughs

Memorandum in Mr. George Burroughs' trial: besides the written evidences that was sworn, several who gave theirs by word of mouth, & Major Browne holding out a heavy gun with one hand.

Thomas Ruck of his sudden coming in after them & that he could tell his thoughts.

Thomas Evans that he carried out barrels [of] molasses & meats etc. out of a canoe whilst his mate went to the fort for hands to help out with them.

Sarah Wilson confessed that the night before Mr. Burroughs was executed, that there was a great meeting of the witches nigh Sarjeant Chandler's, that Mr. Burroughs was there & they had the sacrament &, after they had done, he took leave & bid them stand to their faith, & not own any thing

Martha Tyler saith the same with Sarah Wilson & several others, these since the execution of Mr. Burroughs.

On August 5, 1692, George Burroughs was brought to trial. Cotton Mather wrote an account of the proceedings in his book, *Wonders of the Invisible World,* from minutes taken by Stephen Sewall, the clerk of the court. That Mather's account was never intended to be impartial is made clear by a letter he wrote to Sewall, urging him to send on the minutes as soon as possible, "That I may be the more capable to assist in lifting up a standard against the infernal enemy." In other words, drive on the witch-hunt. Nevertheless, his account seems to be more or less accurate. The testimony it relates corresponds with the written depositions.

Burroughs was hanged on August 19. As we saw in Part 2, from Brattle's letter and Calef's *More Wonders,* he died bravely.

From: Cotton Mather, *Wonders of the Invisible World*

I. The Trial of George Burroughs at a Court of Oyer and Terminer, held in Salem, 1692.

Glad should I have been, if I had never known the name of this man; or never had this occasion to mention so much as the first letters of his name. But the Government requiring some account of his trial to be inserted in this book, it becomes me with all obedience to submit unto the order.

I. This George Burroughs was indicted for witchcrafts, and in the prosecution of the charge against him, he was accused by five or six of the bewitched, as the author of their miseries; he was accused by eight of the confessing witches, as being an head actor at some of their hellish randezvous, and one who had the promise of being a king in Satan's kingdom, now going to be erected: he was accused by nine persons for extraordinary lifting, and such feats of strength, as could not be done without a diabolical assistance. And for other such things he was accused, until about thirty testimonies were brought in against him; nor were these judged the half of what might have been considered for his conviction: however they were enough to fix the character of a witch upon him according to the rules of reasoning, by the judicious Gaule, in that case directed.

II. The court being sensible, that the testimonies of the parties bewitched use to have a room among the suspicions or presumptions, brought in against one indicted for witchcraft, there were now heard the testimonies of several persons, who were most notoriously bewitched, and every day tortured by invisible hands, and these now all charged the spectres of George Burroughs to have a share in their torments. At the examination of this George Burroughs the bewitched people were grievously harassed with preternatural mischiefs, which could not possibly be dissembled; and they still ascribed it unto the endeavours of George Burroughs to kill them. And now upon his trial, one of the bewitched persons testified, that in her agonies, a little black haired man came to her, saying his name was Burroughs and bidding her set her hand unto a book which he showed unto her; and bragging that he was a conjurer, above the ordinary rank of witches; that he often persecuted her with the offer of that book, saying, she should be well, and need fear nobody, if she would but sign it; but he inflicted cruel pains and hurts upon her, because of her denying so to do. The testimonies of the other sufferers concurred with these; and it was remarkable, that whereas biting was one of the ways which the witches used for the vexing of the sufferers, when they cried out of George Burroughs biting them, the print of the teeth would be seen on the flesh of the complainers, and just such a set of teeth as George Burroughs would then appear upon them, which could be distinguished from those of some other mens. Others of them testified, that in their torments, George Burroughs tempted them to go unto a sacrament, unto which they perceived him with a sound of trumpet summoning of other witches, who quickly after the sound would come from all quarters unto the rendezvous. One of them falling into a kind of trance, afterwards affirmed, that George Burroughs had carried her into a very high mountain, where he showed her mighty and glorious kingdoms, and said, He would give them all to her, if she would write in his book; but she told him, they were none of his to give; and refused the motions, enduring of much misery for that refusal.

It cost the court a wonderful deal of trouble, to hear the testimonies of the sufferers; for when they were going to give in their depositions, they would for a long time be taken with fits, that made them uncapable of saying anything. The chief judge asked the prisoner, who he thought hindered these witnesses from giving their testimonies? and he answered, he supposed it was the devil. That honourable person then replied, How comes the devil so loathe to have any testimony born against you? Which cast him into very great confusion.

III. It has been a frequent thing for the bewitched people to be entertained with apparitions of ghosts of murdered people, at the same time that the spectres of the witches trouble them. These ghosts do always affright the beholders more than all the other spectral representations; and when they exhibit themselves, they cry out, of being murdered by the witchcrafts or other violences of the persons who are then in spectre present. It is further considerable, that once or twice, these apparitions have been seen by others at the very same time that they have shown themselves to the bewitched; and seldom have there been these apparitions but when something unusual and suspected had attended the death of the party thus appearing. Some that have been accused by these apparitions, accosting of the bewitched people, who had never heard a word of any such persons ever being in the world, have upon a fair examination freely and fully confessed the murders of those very persons, although these also did not know how the apparitions had complained of them. Accordingly several of the bewitched had given in their testimony, that they had been troubled with the apparitions of two women, who said that they were George Burroughs' two wives, and that he had been the death of them; and that the magistrates must be told of it, before whom if Burroughs upon his trial denied it, they did not know but that they should appear again in the court. Now, George Burroughs had been infamous for the barbarous usage of his two successive wives, all the country over. Moreover, it was testified, the spectre of George Burroughs threatening of the sufferers told them, he had killed (besides others) Mrs. Lawson and her daughter Ann. And it was noted, that these were the virtuous wife and daughter of one at whom this George Burroughs might have a prejudice for his being serviceable at Salem Village, from whence himself had in ill terms removed some years before: and that when they died, which was long since, there were some odd circumstances about them, which made some of the attendents there suspect something of witchcraft, though none imagined from what quarter it should come.

Well, George Burroughs being now upon his trial, one of the bewitched persons was cast into horror at the ghosts of Burroughs' two deceased wives then appearing before him, and crying for vengeance against him. Hereupon several of the bewitched persons were successively called in, who all not knowing what the former had seen and said, concurred in their horror of the apparition, which they affirmed that he had before him. But he, though much appalled, utterly denied that he discerned any thing of it; nor was it any part of his conviction.

IV. Judicious writers have assigned it a great place in the conviction of witches, when persons are impeached by other notorious witches, to be as ill as themselves; especially if the persons have been much noted for neglecting the worship of God. Now, as there might have been testimonies enough of George Burroughs' antipathy to prayer and the other ordinances of God, though by his profession singularly obliged thereunto; so, there now came in against the prisoner the testimonies of several persons, who confessed their own having been horrible witches, and ever since their confessions had been themselves terribly tortured by the devils and other witches, even like the other sufferers; and therein undergone the pains of many deaths for their confessions.

These now testified, that George Burroughs had been at witch-meetings with them; and that he was the person who had seduced and compelled them into the snares of witchcraft: That he promised them fine clothes, for doing it; that he brought poppets to them, and thorns to stick into those poppets, for the afflicting of other people; and that he exhorted them, with the rest of the crew, to bewitch all Salem Village, but be sure to do it gradually, if they would prevail in what they did.

When the Lancashire witches were condemned, I don't remember that there was any considerable further evidence, than that of the bewitched, and then that of some that confessed. We see so much already against George Burroughs. But this being indeed not enough, there were other things to render what had already been produced credible.

V. A famous divine recites this among the convictions of a witch; the testimony of the party bewitched, whether pining or dying; together with the joint oaths of sufficient persons that have seen certain prodigious pranks or feats wrought by the party accused. Now God had been pleased so to leave this George Burroughs that he had ensnared himself by several instances, which he had formerly given of a preternatural strength, and which were now produced against him. He was a very puny man; yet he had often done things beyond the strength of a giant. A gun of about seven foot barrel, and so heavy that strong men could not steadily hold it out with both hands; there were several testimonies, given in by persons of credit and honour, that he made nothing of taking up such a gun behind the lock, with but one hand, and holding it out like a pistol, at arms-end. George Burroughs in his vindication was so foolish as to say, that an Indian was there, and held it out at the same time: Whereas, none of the spectators ever saw any such Indian; but they supposed the Black Man (as the witches call the devil; and they generally say he resembles an Indian) might give him that assistance. There was evidence likewise brought in, that he made nothing of taking up whole barrels filled with molasses or cider, in very disadvantageous postures, and carrying of them through the difficultest places out of a canoe to the shore.

Yea, there were two testimonies that George Burroughs with only putting the fore-finger of his right hand into the muzzle of an heavy gun, a fowling-piece of about six or seven foot barrel, did lift up the gun, and hold it out at arm's end; a gun which the deponents though strong men could not with both hands lift up, and hold out at the butt end, as is usual. Indeed, one of these witnesses was over persuaded by some persons to be out of the way upon George Burroughs' trial; but he came afterwards with sorrow for his withdraw, and gave in his testimony: Nor were either of these witnesses made use of as evidences in the trial.

VI. There came in several testimonies relating to the domestic affairs of George Burroughs which had a very hard aspect upon him; and not only proved him a very ill man; but also confirmed the belief of the character, which had been already fastened on him.

'Twas testified, that keeping his two successive wives in a strange kind of slavery, he would when he came home from abroad pretend to tell the talk which any had with them; That he has brought them to the point of death, by his harsh dealings with his wives, and then made the people about him to promise that in case death should happen, they would say nothing of it; that he used all means to make his wives write, sign, seal, and swear a covenant, never to reveal any of his secrets; that his wives had privately complained unto the neighbours about frightful apparitions of evil spirits, with which their house was sometimes infested; and that many such things have been whispered among the neighbourhood. There were also some other testimonies, relating to the death of people, whereby the consciences of an impartial jury were convinced that George Burroughs had bewitched the persons mentioned in the complaints. But I am forced to omit several passages, in this, as well as in all the succeeding trials, because the scribes who took notice of them, have not supplied me.

VII. One Mr. Ruck, brother in law to this George Burroughs testified, that George Burroughs and he himself, and his sister, who was George Burroughs' wife, going out for two or three miles to gather strawberries, Ruck, with his sister the wife of George Burroughs rode home very softly, with George Burroughs on foot in their company. George Burroughs stepped aside a little into the bushes; whereupon they halted and hallooed for him. He not answering, they went away homewards, with a quickened pace, without any expectation of seeing him in a considerable while; and yet when they were got near home, to their astonishment they found him on foot with them, having a basket of strawberries. George Burroughs immediately then fell to chiding his wife, on the account of what she had been speaking to her brother, of him, on the road: which when they wondered at, he said, He knew their thoughts. Ruck being startled at that, made some reply, intimating that the devil himself did not know so far; but George Burroughs answered, my God makes known your thoughts unto me. The prisoner now at the bar had nothing to answer, unto what was thus witnessed against him, that was worth considering. Only he said, Ruck and his wife left a man with him, when they left him. Which Ruck now affirmed to be false; and when the court asked George Burroughs what the man's name was his countenance was much altered;

nor could he say, who 'twas. But the court began to think, that he then stepped aside, only that by the assistance of the Black Man, he might put on his invisibility, and in that fascinating mist, gratify his own jealous humour, to hear what they said of him. Which trick of rendering themselves invisible, our witches do in their confessions pretend that they sometimes are masters of; and it is the more credible, because there is demonstration that they often render many other things utterly invisible.

VIII. Faltering, faulty, unconstant, and contrary answers upon judicial and deliberate examination, are counted some unlucky symptoms of guilt, in all crimes, especially in witchcrafts. Now there never was a prisoner more eminent for them, than George Burroughs, both at his examination and on his trial. His tergiversations, contradictions, and falsehoods, were very sensible: he had little to say, but that he had heard some things that he could not prove, reflecting upon the reputation of some of the witnesses. Only he gave in a paper to the jury; wherein, although he had many times before granted, not only that there are witches, but also that the present sufferings of the country are the effect of horrible witchcrafts, yet he now goes to evince it, that there neither are, nor ever were witches, that having made a compact with the devil, can send a devil to torment other people at a distance. This paper was transcribed out of Ady, which the court presently knew, as soon as they heard it. But he said, he had taken none of it out of any book; for which, his evasion afterwards was, that a gentleman gave him the discourse in a manuscript, from whence he transcribed it.

IX. The jury brought him in guilty: But when he came to die, he utterly denied the fact, whereof he had been thus convicted.

Nathaniel Hawthorne, one of America's greatest writers. He added a "w" to his name to distance himself from his great-great-grandfather, John Hathorne, the chief magistrate at the examinations of accused witches. Courtesy, Peabody Essex Museum, Salem, Mass.

Arthur Miller's, *The Crucible*. The afflicted girls see spectral visions in the Touring Consortium production, Great Britain, 1988. © Mark Douet/Arena Images.

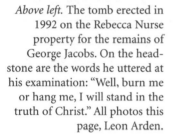

Above left. The tomb erected in 1992 on the Rebecca Nurse property for the remains of George Jacobs. On the headstone are the words he uttered at his examination: "Well, burn me or hang me, I will stand in the truth of Christ." All photos this page, Leon Arden.

Above right. The Rebecca Nurse monument, near the Rebecca Nurse house.

Middle right. The memorial to the twenty men and women executed for witchcraft, next to Salem's ancient burial ground. Each of the twenty slabs is inscribed with the name and dates of a victim. Erected for the centenary of the witch hunt in 1992.

Bottom right. Another centenary memorial, opposite the site of the Salem Village meeting house, where many of the examinations of accused witches took place.

Part IV

THE HISTORIANS

Where do contemporary accounts leave off and historical interpretations begin? In modern terms, when does journalism become history? Robert Calef's *More Wonders of the Invisible World* was finished by 1697, the year Cotton Mather published his *Life of his Excellency Sir William Phips, Knt.* But *More Wonders* was the seventeenth century equivalent of an article by an investigative reporter in the *New Yorker*, the *Life* was part of a history of Massachusetts. Calef told us what happened, Mather explained why. Or, rather, pretended to. He could not face the fact that the witch scare was based on fraud and delusion and claimed its root cause was sorcery. With typical disingenuousness, he conflated the notion of the afflicted girls' fortune-telling, attested to by John Hale, with the supposed practice of witchcraft by the people they accused. Elsewhere in his *Magnalia Christi Americana,* he writes of the Indian medicine men as "horrid sorcerers and hellish conjurers, and such as conversed with demons," suggesting they too played a part in starting the witch-hunt. Thus he invented the myth, persisting to the present, that alien sorcery was the mainspring of the witch panic. As we shall see in Part V, fiction writers seized this notion and ran with it, in turn influencing historians. In later excerpts in this part we trace the course of the legend to its apotheosis in Marion Starkey's half-Negro, voodoo-practicing, spell-chanting Tituba.

Other excerpts show the evolution of the "conspiracy theory," according to which the witch-hunt was planned from the start.

In the last section of this part can be found the fascinating, sometimes groundbreaking, work of historians of the late twentieth century.

6

MYTH AND REALITY

From: Cotton Mather, *The Life of His Excellency Sir William Phipps, Knt.* (London, 1697)

Now the arrival of Sir William Phips to the government of New England, was at a time, when a governor would have had occasion for all the skill in sorcery, that was ever necessary to a Jewish counsellor; a time when scores of poor people had newly fallen under a prodigious possession of devils, which it was then generally thought had been by witchcraft introduced. It is to be confessed and bewailed, that many inhabitants of New England, and young people especially, had been led away with little sorceries, wherein they did secretly those things that were not right against the Lord their God; they would often cure hurts with spells, and practice detestable conjurations with sieves, and keys, and peas, and nails and horseshoes, and other implements, to learn the things for which they had a forbidden and impious curiosity. Wretched books were stolen into the land, wherein fools were instructed, how to become able fortune tellers. . . . And by these books, the minds of many had been so poisoned, that they studied this finer witchcraft; until, 'tis well, if some of them were not betrayed, into what is grosser, and more sensible and capital. Although these diabolical divinations are more ordinarily committed perhaps all over the whole world, than they are in the country of New England, yet, that being a country devoted unto the worship and service of the Lord Jesus Christ above the rest of the world, he signalised his vengeance against these wickednesses, with such extraordinary dispensations, as have not been often seen in other places.

The devils . . . now broke in upon the country, after as astonishing a manner, as was ever heard of. Some scores of people, first about Salem, the centre and first born, of all the towns in the colony, and afterwards in several other places, were arrested with many preternatural vexations upon their bodies, and a variety of cruel torments, which were evidently inflicted from the demons of the invisible world. The people that were infected and infested with such demons, in a few days time, arrived unto such a refining alteration upon their eyes, that they could see their tormentors; they saw a devil of a little stature, and of a tawny colour, attended still with spectres, that appeared in more humane circumstances.

From: Thomas Hutchinson, *The History of the Colony of Massachusetts Bay* (London, 1765)

Thomas Hutchinson (1711–1780) was a much better historian than Cotton Mather. As governor of Massachusetts (1771–1774), he was a man of the Enlightenment, with no time for superstition. But his strengths were his weaknesses. Though much of his analysis is sound he oversimplified by ascribing the whole witch-hunt to fraud and conspiracy.

Volume II begins with the history of witchcraft cases in the New England colonies. It suggests there was widespread disapproval of hanging suspected witches until the *Remarkable Providences* and *Memorable Providences*, and other works, changed the climate of opinion.

From volume 2, chapter 1

Memorable Providences obtained credit sufficient, together with other preparatives, to dispose the whole country to be easily imposed upon by the more extensive and more tragical scene, which was presently after acted at Salem and other parts of the county of Essex. Not many years before, Glanvil published his witch stories in England; Perkins and other Nonconformists were earlier; but the great authority was that of Sir Matthew Hale, revered in New England, not only for his knowledge in the law, but for his gravity and piety. The trial of the witches in Suffolk was published in 1684. All these books were in New England, and the conformity between the behaviour of Goodwin's children and most of the supposed bewitched at Salem, and the behaviour of those in England, is so exact, as to leave no room to doubt the stories had been read by the New England persons themselves, or had been told to them by others who had read them. Indeed, this conformity, instead of giving suspicion, was urged in confirmation of the truth of both; the Old England demons and the New being so much alike. The court justified themselves from books of law, and the authorities of Keble, Dalton and other lawyers, then of the first character, who lay down rules of conviction as absurd and dangerous as any which were practised in New England. The trial of

Richard Hathaway, the impostor, before lord chief justice Holt, was ten or twelve years after. This was a great discouragement to prosecutions in England for witchcraft, but an effectual stop was not put to them until the act of parliament in the reign of his late Majesty. Even this has not wholly cured the common people and we hear of old women ducked and cruelly murdered within these last twenty years. Reproach, then, for hanging witches, although it has been often cast upon the people of New England by those of Old, yet it must have been done with an ill grace. The people of New England were of a grave cast, and had long been disposed to give serious, solemn construction even to common events in providence; but in Old England, the reign of Charles the Second was as remarkable for gaiety as any whatsoever and for scepticism and infidelity as any which preceded it.

Sir William Phips, the governor, upon his arrival, fell in with the opinion prevailing. Mr. Stoughton, the lieutenant-governor, upon whose judgment great stress was laid, had taken up this notion, that although the devil might appear in the shape of a guilty person, yet he would never be permitted to assume the shape of an innocent person. This opinion, at first, was generally received. Some of the most religious women who were accused, when they saw the appearance of distress and torture in their accusers, and heard their solemn declarations, that they saw the shapes or spectres of the accused afflicting them, persuaded themselves they were witches, and that the devil, somehow or other, although they could not remember how or when, had taken possession of their evil hearts, and obtained some sort of assent to his afflicting in their shapes; and thereupon they thought they might be justified in confessing themselves guilty.

It seems, at this day, with some people, perhaps but few, to be the question, whether the accused or the afflicted were under a preternatural or diabolical possession, rather than whether the afflicted were under bodily distempers, or altogether guilty of fraud and imposture. As many of the original examinations have fallen into my hands, it may be of service to represent this affair in a more full and impartial light than it has yet appeared to the world.

In February 1692, a daughter and a niece of Mr. Parris, the minister of Salem village, girls of ten or eleven years of age, and two other girls in the neighbourhood, made the same sort of complaints as Goodwin's children had made two or three years before. The physicians, having no other way of accounting for the disorder, pronounced them bewitched. An Indian woman, who was brought into the country from New Spain, and then lived with Mr. Parris, tried some experiments which she pretended to be used to in her own country, in order to find out the witch. This coming to the children's knowledge, they cried out upon the poor Indian, as appearing to them, pinching, pricking and tormenting them; and fell into fits. Tituba, the Indian, acknowledged that she had learned how to find out a witch, but denied that she was one herself. Several private fasts were kept at the minister's house, and several, more public, by the whole village, and then a general fast through the colony, to seek to God to rebuke Satan, etc. So much notice taken of the children, together with the pity and compassion expressed by those who visited them, not only tended to confirm them in their design, but to draw others into the like. Accordingly, the number of the complainants soon increased, and among them there were two or three women, and some girls old enough for witnesses. These had their fits too, and when in them cried out, not only against Tituba, but against Sarah Osborne, a melancholy distracted old woman, and Sarah Good, another old woman who was bed-rid. Tituba, at length, confessed herself a witch, and that the two old women were her confederates; and they were all committed to prison; and Tituba, upon search, was found to have scars upon her back which were called the devil's mark, but might as well have been supposed those of her Spanish master. This commitment was on the 1st of March. About three weeks after, two other women, of good characters and church members, Corey and Nurse, were complained of and brought upon their examination; when these children fell into fits, and the mother of one of them, and wife of Thomas Putnam, joined with the children and complained of Nurse as tormenting her; and made most terrible shrieks, to the amazement of all the neighbourhood. The old women denied everything; but were sent to prison: and such was the infatuation, that a child Good, about four or five years old, was committed also, being charged with biting some of the afflicted who showed the print of small teeth on their arms. On April 3d, Mr. Parris took for his text, "*Have not I chosen you twelve, and one of you is a devil.*" Sarah Cloyes, supposing it to be occasioned by Nurse's case, who was her sister, went out of meeting. She was presently after complained of for a witch, examined and committed. Elizabeth Proctor was charged about the same time.—Her husband, as every good husband would have done, accompanied her to her examination, but it cost the poor man his life. Some of the afflicted cried out upon him also, and they were both committed to prison.

Instead of suspecting and sifting the witnesses, and suffering them to be cross-examined, the authority, to say no more, were imprudent in making use of leading questions, and thereby putting words into their mouths or suffering others to do it. Mr. Parris was over officious; most of the examinations, although in the presence of one or more of the magistrates, were taken by him.

Hutchinson relies heavily on Calef's *More Wonders* for the rest of his account. But he also reproduces many original documents, including the examinations of Goody Cloyes and Nehemiah Abbot, the examination and confession of Mary Osgood, and the *Return of Several Ministers* consulted by his excellency and the honorable council upon the present witchcraft in Salem Village, of June 15.

He ends thus:

The opinion which prevailed in New England, for many years after this tragedy, that there was something preternatural in it, and that it was not all the effect of fraud and imposture, proceeded from the reluctance in human nature to reject errors once imbibed. As the principal actors went off the stage, this opinion has gradually lessened; and perhaps it is owing to a respect to the memory of their immediate ancestors, that many do not yet seem to be fully convinced. There are a great number of persons who are willing to suppose the accusers to have been under bodily disorders which affected their imaginations. This is kind and charitable, but seems to be winking the truth out of sight. A little attention must force conviction that the whole was a scene of fraud and imposture, begun by young girls, who at first perhaps thought of nothing more than being pitied and indulged, and continued by adult persons, who were afraid of being accused themselves. The one and the other, rather than confess their fraud, suffered the lives of so many innocents to be taken away, through the credulity of judges and juries.

From: George Bancroft, *The History of the United States of America* (1834)

George Bancroft (1800–1891) was the son of a prominent Unitarian minister in Massachusetts, a Harvard graduate, and a Democratic politician and diplomat. His *History of the United States* was enormously popular in its day and makes impressive reading still. His account of the witch-hunt is the first, after Calef's, to note the bitter strife between Samuel Parris and some of his parishioners. He is astute on the role of Cotton Mather but displays an overly optimistic Jacksonian Democrat's faith in the good sense of the people, claiming all responsibility for the tragedy rested not with them but with five or six leaders (contradicting himself, given what he had already said about the strife in Salem Village). Despite the witch-hunt, he insists, the "development of the essential character of New England"—of faith mixed with common sense—continued.

From: volume 3, chapter 19

In Salem Village, now Danvers, there had been between Samuel Parris, the minister, and a part of his people, a strife so bitter, that it had even attracted the attention of the General Court. The delusion of witchcraft would give opportunities of terrible vengeance. In the family of Samuel Parris, his daughter, a child of nine years, and his niece, a girl of less than twelve, began to have strange caprices. "He that will read Cotton Mather's Book of Memorable Providences, may read part of what these children suffered:" and Tituba, an Indian female servant, who had practised some wild incantations, being betrayed by her husband, was scourged by Parris, her master, into confessing herself a witch. The ministers of the neighborhood held, at the afflicted house, a day of fasting and prayer; and the little children became the most conspicuous personages in Salem. Of a sudden, the opportunity of fame, of which the love is not the exclusive infirmity of noble minds, was placed within the reach of persons of the coarsest mould; and the ambition of notoriety recruited the little company of the possessed. There existed no motive to hang Tituba: she was saved as a living witness to the reality of witchcraft; and Sarah Good, a poor woman, of a melancholic temperament, was the first person selected for accusation. Cotton Mather, who had placed witches "among the poor, and vile, and ragged beggars upon earth," and had staked his own reputation for veracity on the reality of witchcraft, prayed "for a good issue." As the affair proceeded, and the accounts of the witnesses appeared as if taken from his own writings, his boundless vanity gloried in "the assault of the evil angels upon the country, as a particular defiance unto himself." Yet the delusion, but for Parris, would have languished. Of his own niece, the girl of eleven years of age, he demanded the names of the devil's instruments who bewitched the band of "the afflicted;" and then became at once informer and witness. In those days, there was no prosecuting officer, and Parris was at hand to question his Indian servants and others, himself prompting their answers, and acting as recorder to the magistrates. . . . A court of oyer and terminer was instituted by ordinance, and Stoughton appointed by the governor and council its chief judge: by the 2nd of June, the court was in session at Salem, making its first experiment on Bridget Bishop, a poor and friendless old woman. The fact of the witchcraft was assumed as "notorious:" to fix it on the prisoner, Samuel Parris, who had examined her before her commitment, was the principal witness to her power of inflicting torture; he had seen it exercised. Deliverance Hobbs had been whipped with iron rods by her spectre; neighbors, who had quarrelled with her, were willing to lay their little ills to her charge; the poor creature had a preternatural excrescence in her flesh; "she gave a look towards the great and spacious meeting-house of Salem,"—it is Cotton Mather who records this,—"and immediately a demon, invisibly entering the house, tore down a part of it." She was a witch by the rules and precedents of Keeble and Sir Matthew Hale, of Perkins and Bernard, of Baxter and Cotton Mather; and, on the 10th of June, protesting her innocence, she was hanged. Of the magistrates at that time, not one held office by the suffrage of the people: the tribunal, essentially despotic in its origin, as in its character, had no sanction but an extraordinary and an illegal commission; and Stoughton, the chief judge, a partisan of Andros, had been rejected by the people of Massachusetts. The responsibility of the tragedy, far from attaching to the people of the colony, rests with the very few, hardly five or six, in whose hands the transition state of the government left, for a season, unlimited influence. Into the interior of the colony the delusion did not spread at all.

The house of representatives, which assembled in June, was busy with its griefs at the abridgment of the old colonial liberties. Increase Mather, the agent, was heard in his own defence; and, at last, Bond, the speaker, in the name of the house, tardily and languidly thanked him for his faithful and unwearied exertions. No recompense was voted. "I seek not yours, but you," said Increase Mather; "I am willing to wait for recompense in another world;" and the general court, after prolonging the validity of the old laws, adjourned to October.

But Phipps and his council had not looked to the general court for directions; they turned to the ministers of Boston and Charlestown; and from them, by the hand of Cotton Mather, they receive gratitude for their sedulous endeavors to defeat the abominable witchcrafts; prayer that the discovery may be perfected; a caution against haste and spectral evidence; a hint to affront the devil, and give him the lie, by condemning none on his testimony alone; while the direful advice is added—"We recommend the speedy and vigorous prosecution of such as have rendered themselves obnoxious." The obedient court, at its next session, condemned five women, all of blameless lives, all declaring their innocence. Four were convicted easily enough; Rebecca Nurse was, at first, acquitted. "The honored court was pleased to object against the verdict;" and, as she had said of the confessing witnesses, "they used to come among us," meaning that they had been prisoners together. Stoughton interpreted the words as of a witch festival. The jury withdrew, and could as yet not agree; but, as the prisoner, who was hard of hearing, and full of grief, made no explanation, they no longer refused to find her guilty. Hardly was the verdict rendered, before the foreman made a statement of the ground of her condemnation, and she sent her declaration to the court in reply. The governor, who himself was not unmerciful, saw cause to grant a reprieve; but Parris had preached against Rebecca Nurse, and prayed against her; had induced "the afflicted" to witness against her; had caused her sisters to be imprisoned for their honorable sympathy. She must perish, or the delusion was unveiled, and the governor recalled the reprieve. On the next communion day, she was taken in chains to the meeting-house, to be formally excommunicated by Noyes, her minister; and was hanged with the rest. "You are a witch; you know you are," said Noyes to Sarah Good, urging a confession. "You are a liar," replied the poor woman; "and if you take my life, God will give you blood to drink."

Confessions rose in importance. "Some, not afflicted before confession, were so presently after it." The jails were filled; for fresh accusations were needed to confirm the confessions. "Some, by these their accusations of others,"—I quote the cautious apologist Hale,—"hoped to gain time, and get favor from the rules." "Some of the inferior sort of people did ill offices, by promising favor thereby, more than they had ground to engage. Some, under these temptations, regarded not as they should what became of others, so that they could thereby serve their own turns. Some have since acknowledged so much." If the confessions were contradictory; if witnesses uttered apparent falsehoods, "the devil," the judges would say, "takes away their memory, and imposes on their brain." And who now would dare to be skeptical? who would disbelieve confessors? Besides, there were other evidences. A callous spot was the mark of the devil: did age or amazement refuse to shed tears; were threats after a quarrel followed by the death of cattle or other harm; did an error occur in repeating the Lord's prayer; were deeds of great physical strength performed,—these all were signs of witchcraft. In some instances, the phenomena of somnambulism would appear to have been exhibited; and "the afflicted, out of their fits, knew nothing of what they did or said in them."

Again, on a new session, six are arraigned, and all are convicted. John Willard had, as an officer, been employed to arrest the suspected witches. Perceiving the hypocrisy, he declined the service. The afflicted immediately denounced him, and he was seized, convicted, and hanged.

At the trial of George Burroughs, the bewitched persons pretended to be dumb. "Who hinders these witnesses," said Stoughton, "from giving their testimonies?"—"I suppose the devil," answered Burroughs. "How comes the devil," retorted the chief judge, "so loath to have any testimony borne against you?" and the question was effective. Besides, he had given proofs of great, if not preternatural muscular strength. Cotton Mather calls the evidence "enough:" the jury gave a verdict of guilty.

John Procter, who foresaw his doom, and knew from whom the danger came, sent an earnest petition, not to the governor and council, but to Cotton Mather and the ministers. Among the witnesses against him were some who had made no confessions till after torture. "They have already undone us in our estates, and that will not serve their turns without our innocent blood;" and he begs for a trial in Boston, or, at least, for a change of magistrates. His entreaties were vain, as also his prayers, after condemnation, for a respite.

Among the witnesses against Martha Carrier, the mother saw her own children. Her two sons refused to perjure themselves till they had been tied neck and heels so long that the blood was ready to gush from them. The confession of her daughter, a child of seven years old, is still preserved.

The aged Jacobs was condemned, in part, by the evidence of Margaret Jacobs, his granddaughter. "Through the magistrates' threatenings and my own vile heart,"—thus she wrote to her father,—"I have confessed things contrary to my conscience and knowledge. But, oh! the terrors of a wounded conscience who can bear?" And she confessed the whole truth before the magistrates. The magistrates refused their belief, and, confining her for trial, proceeded to hang her grandfather.

These five were condemned on the third, and hanged on the nineteenth of August; pregnancy reprieved Elizabeth Procter. To hang a minister as a witch was a novelty; but Burroughs denied absolutely that there was, or could be, such a thing as witchcraft, in the current sense. This opinion wounded the self-love of the judges, for it made them the accusers and judicial murderers of the innocent. On the ladder, Burroughs cleared his innocence by an earnest speech, repeating the Lord's prayer composedly and exactly, and with a fervency that astonished. Tears flowed to the eyes of many; it seemed as if the spectators would rise to hinder the execution. Cotton Mather, on horseback among the crowd, addressed the people, cavilling at the ordination of Burroughs, as though he had been no true minister; insisting on his guilt, and hinting that the devil could sometimes assume the appearance of an angel of light: and the hanging proceeded.

Meantime, the confessions of the witches began to be directed against the Anabaptists. Mary Osgood was dipped by the devil. The court still had work to do. On the ninth, six women were condemned; and more convictions followed. Giles Corey, the octogenarian, seeing that all were convicted, refused to plead, and was condemned to be pressed to death. The horrid sentence, a barbarous usage of English law, never again followed in the colonies, was executed forthwith.

On the twenty-second of September, eight persons were led to the gallows. Of these, Samuel Wardwell had confessed, and was safe; but, from shame and penitence, he retracted his confession, and, speaking the truth boldly, he was hanged, not for witchcraft, but for denying witchcraft. Martha Corey was, before execution, visited in prison by Parris, the two deacons, and another member of his church. The church record tells that, self-sustained, she "imperiously" rebuked her destroyers, and "they pronounced the dreadful sentence of excommunication against her." In the calmness with which Mary Easty exposed the falsehood of those who had selected from her family so many victims, she joined the noblest fortitude with sweetness of temper, dignity, and resignation. But the chief judge was positive that all had been done rightly, and "was very impatient in hearing any thing that looked another way."—"There hang eight firebrands of hell," said Noyes, the minister of Salem, pointing to the bodies swinging on the gallows.

Already twenty persons had been put to death for witchcraft; fifty-five had been tortured or terrified into penitent confessions. With accusations, confessions increased; with confessions, new accusations. Even "the generation of the children of God" were in danger of "falling under that condemnation." The jails were full. It was also observed, that no one of the condemned confessing witchcraft had been hanged. No one that confessed, and retracted a confession, had escaped either hanging or imprisonment for trial. No one of the condemned, who asserted innocence, even if one of the witnesses confessed perjury, or the foreman of the jury acknowledged the error of the verdict, escaped the gallows. Favoritism was shown in listening to accusations, which were turned aside from friends or partisans. If a man began a career as a witch-hunter, and, becoming convinced of the imposture, declined the service, he was accused and hanged. Persons accused, who had escaped from the jurisdiction in Massachusetts, were not demanded, as would have been done in case of acknowledged crime; so that the magistrates acted as if witch-law did not extend beyond their jurisdiction. Witnesses convicted of perjury were cautioned, and permitted still to swear away the lives of others. It was certain, people had been tempted to become accusers by promise of favor. Yet the zeal of Stoughton was unabated, and the arbitrary court adjourned to the first Tuesday in November. "Between this and then," wrote Brattle, "will be the great assembly, and this matter will be a peculiar subject of agitation. Our hopes," he adds, "are here." The representatives of the people must stay the evil, or "New England is undone and undone."

Far different was the reasoning of Cotton Mather. He was met "continually with all sorts of objections and objectors against the work doing at Salem." The obstinate Sadducees, "the witch advocates," who esteemed the executions to be judicial murders, gained such influence as to embarrass the governor. But Cotton Mather, still eager "to lift up a standard against the infernal enemy," undertook the defence of his friends; and he sent to Salem for an account strong enough "to knock down" "one that believed nothing reasonable," promising "to box it about among his neighbors till it come he knows not where at last." Before the opening of the adjourned session of the general court, the indefatigable man had prepared his narrative of "the Wonders of the Invisible World," in the design of promoting "a pious thankfulness to God for justice being so far executed among us." For this book he received the approbation of the president of Harvard College, the praises of the governor, and the gratitude of Stoughton.

On the second Wednesday in October, 1692, about a fortnight after the last hanging of eight at Salem, the representatives of the people assembled; and the people of Andover, their minister joining with them, appeared with their remonstrance against the doings of the witch tribunals. "We know not," say they, "who can think himself safe, if the accusations of children, and others under a diabolical influence, shall be received against persons of good fame." Of the discussions that ensued no record is preserved; we know only the issue. The general court did not place itself in direct opposition to the advocates of the trials: as to legislation, it adopted what King William rejected,—the English law, word for word as it stood in the English statute-book; but they abrogated the special court, establishing a tribunal by public law. Phipps had, instantly on his arrival, employed his illegal court in hanging; the representatives of the people delayed the first assembling of the legal colonial court till January of the following year. Thus an interval of more than three months from the last executions gave the public mind security and freedom; and, though Phipps still conferred the place of chief judge on Stoughton, yet jurors, representing the public mind, acted independently. When the court met at Salem, six women of Andover, at once renouncing their confession, treated the witchcraft but as something so called, the bewildered but as "seemingly afflicted." A memorial of like tenor came from the inhabitants of Andover.

Of the presentments the grand jury dismissed more than half, and, if it found bills against twenty-six, the trials did but show the feebleness of the testimony on which others had been condemned. The same testimony was produced, and there, at Salem, with Stoughton on the bench, verdicts of acquittal followed: "Error expired amidst its worshippers." Three had, for special reasons, been convicted: one was a wife, whose testimony had sent her husband to the gallows, and whose confession was now used against herself. All were at once reprieved, and soon set free.

Still reluctant to yield, the party of superstition were resolved on one conviction. The victim selected was Sarah Daston, a woman of eighty years old, who for twenty years had enjoyed the undisputed reputation of a witch: if ever there were a witch in the world, she, it was said, was one. In the presence of a throng, the trial went forward at Charlestown: there was more evidence against her than against any at Salem; but the common mind was disinthralled, and asserted itself, through the jury, by a verdict of acquittal.

To cover his confusion, Cotton Mather got up a case of witchcraft in his own parish. Miracles, he avers, were wrought in Boston. Believe his statements, and you must believe that his prayers healed diseases. But he was not bloodthirsty; he wished his vanity protected, not his parishioners hanged; and his bewitched neophyte, profiting by his cautions, was afflicted by veiled spectres. The imposture was promptly exposed to ridicule by "a malignant, calumnious, and reproachful man," "a coal from hell," the unlettered but rational and intelligent Robert Calef. Was Cotton Mather honestly credulous? Ever ready to dupe himself, he limited his credulity only by the probable credulity of others. He changes, or omits to repeat, his statements, without acknowledging error, and with a clear intention of conveying false impressions. He is an example how far selfishness, under the form of vanity and ambition, can blind the higher faculties, stupefy the judgment, and dupe consciousness itself. His self-righteousness was complete, till he was resisted. As the recall of Phipps—a consequence of impetuous imbecility—left the government for some years in the hands of Stoughton, the press was restrained: when, at last, the narrative of Calef appeared, Cotton Mather endeavored to shield himself by calling his adversaries the adversaries of religion; and, though hardly seven or eight of the ministers, and no magistrate of popular appointment, had a share in the guilt, he endeavored, but ineffectually, to denounce the book as "a libel upon the whole government and ministry of the land." Denying the jurisdiction of popular opinion, he claims the subject as "too dark and deep for ordinary comprehension," and appeals for a decision to the day of judgment. But the sentence was not delayed. The inexorable indignation of the people of Salem village drove Parris from the place; Noyes regained favor only by a full confession, asking forgiveness always, and consecrating the remainder of his life to deeds of mercy. Sewall, one of the judges, by the frankness and sincerity of his undisguised confession, recovered public esteem. Stoughton and Cotton Mather never repented. The former lived proud, unsatisfied, and unbeloved; the latter attempted to persuade others and himself that he had not been specially active in the tragedy. But the public mind would not be deceived. His diary proves that he did not wholly escape the rising impeachment from the monitor within; and Cotton Mather, who had sought the foundation of faith in tales of wonders, himself "had temptations to atheism, and to the abandonment of all religion as a mere delusion."

The common mind of Massachusetts was more wise. It never wavered in its faith; more ready to receive every tale from the invisible world, than to gaze on the universe without acknowledging an Infinite Intelligence. But, employing a gentle skepticism, eliminating error, rejecting superstition as tending to cowardice and submission, cherishing religion as the source of courage and the fountain of freedom, the common mind in New England refused henceforward to separate belief and reason. To the west of Massachusetts, and to Connecticut, to which the influence of Cotton Mather and its consequences did not extend, we must look for the unmixed development of the essential character of New England; yet there, also, faith and "common sense" were reconciled. In the vicinity of Boston, the skepticism of free inquiry conducted some minds to healthy judgments; others asserted

God to be the true being, the devil to be but a nonentity, and disobedience to God to be the only possible compact with Satan; others, still clinging to the letter of the Bible, yet showed the insufficiency of all evidence for the conviction of a witch; others denied witchcraft, as beyond comprehension, involving a contradiction, and not sustained by the evidence of experience. The invisible world began to be less considered; men trusted more to observation and analysis; and this philosophy, derived from the senses, was analogous to their civil condition. The people in the charter governments could hope from England for no concession of larger liberties. Instead, therefore, of looking for the reign of absolute right, they were led to reverence the forms of their privileges as exempt from change. We hear no more of the theocracy where God was alone supreme lawgiver and king; no more of the expected triumph of freedom and justice anticipated "in the second coming of Christ:" liberty, in Massachusetts, was defended by asserting the sanctity of compact.

From: Charles W. Upham, *Salem Witchcraft*, (Boston, 1867), part 3: "Witchcraft at Salem Village"

Charles Upham, like Hutchinson and Bancroft, is over-simplistic in ascribing almost every aspect of the witch-hunt to conscious fraud and conspiracy. All three lived before the twentieth century's understanding of the unconscious mind. Upham also shared Bancroft's sentimental attachment to the notion of sturdy, sensible farming folk led astray. A Salemite himself, he had a strong motive for finding alien causes for the start of the witch-hunt and develops Mather's myth of the "afflicted" girls, strongly involved in sorcery and magic, into the notion of a wide-ranging spiritualist "circle" led by Tituba and John Indian. However, Upham understood the local political background to the witch-hunt better than anyone till the 1970s, making his history an inclusive exploration of its causes and development.

We left Mr. Parris in the early part of November, 1691, at the crisis of his controversy with the inhabitants of Salem Village, under circumstances which seemed to indicate that its termination was near at hand. The opposition to him had assumed a form which made it quite probable that it would succeed in dislodging him from his position. But the end was not yet. Events were ripening that were to give him a new and fearful strength, and open a scene in which he was to act a part destined to attract the notice of the world, and become a permanent portion of human history. The doctrines of demonology had produced their full effect upon the minds of men, and every thing was ready for a final display of their power. The story of the Goodwin children, as told by Cotton Mather, was known and read in all the dwellings of the land, and filled the imaginations of a credulous age. Deputy-governor Danforth had begun the work of arrests; and persons charged with witchcraft, belonging to neighboring towns, were already in prison.

Mr. Parris appears to have had in his family several slaves, probably brought by him from the West Indies. One of them, whom he calls, in his church-record book, "my negro lad," had died, a year or two before, at the age of nineteen. Two of them were man and wife. The former was always known by the name of "John Indian;" the latter was called "Tituba." These two persons may have originated the "Salem witchcraft." They are spoken of as having come from New Spain, as it was then called,—that is, the Spanish West Indies, and the adjacent mainlands of Central and South America,—and, in all probability, contributed, from the wild and strange superstitions prevalent among their native tribes, materials which, added to the commonly received notions on such subjects, heightened the infatuation of the times, and inflamed still more the imaginations of the credulous. Persons conversant with the Indians of Mexico, and on both sides of the Isthmus, discern many similarities in their systems of demonology with ideas and practices developed here.

Mr. Parris's former residence in the neighborhood of the Spanish Main, and the prominent part taken by his Indian slaves in originating the proceedings at the village, may account for some of the features of the transaction.

During the winter of 1691 and 1692, a circle of young girls had been formed, who were in the habit of meeting at Mr. Parris's house for the purpose of practising palmistry, and other arts of fortune-telling, and of becoming experts in the wonders of necromancy, magic, and spiritualism. . . .

It is quite evident that the part played by the Indian woman on this occasion was pre-arranged. She had, from the first, been concerned with the circle of girls in their necromantic operations; and her statements show the materials out of which their ridiculous and monstrous stories were constructed. She said that there were four who "hurt the children." Upon being pressed by the magistrate to tell who they were, she named Osborne and Good, but did "not know who the others were." Two others were marked; but it was not thought best to bring them out until these three examinations had first been made to tell upon the public mind. Tituba had been apprised of Elizabeth Hubbard's story, that she had been "pinched" that morning; and, as well as "Lieutenant Fuller and others," had heard of the delirious exclamation of Thomas Putnam's sick child during the night. "Abigail Williams, that lives with her uncle Parris," had communicated to the Indian slave the story of "the woman with two legs and wings." In fact, she had been fully admitted to their councils, and made acquainted with all the stories they were to tell. But, when it became necessary to avoid specifications touching parties whose names it had been decided not to divulge at that stage of the business, the wily old servant escapes further interrogation, "I am blind now: I cannot see."

From: Samuel G. Drake, *Annals of Witchcraft in New England* (New York, 1869)

Samuel Drake embellished the notion of the "circle" but without reference to Tituba. His *Annals* consists mainly of reproductions of the trial transcripts.

The principal accusers and witnesses, too, in the whole term of the witchcraft prosecutions were eight females, nearly all young girls, from eleven to twenty years of age. These were Abigail Williams, eleven; Mary Walcott, seventeen; Ann Putnam, twelve; Mercy Lewis, seventeen; Mary Warren, twenty; Elizabeth Booth, eighteen; Sarah Churchill, twenty; and Susannah Sheldon.

Mary Walcott was daughter of Captain John Walcott; Ann Putnam was a daughter of Thomas Putnam; Mercy Lewis was a servant living in Mr. Putnam's family; Mary Warren lived in the family of Mr. John Procter; Elizabeth Booth lived near John Procter; Sarah Churchill lived in the family of George Jacobs, Senr.; Susannah Sheldon lived in the Village.

These females instituted frequent meetings, or got up, as it would now be styled, a club, which was called a circle. How frequent they had these meetings is not stated, but it was soon ascertained that they met "to try projects," or to do or produce superhuman acts. They doubtless had among them some book or books on magic, and stories of witchcraft, which some one or more of their circle professed to understand, and pretended to teach the rest. Yet they were generally very ignorant, for out of the eight but two could write their names. Such were the characters which set in motion that stupendous tragedy, which ended in blood and ruin.

From: M. V. B. Perley, *A Short History of the Salem Witchcraft Trials* (1911)

Perley was also, like Upham, a native of Salem. He uses a vivid imagination to elaborate the image of Tituba, tutor of the dark arts.

John and His Tituba
Rev. S. Parris's Slaves

Mr. Parris brought with him from the Spanish Main, as his slaves, a couple called John Indian and his wife, Tituba. The ignorance of the Spanish population found its summit of pleasure in dancing, singing, sleight of hand, palmistry, fortune-telling, magic, and necromancy (or spirit communication with the dead); and John and his Tituba in all those things were fully up to date.

Parris's Witch School, Apt
Pupils, Their Personnel

To the pastor's house (as he wrote, "When these calamities first began, which was at my house") the village maidens, by surreption, went under the tuition of Tituba. Those of us who have some remembrance of the rise of spiritualism, the phenomenon of table-tipping, and the slightly more refined practice of the élite with scribbling planchet, can picture in some degree Tituba's pupils and how they got there.

From: Winfield S. Nevins, *Witchcraft in Salem Village* (1916) chapter 3, "The Outbreak in Salem Village"

Nevins turns Tituba into a "half negro" and suggests the girls may have claimed she "taught" them rather than afflicted them. He defends everyone else involved in the witch-hunt, from Samuel Parris to Cotton Mather, as well meaning if misguided.

The witchcraft delusion of 1692 undoubtedly had its inception in the home of Rev. Samuel Parris, pastor of the church in Salem Village. In his family were a daughter, Elizabeth, nine years of age; a niece, Abigail Williams, eleven years of age; and a servant, Tituba, half Indian, half negro. The tradition is that the two girls, with perhaps a few other children of the neighborhood, used, during the winter of 1691–2, to assemble in the minister's kitchen and practice tricks and incantations with Tituba. Among the other girls of the neighborhood, some of whom are believed to have been present at a portion of these performances, were Ann Putnam, twelve years of age, daughter of Sergeant Thomas Putnam; Mercy Lewis, seventeen years of age, maid in the family of Sergeant Putnam; Elizabeth Hubbard, seventeen years of age, a niece of the wife of Dr. Griggs, the village physician, and a servant in the family; and Sarah Churchill, aged twenty years, a servant in the family of George Jacobs, Senior. Mercy Lewis had previously lived in the family of Reverend George Burroughs. During the winter these girls held occasional meetings in the neighborhood, usually at the minister's house. Calef says they began to act after a strange and unusual manner, by getting into holes and creeping under chairs and stools, and to use sundry odd postures and antic gestures, uttering foolish, ridiculous speeches, which neither they themselves nor any others could make sense of.

Tituba undoubtedly had familiarity with the strange tricks and jugglery practiced by the semi-barbarous races; and, although we know nothing definite about it, is it not reasonable to presume that she exhibited some of these to Elizabeth Parris and Abigail Williams, who lived in the house with her, and that they told their young friends in the village about the performances; that these friends came secretly to witness the mysterious tricks; that they were instructed in the practice of them, and did practice them for self amusement or the amazement of other young people; and that eventually the business got noised abroad and came to the knowledge of the elder people? They would naturally institute an inquiry. The girls, probably, realized that if the exact truth were known to their elders they would be severely punished; possibly publicly disciplined in church. To prevent this, may they not have claimed that they could not help doing as they did? They undoubtedly had some knowledge of witchcraft, enough at least to enable them to make a pretense of being bewitched. The girls could not for a moment realize the terrible consequences which were to follow. Having taken the first step, they were in the position of all who take a first step in falsehood or any other wrong doing, another step became necessary, and then another. Then they were probably commanded by their elders to tell who caused them to do these strange things; or, as most writers put it, who "afflicted" them. As already stated, they named Tituba, Good and Osborne. Is it possible that we have misunderstood the first statements of these children? Is it possible they did not say Tituba's *apparition caused* them to do certain strange things, but that they said *she taught* them? Is it possible that Parris, to save scandal in his own immediate household, made Tituba declare that she had bewitched the girls? I do not mean to assert that this is the correct version of the outbreak of witchcraft in Salem Village. I only desire to suggest what may have been; something which offers, perhaps, a rational explanation of the beginning of this horrid nightmare. Certainly such a course is as plausible, as reasonable, and has as much basis of fact as any of the theories heretofore advanced.

From: Marion Starkey, *The Devil in Massachusetts* (1949), chapter 2, "Young People's Circle"

It is sad and ironic that this book is widely read to this day. It simplifies and idealizes characters and motives, disregards the local political and historical background, and diminishes the witch-hunt's evil and horror. It also frequently lapses into fiction. In Starkey's hands Tituba becomes a slow-moving, sly, half-negro "big mamma."

There were in the Parris household two slaves, relics of his Barbados venture, the loutish John Indian and his consort, the ageless Tituba, said to be half Carib and half negro. The possession of these slaves lent prestige to the parsonage, for although there were other negro slaves in the community, there were not many. Thanks to the labours of this pair, Mrs Parris, a shadowy, self-effacing woman of whom history says little and tradition only that she was a truly good woman, was able to find time for numerous errands of mercy, and the children to live like little princesses, not to be sure in the sense of enjoying any pampered idleness, but in the sense that their chores consisted of those lighter household tasks that even a princess may learn.

All the heavier household work fell to the slaves. John Indian attended to the livestock and wood-lot, worked in the field, and even on occasion was hired out to give a hand in Deacon Ingersoll's ordinary, cater-cornered across the road from the parsonage. Tituba did the heavier, coarser household chores, boiled and pounded the linen when seasonal wash-days came, fetched water from the well, emptied the slops, scrubbed and sanded the floors.

All these things Tituba did, but not, one gathers, with energy. Her breeding had been in a softer, more languid clime; her life at hard labour in frosty New England was none of her choosing. She found subtle ways of easing her lot, and one of these was idling with the little girls.

Finding opportunity to do so was not difficult, for the children were often left to their tasks under Tituba's direction. The minister spent much of his time afield inspecting the parish, and even at home usually sat safely out of range in his study. Mrs Parris was in the kitchen more often, but even she had frequent charitable errands abroad. Left alone with the children, Tituba had long ago learned to amuse herself in ways that would have got her a thrashing from Parris had he got wind of them in time.

The sport may have started quite harmlessly, possibly even within the hearing of Mrs Parris, with nothing more questionable than reminiscences of life in the Barbados imparted within Tituba's lawful moments of leisure. But there were presently occasions when, in the absence of the elder Parrises, Tituba yielded to the temptation to show the children tricks and spells, fragments of something like voodoo remembered from the Barbados. Once she started, Abigail, thirsting for excitement, must have egged her on to further revelation, conspiring with her to find occasion for the sport, and Betty became a timid accomplice.

Betty's reactions to these sessions are not on record—no more than anyone else's, for no one was ever to be wholly truthful about what went on in the parsonage kitchen. However, the child's painfully overdeveloped conscience could not have missed the scent of evil in these enterprises, and above all she knew the guilt of keeping a secret from her parents.

Yet Betty did not give Abigail and Tituba away, no matter how guilty and frightened she became. For one thing, daring Abigail had long ago become her leader in most private matters; for another, Betty was devoted to Tituba, whose special pet she was. The half-savage slave loved to cuddle the child in her own snuggery by the fire, stroke her fair hair and murmur to her old tales and nonsense rhymes. Never from her own mother had the child received such affection, for though godly parents loved their children as much as any heathen, they would not risk spoiling them. Basking in this warmth, Betty gave an almost hypnotic attention to the slurred Southern speech and tricksy ways of Tituba. Well she knew in her upright Puritan heart that she was tampering with the forbidden, but she could no more resist than she could lift a hand to free herself from the spell of an evil, thrilling dream.

Abigail knew more explicitly than Betty that what she was doing was none of God's work; even her heart may have known its secret pangs of guilt. But Abigail was so constructed that up to a point the guilt only added zest to the adventure.

From: Chadwick Hansen, *Witchcraft at Salem* (New York, 1969)

Someone, sometime, was bound to come up with the theory that some of the accused witches at Salem really were practicing witchcraft. Chadwick Hansen makes a coherent, if unconvincing, case for this. His book includes an excellent explanation of the onset of the girls' fits as due to clinical hysteria but suggests that it was the fear of witchcraft that caused that hysteria. The fear was so strong, he claims, because the witchcraft was real.

From: Chapter 5

Bridget Bishop was in all probability a practicing witch. She had a long-standing reputation for witchcraft; it was rumored that she had bewitched her first husband (a Goodman Wasslebee) to death. In 1679/80, during her second marriage (to Thomas Oliver), she had been brought before the Court of Assistants for witchcraft. The records of that trial do not survive, but it is probable that a major factor in her release at the time was the good opinion of her clergyman, John Hale of Beverly, who was then "hoping better of Goody Bishop" than others in the community. But Hale had changed his mind by 1692. Her present husband, Edward Bishop, had accused her of witchcraft; two women testified that he had said "the Devil did come bodily unto her, and that she was familiar with the Devil, and that she sat up all the night long with the Devil." She was well aware of her reputation. Once she had asked William Stacey "whether his father would grind her grist. He put it to her why she asked. She answered, because folks counted her a witch." She also had the malice requisite to the craft. During her examination, when Hathorne used the bullying techniques he had used on others, she startled him with an open threat. "If I were any such person [a witch]," she told him, "you should know it." [I.e., she would *make* him know it.]

But there was much more against Bridget Bishop than her reputation and her malice. Two men testified that

> being employed by Bridget Bishop, alias Oliver, of Salem to help take down the cellar wall of the old house she formerly lived in, we the said deponents, in holes in the old wall belonging to the said cellar, found several puppets made up of rags and hogs' bristles with headless pins in them with the points outward. . . .

The doll with pins in it is the classic charm of black magic, and burying it in a wall is still a technique of witches; such charms have been found in the walls of rural English cottages in the twentieth century. To be sure, the evidence was circumstantial—nobody had seen Bridget Bishop stick the pins in the dolls or bury them in the walls. But she could, according to Cotton Mather, give no account of them to the court "that was reasonable or tolerable." Coupled with the other testimony against her, that concerning the dolls was extremely incriminating. It would have been quite enough to get her hanged in seventeenth-century England or burned in Scotland or on the Continent. It is probable that Bridget Bishop was indeed a practicing witch.

There is one more piece of evidence which probably applies to her use of image magic. Samuel Shattuck, a Quaker who was the local dyer, testified that she had brought him for dyeing "sundry pieces of lace, some of which were so short that I could not judge them fit for any use." Upham, in the nineteenth century, interpreted this to mean that Bridget Bishop was wearing clothing of a style incomprehensible to a simple Quaker and later writers have followed him in this interpretation, coupling with it the fact that Bridget Bishop often wore a "red paragon bodice" and leaving the impression that she dressed in a higher or more flashy fashion than the community thought proper. But red was not an unusual color for clothing in seventeenth-century New England, and Shattuck said nothing about the cut of the laces she brought him for dyeing. He said the pieces were *too small* to be of any use. If Bridget Bishop had been dressing extravagantly wouldn't her laces have been *larger* than usual? It would seem that what Shattuck meant was that the pieces of lace were too small to be worn by a human being. But they would not have been too small for dressing a witch's doll, which is often clothed in the same materials and colors as the clothing worn by the victim.

Shattuck, like other seventeenth-century common folk, had quite a smattering of occult information, which he was not above putting to use. One of his children had, years ago, been unaccountably ill of fits; "his mouth and eyes drawn aside . . . in such a manner as if he was upon the point of death." A passing stranger suggested the child was bewitched and offered to take the boy to Goodwife Bishop's and scratch her face (drawing blood from a witch's face was a common means of breaking her spells). Shattuck agreed, and added some white magic of his own: "I gave him money and bid him ask her for a pot of cider." (Obtaining property and subjecting it to occult abuse was a common technique of both white and black magic.) But Goodwife Bishop was not to be taken in. She refused to sell the cider and chased the stranger off with a spade. Not only did she avoid having her face scratched; she scratched the face of Shattuck's son. "And ever since," said Shattuck,

> this child hath been followed with grievous fits as if he would never recover more, his head and eyes drawn aside so as if they would never come to rights more; lying as if he were in a manner dead, falling anywhere, either into fire or water if he be not constantly looked to; and generally in such an uneasy and restless frame, almost always running to and fro, acting so strange that I cannot judge otherwise but that he is bewitched, and by these circumstances do believe that the aforesaid Bridget Oliver, now called Bishop, is the cause of it. And it has been the judgment of doctors . . . that he is under an evil hand of witchcraft.

Notice again how willing the medical profession was to diagnose witchcraft. In fact, the seventeenth-century physician was apt to attribute everything he could not explain organically to witchcraft, just as the twentieth-century physician is apt to call whatever he cannot understand psychosomatic. But notice also that the child's symptoms are identifiably hysterical, and therefore may well have been due to his frightening experience with Bridget Bishop.

Certainly other persons were terrified of her and had hysterical hallucinations as a result of their terror. Richard Coman testified that about eight years before he had been in bed with his wife, with a light burning in the room.

> I being awake did then see Bridget Bishop of Salem, alias Oliver, come into the room we lay in and two women more with her, which two women were strangers to me. I knew them not, but said Bishop came in her red paragon bodice and the rest of her clothing which she then usually did wear. . . . And quickly after they appeared the light was out, and the curtains at the foot of the bed opened, where I did see her. And presently [she] came and lay upon my breast or body and so oppressed me that I could not speak nor stir, no not so much as to awake my wife, although I endeavored much so to do it. The next night they all appeared again in like manner and the said Bishop, alias Oliver, took hold of me by the throat and almost hauled me out of the bed. The Saturday night following, I having been that day telling of what I had seen and how I suffered the two nights before, my kinsman William Coman told me he would stay with me and lodge with me and see if they would come again, and advised me to lay my sword athwart my body. [The hilt of a sword, being shaped like a cross, was thought to be a protection against witches and evil spirits.] Quickly after we went to bed that said night, and both well awake and discoursing together, in came all the three women again, and said Bishop was the first as she had been the other two nights. So I told him, "William, here they be all come again." And he was immediately struck speechless and could not move hand or foot. And immediately they got hold of my sword and strived to take it from me, but I held so fast as they did not get it away. And I then had liberty of speech [having been able to hold on to the sign of the cross; notice again how magic works in a society which believes in it] and called William, also my wife, and Sarah Phillips that lay with my wife, who all told me afterwards they heard me but had not power to speak or stir. . . . And the first that spake was Sarah Phillips, and said, "In the name of God, Goodman Coman, what is the matter with you?" So they all vanished away.

Presumably the hallucination ended because the name of God had been invoked, just as Coman had regained his speech by holding to the symbol of the cross.

Samuel Gray had a similar experience fourteen years before, when he woke to

> see a woman standing between the cradle in the room and the bedside and [she] seemed to look upon him. So he did rise up in his bed and it vanished. . . . Then he went to the door and found it locked. And unlocking and opening the door he went to the entry door and looked out, and then again did see the same woman he had a little before seen in the room, and in the

> same garb she was in before. Then he said to her, "In the name of God, what do you come for?" Then she vanished away. So he locked the door again and went to bed. And between sleeping and waking he felt something come to his mouth or lips, cold, and thereupon started and looked up, and again did see the same woman with something between both her hands, holding it before his mouth. Upon which she moved, and the child in the cradle gave a great screech out, as if it was greatly hurt, and she disappeared. And taking the child up [he] could not quiet it in some hours. From which time the child, that before was a very likely thriving child, did pine away and was never well (although it lived some months after, yet in a sad condition) and so died. Some time after, within a week or less, he did see the same woman in the same garb or clothes that appeared to him as aforesaid, . . . although he knew not her nor her name before. Yet both by her garb and countenance doth testify that it was the same woman that they now call Bridget Bishop, alias Oliver, of Salem.

The death of the child cannot be explained on natural grounds except by suggesting that there was something wrong with it quite unrelated to its father's experience. Nor can one account for Gray's having hallucinations of Bridget Bishop before he knew her or knew her name except by suggesting that he was mistaken. But the next experiences—those of John Louder—need no explanation. They fit the pattern of hysterical hallucinations we have seen before.

> About seven or eight years since, I then living with Mr. John Gedney in Salem . . . had some controversy with Bridget Bishop, the wife of Edward Bishop of Salem, sawyer, about her fowls that used to come into our orchard or garden. Some little time after which, I going well to bed, about the dead of the night felt a great weight upon my breast, and awakening looked and, it being bright moonlight, did clearly see said Bridget Bishop or her likeness sitting upon my stomach. And putting my arms off of the bed to free myself from that great oppression, she presently laid hold of my throat and almost choked me, and I had no strength or power in my hands to resist or help myself. And in this condition she held me to almost day. Some time after this my mistress, Susannah Gedney, was in our orchard and I was then with her, and said Bridget Bishop being then in her orchard which was next adjoining to ours, my mistress told said Bridget that I said or affirmed that she came one night and sat upon my breast as aforesaid, which she denied and I affirmed to her face to be true, and that I did plainly see her, upon which discourse with her she threatened me. And some time after that I, not being very well, stayed at home on a Lord's Day. And on the afternoon of said day,

> the doors being shut, I did see a black pig in the room coming towards me. So I went towards it to kick it and it vanished away. [Notice again that hallucinations vanish if the subject is able to speak or move.] Immediately after I sat down . . . and did see a black thing jump into the window. And [it] came and stood just before my face. . . . The body of it looked like a monkey, only the feet were like a cock's feet with claws, and the face somewhat more like a man's than a monkey's. And I being greatly affrighted, not being able to speak or help myself by reason of fear, I suppose, so the thing spoke to me and said, "I am a messenger sent to you. For I understand you are troubled in mind, and if you will be ruled by me you shall want for nothing in this world." Upon which I endeavored to clap my hands upon it, and said, "You Devil, I will kill you," but could feel no substance. And it jumped out of the window again and immediately came in by the porch, although the doors were shut, and said, "You had better take my counsel." Whereupon I struck at it with a stick but struck the groundsill and broke the stick, but felt no substance, and that arm with which I struck was presently disenabled. Then it vanished away and I opened the back door and went out, and going towards the house-end I espied said Bridget Bishop in her orchard going towards her house, and seeing her had no power to set one foot forward but returned in again. And going to shut the door I again did see that or the like creature that I before did see within doors, in such a posture as it seemed to be going to fly at me. Upon which I cried out, "The whole armor of God . . . be between me and you!" So it sprang back and flew over the appletree, flinging the dust with its feet against my stomach, upon which I was struck dumb and so continued for about three days time. And also it shook many of the apples off from the tree which it flew over.

At her trial Bridget Bishop denied knowing John Louder, although it was common knowledge that they had been next-door neighbors and had frequently quarreled. The gratuitous lie must have hurt her, but not nearly so much as the other evidence against her.

There is, unfortunately, no way of knowing whether Bridget Bishop was actually using charms or spells against Richard Coman, or Samuel Gray, or John Louder. But their testimony is eloquent evidence of the power which accompanied a reputation for witchcraft. And the dolls, the pieces of lace too short for use, and the scratching of the Shattuck child's face all suggest that Bridget Bishop had consciously sought such power, that she was in fact a witch, as the community believed her to be.

Bridget Bishop was not the only witch in Essex County; before they were through the magistrates had found others who were guilty of practicing black magic. One of them was Candy, a Negro slave from Barbados, who was examined on the fourth of July. Yes, she said, she was a witch. But she had not been a witch in Barbados, nor had her mother been a witch. Her mistress, Mrs. Hawkes, had made her a witch in this country, by bringing her a book in which she made her mark. "How did you afflict or hurt these folks?" Hathorne asked her. "Where are the puppets you did it with?" She asked permission to leave the room, and get them. The magistrates sent someone with her and she returned shortly carrying "a handkerchief wherein several knots were tied, rags of cloth, a piece of cheese and a piece of grass." At the sight of these

> Mary Warren, Deliverance Hobbs, and Abigail Hobbs . . . were greatly affrighted and fell into violent fits. And all of them said that [the specters of] the Black Man and Mrs. Hawkes and the Negro stood by the puppets or rags and pinched them, and then they were afflicted. And when the knots were untied yet they continued as aforesaid.

The accounts do not tell us what the cheese was used for. But Candy was forced to swallow the grass "and that night she was burned in her flesh." The magistrates had, apparently, decided to experiment rather thoroughly with these charms. A piece of one of the rags was burned "and one of the afflicted . . . was presently burned on the hand." Another piece was put under water and two of the afflicted "were choked, and strived for breath as if under water." Another ran down to the river "as if she would drown herself," but they stopped her. It does not seem to have occurred to anyone at the time that in experimenting with these charms the magistrates were themselves practicing witchcraft, and with dramatic and conspicuous success. Nor did it occur to anyone to notice that the experiments suggested that the malignant power must reside not in the witch but in the charms themselves or in the Devil's power that lay behind them, since they worked equally well whether they were manipulated by a confessed witch or by a godly magistrate. John Hale was to reflect on these experiments months later and reach a startling and original conclusion.

Another person who had clearly practiced witchcraft was Wilmot "Mammy" Redd, who had for many years been the town witch of Marblehead. The most interesting and most damning evidence against her concerned a quarrel she had with a Mrs. Simms of Salem Town, who suspected Mammy Redd's maid of stealing her linen. The quarrel grew so hot that Mrs. Simms threatened to swear out a warrant against the maid, upon which Mammy Redd pronounced a curse. Two witnesses swore to the substance of the curse, which was that Mrs. Simms "might never *mingere* [urinate] nor *cacare* [defecate]" until she let her alone. And sure enough, Mrs. Simms was shortly "taken with the distemper of the dry belly-ache, and so continued many months" until she left the area. At her preliminary examination, on May 31, Mammy Redd was reserved if not downright evasive. Hathorne may well have been interested in her professional opinion on the condition of the afflicted persons. In any case, he asked her repeatedly what she thought ailed them. But she would only answer, "I cannot tell." Finally he asked her directly whether she did not think it was witchcraft, but again she replied, "I cannot tell." "And being [again] urged for her opinion in the case, all she would say was, 'My opinion is they are in a sad condition.'"

Bridget Bishop, Candy, and Wilmot Redd had practiced malefic witchcraft. There were others who may or may not have practiced it—the evidence is insufficient—but who had clearly used their reputation for occult power to gain illegitimate personal ends. One of these was Dorcas Hoar of Beverly, a parishioner of the Reverend John Hale. She had been dabbling in the occult for years; Hale testified that "about twenty-two years ago" she told him she had borrowed a book on palmistry, containing rules on how to know the future. "But I telling her it was an evil book and evil art, she seemed to me to renounce or reject all such practices, whereupon I had great charity for her several years." Hale's charity was wasted, however, since Dorcas Hoar continued telling people's futures, sometimes through reading their faces as well as through reading their palms. Fortunetelling is often only white magic. But it easily becomes black magic when it concerns itself with the time or manner of the subject's death. In such cases the fortuneteller is often suspected, and not without reason, of assisting fortune. Precisely this had happened with Dorcas Hoar, who had told it about "that she should live poorly so long as her husband William Hoar did live, but the said Will should die before her and after that she should live better." He did die before her (not the only instance in which she had correctly foretold the order of death), and the community was so suspicious that an autopsy was held. She was enraged at that, but nothing had ever come of it.

Eight years after Hale first remonstrated with Dorcas Hoar he discovered

> an evil practise [which] had been between a servant of mine and some of said Hoar's children in conveying goods out of my house to the said Hoars. And I had a daughter Rebecca, then between eleven and twelve years old, whom I asked if she knew of the Hoars' stealing. She told me yea, but [she] durst not reveal it to me. And one reason was [that] she was threatened that Goody Hoar was a witch, and had a book by which she could tell what said Rebecca did tell me in my house. And if the said Rebecca told me of the stealing, the said Hoar would raise the Devil to kill her or bewitch her or words to that effect. But whether the said Dorcas herself or her children told Rebecca these words I remember not. I asked Rebecca if she saw the book.

> She said yes, she was showed that book, and there were many streaks and pictures in it by which (as she was told) the said Hoar could reveal and work witchcrafts. . . . [Both fortune-telling manuals and grimoires are, of course, full of diagrams.] "And," said she, "now I have told you of the stealing Goody Hoar will bewitch me." I [tried to persuade] my daughter not to think so hardly of Goody Hoar. But she replied, "I know Goody Hoar is a witch" (or to that effect), and then told stories of strange things that had been acted in or about my house when I and my wife were abroad to fright[en] said Rebecca into silence about the theft, which said Rebecca judged to be acts of witchcraft. The particulars I have now forgotten. . . . And after my daughter's death a friend told me that my daughter said to her [that] she went in fear of her life by the Hoars till quieted by the scripture, "Fear not them which can kill the body."

Theft was not a capital crime in seventeenth-century New England (although it was in seventeenth-century England, and remained so into the nineteenth century). But theft under these particularly repulsive circumstances would have been enough to get Goodwife Hoar executed in any part of seventeenth-century Western civilization. Indeed, the wonder is that Hale had not prosecuted her at the time. The most likely explanation of his failure to do so is his frequently demonstrated benevolence. He was always "hoping better" of people—even of such reprobates as Bridget Bishop and the Hoars.

The other person who used a reputation for occult power for illegitimate ends was the Reverend George Burroughs, who had been minister of Salem Village from 1680 to 1682 and was now serving a parish in Maine. On April 20 the apparition of a minister appeared to Ann Putnam, Jr. (who had been only two years old when Burroughs left Salem Village), at which "she was grievously affrighted and cried out, Oh dreadful, dreadful! Here is a minister come. What, are ministers witches too?" Like other witch apparitions he tortured her, and the torture included choking, as in so many other cases. He also tempted her "to write in his book," but she refused, scolding him "that he which was a minister, that should teach children to fear God, should come to persuade poor creatures to give their souls to the Devil." She asked him to tell her who he was so that she might complain of him to the authorities. Rather inconsistently, he told her, and went on to volunteer the information that he had bewitched many people to death, including his first two wives. (This was only one of several occasions when specters incriminated the persons they represented.)

Two weeks later the apparition was back, telling Ann that the specters of his first two wives would shortly appear to her but that they would tell a great many lies, to which she must not listen.

> Then immediately appeared to me the form of two women in winding-sheets, and napkins about their heads, at which I was greatly affrighted. And they turned their faces towards Mr. Burroughs and looked very red and angry and told him that he had been a cruel man to them, and that their blood did cry for vengeance against him, and also told him that they should be clothed with white robes in Heaven when he should be cast into Hell. And immediately he vanished away. And as soon as he was gone the two women turned their faces towards me and looked as pale as a white wall, and told me that they were Mr. Burroughs' two first wives and that he had murdered them. And one told me that she was his first wife, and he stabbed her under the left arm and put a piece of sealing-wax on the wound. And she pulled aside the winding-sheet and showed me the place, and also told me that she was in the house [where] Mr. Parris now lived where it was done. And the other told me that Mr. Burroughs and that wife which he hath now killed her in the vessel as she was coming to see her friends, because they would have one another.

Burroughs' specter appeared in the hallucinations of a number of other people, including Susannah Sheldon, who reported that his specter told her he "had killed two of his wives—the first he smothered and the second he choked." Nobody seems to have noticed that the specters differed about the means by which the supposed murders were done. Or perhaps the discrepancy was attributed to the fact that it was Burroughs' specter speaking on one occasion and those of his wives on the other. In any case, it is easy to discover the source for these particular hallucinations, since Burroughs had indeed been a cruel man to his wives. Among other things, he was constantly suspicious of them and of others. He tried to force them to "write, sign, seal, and swear a covenant never to reveal any of his secrets." And whenever he was absent from them he would, on his return, proceed to tell them what they had been saying about him.

The testimony of his brother-in-law, Goodman Ruck, is particularly enlightening here. Ruck and his sister and Burroughs had gone out to gather strawberries, and Burroughs

> stepped aside a little into the bushes, whereupon they halted and hallooed for him. He not answering, they went away homewards with a quickened pace without any expectation of seeing him in a considerable while. And yet when they were got near home, to their astonishment they found him on foot with them, having a basket of strawberries. [Burroughs] immediately then fell to chiding his wife on the account of what she had been speaking to her brother of him on the road, which, when they wondered at [it], he

> said he knew their thoughts. Ruck, being startled at that, made some reply intimating that the Devil himself did not know so far. But [Burroughs] answered, "My God makes known your thoughts unto me."

What had happened, apparently, was that Burroughs had simply stepped out of sight in the bushes and then followed his wife and his brother-in-law home, keeping within hearing but out of sight. Then he had repeated their conversation to them and made them believe that he knew it not from eavesdropping but from occult powers. When Burroughs said "My God makes known your thoughts unto me," both he and his hearers understood his god to be the Devil; the Christian God does not deal in the occult, particularly at the level of family gossip, but the Devil does. Now he was about to pay for the illegitimate power he had sought, but he tried to evade the payment with a clumsy lie. He had not been left alone, he said. His wife and brother-in-law had left a man with him. Ruck denied it, and when the magistrates asked Burroughs what this man's name was, "his countenance was much altered, nor could he say who 'twas."

Burroughs seems, in fact, to have been an habitual liar. At his trial, as part of his defense, he read a paper arguing that witches cannot send a Devil to torment people by making a covenant with the Devil. The court immediately recognized this paper as copied out of Thomas Ady's *A Candle in the Dark.* Burroughs "said he had taken none of it out of any book." When he was flatly charged with plagiarism he barely wriggled out of the contradiction he had created by saying that "a gentleman gave him the discourse in a manuscript, from whence he transcribed it." This devious half-lie, coupled with his other lies, told very heavily against him—a clergyman especially was supposed to be a man of good faith; it was the Devil who was the Prince of Lies. It is quite possible that George Burroughs was a worshipper of that prince. Certainly he was no orthodox Puritan. He had conspicuously avoided taking communion—he said it was so long since he had taken it that he could not tell how long—and he had baptized only the eldest of his children. But one cannot be certain. Perhaps he was only a liar who liked to boast of occult powers.

Certainly he boasted of his physical powers. He was, apparently, a very strong man, although slightly built. Some of the stories told of him are incredible: that he held up a seven-foot fowling piece by inserting his forefinger in the muzzle, or that he lifted a barrel of molasses by inserting two fingers in the bung. Burroughs had told some of these stories of himself; now they were coming back to haunt him, since they seemed to the community evidence of a strength that was clearly preternatural.

While the accusation of a minister was shocking, it was by no means unusual. Renegade members of the clergy have played a large part in the history of witchcraft both in fact and in fiction. It should be remembered that Morgan le Fay, King Arthur's sister, was supposed to have learned her evil craft in the nunnery where she was educated, that Benvenuto Cellini's sorcerer-friend was a priest, and that a renegade priest is supposed to be necessary to the performance of a Black Mass. So Massachusetts found no difficulty in reconciling George Burroughs' occupation with his reputation as a wizard. On the contrary, they felt when they arrested him that they had laid hands on the leader of the demonic conspiracy.

Beside the black magic of Bridget Bishop, Candy, and Wilmot Redd and the illegitimate use of a reputation for occult power by the Hoar family and by George Burroughs, the examining magistrates turned up evidence of much trafficking in the occult that is best classified as white witchcraft. We have seen that the events at Salem began with experiments made by Elizabeth Parris and Abigail Williams with the egg and glass, and that a witch cake was used to find out the names of the first witches. Similar methods of obtaining knowledge were commonly used, especially the sieve and shears, a method of divining not unlike the contemporary ouija board. Two persons are required. Each holds one handle of a pair of shears, and a sieve is held suspended between the points of the shears. Then questions are asked, and the answer depends on the movements of the sieve. Another common method of divining was the key and Bible, in which a key is inserted between the leaves of a Bible and the answer to the question is found in the words to which the key points.

Beside divining, there was much white magic involved in the medical practice of the time, which liberally employed both spells and charms. The most entertaining example of the latter to be found in the Salem documents has to do with what Robert Calef called "the burning [of] the mare's fart." Isaac Cummings, Senior, had a mare which fell suddenly sick—so suddenly that he thought she must have been ridden all night by witches. He sent for Thomas Andrews of Boxford to help cure the animal, and Andrews tried a number of remedies without success.

> "But," said he, "I cannot tell but she may have the belly-ache. And," said he, "I will try one thing more." My brother Andrews said he would take a pipe of tobacco and light it and butt it into the fundament of the mare. I told him that I thought it was not lawful. [The idea that this remedy was unlawful is probably a result of the use of tobacco in it. Tobacco was an "Indian weed" and used in Indian ceremony and medicine. The Puritans, like other seventeenth-century Christians, thought the Indians to be Devil worshippers and thought of their medicine men as magicians.] He said it was lawful for man or beast. Then I took a clean pipe and filled it with tobacco and did light it,

> and went with the pipe lit to the barn. Then the said Andrews did use the pipe as he said before he would, and the pipe of tobacco did blaze and burn blue. [Gaseous nitrogenous waste does burn with a blue color.] Then I said to my brother Andrews, "You shall try no more; it is not lawful." He said, "I will try again once more," which he did. And then there arose a blaze from the pipe of tobacco which seemed to me to cover the buttocks of the said mare. The blaze went upward towards the roof of the barn and in the roof of the barn there was a great crackling, as if the barn would have fallen or been burnt.

At this point, according to Cummings' son, the father declared that "he had rather lose his mare than his barn," and the experiments ended for that day. But Cummings conquered his misgivings rapidly. "The next day, being Lord's day, I spoke to my brother Andrews at noon to come to see the said mare, and said Andrews came. And what he did I say not."

One of the commonest countercharms for a bewitched animal was to cut a piece off of it—frequently an ear—and burn it or boil it. A neighbor of Cummings', John Hunkins, suggested this countercharm to him in the evening of that same Sunday. But Cummings would have no part in working further magic on the Sabbath. "I said no, not today. But if she lived till tomorrow morning he might cut off a piece of her and burn [it] if he would." No sooner had he said this than the mare fell dead.

This kind of countercharm verged on black magic because it was supposed not only to break the witch's spell but to injure the witch or compel her presence. It could be used with people as well as with animals, although you did not, of course, cut off the person's ear. You cut some of their hair or took some of their urine, and boiled it. The Quaker Samuel Shattuck, whom we have seen before engaged in an occult contest with Bridget Bishop, once tried this countercharm when he thought his child bewitched by one Mary Parker. Directly after Goodwife Parker had visited the Shattuck house the child

> was taken in a strange and unusual manner as if his vitals would have broke out his breast-bone, drawn up together to the upper part of his breast, his neck and eyes drawn so much aside as if they would never come to right again. He lay in so strange a manner that the doctor and others did believe he was bewitched. Some days after, some of the visitors cut some of his hair off to boil [in Shattuck's testimony it is always anonymous visitors who work the charms], which they said although they did [it] with great tenderness the child would shriek out as if he had been tormented. They put his hair in a skillet over a fire which stood plain on the hearth. And as soon as

> they were gone out of the room it was thrown down, and I came immediately into the room and could see no creature in the room.

They put the skillet back on the fire, and after the child's hair had boiled awhile Goodwife Parker came to the house on the pretense of selling chickens, although Shattuck found on later investigation that she had no chickens to sell. So the experiment was considered a success, on the grounds that it had compelled the presence of the witch. Unfortunately it did not help the child, who "continued in a very sad condition followed with very solemn fits, which hath taken away his understanding."

Boiling urine was a far more common countercharm than boiling hair, although it was, in colonial history, often attended with difficulties. In 1682, for example, a meeting of prominent Quakers in New Hampshire, including Samuel Jennings, governor of West Jersey, Walter Clark, deputy governor of Rhode Island, and Thomas Maule of Salem, was troubled by persistent poltergeist activity, especially stone-throwing. The family at whose house they met tried a number of ways to rid themselves of these "lapidary salutations," including the following experiment:

> They did set on the fire a pot with urine and crooked pins in it, with [the] design to have it boil, and by that means to give punishment to the witch or wizard (that might be the wicked procurer or contriver of this stone affliction) and take off their own, as they had been advised. This was the effect of it: as the liquor began to grow hot a stone came and broke the top or mouth of it, and threw it down and spilt what was in it; which being made good again, another stone, as the pot grew hot again, broke the handle off; and being recruited and filled the third time was then with a third stone quite broke to pieces and split; and so the operation became frustrate and fruitless.

Another failure was recorded by Cotton Mather in his *Memorable Providences.* A man having fallen ill, and witchcraft being suspected, his friends "went to the traditional experiment of bottling urine; but they could get no urine from him, a strange hole through the urinary passage shedding the water before they could receive it into the vessel." The man died shortly afterward and the body was examined by a jury. "An hole was found quite through his yard, which hindered their saving of any urine and gave a terrible torture to him." Everyone concluded that he had been bewitched, but in the absence of evidence sufficient to convict a witch the case went no further.

Mather did not approve of what he called "the urinary experiment," on the grounds that it was using "a charm against a charm, or . . . a Devil's shield against a Devil's sword." Nevertheless, careful scholar that he was, he recorded the opinion that it was not sufficient to boil steel filings with the urine. "I suppose the urine must be bottled with nails and pins, and such instruments in it as carry a show of torture with them, if it [is to] attain its end."

But the instance of urine-boiling which came before the Salem magistrates was not a failure, but a success. A doctor by the comically appropriate name of Roger Toothaker had boasted to one Thomas Gage

> that his daughter had killed a witch. And I asked him how she did it. And said Toothaker answered readily that his daughter had learned something from him. I asked by what means she did it. And he said that there was a certain person bewitched, and said person complained of being afflicted by another person. . . . And further, said Toothaker said that his said daughter got some of the afflicted person's urine and put it into an earthen pot, and stopped said pot very close and put said pot into a hot oven, and stopped up said oven.

The next morning the witch was dead; apparently she was bewitched to death.

Most of the physical effects of witchcraft are attributable to hysteria, but not death. People do not die of hysteria. But death, like the hysterical symptoms of bewitchment, begins with the victim's fear of the witch's power.

Witchcraft deaths have been reported for a very long time, yet it is only recently that they have received serious medical attention. In 1942 Dr. Walter B. Cannon of Harvard Medical School published an article entitled "'Voodoo' Death," in which he began by acknowledging that "the phenomenon is so extraordinary and so foreign to the experience of civilized people that it seems incredible." And yet, he thought, it had been so widely reported, for so long, and by such dependable observers that it clearly deserved careful investigation. Cannon was unaware that death is frequently reported in the literature of European and American witchcraft, but he did know that it had been reported from primitive cultures in South America, Africa, Australia, New Zealand, the Pacific islands, and Haiti, over a period of time from 1587 to the present. He quotes several such reports, two of which are well worth repeating here. The first is from Africa:

> I have seen more than one hardened old Hausa soldier dying steadily and by inches because he believed himself to be bewitched; no nourishment or medicines that were given to him had the slightest effect either to check the mischief or to improve his condition in any way, and nothing was able to divert him from a fate which he considered inevitable. In the same way, and under very similar conditions, I have seen Kru-men and others die in spite

> of every effort that was made to save them, simply because they had made up their minds, not (as we thought at the time) to die, but that being in the clutch of malignant demons they were bound to die.

The second describes the effect of magic bone-pointing among Australian aborigines:

> The man who discovers that he is being boned by an enemy is, indeed, a pitiable sight. He stands aghast, with his eyes staring at the treacherous pointer, and with his hands lifted as though to ward off the lethal medium, which he imagines is pouring into his body. His cheeks blanch and his eyes become glassy and the expression of his face becomes horribly distorted. . . . He attempts to shriek but usually the sound chokes in his throat, and all that one might see is froth at his mouth. His body begins to tremble and the muscles twist involuntarily. He sways backwards and falls to the ground, and after a short time appears to be in a swoon; but soon after he writhes as if in mortal agony, and, covering his face with his hands, begins to moan. After a while he becomes very composed and crawls to his wurley. From this time onwards he sickens and frets, refusing to eat and keeping aloof from the daily affairs of the tribe. Unless help is forthcoming in the shape of a counter-charm administered by the hands of the Nangarri, or medicine man, his death is only a matter of a comparatively short time. If the coming of the medicine man is opportune he might be saved.

In all cases death comes inexorably and in a relatively short time. As one observer put it, "the victims die . . . as though their strength ran out as water." The only known cure was a countercharm, and when this was successfully employed recovery was so rapid and complete that Western observers found it remarkable. (Since Cannon's article was published, two doctors have reported their experiences in curing bewitched patients. Dr. John E. Snell of Tufts University has successfully used hypnosis to cure both southern whites and Negroes who believed themselves bewitched. A Hawaiian physician, Dr. Harold M. Johnson, has reported both severe skin lesions and death among the victims of Kahuna sorcerers. He has succeeded in curing bewitched patients by giving them methylene blue tablets, which turns their urine blue and persuades them that a powerful countercharm has been worked on their behalf.)

Cannon suggested that witchcraft death might well be a genuine phenomenon, and also put forward a hypothetical explanation. "It may be explained," he thought, "as due to shocking emotional stress—to obvious or repressed terror." It would occur, he felt, chiefly in primitive cultures,

> among human beings so primitive, so superstitious, so ignorant that they are bewildered strangers in a hostile world. Instead of knowledge they have a fertile and unrestricted imagination which fills their environment with all manner of evil spirits capable of affecting their lives disastrously.

Therefore he published his article in *American Anthropologist* rather than in one of the medical journals, presumably feeling that an anthropological audience would have better opportunities for testing his hypothesis than a medical one. Yet he did note that there were two "civilized" environments that might produce such deaths. Battlefield deaths had been reported in which the wounds were superficial and a postmortem revealed no serious injury. And apparently some patients found a hospital as terrifying an environment as a battlefield, and at least one doctor was very much aware of this:

> That the attitude of the patient is of significant importance for a favorable outcome of an operation is firmly believed by the well-known American surgeon, Dr. J. M. T. Finney, for many years Professor of Surgery at the Johns Hopkins Medical School. He has publicly testified [1934], on the basis of serious experiences, that if any person came to him for a major operation, and expressed fear of the result, he invariably refused to operate.

Cannon's hypothesis was tested in the Psychobiological Laboratory at Johns Hopkins Medical School by Curt P. Richter, who published his findings in 1957 in an article entitled "On the Phenomenon of Sudden Death in Animals and Man." Richter encountered the phenomenon while testing the survival times of wild versus domesticated rats, which he placed in water-filled beakers to swim until they drowned. The statistics he was obtaining were most irregular because some of the rats, especially the wild rats, died much more rapidly than others, and for no assignable reason. It occurred to Richter that these rats might be dying the same psychogenic death as human victims of witchcraft, and he therefore set out to test the cause of death. Cannon had suggested that fear might be the emotional cause, with consequent overstimulation of the sympathicoadrenal system, acceleration of the heart beat, and death with the heart contracted in systole. But Richter found that while acceleration of the heart beat was the initial reaction, it was shortly followed by a steady, gradual decrease in rate, with the heart eventually stopping in diastole, like a run-down clock. This meant that the emotional cause of death was not fear but hopelessness, produced by the rat's conviction that there was no possible means of escape, with consequent over-stimulation of the parasympathetic rather than the sympathicoadrenal system.

Richter tested his findings by pretreatment with atropine and with colinergic drugs, and also by adrenalectomy and thyroidectomy. He also tried training the rats. By immersing them briefly and then removing them from water he taught them that their situation was not hopeless. Rats so trained did not die psychogenic deaths but produced constant swimming endurance records. Finally, he discovered that if rats about to die a psychogenic death were removed from the beaker they recovered rapidly, precisely like the human witchcraft victim who has been reprieved by a countercharm.

In short, Richter found that the first response in such cases was fear but that the emotional cause of death was the hopelessness that succeeded fear, and that death could be prevented either by restoring hope or by training the subject to be hopeful in a particular situation. He agreed with Cannon that the incidence of this kind of death would probably vary

> inversely as the degree of civilization, or domestication, of the individual, since it occurs more frequently in wild than in domesticated rats and so far has been described chiefly in primitive man, that is to say, in creatures living in precarious situations.

But he noted that there did seem to be instances of the phenomenon in so-called "civilized" contexts, and not only in the hospital or on the battlefield. "Many instances are at hand," he said, "of sudden death from fright, sight of blood, hypodermic injections, or from sudden immersion in water." He concluded by reporting the experience of Dr. R. S. Fisher, coroner of the City of Baltimore, who had found that "a number of individuals die each year after taking small, definitely sublethal doses of poison, or after inflicting small, nonlethal wounds on themselves; apparently they die as a result of the belief in their doom."

Richter's findings throw much new light on the history of Massachusetts witchcraft. They should enable us at long last to take as seriously as it deserves Cotton Mather's detailed account of his treatment of the Goodwin girl. When he gave her religious sustenance by spelling the crucial words she was unable to hear spoken (a technique he would use again, as we shall see, in 1693), he may have been saving his patient from much more than convulsive fits. By giving her continued hope he may literally have been keeping her alive.

Richter's findings also explain the frequent reports of death in both European and American witchcraft cases. There are about a dozen such reports in the documents of Salem witchcraft, but in most instances one cannot be at all certain of the actual cause of death. Even when death does appear to be psychogenic it is usually impossible to say whether the victim's hopelessness was simply a result of private fears or whether those fears had their origin in a specific magical act. But with Roger Toothaker and his daughter there is enough to reconstruct the probable course of events with some degree of accuracy. We have seen, in the deadly earnest contests of charm and countercharm between Samuel Shattuck and Bridget Bishop and between Shattuck and Mary Parker, the seriousness with which seventeenth-century people took occult combat.

Toothaker accepted such a combat on behalf of a person he believed bewitched. He taught his daughter the classic countercharm of boiling the victim's urine in a pot. Probably he threatened the witch with this countercharm, or boasted of it to the neighbors, because the next morning the witch was dead. It is the right period of time for a witchcraft death, and therefore it is quite likely that this woman died of knowing that her victim's urine was being boiled in a pot.

It should be clear by now that our historians have erred in their assumption that there was no witchcraft practiced at Salem, or that if there was it was of little consequence. The documents, rightly read, present us a far different picture. In Bridget Bishop, Candy, and Mammy Redd we have three people who practiced black magic, and with demonstrable success. In the Hoar family and George Burroughs we have people who established a reputation for black magic and then traded on it, although whether they were actually witches remains uncertain. There are other cases, like those of Sarah Good and Samuel Wardwell, which I have not treated in detail because the evidence is suspicious but not conclusive, and one can only guess that some of them were probably practicing witchcraft. Finally, we have a variety and abundance of white magic, some of which merges with the black because it was intended to harm the witch. And if the testimony concerning Roger Toothaker and his daughter may be taken at face value—and there is reason to believe it may—we have one case of murder by witchcraft—one case in which occult means were used to take a human life away.

From: Paul Boyer and Stephen Nissenbaum, *Salem Possessed: The Social Origins of Witchcraft,* (Cambridge, 1974), chapter 4, "Salem Town and Salem Village: The Dynamics of Factional Conflict"

In the last quarter of the twentieth century, historical studies of the Salem episode have largely stopped recycling familiar material and looked harder at the evidence or even unearthed new evidence. The most valuable work has been done by Paul Boyer and Stephen Nissenbaum, who not only assembled the *Salem Witchcraft Papers* and *Salem-Village Witchcraft* but wrote the incisive study *Salem Possessed.*

This argues that the witch-hunt was caused, at the most fundamental level, by the conflict between the new entrepreneurial world represented by Salem Town and the old Puritan world of third-generation Salem Village farmers. Making brilliant use of the documentary and demographic evidence, the authors show the economic and philosophical underpinning of the factions whose enmity climaxed in the tragedy of 1692.

Chapter 4 describes the differences between the two factions in the village, one led by the Porter family, the other by the Putnams. The first faction desired close connection with the town, while the second wanted a completely independent village. These unresolved aims had caused conflict for decades.

But still we have not penetrated to the heart of the matter. For our narrative of Salem Village's ordeal, even supplemented by an examination of her two rival factions, raises as many questions as it answers. How, after all, could such a dispute have escalated to so bitter and deadly a level? Why were the two sides so long unable to find any political means of resolving the impasse? And, moving back one step further, why should the presence of differing economic interests have polarized the Village in the first place into such vindictive and implacable camps? Even granting the existence of two opposing sides, why did not each one simply pursue its particular interests and tacitly accept the right of the other to do the same?

In one sense, of course, Salem Village factionalism poses no "problem." There were, after all, concrete issues at stake, and significant, measurable differences between the two groups. And yet, as one follows these disputes over the years, their *intensity* so often seems out of proportion to the ostensible issues. In 1687, in one of many similar observations made over the years, a committee of outside arbitrators commented on "the settled prejudice and resolved animosity" which their probe of Village conditions had uncovered. Samuel Parris's early church records made clear that conditions, if anything, grew worse in the period immediately preceding 1692. And, of course, the witchcraft trials themselves offer the most persuasive evidence of the passionate emotions which underlay these longstanding divisions.

To understand this intensity, we must recognize the fact—self-evident to the men and women of Salem Village—that what was going on was not simply a personal quarrel, an economic dispute, or even a struggle for power, but a mortal conflict involving the very nature of the community itself. The fundamental issue was not who was to control the Village, but what its essential character was to be. To the Puritans of seventeenth-century New England, no social or political issue was without its moral dimension as well. For a community was more than simply a collection of individuals who happened to live and work together; it was itself an organism with a reality and an existence distinct from that of its component parts.

John Winthrop, the first governor of colonial Massachusetts, fully articulated this theme as early as 1630 in his lecture aboard the ship *Arabella,* as the first large contingent of Puritan settlers was sailing toward New England. "[W]e must be knit together in this work as one man," he declared; "We must delight in each other, . . . rejoice together, mourn together, labor and suffer together, always having before our eyes our commission and community in the work, our community as members of the same body." Since each community was almost literally a "body," the individuals who composed it could neither logically nor practically regard themselves as autonomous creatures with their own "particular" interests. For a person to pursue such a self-determined course was as destructive and, ultimately, as absurd as for one part of the human body to pursue *its* own good: for a hand to refuse to release to the mouth the food it held in its grasp, for example, or for the mouth to refuse to pass along that food to the stomach. "Self-interest" was like that. If left uncontrolled, it could result only in the failure of the community and of every person within it.

From infancy, a Puritan was raised to distrust his private will, to perceive it as the "old Adam" which, above all, constituted original sin. It was this innate self-interest—more than sexual lust, more than any of the "sins" we commonly (and mistakenly) think of as particularly repugnant to the Puritans—that had to be tamed if it could not be eradicated.

Thus, Winthrop's insistence that the men and women aboard the *Arabella* were "members of the same body" was no casual figure of speech or sentimental paean to a vague commonality of feeling. It was, for Winthrop, a statement of certain very specific social and economic policies—policies which he enunciated again and again in his lecture: "We must be willing to abridge ourselves of our superfluities, for the supply of others' necessities"; "The care of the public must oversway all private respects"; "We must not look only on our own things, but also on the things of our brethren." And Winthrop's scheme contained an enforcement procedure as well: the constant scrutiny and regulation of all facets of individual behavior in order to nip in the bud deviations that threatened the interests of the community as a whole.

The important thing is not whether very many people actually behaved in this fashion (almost certainly most of them did not), but rather the fact that when they did not act in this way—when they pursued their self-interest at the expense of the greater good of the whole—they felt that they were not behaving properly.

By the end of the seventeenth century, however, this sense that there was a dangerous conflict between private will and public good had become seriously eroded in many quarters by two generations of population growth, geographic dispersal, and economic opportunity: the emergence of pre-industrial capitalism. By the next century all that would remain would be a general sense that there were *some* limits beyond which an individual might not venture in pursuing his private interests. This qualification aside, however, New England towns of the 1700's conceded that they were made up of a diverse mixture of imperfect and self-seeking human beings, and they largely abandoned the effort to be anything more.

To be sure, factional conflicts, intra-town fights, and rural-urban struggles continued to be bitter enough in the eighteenth century, but they no longer involved the conviction that the fate of the community itself was hanging in the balance. Factions might temporarily fall from power, but that was all. Whatever their rhetoric, all sides recognized at heart that the stakes for which they played, while vital to their immediate interests, were nevertheless limited. The crucial change in the eighteenth century, then, was not in the frequency of conflicts, or in the objective issues that produced them, but in their diminished moral resonance. By mid-century, certainly, the fundamental questions as to the nature and structure of the social order had been resolved—and resolved on the side of individual freedom.

But in the 1690's, it was still possible for the farmers of the pro-Parris faction to believe that the outcome of this shadowy struggle remained very much in question. Thus, for them, Salem Town was not suspect just because of its vaguely hostile political climate, or because it was following a different line of economic development, but because the total thrust of that commercial development represented a looming *moral* threat with implications of the most fundamental sort.

As we have seen, Salem Village itself in the late seventeenth century was neither a haven of pastoral tranquility nor an embodiment of John Winthrop's public-mindedness. And yet, coupled with the inescapable realities of social turbulence and diminished opportunity was the sense that if any place *could* offer shelter against sweeping social change and provide a setting where the Puritan social vision might yet be realized, it would likely be an agricultural, essentially noncommercial settlement such as Salem Village. The very nature of farm life, with its settled routines and seasonal rhythms, offered at least the illusion of social stability and continuity—and perhaps, in comparison to what was happening in Salem Town, it was more than illusion.

Thus the merchant capitalists who controlled the Town—and to an extent the Village, too—were not merely outsiders; they were outsiders whose careers could be seen as a violation of much that is contained in the word "Puritan." As Bernard Bailyn has put it, commenting on Massachusetts commercial development in these very decades:

> In the larger port towns of provincial New England, particularly those in continuous touch with Europe, the business community represented the spirit of a new age. Its guiding principles were not social stability, order, and the discipline of the senses, but mobility, growth, and the enjoyment of life. Citizens of an international trading world as well as of New England colonies, the merchants took the pattern for their conduct not from the Bible or from parental teachings but from their picture of life in Restoration England.

It may not be necessary to go quite this far in describing the merchant elite of Salem; and, in any case, Bailyn's description would apply to only a handful of the anti-Parris Villagers, since they were not themselves merchants, but mainly farmers who to a degree identified their interests with those of the Town's commercial element. Still, under the circumstances, it was only too easy for Parris's supporters to see the minister's opponents in terms like these. The anti-Parris leaders may have lived *in* the Village, but they were not *of* the Village.

It is tempting simply to label the pro-Parris faction as "Puritans," their opponents as "capitalists," and let it go at that. But we know from experience that human beings rarely fit quite so neatly into such categorical boxes. And as the work of several generations of scholars has made clear, the relationship between Puritanism and capitalism is itself deeply ambiguous. In any case, the pro-Parris Villagers were certainly no more a group of Winthrop's self denying communitarians than their opponents were the materialistic individualists we commonly associate with nineteenth-century entrepreneurship. The similarities between our two little microcosmic groups would probably, to most modern eyes, have seemed far more noticeable than the subtle differences of emphasis and priority which set them apart.

And, still further, at a time when one world view was imperceptibly yielding to another, each faction must have shared enough of the other's outlook to feel its power and be drawn to it. The anti-Parris men must at times have sensed with a pang what they were giving up in turning toward the burgeoning Town and away from the Village. And the pro-Parris Villagers, for their part, must have felt deeply the lure of the forces which were transforming the Town: the very forces they feared and despised. This, too, helps us understand the intensity of the conflict. For the Villagers were not only at war with each other; they were also at war with themselves.

Why Salem Village?

But many New Englanders must have been at war with themselves at the end of the seventeenth century, and for these very reasons. And many communities were undergoing factional struggles in this period when such conflicts were often invested with a particular freight of moral significance. Yet none experienced the kind of convulsion which prostrated Salem Village. Nowhere else did members of one faction willingly connive in the prosecution and, in certain cases, the deaths, of scores of persons they in some way identified with the other side. What was it that reduced the Salem Village struggle ultimately to a kind of total war?

The answer, obvious perhaps, seems to lie in the convergence of a specific and unlikely combination of historical circumstances at this particular time and place.

To begin with, *physical setting.* If the Village had been an isolated agricultural community, off in the back country, then Salem Town would hardly have loomed so large in its consciousness. A dissident group might still have arisen, but its presence, lacking any nearby source of real or symbolic support, would not have seemed so acutely threatening to the Village's stability.

Lack of autonomy. But whatever its physical proximity to the Town, if Salem Village had been granted full political and ecclesiastical independence in 1672 (or even, conceivably, in 1689) it might have been able to develop strong institutions of its own—institutions which would have given it the political strength to resolve its factional problems.

But a *taste of independence.* If, alternatively, "Salem Farms" had remained completely a part of the Town, the region would not have developed any institutions at all—meetinghouse, legal meetings, Committee, or minister—and so would have had no peg on which to hang its separatist impulses. Even though serious problems would certainly have persisted after 1672, a single town, physically and institutionally undivided, might have been able to contain those problems within tolerable limits.

Coupled with a *lack of power in Town politics.* The Villagers were, after all, still able to vote in Town elections and eligible to hold Town offices. If they had enjoyed anything like political parity with the Town, their political impulses might have found meaningful expression, and their grievances at least partial resolution. But as matters turned out, their numerical weakness was such that only on rare occasions were they able to use the Town's political apparatus as a weapon in Village conflicts. (The contrast here between Salem and other towns which experienced similar separatist conflicts in these years is striking. In Dedham, Massachusetts, for example, no fewer than five distinct outlying communities managed early in the eighteenth century to form ad hoc political alliances with each other which enabled them to maneuver very effectively in the arena of Dedham politics.)

Finally, *a weak stick in Boston.* If authorities at the provincial (not to say the imperial) level had exerted a stronger and more consistent hand in settling matters, Salem Village factionalism would certainly never have flowered as luxuriantly as it did. But like vacillating or argumentative parents, the provincial authorities evoked neither affection nor deference from either Village faction. Those authorities had to be reckoned with at every point, to be sure, but more as an unpredictable and capricious obstacle than as a firm source of policy.

If any one of these circumstances had been significantly different, it is possible that Salem would be remembered today simply as the oldest town in the colony, and as the home of Nathaniel Hawthorne—not as the site of one of the most notorious events in New England history.

But the trials came. Unable to relieve their frustrations politically, the members of the pro-Parris faction unconsciously fell back on a different and more archaic strategy: they treated those who threatened them not as a political opposition but as an aggregate of morally defective individuals. Given the social assumptions which prevailed in seventeenth-century New England, it was a perfectly normal procedure for a town to rid itself of deviant or threatening individuals—by changing them if possible, by exile or execution if necessary. A long succession of people, including a number of isolated "witches," had learned that fact in the most vivid way possible. But what confronted Salem Village, as seems clear in retrospect, was not a handful (even a large handful) of "deviants." It was a group of people who were on the advancing edge of profound historical change. If from one angle they were diverging from an accepted norm of behavior, from another angle their values represented the "norm" of the future. In an age about to pass, the assertion of *private will* posed the direst possible threat to the stability of the community; in the age about to arrive, it would form a central pillar on which that stability rested. By treating their "enemies" as deviants, the pro-Parris Villagers of the 1690's chose to proceed as if nothing fundamental had changed in New England society—another attempt, perhaps, to convince themselves that nothing really had.

From: Linnda R. Caporael, "Ergotism: The Satan Loosed in Salem?" *Science,* 192 (April 2, 1976).

Linnda R. Caporael argues that convulsive ergotism may have been a physiological basis for the Salem witchcraft crisis in 1692. Much of her reasoning seems cogent but does not adequately explain why the condition should have struck only in Salem Village at that time. She uses as an argument for her case that the "witchcraft episode . . . ended unexpectedly for no apparent reason." But there were a great many reasons, one of which was that the afflicted girls overreached themselves and started accusing the highest in the land.

Numerous hypotheses have been devised to explain the occurrence of the Salem witchcraft trials in 1692, yet a sense of bewilderment and doubt pervades most of the historical perspectives on the subject. The physical afflictions of the accusing girls and the imagery of the testimony offered at the trials seem to defy rational explanation. A large portion of the testimony, therefore, is dismissed as imaginary in foundation. One avenue of understanding that has yet to be sufficiently explored is that a physiological condition, unrecognized at the time, may have been a factor in the Salem incident. Assuming that the content of the court records is basically an honest account of the deponents' experiences, the evidence suggests that convulsive ergotism, a disorder resulting from the ingestion of grain contaminated with ergot, may have initiated the witchcraft delusion.

Suggestions of physical origins of the afflicted girls' behavior have been dismissed without research into the matter. In looking back, the complexity of the psychological and social factors in the community obscured the potential existence of physical pathology, suffered not only by the afflicted children, but also by a number of other community members. The value of such an explanation, however, is clear. Winfield S. Nevins best reveals the implicit uncertainties of contemporary historians.

> I must confess to a measure of doubt as to the moving causes in this terrible tragedy. It seems impossible to believe a tithe of the statements which were made at the trials. And yet it is equally difficult to say that nine out of every ten of the men, women and children who testified upon their oaths, intentionally and wilfully falsified. Nor does it seem possible that they did, or could invent all these marvelous tales; fictions rivaling the imaginative genius of Haggard or Jules Verne.

The possibility of a physiological condition fitting the known circumstances and events would provide a comprehensible framework for understanding the witchcraft delusion in Salem.

Background

Prior to the Salem witchcraft trials, only five executions on the charge of witchcraft are known to have occurred in Massachusetts. Such trials were held periodically, but the outcomes generally favored the accused. In 1652, a man charged with witchcraft was convicted of simply having told a lie and was fined. Another man, who confessed to talking with the devil, was given counsel and dismissed by the court because of the inconsistencies in his testimony. A bad reputation in the community combined with the accusation of witchcraft did not necessarily insure conviction. The case against John Godfrey of Andover, a notorious character consistently involved in litigation, was dismissed. In fact, soon after the proceedings, Godfrey sued his accusers for defamation and slander and won the case.

The supposed witchcraft at Salem Village was not initially identified as such. In late December 1691, about eight girls, including the niece and daughter of the minister, Samuel Parris, were afflicted with unknown "distempers." Their behavior was characterized by disorderly speech, odd postures and gestures, and convulsive fits. Physicians called in to examine the girls could find no explanation for their illness, and in February one doctor suggested the girls might be bewitched. Parris seemed loath to accept this explanation at the time and resorted to private fasting and prayer. At a meeting at Parris's home, ministers from neighboring parishes advised him to "sit still and wait upon the Providence of God to see what time might discover."

A neighbor, however, took it upon herself to direct Parris's Barbados slave, Tituba, in the concocting of a "witch cake" in order to determine if witchcraft was present. Shortly thereafter, the girl made an accusation of witchcraft against Tituba and two elderly women of general ill repute in Salem Village, Sarah Good and Sarah Osborne. The three women were taken into custody on 29 February 1692. The afflictions of the girls did not cease, and in March they accused Martha Corey and Rebecca Nurse. Both of these women were well respected in the village and were convenanting members of the church. Further accusations by the children followed.

Examinations of the accused were conducted in Salem Village until 11 April by two magistrates from Salem Town. At that time, the examinations were moved from the outlying farming area to the town and were heard by Deputy Governor Danforth and six of the ablest magistrates in the colony, including Samuel Sewall. This council had no authority to try accused witches, however, because the colony had no legal government—a state of affairs that had existed for years. By the time Sir William Phipps, the new governor, arrived from England with the charter establishing the government of Massachusetts Bay Colony, the jails as far away from Salem as Boston were crowded with prisoners from Salem awaiting trial. Phipps appointed a special Court of Oyer and Terminer, which heard its first case on 2 June. The proceedings resulted in conviction, and the first condemned witch was hanged on 10 June.

Before the next sitting of the court clergymen in the Boston area were consulted for their opinion on the issue pending. In an answer composed by Cotton Mather, the ministers advised "critical and exquisite caution" and wished "that there may be as little as possible of such noise, company and openness as may too hastily expose them that are examined." The ministers also concluded that spectral evidence (the appearance of the accused's apparition to an accuser) and the test of touch (the sudden cessation of a fit after being touched by the accused witch) were insufficient evidence for proof of witchcraft.

The court seemed insensitive to the advice of the ministers, and the trials and executions in Salem continued. By 2 September, 19 men and women had been sent to the gallows, and one, Giles Corey, had been pressed to death, an ordeal calculated to force him to enter a plea to the court so that he could be tried. The evidence used to obtain the convictions was the test of touch and spectral evidence. The afflicted girls were present at the examinations and trials, often creating such pandemonium that the proceedings were interrupted. The accused witches were, for the most part, persons of good reputation in the community; one was even a former minister in the village. Several notable individuals were "cried out" upon, including John Alden and Lady Phipps. All the men and women who were hanged had consistently maintained their innocence: not one confessor to the crime was executed. It had become obvious early in the course of the proceedings that those who confessed would not be executed.

On 17 September 1692, the Court of Oyer and Terminer adjourned the witchcraft trials until 2 November; however, it never met again to try that crime. In January 1693 the Superior Court of Judicature, consisting of the magistrates on the Court of Oyer and Terminer, met. Of 50 indictments handed in to the Superior Court by the grand jury, 20 persons were brought to trial. Three were condemned but never executed and the rest were acquitted. In May Governor Phipps ordered a general reprieve, and about 150 accused witches were released. The end of the witchcraft crisis was singularly abrupt.

Tituba and the Origin Tradition

Repeated attempts to place the occurrences at Salem within a consistent framework have failed. Outright fraud, political factionalism, Freudian psychodynamics, sensation seeking, clinical hysteria, even the existence of witchcraft itself, have been proposed as explanatory devices. The problem is primarily one of complexity. No single explanation can ever account for the delusion; an interaction of them all must be assumed. Combinations of interpretations, however, seem insufficient without some reasonable justification for the initially afflicted girls' behavior. No mental derangement or fraud seems adequate in understanding how eight girls, raised in the soul-searching Puritan tradition, simultaneously exhibited the same symptoms or conspired together for widespread notoriety.

All modern accounts of the beginnings of Salem witchcraft begin with Parris's Barbados slave, Tituba. The tradition is that she instructed the minister's daughter and niece, as well as some other girls in the neighborhood, in magic tricks and incantations at secret meetings held in the parsonage kitchen. The odd behavior of the girls, whether real or fraudulent, was a consequence of these experiments.

The basis for the tradition seems two-fold. In a warning against divination, John Hale wrote in 1702 that he was informed that one afflicted girl had tried to see the future with an egg and glass and subsequently was followed by a "diabolical molestation" and died. The egg and glass (an improvised crystal ball) was an English method of divination. Hale gives no indication that Tituba was involved, or for that matter, that a group of girls was involved. I have been unable to locate any reference that any of the afflicted girls died prior to Hale's publication.

The other basis for the tradition implicating Tituba seems to be simply the fact that she was from the West Indies. The Puritans believed the American Indians worshiped the devil, most often described as a black man. Curiously, however, Tituba was not questioned at her examination about activities as a witch in her birthplace. Historians seem bewitched themselves by fantasies of voodoo and black magic in the tropics, and the unfounded supposition that Tituba would inevitably be familiar with malefic arts of the Caribbean has survived.

Calef reports that Tituba's confession was obtained under duress. She at first denied knowing the devil and suggested the girls were possessed. Although Tituba ultimately became quite voluble, her confession was rather pedestrian in comparison with the other testimony offered at the examinations and trials. There is no element of West Indian magic, and her descriptions of the black man, the hairy imp, and witches flying through the sky on sticks reflect an elementary acquaintance with the common English superstitions of the time.

Current Interpretations

1) *Fraud.* Various interpretations of the girls' behavior diverge after the discussion of its origins. The currently accepted view is that the children's symptoms of affliction were fraudulent. The girls may have perpetrated fraud simply to gain notoriety or to protect themselves from punishment by adults as their magic experiments became the topic of rumor. One author supposes that the accusing girls crave "Dionysiac mysteries" and that some were "no more seriously possessed a pack of bobby-soxers on the loose. The major difficulty in accepting the explanation of purposeful fraud is the gravity of the girls' symptoms: all the eyewitness accounts agree to the severity of the affliction.

Upham appears to accept the contemporaneous descriptions and ascribes to the afflicted children the skills of a sophisticated necromancer. He proposes that they were able ventriloquists, highly accomplished actresses, and by long practice could "bring the blood to the face, and send it back again." These abilities and more, he assumes, the girls learned from Tituba. As discussed above, however, there is little evidence that Tituba had any practical knowledge of witchcraft. Most colonists, with the exception of some of the accused and their defenders, did not appear even to consider pretense as an explanation for the girls' behavior. The general conclusion of the New Englanders after the tragedy was that they suffered from demonic possession.

2) *Hysteria.* The advent of psychiatry provided new tools for describing [and] interpreting the events at Salem. The term "hysteria" has been used with varying degrees of license and the accounts of hysteria always begin in the kitchen with Tituba practicing magic. Starkey uses the term in the loose sense: the girls were hysterical, that is overexcited, and committed sensational fraud in a community that subsequently fell ill to "mass hysteria." Hansen proposes the use of the word in a stricter, clinical sense of being mentally ill. He insists that witchcraft really was practiced in Salem and that several of the executed were practicing witches. The girls' symptoms were psychogenic, occasioned by guilt at practicing fortune-telling at their secret meetings. He states that the mental illness was catching and that the witnesses and majority of the confessors became hysterics as a consequence of their fear of witchcraft. However, if the girls were not practicing divination, and if they did indeed develop true hysteria, then they must all have developed hysteria simultaneously, hardly a credible supposition. Furthermore, previous witchcraft accusations in other Puritan communities in New England had never brought on mass hysteria.

Psychiatric disorder is used in a slightly different sense in the argument the witchcraft crisis was a consequence of two party (pro-Parris and anti-Parris) factionalism in Salem Village. In this account, the girls are unimportant factors in the entire incident. Their behavior "served as a kind of Rorschach test into which adults read their own concerns and expectations." The difficulty with linking factionalism to the witch trials is that supporters of Parris were also prosecuted while some non-supporters were among the most vociferous accusers. Thus, it becomes necessary to resort to projection, transference, individual psychoanalysis, and numerous psychiatric disorders to explain the behavior of the adults in the community who were using the afflicted children as pawns to resolve their own personal and political differences.

Of course, there was fraud and mental illness at Salem. The records clearly indicate both. Some depositions are simply fanciful renditions of local gossip or cases of malice aforethought. There is also testimony based on exaggerations of nightmares and inebriated adventures. However, not all the records are thus accountable.

3) *Physiological explanations.* The possibility that the girls' behavior had a physiological basis has rarely arisen, although the villagers themselves first proposed physical illness as an explanation. Before accusations of witchcraft began, Parris called in a number of physicians. In an early history of the colony, Thomas Hutchinson wrote that "there are a great number of persons who are willing to suppose the accusers to have been under bodily disorders which affected their imagination." A modern historian reports a journalist's suggestion that Tituba had been dosing the girls with preparations of jimsonweed, a poisonous plant brought to New England from the West Indies in the early 1600's. However, be-

cause the Puritans identified no physiological cause, later historians have failed to investigate such a possibility.

Ergot

Interest in ergot (*Claviceps purpura*) was generated by epidemics of ergotism that periodically occurred in Europe. Only a few years before the Salem witchcraft trials the first medical scientific report on ergot was made. Denis Dodart reported the relation between ergotized rye and bread poisoning in a letter to the French Royal Académie des Sciences in 1676. John Ray's mention of ergot in 1677 was the first in English. There is no reference to ergot in the United States before an 1807 letter by Dr. John Stearns recommending powdered ergot sclerotia to a medical colleague as a therapeutic agent in childbirth. Stearns is generally credited with the "discovery" of ergot; certainly his use prompted scientific research on the substance. Until the mid–19th century, however, ergot was not known as a parasitic fungus, but was thought to be sunbaked kernels of grains.

Ergot grows on a large variety of cereal grains—especially rye—in a slightly curved, fusiform shape with sclerotia replacing individual grains on the host plant. The sclerotia contain a large number of potent pharmacologic agents, the ergot alkaloids. One of the most powerful is isoergine (lysergic acid amide). This alkaloid, with 10 percent of the activity of D-LSD (lysergic acid diethylamide), is also found in ololiuqui (morning glory seeds), the ritual hallucinogenic drug used by the Aztecs.

Warm, damp, rainy springs and summers favor ergot infestation. Summer rye is more prone to the development of the sclerotia than winter rye, and one field may be heavily ergotized while the adjacent field is not. The fungus may dangerously parasitize a crop one year and not reappear again for many years. Contamination of the grain may occur in varying concentrations. Modern agriculturalists advise farmers not to feed their cattle grain containing more than one to three sclerotia per thousand kernels of grain, since ergot has deleterious effects on cattle as well as on humans.

Ergotism, or long-term ergot poisoning, was once a common condition resulting from eating contaminated rye bread. In some epidemics it appears that females were more liable to the disease than males. Children and pregnant women are most likely to be affected by the condition, and individual susceptibility varies widely. It takes 2 years for ergot in powdered form to reach 50 percent deterioration, and the effects are cumulative. There are two types of ergotism—gangrenous and convulsive. As the name implies, gangrenous ergotism is characterized by dry gangrene of the extremities followed by the falling away of the affected portions of the body. The condition occurred in epidemic proportions in the Middle Ages and was known by a number of names, including *ignis sacer*, the holy fire.

Convulsive ergotism is characterized by a number of symptoms. These include crawling sensations in the skin, tingling in the fingers, vertigo, tinnitus aurium, headaches, disturbances in sensation, hallucination, painful muscular contractions leading to epileptiform convulsions, vomiting, and diarrhea. The involuntary muscular fibers such as the myocardium and gastric and intestinal muscular coat are stimulated. There are mental disturbances such as mania, melancholia, psychosis, and delirium. All of these symptoms are alluded to in the Salem witchcraft records.

Evidence for Ergotism in Salem

It is one thing to suggest convulsive ergot poisoning as an initiating factor in the witchcraft episode, and quite another to generate convincing evidence that it is more than a mere possibility. A jigsaw of details pertinent to growing conditions, the timing of events in Salem, and symptomology must fit together to create a reasonable case. From these details, a picture emerges of a community stricken with an unrecognized physiological disorder affecting their minds as well as their bodies.

1) *Growing conditions.* The common grass along the Atlantic Coast from Virginia to Newfoundland was and is wild rye, a host plant for ergot. Early colonists were dissatisfied with it as forage for their cattle and reported that it often made the cattle ill with unknown diseases. Presumably, then, ergot grew in the New World before the Puritans arrived. The potential source for infection was already present, regardless of the possibility that it was imported with English rye.

Rye was the most reliable of the Old World grains and by the 1640's it was a well-established New England crop. Spring sowing was the rule; the bitter winters made fall sowing less successful. Seed time for the rye was April and the harvesting took place in August. However, the grain was stored in barns and often waited months before being threshed when the weather turned cold. The timing of Salem events fits this cycle. Threshing probably occurred shortly before Thanksgiving, the only holiday the Puritans observed. The children's symptoms appeared in December 1691. Late the next fall, 1692, the witchcraft crisis ended abruptly and there is no further mention of the girls or anyone else in Salem being afflicted.

To some degree or another all rye was probably infected with ergot. It is a matter of the extent of infection and the period of time over which the ergot is consumed rather than the mere existence of ergot that determines the potential for ergotism. In his 1807 letter written from upstate New York, Stearns advised his medical colleague that, "On examining a granary where rye is stored, you will be able to procure a sufficient quantity [of ergot sclerotia] from among that grain." Agricultural practice had not advanced, even by Stearns's time, to widespread use of methods to clean or eliminate the fungus from the rye crop. In all probability, the infestation of the 1691 summer rye crop was fairly light: not everyone in the village or even in the same families showed symptoms.

Certain climatic conditions, that is, warm, rainy springs and summers, promote heavier than usual fungus infestation. The pattern of the weather in 1691 and 1692 is apparent from brief comments in Samuel Sewall's diary. Early rains and warm weather in the spring progressed to a hot and stormy summer in 1691. There was a drought the next year, 1692, thus no contamination of the grain that year would be expected.

2) *Localization.* "Rye," continues Stearns, "which grows in low, wet ground yields [ergot] in greatest abundance." Now, one of the most notorious of the accusing children in Salem was Thomas Putnam's 12-year-old daughter, Ann. Her mother also displayed symptoms of the affliction and psychological historians have credited the senior Ann with attempting to resolve her own neurotic complaints through her daughter. Two other afflicted girls also lived in the Putnam residence. Putnam had inherited one of the largest landholdings in the village. His father's will indicates that a large measure of the land, which was located in the western sector of Salem Village, consisted of swampy meadows that were valued farmland to the colonists. Accordingly, the Putnam farm, and more broadly, the western acreage of Salem Village, may have been an area of contamination. This contention is further substantiated by the pattern of residence of the accusers, the accused, and the defenders of the accused living within the boundaries of Salem Village. Excluding the afflicted girls, 30 of 32 adult accusers lived in the western section and 12 of the 14 accused witches lived in the eastern section, as did 24 of the 29 defenders. The general pattern of residence, in combination with the well-documented factionalism of the eastern and western sectors, contributed to the progress of the witchcraft crisis.

The initially afflicted girls show a slightly different residence pattern. Careful examination reveals plausible explanations for contamination in six of the eight cases.

Three of the girls, as mentioned above, lived in the Putnam residence. If this were the source of ergotism, their exposure to ergotized grain would be natural. Two afflicted girls, the daughter and niece of Samuel Parris, lived in the parsonage almost exactly in the center of the village. Their exposure to contaminated grain from western land is also explicable. Two-thirds of Parris's salary was paid in provisions; the villagers were taxed proportionately to their land holding. Since Putnam was one of the largest landholders and an avid supporter of Parris in the minister's community disagreements, an ample store of ergotized grain would be anticipated in Parris's larder. Putnam was also Parris's closest neighbor with afflicted children in residence.

The three remaining afflicted girls lived outside the village boundaries to the east. One, Elizabeth Hubbard, was a servant in the home of Dr. Griggs. It seems plausible that the doctor, like Parris, had Putnam grain, since Griggs was a professional man, not a farmer. As the only doctor in town, he probably had many occasions to treat Ann Putnam, Senior, a woman known to have much ill health. Griggs may have traded his services for provisions or bought food from the Putnams.

Another of the afflicted, Sarah Churchill, was a servant in the house of a well off farmer. The farm lay along the Wooleston River and may have offered good growing conditions for ergot. It seems probable, however, that Sarah's affliction was a fraud. She did not become involved in the witchcraft persecutions until May, several months after the other girls were afflicted, and she testified in only two cases, the first against her master. One deponent claimed that Sarah later admitted to belying herself and others.

How Mary Warren, a servant in the Proctor household, would gain access to grain contaminated with ergot is something of a mystery. Proctor had a substantial farm to the southeast of Salem and would have had no need to buy or trade for food. Both he and his wife were accused of witchcraft and condemned. None of the Proctor children showed any sign of the affliction; in fact, three were accused and imprisoned. One document offered as evidence against Proctor indicates that Mary stayed overnight in the village. How often she stayed or with whom is unknown.

Mary's role in the trials is particularly curious. She began as an afflicted person, was accused of witchcraft by the other afflicted girls, and then became afflicted again. Two depositions filed against her strongly suggest, however, that at least her first affliction may have been a consequence of ergot poisoning. Four witnesses attested that she believed she had been "distempered" and during the time of her affliction had thought she had seen numerous apparitions. However, when Mary was well again, she could not say that she had seen any specters. Her second affliction may have been the result of intense pressure during her examination for witchcraft crimes.

Ergotism and the Testimony

The utmost caution is necessary in assessing the physical and mental states of people dead for hundreds of years. Only the sketchiest accounts of their lives remain in public records. In the case of ergot, a substance that affects mental as well as physical states, recognition of the social atmosphere of Salem in early spring 1692 is basic to understanding the directions the crisis took. The Puritans' belief in witchcraft was a totally accepted part of their religious tenets. The malicious workings of Satan and his cohorts were just as real to the early colonists as their belief in God. Yet, the low incidence of witchcraft trials in New England prior to 1692 suggests that the Puritans did not always resort to accusations of black magic to deal with irreconcilable differences or inexplicable events.

The afflicted girls' behavior seemed to be no secret in early spring. Apparently it was the great consternation that some villagers felt that induced Mary Sibley to direct the making of the witch cake of rye meal and the urine of the afflicted. This concoction was fed to a dog, ostensibly in the belief that the dog's subsequent behavior would indicate the action of any malefic magic. The fate of the dog is unknown; it is quite plausible that it did have convulsions, indicating to the observers that there was witchcraft involved in the girls' afflictions. Thus, the experiments with the witch cake, rather than any magic tricks by Tituba, initiated succeeding events.

The importance of the witch cake incident has generally been overlooked. Parris's denouncement of his neighbor's action is recorded in his church records. He clearly stated that, until the making of the cake, there was no suspicion of witchcraft and no reports of torturing apparitions. Once a community member had gone "to the Devil for help against the Devil," as Parris put it, the climate for the trials had been established. The afflicted girls, who had made no previous mention of witchcraft, seized upon a cause for their behavior—as did the rest of the community. The girls named three persons as witches and their afflictions thereby became a matter for the legal authorities rather than the medical authorities or the families of the girls.

The trial records indicate numerous interruptions during the proceedings. Outbursts by the afflicted girls describing the activities of invisible specters and "familiars" (agents of the devil in animal form) in the meeting house were common. The girls were often stricken with violent fits that were attributed to torture by apparitions. The spectral evidence of the trials appears to be the hallucinogenic symptoms and perceptual disturbances accompanying ergotism. The convulsions appear to be epileptiform.

Accusations of choking, pinching, pricking with pins, and biting by the specter of the accused formed the standard testimony of the afflicted in almost all the examinations and trials. The choking suggests the involvement of the involuntary muscular fibers that is typical of ergot poisoning; the biting, pinching, and pricking may allude to the crawling and tingling sensations under the skin experienced by ergotism victims. Complaints of vomiting and "bowels almost pulled out" are common in the depositions of the accusers. The physical symptoms of the afflicted and many of the other accusers are those induced by convulsive ergot poisoning.

When examined in the light of a physiological hypothesis, the content of so-called delusional testimony, previously dismissed as imaginary by historians, can be reinterpreted as evidence of ergotism. After being choked and strangled by the apparition of a witch sitting on his chest, John Londer testified that a black thing came through the window and stood before his face. "The body of it looked like a monkey, only the feet were like cock's feet, with claws, and the face somewhat more like a man's than a monkey . . . the thing spoke to me."

Joseph Bayley lived out of town in Newbury. According to Upham, the Bayleys, en route to Boston, probably spent the night at the Thomas Putnam residence. As the Bayleys left the village, they passed the Proctor house and Joseph reported receiving a "very hard blow" on the chest, but no one was near him. He saw the Proctors, who were imprisoned in Boston at the time, but his wife told him that she saw only a "little maid." He received another blow on the chest, so strong that he dismounted from his horse and subsequently saw a woman coming toward him. His wife told him she saw nothing. When he mounted his horse again, he saw only a cow where he had seen the woman. The rest of Bayley's trip was uneventful, but when he returned home, he was "pinched and nipped by something invisible for some time." It is a moot point, of course, what or how much Bayley ate at the Putnams', or that he even really stayed there. Nevertheless, the testimony suggests ergot. Bayley had the crawling sensations in the skin, disturbances in sensations, and muscular contractions symptomatic of ergotism. Apparently his wife had none of the symptoms and Bayley was quite candid in so reporting.

A brief but tantalizing bit of testimony comes from a man who experienced visions that he attributed to the evil eye cast on him by an accused witch. He reported seeing about a dozen "strange things" appear in his chimney in a dark room. They appeared to be something like jelly and quavered with a strange motion. Shortly, they disappeared and a light the size of a hand appeared in the chimney and quivered and shook with an upward motion. As in Bayley's experience, this man's wife saw nothing. The testimony is strongly reminiscent of the undulating objects and lights reported in experiences induced by LSD.

By the time the witchcraft episode ended in the late fall 1692, 20 persons had been executed and at least two had died in prison. All the convictions were obtained on the basis of the controversial spectral evidence. One of the commonly expressed observations about the Salem Village witchcraft episode is that it ended unexpectedly for no apparent reason. No new circumstances to cast spectral evidence in doubt occurred. Increase Mather's sermon on 3 October 1692, which urged more conclusive evidence than invisible apparitions or the test of touch, was just a stronger reiteration of the clergy's 15 June advice to the court. The grounds for dismissing the spectral evidence had been consistently brought up by the accused and many of their defenders throughout the examinations. There had always been a strong undercurrent of opposition to the trials and the most vocal individuals were not always accused. In fact, there was virtually no support in the colonies for the trials, even from Boston, only 15 miles away. The most influential clergymen lent their support guardedly at best; most were opposed. The Salem witchcraft episode was an event localized in both time and space.

How far the ergotized grain may have been distributed is impossible to determine clearly. Salem Village was the source of Salem Town's food supply. It was in the town that the convictions and orders for executions were obtained. Maybe the thought processes of the magistrates, responsible and respected men in the Colony, were altered. In the following years, nearly all of them publicly admitted to errors of judgment. These posttrial documents are as suggestive as the court proceedings.

In 1696, Samuel Sewall made a public acknowledgment of personal guilt because of the unsafe principles the court followed. In a public apology, the 12 jurymen stated, "We confess that we ourselves were not capable to understand nor able to withstand the mysterious delusion of the Powers of Darkness and Prince of the Air . . . [we] do hereby declare that we justly fear that we were sadly deluded and mistaken." John Hale, a minister involved in the trials from the beginning, wrote, "such was the darkness of the day . . . that we walked in the clouds and could not see our way."

Finally, Ann Putnam, Jr., who testified in 21 cases, made a public confession in 1706.

> I justly fear I have been instrumental with others though ignorantly and unwittingly, to bring upon myself and this land the guilt of innocent blood; though what was said or done by me against any person I can truly and uprightly say before God and man, I did it not for any anger, malice or ill will to any person, for I had no such things against one of them, but what I did was ignorantly, being deluded of Satan.

One Satan in Salem may well have been convulsive ergotism.

Conclusion

One could reasonably ask whether, if ergot was implicated in Salem, it could have been implicated in other witchcraft incidents. The most cursory examination of Old World witchcraft suggests an affirmative answer. The district of Lorraine suffered outbreaks of both ergotism and witchcraft persecutions periodically throughout the Middle Ages until the 17th century. As late as the 1700's, the clergy of Saxony debated whether convulsive ergotism was symptomatic of disease or demonic possession. Kittredge, an authority on English witchcraft, reports what he calls "a typical case" of the early 1600's. The malicious magic of Alice Trevisard, an accused witch, backfired and the witness reported that Alice's hands, fingers, and toes "rotted and consumed away." The sickness sounds suspiciously like gangrenous ergotism. Years later, in 1762, one family in a small English village was stricken with gangrenous ergotism. The Royal Society determined the diagnosis. The head of the family, however, attributed the condition to witchcraft because of the suddenness of the calamity.

Of course, there can never be hard proof for the presence of ergot in Salem, but a circumstantial case is demonstrable. The growing conditions and the pattern of agricultural practices fit the timing of the 1692 crisis. The physical manifestations of the condition are apparent from the trial records and contemporaneous documents. While the fact of perceptual distortions may have been generated by ergotism, other psychological and sociological factors are not thereby rendered irrelevant; rather, these factors gave substance and meaning to the symptoms. The content of hallucinations and other perceptual disturbances would have been greatly influenced by the state of mind, mood, and expectations of the individual. Prior to the witch cake episode, there is no clue as to the nature of the girls' hallucinations. Afterward, however, a delusional system, based on witchcraft, was generated to explain the content of the sensory data. Valins and Nisbett, in a discussion of delusional explanations of abnormal sensory data, write, "The intelligence of the particular patient determines the structural coherence and internal consistency of the explanation. The cultural experiences of the patient determine the content—political, religious, or scientific—of the explanation." Without knowledge of ergotism and confronted by convulsions, mental disturbances, and perceptual distortions, the New England Puritans seized upon witchcraft as the best explanation for the phenomena.

From: James E. Kences, *Some Unexplored Relationships of Essex County Witchcraft to the Indian Wars of 1675 and 1687 (July 1984)*, Essex Institute Historical Collections

In section 1 James Kences explains that the lives of the people of colonial Massachusetts were dominated by their relationships with the Indians. The towns of Essex County had to supply militia and money to defend communities further north, where the heaviest fighting occurred, and were in constant danger of massacre themselves. In the 1690s the military alliance of the Indians and French added a new, terrifying dimension.

In section 2 Kences suggests that the tensions among Salem Village's opposing factions were exacerbated by the village's being inadequately defended, especially from the sea. Many of the advocates of a Salem

Village church were also active in trying to improve village defenses, whereas the enemies of the church appear to have been far less concerned with defense issues.

volume 120, section 3

On 25 January 1692 a messenger conveying news of a catastrophe galloped south toward Boston on the Ipswich Road, which passed Salem Village; earlier that day, and only forty miles distant, a war party comprised of 150 Abanaki Indians had attacked "wretchedly secure" York, Maine, on the Agamenticus River. The homes of 300 or 400 persons had been burned, and the community's minister, Shubael Dummer, had perished with about 50 other persons. The Reverend George Burroughs, minister at neighboring Wells, Maine, supplied authorities at Boston with a graphic report of the "pillours of smoke, ye raging of ye merciless flames, ye insultations of ye heathen enemy, shouting, shooting, hacking . . . & dragging away [80] others [to Canada]."

Contemporary observers felt that York had not been sufficiently vigilant, "dwelling in unguarded houses." Actually, one of the reasons York fell was that as a typical agricultural village of late seventeenth-century New England, its homes and farms were too widely scattered to be adequately protected if attacked. Salem Village was clearly aware of the dangers of this type of scattering, having addressed this problem in its previously mentioned 1667 petition to the Massachusetts legislature. That document portrayed a community whose inhabitants were so widely separated "one from another, some a mile, some further" that even "six or eight watches will not serve."

One of the villagers opposed to Parris, Peter Cloyce, was a former inhabitant of York whose wife, Sarah, would eventually be hanged as a witch in August of 1692. Every Indian war had brought refugees to Essex County towns from the "eastward." These persons generally returned to their homes when hostilities ceased, but some stayed. Two victims of the 1692 witch hunt, Abigail Hobbs of Topsfield and Anne Pudeator of Salem Town, had originally lived in Casco or Falmouth, Maine, until the Indians forced their migration south. In her confession Hobbs said that she had first seen the devil in the Maine woods. Goody Pudeator, who was hanged, still had children living at Casco at the time of her death.

Among the small group of the accusing "afflicted girls" who lived in Salem Village was Susanah Sheldon, the daughter of yet another refugee family from Black Point, Maine. Not only had the family of this seventeen-year-old been driven from Maine in 1675 during King Philip's War and again in William's War, but her twenty-four-year-old brother, Godfrey, had been killed at the "eastward" in early July of 1691.

Though Susanah Sheldon may have justly harbored a deep hatred or fear of the Indians as a result of her experiences, almost every one of the girls at one time or another during the witch hunt also revealed a dread of the heathen. Mary Walcott, the "afflicted" stepdaughter of the village's militia captain, accused Captian John Alden of witchcraft because he "[sold] powder and shot to the Indians and French, and [lay] with Indian squaws and had Indian papooses." This abuse of Alden might well have been engendered by his having negotiated a truce with the Indians that led indirectly to the attack upon York when the French sought to revive their alliance with the northern tribes. Alden's association with the York massacre took another form as well, for he had been responsible for securing the redemption of the captives.

Eleven-year-old Ann Putnam, another of the "afflicted" children, accused George Burroughs, the village's former minister and the survivor of two Indian massacres in Maine, of having murdered the son of Deodat Lawson while young Lawson was a chaplain in the service of Sir Edmund Andros, saying that the chaplain had "preached soe to the souldiers." She also claimed that Burroughs had "bewicthed [*sic*] a grate many souldiers to death at the eastword."

It was, though, Mercy Lewis, the Putnam family's seventeen-year-old servant, who uttered the most direct denunciation of the Indians or heathen, and she did so in a manner characteristic of the New England Puritans when she derived her language directly from the Bible. The Reverend Lawson witnessed the unusual display, as Mercy "sang the song in the fifth of Revelation, and the 110 Psalm, and the 149 Psalm." In both of these Psalms, the word *heathen* occurs:

> He shall judge among the heathen, he shall fill the places with the dead bodies: he shall wound the heads over many countries.
>
> **Psalm 110:6**

> Let the high praises of God be in their mouth, and a twoedged sword in their hand;
>
> To execute vengeance upon the heathen, *and* punishments upon the people.
>
> **Psalm 149:6–7**

Mercy Lewis's confusion over the identities of Indians and witches was as much a product of Puritan influences upon her as these Biblical quotations. During the most discouraging moments of her captivity, Mrs. Rowlandson similarly found security in the Psalms. On one occasion it was to alleviate her anxiety over the welfare of her ill son and missing daughter:

I repaired under these thoughts to my Bible (my great comfort in that time) and that scripture came to my hand, "Cast thy burden upon the Lord, and he shall sustain thee," Psalm 55:22.

According to Samuel Parris, the New England Puritans belonged to the family of man, but were distinct from all other peoples because God had created them for a special mission. This was as much a convention of Puritan thought as was the reliance upon the Bible. But Parris had an unusual way of introducing the idea which stressed kinship of Puritan and pagans; "we are all one by nature," he once informed the Salem Village congregation, "with Egyptians, Turks, Pagans, Indians and Ethiopians."

section 4

During the first year of King William's War, Cotton Mather exhorted readers to:

> tell mankind that there are Devils and Witches: and that those night-birds least appear where the Day-light of the Gospel comes, yet New England has had examples of their existence and operation: and that not only the wigwams of Indians, where the pagan powaws often raise their masters, in the shapes of bears and snakes and fires but also in the homes of white English men and women.

That same year, 1699, the captive John Gyles was warned by "an old squaw" to whom he had confided his desire to observe an Indian powow in progress, "that if they knew of my being there, they would kill me. . . . When she was a girl she had known young persons to be taken away by a hairy man." Gyles was in danger of being carried off by the "hairy man" also if the wizards had discovered him.

The near encounter with the "hairy man" reflected a consensus opinion of seventeenth-century New England; the Elect perceived themselves as having been encroached upon by unregenerates who acted as the instruments of Satan to obstruct or destroy their labors for God in the wilderness of the New World, and they believed as well that the devil had inspired the Indians to go to war, and to perpetrate massacres. Each story of atrocity or torture served to reinforce these simple ideas and helped to make the affinities all the more apparent. Increase Mather observed that the "barbarous Indians (like their Father the Devil . . . delighted in crueltyes)."

For the inhabitants of Essex County in 1692 this belief had important consequences. Witchcraft appears to have been generally regarded as a preliminary weakening of a community's moral strength or resistance, so that the inhabitants might eventually fall victim to the Indians and French. This can be inferred from Cotton Mather's revelation learned from:

> one who was executed at Salem for witchcraft who confessed that at their cheef witch-meetings, there had been present some French Canadiens, and some Indian sagamores to concert the methods of ruining New England.

Essex County had already displayed signs of what social psychologists refer to as "invasion neurosis," the extreme tension of anticipating an attack which does not materialize. The tendency of the county's population to react to rumour and to sense imminent danger was exemplified by two incidents which occurred during King William's War. In the first case, there was just cause for fear; an escaped slave revealed details of a conspiracy which a fanatic French sympathizer named Isaac Morril had organized in the autumn of 1690. Morril not only planned to overwhelm northern Essex County with 500 Indians and 300 French soldiers, he also hoped to incite servants to murder their masters and to fight beside him as allies. . . . Morril's preparations had included an alarmingly thorough reconnaisance of the region's garrisons, which, according to witnesses Robert and Elizabeth Long, he had inspected while carrying a concealed weapon on his person.

A much stranger example of war hysteria occurred at the town of Gloucester in the summer of 1692, but this episode seems largely to have been the fault of that town's excitable minister, the Reverend John Emerson. A potential source of trouble for the town had surfaced two years earlier, when in July of 1690, Emerson had implored Maj. Wait Winthrop to release forty-seven members of the village's militia company who had been impressed into the army which was then being assembled for the attack upon Quebec. Otherwise, Emerson complained, "wee must all be forced to leave the towne for we are not able to stay any longer after they are gone." The extraordinary levy, if enacted, would have divested the town of two-thirds of its men, and the group of fifteen soldiers that would be retained to defend Gloucester would have been easily overwhelmed by a French raiding party which tried "to breake in upon" the town.

Emerson's anxiety over possible attack appears to have been contagious, for in late June of 1692 Ebenezer Babson reported to him of the occurrence of furtive activity in the vicinity of his house. Babson had seen, or so he told the minister, "men which looked like Frenchmen" moving stealthily through the swamps. Upon hearing this rumour, several persons abandoned their farms and fled to the garrisons to evade what by that time Emerson thought to be the "Devil and his agents." In a letter written to Cotton Mather after the panic had subsided, Emerson described some of the strange happenings witnessed by the town that summer which included an account of Babson's encounter with the nebulous enemy:

> Bapson . . . saw three men walk softly out of the swamp . . . being within two or three rod[s] of them he shot, and as soon as his gun went off they all fell down. Bapson then running to his supposed prey, cried out unto his companion . . . "he had killed three!" "he had killed three!" But coming about unto them they all rose up.

At Gloucester, the rapid shift in interpretation of the menace as first an actual enemy, and then to one of supernatural origin, was due in part to the memory of the 1653 and 1657 witchcraft outbreaks in the town, and also to the mind-set of Essex County in 1692. The critics of the witchcraft trials who have condemned the Puritans for callousness and lack of sophistication have largely ignored the evidence in the confessions, of "witch militias" and nests of witches at garrisons, such as Chandler's garrison in Andover—the kind of information which only helped to further aggravate "invasion neurosis." The Reverend Deodat Lawson recorded many examples of these admissions in his *Brief and True Narrative*, and he shows—through an aggressive confrontation between the "afflicted" girls and Martha Corey—that the witch militia appeared as real as that which Jonathan Walcott captained in Salem Village; "the afflicted persons asked Corey why she did not go to the Company of Witches which were before the Meeting house mustering? Did she not hear the drum beat?" The "company," as Lawson later explained, was composed of "about 23 or 24" individuals.

Boyer and Nissenbaum argue that the witchcraft accusations were influenced by the conscious and even subconscious resentments among the faction that supported the church in response to gestures of disloyalty by its enemies. Such a gesture seems implicit in a June 1690 notice from the colonial government to the officers of the Beverly troop. Those officers were assured that if they could "make up a number of forty able Troopers . . . with the addition of those of Salem Village now listed with them they may continue" as a troop.

Eligibility for the troop of horse—one of the most prestigious branches of the colonial service—was determined by wealth, as the trooper was expected to purchase his own costly accoutrements: a horse, saddle and equippage, carbine, pistols, and a sword or cutlass. These acquisitions were beyond the means of the majority of Parris's supporters, who lived too far west of Beverly to have frequented the town. The men, whoever they might have been, probably lived on the Ipswich Road, close to the taverns and shops alien to the less worldly farmers.

It is possible that wartime disloyalty was the nucleus of discontent that resulted in the spread of accusations of witchcraft to the town of Andover, which soon rivaled Salem Village in the number of arrests. The source of trouble in Andover was exposed when the government attempted to reorganize the Upper

Regiment, the regiment of militia in northwestern Essex County, by transferring the Boxford militia from that unit to another regiment in the county. A group of men from Andover promptly sent a petition to Boston to protest the action because the two towns:

> [lay] soe neare to each other & ready upon all occasions of ye enemy's approach to releive each other, which if disjoyned wee cannot doe, & for many other reasons we humbly pray . . . that Boxford might still continue as part of ye upper Regiment.

The "many other reasons" alluded to in this petition signed by Captain John Osgood, John Barker, and Stephen Johnson, who were to be in 1692 the husbands and fathers of ten Andover witches, suggest that these families may have begun to gravitate toward Boxford. There is no direct evidence of any ambitions to secede from Andover, as it was never formally asserted; there are, however, occasional expressions of close association, such as the extensive land holdings of the Barker family in Boxford.

After having witnessed Rowley's experience with secession, the Andover selectmen would have been especially alert to prevent any attempted move, and this inchoate faction, if any factionalism actually existed, may have been on their minds during the summer of 1692, when Joseph Ballard "sent horse and man" to Salem Village to fetch little Ann Putnam so that she might discover the cause of his wife's illness—an action that resulted in an epidemic of witchcraft accusations in Andover. Ballard's ailing wife, Elizabeth (Phelps) Ballard was related to Thomas Chandler, the keeper of the infested garrison house, through the marriage of two of his children, daughter Sarah and son William, to members of the Phelps family in 1682 and 1687.

Two possible exhibitions of disloyalty at Salem Village and an adjacent town symbolized the disintegration of the communal covenant that was so important to the Puritans. As Boyer and Nissenbaum have shown, Samuel Parris espoused this particular theme obsessively from 1689 until 1692. In January of 1690, Parris informed his congregation, "there is no trust to a rotten hearted person, whatever friendship may be pretended." Parris also tended to portray the church as a fortress—and in a real sense a garrison house—and its communicants as soldiers obligated to defend it:

> Christ furnisheth the believer with skill, strength, courage, weapons and all military accomplishments for victory . . . the Lord Jesus sets them forth, furnisheth them with all necessaries for battle. The Lord Jesus is the true believer's magazine. [19 July 1691]

Cotton Mather reported after his detailed discussions with the "afflicted" Mercy Short about her spectral visions:

> that at such times the spectres went away to ther witch-meetings: but that when they returned the whole crew, besides her daily troublers look'd in upon her, to see how the work was carried on: that there were French Canadiens and Indian sagamores among them, diverse of whom shee knew.

Her familiarity with the enemy resulted from Mercy's experiences as a survivor of an Indian massacre and as a redeemed captive. She was the daughter of Clement Short, a farmer from the small southern New Hampshire coastal community of Salmon Falls.

Mercy's ordeal had begun on 18 March 1690 when a war party led by the French-Canadian, Hertel, simultaneously assaulted the settlement's three garrison houses. Surprised and defenseless, Salmon Falls was destroyed; thirty-four people were killed and another fifty-four were captured. On that day the Indians and French "horribly butchered Mercy's father, her mother, her brother, her sister and others of her kindred." Three other brothers and two sisters were carried off to Canada. Mercy Short had in common with the "afflicted" of Salem Village her age and lack of family, as well as the severe form of dislocation that she had suffered as a result of the Indian attack.

Six of the eight "afflicted" girls in Salem Village were not living in their parent's households in 1692. Some of them worked as servants, and others lived in the homes of relatives. The deliberate separation of teen-aged children from their parents was a fundamental idea of the social or family ethic of New England Puritanism. Edmund S. Morgan maintains that this practice of "putting children out" as apprentices or to live with other families was often done for the purpose of establishing a "necessary distance between parent and child." A recent contrasting view accounts for the behavior as an intuitive response by parents concerned with "insulating themselves to some extent against the shock that the death of a child might bring."

Separation from parents was also a frequent theme of Puritan ministers in their dialogues with children. Cotton Mather explained gravely to youthful listeners, "That which will exceedingly Aggravate [the] *Torments* of your *Damnation,* will be the Encounter which you shall have with your Godly Parents," for on that Day of Judgement such children will see their parents concur in their condemnation and will hear them say, "We now know them no more, Let them depart among the Workers of Iniquitie."

The Reverend Michael Wigglesworth employed the imagery of separation in his poem "The Day of Doom," composed in the 1660s:

The tender Mother will own no other
of all her num'rous brood,
But such as stand at Christ's right hand,
acquitted through his Blood.

A grim specter seen by the "afflicted" girls Mary Walcott and Susanah Sheldon during the witchcraft episode seems the embodiment of the Puritan Father. This specter, which the girls called the "shining man," had once interceded to rescue Susanah Sheldon from the witchspectre of John Willard. The shining man then commanded her to tell what:

> I had heard and seen to Mr. Hathorn this Willard being there present tould mee if I did hee would cutt my throate. At this same time and place this Shining Man told mee that if I did goe to tell this to Mr. Hathorn that I should be well goeing and coming but I should be afflicted there, then said I to the Shining Man hunt Willa[r]d away and I would beleeve what he said that he might not chock mee with that the Shining Man held up his hand and Willard vaneshed away.

Children who were denied genuine closeness to their parents through emotional or physical distance were sometimes brought closer together as an artificial family; but such an intimate unit can work only as long as conditions are not too demanding. False families of "disaster" children tended only to cultivate their fears.

Regarding the above, it was not the January 1692 York massacre alone which forced the children to behave this way, but rather the earlier massacres at Salmon Falls and Falmouth, Maine, in March and May of 1690 respectively, which the girls still remembered two years later when York fell.

The critical factor in the children's response to the 1690s massacres could have been Mrs. Ann Putnam, whose eleven-year-old daughter and namesake had accused the Reverend Burroughs of murder. Prior to her 1678 marriage to Lt. Thomas Putnam, Jr., immediately after King Philip's War, Ann Carr had lived in Salisbury, in the extreme northern part of Essex County. Her father (George Carr) had owned, in addition to a large estate, a shipworks and ferry, and upon his death in 1682, his widow and one of his sons took control of the entire enterprise, not only causing enmity between them and Ann, but even producing litigation.

In August of 1672, through the marriage of her brother William Carr to Elizabeth Pike, Ann (Carr) Putnam became a relation of Maj. Robert Pike, the individual who in May of 1690 was appointed commander in chief of all Massachusetts militia forces in New Hampshire and Maine. A year before her own marriage, while she still lived in Salisbury, Ann Putnam had witnessed a violent argument between Major Pike and the Reverend John Wheelright during which the town of Salisbury divided itself into factions around the two men. Wheelright had succeeded one morning in having Pike excommunicated when during an Indian alarm he took advantage of the absence of the soldier's supporters from the meeting house.

On 13 September 1677 the Massachusetts government severely reprimanded both individuals: Major Pike for having:

> shewed himselfe too litigious in impeaching him [Wheelright] with soe many articles under his hand, thereby creating great disturbance to the church & place, & alsoe much contempt of sd. Wheelright's person & office. . . . But neither can wee excuse Mr. Wheel- of too much precipitancy in pronouncing a sentance of excommunication against sd. Pike without further triall for repentance according to the vote of the church if he repent.

Ann Carr's brother William was one of Pike's supporters who signed a complaint against Wheelright in May of 1677. The Massachusetts officials castigated these men for having contributed greatly to the disruption of the town:

> Wee cannot but condemne that evill practice of those of the church & towne that did endeavour in their petition to the Generall Court to eject off Mr. Wheelright from his ministry.

In 1685 another scandal engulfed the Carr family, and again Major Robert Pike was involved, as revealed in a reference from the diary of Samuel Sewall:

> Mr. Stoughton also told me of George Car's wife being with child by another man, tells the father, Major Pike sends her down to prison. Is the Governour's grandchild by his daughter Cotton.

Mrs. Putnam's perception of these negative events might have had a direct bearing on her reaction to the 1690 massacres; being herself a victim of early parental separation and an individual who probably felt considerable ambivalence toward her family, the fragmentary reports of an Indian massacre at Salmon Falls, only fifteen miles from where she had spent her childhood, might well have revived these feelings in the adult Ann Putnam, and made her anxious for the safety of relatives or family friends, and she could have manifested that anxiety to her daughter. The evidence in a preponderance of recent studies concerning the effects of war and natural catastrophe upon children suggests that the most vulnerable children in such situations are those whose mothers are easily agitated and whose fathers react angrily or aggressively. There is no evidence of isolated children being particularly disturbed; rather, "each problem proved to be that of a disturbed family."

A striking modern example of a "vulnerable" child's hallucinating devils and witches can be found in an early 1970s report of an eleven-year-old Catholic girl from Northern Ireland who, after having been subjected to a gas attack and to contact with a bloodied body, had the first of her hallucinations. She said that the figure she saw was "a tall man with a big hat, brightly colored coat and frightening eyes. He was, he said, a Protestant, because he was 'evil' and was trying to kill her."

Normally, following a disaster or some other frightening experience, children attempt to comprehend what has happened to them through play-acting, or by constantly talking about the episode—a means of "ventilating" those aspects of the event that most trouble them. Attentive parents recognize the signs and respond, but if the parents are not alert to the signs or remain too anxious in the aftermath, the signs are not perceived, and the child shows nervous symptoms instead. In 1692, in Salem Village, the girls described sensations of biting, strangulation, convulsions, and hallucinations. The combination of the parental distance endemic to New England Puritanism and the tensions of factional conflict doubtless prevented the Salem parents from recognizing what was wrong with their children.

Further, the quality of communication in 1690 probably resulted in the children's learning about the massacres in successive waves of rumor and misinformation as messengers, soldiers, and other witnesses traveled south to Boston with inflated reports of casualties and destruction. In addition, many of the girls were approaching marriageable age and were powerless to stop the departures of eligible men in their early twenties to the "eastward" and the war. As many as seven men ranging in age from sixteen years to their mid twenties perished in King William's War:

1690

April 17, John Bishop (18 years) killed with ye Indians.
September 21, Nicholas Reed (18 years) Edward Putnam's man killed with ye Indians.

1691

July 3, Godfrey Sheldon (24 years) killed by ye Indians.
July 4, Thomas (18 years) killed at Casko.
July 5, Edward Crocker(19 years) killed at Casko.
July 6, George Bogwell(16 years) killed at Casko.

1693

June, William Tarbell, soldier at ye Eastward.

If the girls' different anxieties relating to Indian massacre had remained unresolved from the spring of 1690 to the time of the York massacre in January 1692, that incident would have revived all of the old fears and uncertainties surrounding Salmon Falls and Falmouth in March and May 1690, perhaps accounting for the apparent concentration of afflictions and arrests on specific days and weeks in the spring of 1692.

This was not the first example in New England of witchcraft accusations being generated by Indian war. At the town of Scituate in Plymouth Colony in March of 1677, Mary Ingham was accused by Mehittable Woodworth of being the cause of her violent fits. . . . While at the time of Ingham's accusation the town was entirely free of an Indian menace, exactly one year earlier, in March of 1676, the town of Scituate remained under constant threat of Indian attack for two months.

From late February of 1676 Indian raids had occurred within a ten-mile radius of Scituate on the average of once a week with assaults upon Weymouth, Braintree, Bridgewater, and Attleborough. Then, on Sunday, 12 March 1676, the Indians penetrated to the center of Plymouth and massacred eleven persons at Clark garrison house. Less than two weeks later, Captain Michael Peirse of Scituate and forty-two soldiers—fourteen of them Scituate men—were massacred by the Indians five miles north of Providence.

On 19 April 1676 the destruction of the war reached the immediate environs of Scituate when John Jacob was killed by the Indians at the adjacent town of Hingham. The following day the Indians burned five houses at Hingham and then advanced south to Scituate and burned nineteen houses in the town; exactly one month later on 20 May 1676 the Indians attacked again and destroyed the mill of Cornet Robert Stetson, father to Robert Stetson, Jr., whose house had been burned in April. Plymouth Court records of July 1676 reveal a controversy between the Stetson and Woodworth families involving the birth of an illegitimate child to Elizabeth Woodworth that was apparently fathered by Stetson, Jr.

Mehittable Woodworth was probably a "vulnerable" child long before February 1676, and the progress her phobia took can be easily traced from the moment of the first attack near her town and her correct anticipation of a second, a third, and fourth visitation. The embarrassment of a local scandal and the targeting of the Stetsons by the Indians might also have frightened her.

Hysterical behavior triggered by the first or second anniversaries of critical events was the common element in both the Scituate and Salem Village episodes. In late February of 1692 Tituba (Samuel Parris's Carib Indian slave), Sarah Osborne, and Sarah Good were the first women to be arrested for witchcraft. Three more women were accused in March. On 18 March 1692—the second anniversary of Salmon Falls—Ann (Carr) Putnam claimed to have been afflicted by the specter of Martha Corey, stating that Corey had "tortured me so as I cannot express, ready to tear me all to pieces." Goody Corey was summarily arrested as was Rebecca Nurse, also largely as a result of "severe spectral afflictions which befell the elder Ann Putnam between March 19 and 24."

The cluster of arrests for witchcraft in late May 1692—the anniversary of Falmouth or Casco—was quite large; thirty arrests were made in a twenty-day period. Of those, ten arrests occurred on 28 May and were the result of spectral afflictions experienced by Mary Walcott. Among those arrested that day were Captain John Alden, Martha Carrier, and Martha Toothaker—the Billerica woman who had dreamed of fighting Indians. A fourth arrestee, Captain John Floyd of Rumney Marsh, had, like Alden, associations with the York massacre, having been in command of the militia (including Salem men) which had found the town in ruins. On 27 January 1692 he had written to his superiors, "The 25 of this instant I having information that York was destroyed made the greatest hast that I could with my Company for their reliefe if there were any left which I did hardly expect."

The "afflicted" may have accused men who had been prominently involved in the prosecution of the Indian because of the simple conviction that persons who had been in close contact with the Indians and survived were in fact witches; those who had died, like Godfrey Sheldon, were true Christians. This assumption would have been consistent with the Puritan belief that Indians and witches were synonymous, and may even have been responsible for the process of affliction itself. The "afflicteds'" perception of Indian war had always been a distorted one, especially for the three seventeen-year-olds, Mary Walcott, Mercy Lewis, and Susanah Sheldon, who were infants in 1675 and 1676. In the early 1680s, when these girls were between five and six years of age, King Philip's War was still a vivid memory—the ruins, the wounded, and the widowed women were very likely all around them. And the Puritans produced a considerable war literature: histories, captivity narratives, and memorial sermons, which further contributed to the symbolization of the war. Just how much the "afflicted" knew about Philip's War from this literature is impossible to determine. It does, however, seem plausible that at some time while they were growing up, the girls became familiar with the "cenotaphic" hills in the village which, although bearing the names of earlier owners of the properties (Davenport, Leach, Smith, Thorndike, and Whipple) also seemed to memorialize their direct descendants who fought or were killed by Indians in King Philip's War. The map shown in figure 4 shows the location of the hills and the properties of individuals (called "accusers" and "defenders" by Boyer and Nissenbaum) who represented opposing factions in the witchcraft dispute.

By 1692 the village girls' fear of the Indian had advanced to such an irrational state that they were unable to think directly about him; instead, they used the witch as his symbolic substitute—and a witch was any person who distressed either the girls or their parents. As previously noted, the "afflicted" would also have held such people responsible for the failure of their parents to supply needed emotional support.

The charging of the Reverend George Burroughs, "the little black minister from Casco Bay," is the best illustration of how actively the girls sought agents of the war at a symbolic level. Burroughs was regarded as the source—even the mastermind—of the spectral assault which emerged from his "eastward" domain, and the "afflicted" girls had been inclined to perceive the world typologically—especially in light of Samuel Parris's encouragement to reduce complex disagreements to distinctions of good and evil. The influence of Parris and their ingrained fear of the Indian made it easy for the girls to see the "eastward" as an allegorical hell, and even to interpret the events of the war as signs that the end of the world was approaching.

Evidence for a too-literal misreading of Revelations in 1692 comes from two sources—Deodat Lawson, who heard the possessed Mercy Lewis sing:

> Thou art worthy to take the book and to open the seals therof: for thou wast slain and has redeemed us to God by thy blood.
>
> **Revelations 5:9**

and from occasional reference to the existence of a seal on the forehead of a specter of the witch's victim—possibly traceable to Revelations 9, which is most suggestive as a plan for the infestation of the region by witches, in that it describes an assault by locusts following the opening of a "bottomless pit."

The act of opening the pit was represented by "the smoke of a great furnace [which darkened] the sun and the air," an image of which the York massacre could be a symbolic equivalent. The locusts which appeared had been "commanded [not to] hurt the grass of the earth, neither any green thing, neither any tree, but only those men which have not the seal of God in their forehead," and the pain which they were to inflict was to cause "the torment of a scorpion when he striketh a man." The parallel between the Biblical locusts and the Essex County witches is evident even in the description of their appearance:

> And they had hair as the hair of women, and their teeth were as the teeth of lions.
>
> And they had breastplates, as it were breastplates of iron: and the sound of their wings was as the sound of chariots of many horses running to battle.

> And they had a king over them which is the angel of the bottomless pit.
> **Revelations 9: 8, 9, 10**

Abigail Williams, who lived in the Reverend Parris's home was, with the minister's daughter, one of the first to have been afflicted, displaying behavior imitative of these locusts in the presence of Deodat Lawson. The incident occurred on 19 March 1692, and Lawson noted that she was "hurryed with violence to and fro in the room, sometimes making as if she would fly, stretching up her arms as high as she could, and crying 'Whish, Whish, Whish' several times." Abigail next debated with a specter, and then retreated from it "to the fire and begin to throw fire brands about the house, and run up against the back, as if she would run up chimney."

In this compact allegorical drama, Abigail Williams seems to have performed the parts of both the locust and its victim. Mercy Lewis had attempted to inform Lawson in the same indirect way with recitations against the heathen, but Lawson and his colleagues never understood the New Testament allusion, and the frustrated girls soon advanced from play-acting to "fits."

In February of 1692 Abigail Williams developed an illness and suffered with "pains in her head and other parts" throughout that month. This illness, which was coincident with Tituba's first supposed contact with the devil, is significant because the devil had constantly advised Tituba to "doe hurt" to the children "and pinch them." Tituba attempted to resist the devil and to ignore his orders, but said she was coerced into obedience:

> they hall me [away] and make me pinch Betty, and the next Abigaill, and then quickly went away altogether.

Like the children, Tituba was also hallucinating, but for different reasons. The emphasis upon physical injury in her fantasies—particularly acts against Elizabeth Parris—seems derived from a psychological conflict made worse by her frequent dislocation from a familiar place. Tituba's impulse to pinch seemed to Abigail Williams like the torments of the Biblical locusts, and as further reinforcement, Tituba as an Indian could be linked at a symbolic level to the fiendish Indians of the "eastward."

section 5

The more accurate historical understandings of the witch hunts have during the last few decades resulted largely from an effort to comprehend the event more as a social phenomenon than as a crime. Practically all of the agents involved in the events of 1692—witches, judges, and ministers—have been perceived as having behaved as the culture expected they should; but this objectivity has not been extended to the "afflicted" girls. While they are no longer accused of fraud, it has become easier to dismiss them as being insignificant. The spectrum of analysis regarding the cause of the afflictions has embraced ergot poisoning, hysterical symptoms owing to fear of magic, and antecedents of the revivalism of the eighteenth century. The Indian war and the complex of fears which it might have generated would, in contrast with these other conjectures, help to make the girls' behavior comprehensible as a contemporary and appropriate response under very real emotional stress.

The 1692 witch hunt was very much a product of King William's War, which seemed not only to have exacerbated village factionalism, but to have promoted the further alienation of Salem Village from Salem Town. For two and a half years, Samuel Parris had—on a weekly basis—impressed upon his congregration the fact that they might be betrayed, and that they would have to be vigilant to survive. Less sophisticated persons might have easily confused his rhetoric with admonitions about the war in the "eastward"; and among these less sophisticated individuals were the female children who were deprived of an active role in the war and were thus forced to stand helplessly by as spectators to the massacres. The magnitude of the witch hunts increased, because these same girls influenced the spread of accusations into the frontier towns of Andover and Billerica, where massacres had taken place and where the people were uneasy.

New England Puritanism transformed the anxieties of children in wartime into a witch panic, because Puritans regarded the relationship of Indian and witch as fundamental to a perception of Indian war; nor was theirs a religion which could accommodate itself to the needs of children or be sympathetic in dealing with their fears. Finally, Puritanism was oriented toward Biblical symbolism, which greatly affected the colonists' outlook upon the present. Indian wars and captivities were described in epic language, and the Indian's power was exaggerated so that his defeat would appear more meaningful and heroic. The mundane and the accidental aspects of Indian war should have helped the girls to see the Indians more realistically, but the Puritan emphasis was on the heathen's devil-inspired omniscience and omnipotence; it is thus not difficult to see how fear of Indians evolved into a deep-rooted belief that they were creatures of the devil. It is somewhat ironic that this dark vision of the Indian is clearly apparent even in an official directive to one of the men who would himself later be accused of witchcraft. The instructions that were delivered to Captian John Alden following his assignment to redeem the York captives from the Indians reminded him that:

> it will be necessary that you represent unto them their baseness, treachery and barbarities practised in carrying on of this warr . . . haveing alwaies declined a fair pitch battle acting [instead] like bears and wolves.

This grisly analogy shows how much the Indian's diabolic nature seemed to be an established reality in 1692, not only to the "afflicted" of Salem Village, but to the authorities of law and order as well.

From: Enders A. Robinson, *The Devil Discovered,* (New York, 1991), chapter 7, "Collusion and Conspiracy"

Enders Robinson, a descendant of one of the hanged witches, Samuel Wardwell, explores some unexpected as well as some obvious connections between the participants in the witch-hunt. He develops a "conspiracy theory" that goes beyond Upham's, claiming that Thomas Putnam and his allies planned the witch-hunt even as the girls had their first fits. They then conspired with local ministers and magistrates and the Boston Puritan "old guard" to continue the convictions. Robinson's book is important in showing how different vested interests worked together, if not necessarily by the careful planning he suggests, then by always seizing the opportunities presented.

The Rev. Samuel Parris, age thirty-nine in 1692, was a founding member of the conspiracy and a prime conspirator. He lived in the Salem Village parsonage with his wife Elizabeth, age forty-four, their daughter Elizabeth Parris, called Betty, age nine, and his niece Abigail Williams, age eleven. Also he owned two slaves, Tituba and her husband, John Indian. The names of Betty and Abigail appeared on the first complaint, filed on February 29, 1692. It states that Betty and Abigail were afflicted by Sarah Good, Sarah Osborne, and Tituba. The complaint was filed by Thomas Putnam, his brother Edward Putnam, Joseph Houlton and Thomas Preston. Parris' name does not appear. Thomas Preston, in putting his name on this complaint, had been duped by the conspiracy. The son-in-law of Rebecca Nurse, he quickly realized his folly and withdrew his support for the witchcraft proceedings.

Betty was an active participant in the courtroom until early April, when the Rev. Parris withdrew her from further participation and sent her to live in Salem Town with the family of Stephen Sewall. The youngest of the afflicted girls, Betty was beginning to show preliminary symptoms of a mental breakdown. At his wife's insistence, he drew the line at the health of their daughter. His niece Abigail Williams was made of sterner stuff. After Betty left the circle, Abigail Williams and Ann Putnam, Jr. continued as the most active of the group. They were now also the youngest.

In all, Abigail alleged she was afflicted by forty-four persons. She testified against many in court. Even Joseph Hutchinson, a member of the fringe group of the conspiracy, was upset by the outrageous lies of Abigail Williams. In a deposition he tried to discredit Abigail's veracity. Because Abigail was the niece of the Rev. Parris, Hutchinson's deposition did little good.

Dr. William Griggs was another founding member of the conspiracy. Dr. Griggs and the Rev. Parris were often brought together by their professional interests. In those days the approaches of physician and cleric in dealing with sickness were similar, converging somewhere between the occult and faith healing. The physical (sickness) and the spiritual (sin) were regarded as parts of the same whole. As already seen, Cotton Mather himself had studied medicine before entering the clergy.

Originally from Boston, Dr. Griggs was the first physician to practice in Salem Village. In 1692, he was about seventy-seven years old and his wife, whose maiden name was Rachel Hubbard, was sixty-four years old. The Hubbard family was distinguished, whereas Griggs came from modest beginnings. Not particularly successful, he paid a tax of only sixteen shillings in Salem Village in 1690. In 1692 Dr. Griggs was not reluctant to see some of the Salem Village midwives arrested for witchcraft, since they had been dispensing medicine which was generally regarded as more beneficial than his own. For example, testimony against Elizabeth Proctor, an accused witch, claimed that she was responsible for the death of a man because Dr. Griggs had not been sent for "to give him physic."

Elizabeth Hubbard, the great niece of Dr. Griggs' wife, was living with the old couple and working as their servant. Elizabeth was a good friend of Mary Walcott; both seventeen, they spent much time together. Dr. Griggs' house was only about one half of a mile from Jonathan Walcott's house. However, on February 16, 1692, close to the start of the witch hunt, Dr. Griggs bought a better house, situated close to the Beverly line, nearly three miles from the Walcott house. Elizabeth still visited the Walcott house, but now she often spent the night. Ann Putnam, Jr. and Mercy Lewis lived at Thomas Putnam's house, over a mile from the Walcott house. Ann managed to visit the Walcott house regularly to see her aunt and play with the children. Mercy Lewis often went with Ann; Mercy was the same age as Elizabeth Hubbard and Mary Walcott. Ann, only twelve, was friends with Abigail Williams, age eleven, who lived in the Rev. Parris' parsonage, the nearest house to the Walcott house, just a few hundred feet away. Also at the parsonage was little Elizabeth Parris, age nine. These six girls, the two Elizabeths, Mary, Ann, Mercy, and Abigail, made up the inner circle.

If as a physician, Dr. Griggs refrained from filing any legal complaints, we see his hand in the actions of his servant, Elizabeth Hubbard. Elizabeth Hubbard maintained a spiteful and malicious role throughout the witchcraft scare. In a deposition, Clement Coldum stated that on May 29, 1692 "I asked her if she was not afraid of the Devil? She answered me no, she could discourse with the Devil as well as with me." Coldum was ready to testify under oath as to his testimony. James Kettle was also willing to testify against Elizabeth and stated "the last of May, having some discourse with Elizabeth Hubbard, I found her to speak several untruths." The records show that she was afflicted by seventeen persons, and she testified against many.

On February 10, 1693, when the witchcraft craze was coming to an end, Dr. Griggs, "being aged and infirm," conveyed his newly purchased house to his son, Jacob Griggs of Beverly. When Dr. Griggs died in 1698, his library consisted of "nine physic books," worth 30 shillings, and "bibles & other books," worth 15 shillings. His medical equipment included a case of lances, two razors, a saw, and seven instruments for chirurgeon [surgeon]. His wife survived him, living to be ninety.

Sergeant Thomas Putnam, age thirty-nine, a founding member of the conspiracy, acted as ringleader. Much can be learned by looking at events from the perspective of this man, the chief filer of the legal complaints that led to the arrest of alleged witches. Repeatedly he claimed that his eldest daughter, Ann Putnam, Jr., and his servant Mercy Lewis were afflicted and tormented by a multitude of witches. He demanded justice.

His wife Ann Putnam, Senior, age thirty, entered into this macabre play-act as an afflicted person on a number of occasions. In fact she was in court almost as often as her daughter and her servant, all of them acting out the afflictions of witchcraft. Together, the three were responsible for the spectral evidence leading to many imprisonments, some of which resulted in death.

Mother Ann and daughter Ann were a particularly formidable pair of actors. People from miles around trooped into the courtroom to watch their performances under bewitchment. They regarded their afflictions as a matter of life and death. During the course of the witch hunt, Ann Putnam, Jr. alleged that she was afflicted by a total of sixty-two persons. She testified against many people in court, and gave a number of affidavits.

In 1692 Mercy Lewis was a well-educated young woman. She was born in 1675, the daughter of Philip Lewis of Casco, Maine. The town was destroyed by the Indians in 1676. For the duration of the war, no white person ventured within this desolate locality, but after the conclusion of peace in November 1678, resettlement slowly took place. The Lewis family settled on Hogg Island as tenants of Edward Tyng. Tyng's main residence was on the Neck, the most desirable location in Casco, and the center of the present-day city of Portland. His closest neighbor was the minister, the Rev. George Burroughs.

When Mercy Lewis' parents were both killed by the Indians in 1689, she was taken into the house of the Rev. Burroughs. In 1690, as the only minister for all the towns between Casco and Wells, Maine, he took up residency in Wells. Because of the danger of repeated Indian attacks in Maine, Mercy was placed in the home of William and Rachel Bradford. Mercy lived a part of a year with them, during which they did "judge in the matter of conscience of speaking the truth and untruth, she would stand stiffly [original document torn]." She was finally placed as a servant in the home of Sergeant Thomas Putnam in Salem Village. According to the records she was afflicted by fifty-one persons. She testified against scores of people in court, and gave many affidavits against the accused witches. In her deposition against George Burroughs, she stated, "I saw the apparition of George Burroughs, whom I very well knew. He brought to me a new fashioned book, and told me I might write in that book, for that was a book that was in his study when I lived with them. But I told him, I did not believe him, for I had often been in his study, but I never saw that book there. But he told me that he had several books in his study which I never saw in his study, and he could raise the Devil."

Although Sergeant Thomas Putnam operated mostly in the background, he did step out in the open to file legal complaints; indeed, he filed more than anyone else. In addition, he testified in a great number of cases, including those of Sarah Buckley, the Rev. George Burroughs, Martha Carrier, Giles and Martha Corey, Mary Easty, Sarah Cloyce, Thomas Farrar, Senior, Dorcas Hoar, George Jacobs, Senior, Susannah Martin, Rebecca Nurse, Elizabeth and John Proctor, Sarah Proctor, Tituba, and John Willard. Of these people, ten were executed, and two condemned to death but reprieved at the final moment.

Sergeant Thomas Putnam's brother, Deacon Edward Putnam, age thirty-eight in 1692, was a member of the conspiracy and his closest ally in carrying out the witch hunt.

Another member, Captain Jonathan Walcott, was the father of Mary Walcott by his first wife. At the time of the witch hunt, he was fifty-two, and married to his second wife, Deliverance, the sister of Thomas and Edward Putnam. Not only did Captain Walcott encourage his daughter Mary Walcott to act out the role of an afflicted girl, but he testified with great effectiveness against many accused witches himself.

Records show that Mary Walcott alleged that she was afflicted by fifty-nine persons. She gave many affidavits and frequently testified in court against people. Mary Walcott and Ann Putnam, Jr. were taken to Andover on June 11, 1692, to initiate a witch hunt in that area. Again, on July 26, the two girls visited that town to spur on the Andover witch hunt.

Thomas and Edward Putnam's sister Ann had been married to William Trask. Both she and William had died by 1692. Still, the Trask family helped the Putnams in the witch hunt. John Trask appeared as a witness against Sarah Bishop, the wife of Edward Bishop, Jr.

Sergeant Thomas Putnam's two uncles John Putnam, Senior and Nathaniel Putnam were eager to help. They were members of the conspiracy, but were not as active as the younger Putnams.

John Putnam Senior, had married Rebecca Prince, step-daughter of John Gedney, Senior, the wealthy owner of the Ship Tavern in Salem Town. In 1692 John Putnam, Senior believed that his nephews, the two Prince boys, were being cheated out of their inheritance by Sarah Osborne. To destroy Sarah Osborne, John Putnam, Senior saw to it that she was one of the first three witches accused. Sarah Osborne died in prison a couple of months later. John Putnam, Senior also took his revenge on the Rev. George Burroughs by testifying against him in the witchcraft trials.

John Putnam, Senior's son, Constable Jonathan Putnam, was also a member. He and his first cousin, Edward Putnam, signed the complaint that put Rebecca Nurse behind bars, as well as the complaint that put four-year-old Dorcas Good into chains.

The other uncle, Nathaniel Putnam, signed the complaint against Elizabeth Paine and Elizabeth Fosdick. His son, Constable John Putnam, Jr., also a member of the conspiracy, signed several complaints and testified against many.

Lieutenant Nathaniel Ingersoll, the innkeeper, was the final member of the conspiracy. He was the uncle of Captain Jonathan Walcott. Lieutenant Ingersoll worked closely with Sergeant Thomas Putnam and Captain Walcott to keep the flames burning. With a wary eye toward maintaining goodwill so as not to impair the profits of his tavern, Ingersoll signed only a few complaints. However, when called as witness he gladly testified against those accused. It was no coincidence that two of his competitors in Salem Village, tavern-owners John Proctor and Edward Bishop, Jr. were both arrested for witchcraft, and that Proctor paid with his life.

Except for the departure of Elizabeth Parris, the inner circle of afflicted girls remained unchanged throughout the witch hunt. Of the six girls, only three, Elizabeth Parris, Ann Putnam, Jr., and Mary Walcott, were living in their parents' homes. The other three, having lost one or both parents, had been placed in the conspirators' households, and, except for Abigail Williams, were servants.

Since none of the four girls in the outer circle of afflicted lived in the households of conspirators, they required careful control at all times.

The daughter of George and Elizabeth Booth of Salem Village, Elizabeth Booth, age eighteen, was a member of the outer circle, participating in examinations, inquests, and trials. Not a favorite of the conspiracy, her name was only chosen for use on a couple of complaints. It appears on the warrant for the arrest of John Alden, Jr. (Alden, the sea captain and trader who worked his ship along the Maine coast, had engaged in the fur trade with Indian friends before King William's War.) Elizabeth's actions as an afflicted girl were supported by her mother and younger sister, Alice, age fourteen. On October 11, 1692, nineteen days after the executions on September 22, Elizabeth Booth married Jonathan Pease, age twenty-three, and started a family of her own. Her afflictions were over; of the witches whose apparitions had hurt her, John Proctor and Wilmot Redd had been hanged, Giles Corey pressed to death, and the pregnant Elizabeth Proctor was in prison, sentenced to death, but under reprieve until the child was born.

Susannah Sheldon, age eighteen, another member of the outer circle, suffered from a deep and abiding fear of the Indians. Her parents, Rebecca (Scadlock) and William Sheldon had resided in Saco, Maine, but were driven out by the Indians in 1676 during King Philip's War. Susannah, only a baby at the time, barely escaped death as the family fled the slaughter which ensued. Taking up residence in Salem, the family returned to Saco as soon as it was safe. With the outbreak of King William's War, the Indians again destroyed their farm. The family escaped death, but this time Susannah's father was badly wounded in trying to protect her. The family then moved to Salem Village.

Susannah's older brother, Godfrey, age twenty-four, encountered the Indians in Maine on July 3, 1690 in the service of his country. Surprised in an ambush, some of the soldiers panicked and tried to flee. Godfrey was last seen alive being pursued into the forest by a stout Indian, brightly daubed in warpaint, a gun in one hand and a hatchet in the other. Godfrey's hacked body was later found without its scalp.

Susannah's father, crippled by his wounds, fell and cut his knee. He died two weeks later, on December 2, 1691, less than three months before the witchcraft outbreak. Susannah stayed on in Salem Village with her widowed mother and remaining siblings. Having lost everything to the Indians, they were almost destitute. Cotton Mather and other divines were constantly railing that witches and Indians both were agents of the Devil. The records show that Susannah was afflicted by eleven alleged witches, and bore witness against them in examinations, inquests, and trials.

Mary Warren, age twenty, who proved to be the most faithful and dependable member of the outer circle, was an orphan. At the outset of the witch hunt she was a servant in the household of John Proctor of Salem Farms, a part of Salem township just south of Salem Village. Both John Proctor and his wife were imprisoned on April 11, 1692. On April 18, one week later, Mary herself was accused and imprisoned. The complaint was filed by Ezekiel Cheever and John Putnam, Jr. for afflicting the inner circle girls.

Parris' description of Mary Warren's examination on April 19 is dramatic. At the end he notes "that not one of the sufferers was afflicted during her examination after once she began to confess, though they were tormented before." She was imprisoned at Salem, where she was examined and accused her master, John Proctor, and his wife Elizabeth, as well as Giles Corey.

Mary Warren displeased the conspirators when she wanted to tell the truth. Imprisoned witches Mary Easty, Edward Bishop, Jr. and his wife, Sarah, gave the following deposition which states how Mary Warren discredited the afflicted girls. "About three weeks ago today, when we were in Salem Jail, we heard Mary Warren several times say that the magistrates might as well examine Keyser's daughter, who has been distracted many years, and take notice of what she said as well as any of the afflicted persons. Mary Warren said when I was afflicted I thought I saw the apparitions of a hundred persons. She said her head was distempered; that she could not tell what she said. And Mary told us that when she was well again, she could not say that she saw any of [the] apparitions at the time aforesaid."

Early in June, however, Mary Warren was released and allowed to continue her active participation in the afflicted group. Altogether she claimed to have been afflicted by fourteen persons.

Sarah Churchill, age twenty, was the second most dependable member of the outer circle. She came from a family in Saco, Maine, with considerable property and a heritage of English gentry. After her parents had been killed by the Indians, she was reduced to the position of servant in the household of George Jacobs, Senior of Salem. Soon after the outbreak of the witch hunt, she became one of the afflicted. Jacobs called the afflicted girls "bitch witches" and was otherwise very disrespectful of her. Sarah was often in court as part of the afflicted group. She was also a witness against her master.

George Jacobs, Senior was imprisoned on May 10, as was his granddaughter, Margaret Jacobs. Shortly thereafter, Sarah Churchill herself was accused and imprisoned. Her name appeared on the list of those in Salem Prison, along with Mary Warren. Sarah Churchill had angered the conspiracy because she, too, wanted to tell the truth. Sarah Ingersoll, who worked in the tavern, gave this deposition. "Sarah Churchill after her examination came to me crying. She said she had lied in saying that she set her hand to the Devil's book. She lied because they threatened her and told her they would put her into the dungeon, along with the Rev. Burroughs. She said she had undone herself in belying herself and others. She said also that if she told Mr. Noyes [assistant minister at Salem] but once that she had set her hand to the book, he would believe her, but, if she told the truth and said that she had not set her hand to the book a hundred times, he would not believe her." Sarah Ingersoll was the daughter of conspirator Nathaniel Ingersoll.

On June 1 Sarah Churchill testified that her master, George Jacobs, Senior, as well as Ann Pudeator and Bridget Bishop, made her a witch. Sarah's imprisonment was of short duration, as she was in court again on July 2 to testify against Ann Pudeator.

Mary Warren and Sarah Churchill were the only two afflicted girls to be imprisoned, albeit briefly. Both were taken shortly after their masters had been incarcerated. The extant depositions show that the two were distressed with the roles they were playing in the witch hunt, and wanted to tell the truth. But naturally, being terrified in prison, they preferred to return to their acting. Each twenty-years old, they were older than all the rest of the afflicted in the circle, and as servants and orphans they stood alone in a dangerous world.

John Indian, husband of Tituba, was used in court as an afflicted person. He could reliably demonstrate how grievously he was tormented by whomever was under examination. No doubt he was convinced that he would stand a better chance of survival among the afflicted than among the accused, and sensibly, he played his part well. It is most probable that others who joined the ranks of the afflicted from time to time acted from the same pragmatic standpoint. None, however, gained admittance to the favored circles, inner or outer, of the Salem Village afflicted.

When it was formed in February 1692, the nascent conspiracy never could have guessed the extremes to which they would be allowed to go. Its members suspected that vindictive people in Salem Village and neighboring communities would support their cause of rooting out certain undesirable people as witches. They trusted that the powerful personage, John Hathorne, who gave original encouragement would continue in his support. What they could not foresee, however, was that the highest level of government, the ruling, old-guard Puritans, would not only act in collusion to support their cause of destroying the "enemies of the church," but would give them a free hand in determining who those enemies were.

It did not take long for the conspiracy to find this out; the crucial day was April 11, 1692. On that day two witches, Sarah Cloyce and Elizabeth Proctor, were examined in the large meetinghouse in Salem Town. The aged and ill governor, Simon Bradstreet, now only a figurehead, did not attend. But members of the ruling old guard did: Thomas Danforth (the deputy governor), Isaac Addington of Boston (the secretary of the province), Major Samuel Appleton of Ipswich, James Russell of Charlestown, Captian Samuel Sewall of Boston, Jonathan Corwin, and, of course, John Hathorne, the last five being assistants to the governor. The examinations were officially described as taking place "at a council held at Salem." These Council members concurred in the methods used by the conspiracy, thereby stamping the witch hunt with their seal of approval. William Stoughton was the only one of this core of high ranking men who was not present at the meeting. The overwhelming evidence of the complicity of the ruling old guard was born out in all events which followed.

In the Salem Village witch hunt, a hierarchical structure exists. The pyramid has the sponsors at the top, made up of several clergy in collusion with the old-guard Puritan rulers. They sanctioned the agents, consisting of the accusers and the afflicted circle of girls. Under them are the people who suffered, predominantly women, accused as witches. At the base is the mass of the populace who either were not affected directly, or were brought in on special occasions to provide malicious gossip about their accused neighbors.

From: Frances Hill, *A Delusion of Satan: The Full Story of the Salem Witch Trials* (New York, 1995), chapter 12, "Diabolical Malice"

My purpose in writing this book was to give an up-to-date, historically accurate, popular account of the Salem witch-hunt that would point up its essential similarities to other witch-hunts. It was also intended to convey the depth of the horror of what happened, all too easily forgotten both in the narration of the "good stories" in which the episode abounds and in the analyses of root causes.

The child Dorcas Good, who appears in this chapter, was four and a half years old.

The jails in Ipswich, Salem, and Boston, among which the accused witches were dispersed, were places not just of privation but of horror. They must have seemed to their prisoners indistinguishable from the last destination of sinners. As the most dangerous inmates, the witches were kept in the dungeons. These were perpetually dark, bitterly cold, and so damp that water ran down the walls. They reeked of unwashed human bodies and excrement. They enclosed as much agony as anywhere human beings have lived.

The stone dungeons of the Salem Town prison were discovered in the 1950s in St. Peter Street when the site was excavated to build a New England Telephone Company building. In 1692 they stood under a wooden structure, twenty feet square, known as the "witch jail." Since they were so close to the banks of a tidal river, they were probably infested with water rats. Certainly they were a breeding ground for disease.

All prisoners endured huge physical suffering. They were kept hungry and thirsty and in winter desperately cold. But accused witches were worse off than the other unfortunates. Their limbs were weighed down and their movements restricted by manacles chained to the walls, so that their specters could less easily escape to wreak havoc. They were treated by wardens and visitors with deliberate cruelty, fair game for sadism since they were enemies of God and mankind. Body searches for "witches' teats" afforded ample opportunities for rough treatment. Such teats, supposedly nipples for familiars to suck on, consisted of any mole, wart, pimple, or growth that could be considered unnatural. Much of the searching was in and around the accused witch's genitals. Eventually many of the accused were tortured, by an assortment of methods, to elicit confessions.

These wretches' only comfort, if comfort it was, was each other's company. Normally several prisoners would be locked up together, though on occasion someone was confined alone to a cell so tiny as to allow inadequate space to lie or even sit down. Of course, company was sometimes not comfort but additional torture. This must have been so in the jail in Boston: Tituba, Sarah Osborne, and Sarah Good could scarcely have afforded each other much solace. Sarah Osborne, bedridden before she was jailed, must have suffered past imagining. She died, still in jail, two months later.

As unimaginable as Sarah Osborne's anguish are Dorcas Good's terror and bewilderment when she was taken from Salem to join the other three. Deodat Lawson said that when he saw her at Ingersoll's tavern, before her examination, she looked as "hale and well as other children." Two weeks later she was removed from Salem jail, no doubt already thinner, larger-eyed, more frightened, and altogether less hale and well, to travel all day by horseback, behind the constable on a pillion, and be sent underground once again into darkness and cold. In this new hell was a new horror that surpassed every other. She was loaded with irons and chained to a wall. Though it is impossible to imagine her feelings, it is all too easy to imagine her screams.

No doubt, even in her first agony she was, at best, largely ignored by the adults around her. Distraught prisoners and cruel wardens lack the motive or impulse to care for a child. It is unlikely that even her mother had much love left to give her. A new baby she had brought into prison had already died or was dying.

Dorcas was to spend many months without seeing the light of the sun, unable to run or walk and with nothing to play with but the rags she was wearing. The little fingers that picked at and twisted and folded the torn, filthy cloth were the only part of her being she could move without hindrance or pain. At first she may have shouted and wept. Perhaps she banged her head on the wall she was chained to. But, like all small children without care, stimulation, or love, in the end she went silent, rocking to and fro, as far as her chains would allow, or lying still, staring blankly.

Eighteen years later her father, William Good, was to write that "she was in prison seven or eight months and being chained in the dungeon was so hardly used and terrified that she hath ever since been very chargeable, having little or no reason to govern herself." By "very chargeable" he meant a financial burden: When she came out and for the rest of her days, he had to pay a keeper to care for her.

How could it happen? How could God-fearing, law-abiding citizens send a four-year-old into hell? Charles Upham argues that "the managers" of the witch-hunt, by whom he means Samuel Parris, Thomas Putnam, and perhaps Edward Putnam, Jonathan Putnam, and Dr. Griggs, wanted to "utterly overwhelm the influence of all natural sentiment in the community" by proceeding against a little child as well as a "venerable and infirm great-grandmother." This theory has the merit of providing a rational, if evil, motive for Dorcas Good's imprisonment. But it strains our credulity. The evidence is lacking. It appears far more probable that the girls called Dorcas's name without prompting. Dorcas, as the child of a witch, was automatically under suspicion herself, despite her young age. She must have accompanied her mother on her begging expeditions; she may have copied her irascible words and behavior. She was very likely transformed in the girls' minds to a little creature of pure malevolence. They may have seen in her sharp, hungry looks and heard in her muttering a frightening mirror of their own angry need. They would have longed to smash such a mirror. But they may also have seen in her running and skipping, her clinging to her mother's long skirts, her weeping and laughing, the enviable freedom of behavior accorded, even by the Puritans, to very early childhood. Dorcas was at the age of some of their siblings who were still allowed to play, to display hurt and fear and warm love. Murderous feelings toward those brothers and sisters may have focused on this little outcast.

In certain social and psychological conditions all empathy is destroyed and there is only a furious desire to hurt, even kill. In naming Dorcas, and the other accused witches, the afflicted girls indulged to the full those impulses that are more often overt in the furious young—children and adolescents who have been overcontrolled or unloved or otherwise made to feel worthless—than in their more socialized elders. Adults find excuses for cruelty. When they kill there is almost always a motive. Committers of sex crimes find rationalizations. Even madmen hear voices telling them that their victims are evil. When children kill, as in the recent case in Liverpool, England, in which two ten-year-olds murdered the toddler James Bulger, there is often no motive, just unrationalized fury and pain.

We cannot know whether the furious children of Salem believed the available excuse for sending people to their deaths. Without question the adults did. As a pretext for cruelty, witchcraft is perfect. The witch is the embodiment of evil and her destruction is not just laudable but necessary. For the destroyer, terrified of his own evil impulses, the satisfaction is twofold. The impulse to hurt and destroy is assuaged. At the same time the wickedness inside himself is projected onto the witch and eliminated. Through the mouths of their wild, merciless children the people of Salem guiltlessly condemned those they wished to see dead.

No doubt the adult Putnams and others had no special desire that Dorcas should suffer. They did not rejoice in her agony as they almost certainly did rejoice, however secretly, in that of Martha Corey and Rebecca Nurse. But their satisfaction in the witch-hunt made them indifferent to Dorcas's pain. The same seems to have been true of the rest of the populace; no protests were made on the child's behalf. Of course, Dorcas was the daughter of an outcast. Had she been the child of a respectable family, she might have had relations to speak for her.

The Salem witch-hunt, like all witch-hunts, was conducted not by an individual acting alone but by a group. All types of groups are capable of behaving in ways that would shock the consciences of their individual members. But those that espouse a morality of censure and blame rather than compassion and empathy are utterly merciless toward objects of hatred. The more a group idealizes itself, its own values, and its God, the more it persecutes both other groups and the dissenters in its midst. In doing so it protects those it prizes from any aggression they arouse by deflecting it.

The "afflicted girls" and Puritan society were both groups espousing a morality of censure and blame to as great a degree as any fanatical nation or sect in world history. In their witch-hunt, as in all witch-hunts, the destructive rage of certain individuals was complemented by the compliance of the rest of the community. Thus cruelty was countenanced that seems beyond what should be humanly possible.

It must have been in a mood of somber relief, close to restrained exhilaration, that the congregation trooped out of the meetinghouse after Rebecca and Dorcas were led to the dungeons. Over cider and cakes at Ingersoll's tavern, each individual's conviction that the great-grandmother and the child were servants of Satan merged in consensus. Men and women swapped memories of Benjamin Holton's demise after Rebecca chastised him for losing control of his pigs and of Dorcas's wicked looks and strange ways.

After two hours everyone moved back down the road and reentered the meetinghouse. As they settled into their pews, the atmosphere was calmer than it had been in that place for some time, though full of expectancy. Deodat Lawson mounted the pulpit, said a prayer, and read out his text. It began: "And the Lord said unto Satan, the Lord rebuke thee, O Satan. . . ." The congregation were about to enjoy the stimulating yet soothing activity of listening to a sermon that would clarify their thoughts while confirming their opinions.

Lawson began by reminding them of Satan's history as a mutinous angel and his aim of destroying mankind. Summarizing part of Zechariah, he said that Christ fought Satan on behalf of Joshua, whom Satan despised "by reason of his filthy garments." Christ rebuked Satan but took his censure to heart, giving Joshua a "change of raiment."

It is hard to imagine the youthful members of a present-day congregation keeping a straight face at this tale of Satan's snobbish contempt for Joshua's wardrobe and Christ's acting as a valet. However, there is no evidence of the existence of humor in Salem. Besides, the merging of the concrete, everyday world and the supernatural, found in this passage, was commonplace, not bizarre, to the Puritans. Satan and Christ were for them visible persons as well as mystical entities. The natural and supernatural in their eyes were essentially one. Presumably nobody smiled.

Lawson went on to give numerous other, more drastic examples of Satan's malignity. He stressed that the Evil One attacks people's souls *and* their bodies. Revealing his hidden agenda, he slipped a crucial message into his catalogue of Satan's evil ways, claiming that local examples of devilish attacks were clearly the "effects of diabolical malice and operations and . . . cannot rationally be imagined to proceed from any other cause whatsoever." He talked of the deep humiliation of "visible members of this church [being] under the awful accusations, and imputations, of being the instruments of Satan."

He also warned against giving way to envy, malice, and hatred of neighbors and of the danger of rashly censuring others or making false accusations. However, he went on to advise of the wrongfulness of bearing a grudge against those who unwittingly made such false accusations. He spoke against superstitious means of finding out witches or guarding against their activities. But he exhorted the congregation to "arm, arm, arm" against Satan, that by "the shield of faith, ye and we all may resist the fiery darts of the wicked."

Later Lawson was to dedicate the printed version of his sermon to the magistrates Bartholomew Gedney, John Hathorne, and Jonathan Corwin and the Salem ministers John Higginson and Nicholas Noyes. But it seems from the text as a whole that, though Lawson was following the Parris/Putnam line, he was not merely performing to order. No doubt he sincerely believed all or most of what he was saying and felt he was doing his duty in saying it. As a minister, he instinctively favored a view that ascribed fits and visions, instead of to mere human delinquency, to the supernatural forces he was paid to explain to the populace.

He may have hoped to promote his career, gaining greater fame and respect, by associating himself with the witch finders. This proved a wrong judgment. Eventually he went back to England, his career not aided but blighted. He ended as an ignominious failure, reduced to sending letters to friends begging for food, clothes, and fuel for his destitute family. He is referred to in passing by an associate, without amplification, as "the unhappy Deodaty Lawson." This unfortunate, if well-meaning, dupe of Parris and the Putnams lacked even the consolation of knowing that his "brief and true narrative" would make his name live in history.

It is observable in the modern-day witch-hunt that therapists often argue that child sex abuse actually happened when there seems ample cause to suspect it the product of fantasy. Those therapists, as they promote prosecutions, do not seem to have any particular animus toward the accused but, directly and indirectly, merely to be furthering their professional interests.

Lawson was well aware, when giving his sermon, that not everyone in Salem Village found it as impossible as he did to imagine that the torments of the afflicted proceeded from "any other cause" but the devil. Otherwise he would not have made his claims with such stridency. The undercurrent of skepticism that had been there from the start in Salem Village was growing stronger. It had swelled with the accusations against the two respected church members Martha Corey and Rebecca Nurse. Joseph Putnam had told his estranged half-brothers that he had a gun loaded and a horse saddled in case the marshal came to arrest him. He had no doubt of the political direction the witch-hunt was taking and assumed himself a prime target. As it happens, he was never named. This may have been because he, together with his friend and father-in-law Israel Porter, was too respected and powerful a local figure.

Rebecca Nurse's friends and relations, including Israel, were soon to mount a petition in her favor. It was to be signed by thirty-nine people, including the Sarah Holton who had accused her of bewitching her husband. Knowing Rebecca was in jail and might hang must have made her think twice.

The day after Lawson's sermon, equally serious doubts were far more violently expressed by someone who should have known better, from the point of view of his personal safety. John Proctor, the successful farmer, entrepreneur, and tavern keeper, meeting Samuel Sibley on the road to Salem Village from his house on the edge of the town, said he had allowed his "jade," that is, servant, Mary Warren, to go to the village the day before to attend Rebecca Nurse's examination as one of the afflicted girls. Now he very much wished he had not. He continued by saying that if the girls were left to their own devices, "we should all be devils and witches quickly" and suggested they ought to be whipped. He was going to bring his maid home to "thrash the devil out of her." He had threatened to thrash her when she had first been taken with fits and had kept her "close to her spinning wheel." As a result she had had no more fits till the next day when he was away, "and then she must have her fits again forsooth." He cried, of the afflicted girls, "Hang them! Hang them!"

John Proctor was to rue his rash words. The witch-hunt, whatever else it was, was becoming, ever more inexorably, a battle of wills.

From: Elaine G. Breslaw, *Tituba, Reluctant Witch of Salem: Devilish Indians and Puritan Fantasies* (New York, 1996), "Introduction"

Elaine Breslaw has performed an invaluable service in finally laying to rest the disturbed spirit that has haunted Salem witch trial studies for at least a hundred years: the half-Negro, voodoo-practicing, spell-chanting Tituba.

The Amerindian slave woman called Tituba was among the first three persons to be accused of witchcraft in Salem, Massachusetts, in 1692. The other two—Sarah Osborne and Sarah Good—vehemently protested their innocence. But Tituba confessed and thereby gave the Salem magistrates reasons to suspect that the Devil's followers had invaded their midst. Nineteen people were subsequently hanged for witchcraft, one man was pressed to death, and close to two hundred were accused of witchcraft; over fifty of them confessed. The lives and fate of accused and accusers have captivated the American imagination.

Tituba, however, in spite of her central and early role in that witch-hunt, has attracted little serious attention. The Salem records provide very sparse details about her background and few scholars have turned to alternate sources for information on her life. She has no descendants who can speak for her or spark new interest in her guilt or innocence. Surprisingly, there has been minimal interest in her ethnicity or the relationship of her racial background to the accusations. Most important, the multicultural dimensions of Tituba's confession, the most significant evidence of a diabolical conspiracy in Salem, have been either misunderstood or ignored.

Tituba's roles in that tragedy, as both victim and willing participant, as both scapegoat and manipulator of Puritan fears, beg for reexamination. Tituba is here viewed in the context of the Salem events as a woman, as a slave, as an American Indian, and as an outsider in a Puritan society. This biography brings the American Indian slave woman to the forefront of events that so overwhelmed her contemporaries they almost destroyed their own society.

Tituba the storyteller prolonged her life in 1692 through an imaginative ability to weave and embellish plausible tales. In the process of confessing to fantastic experiences, she created a new idiom of resistance against abusive treatment and inadvertently led the way for other innocents accused of the terrible crime of witchcraft. Her resistance, a calculated manipulation of the Puritan fears, was intimately related to her ethnic heritages. Puritans were predisposed to believe that Indians willingly participated in Devil worship. That perception of Indians as supporters of the Devil encouraged Tituba to fuel their fantasies of a diabolical plot. As she hesitantly capitalized on Puritan assumptions regarding Satanism, Tituba drew on the memories of her past life for the wondrous details of a story so frightening in its implications that she had to be kept alive as a witness.

Interest in Tituba and her role in the 1692 events has traditionally focused on her supposed indoctrination of a group of girls into a witchcraft molded by the practice of voodoo. In the accepted wisdom, Tituba stood at the center of a circle of girls practicing sorcery derived from African folklore. Her confession notwithstanding, there is no proof that Tituba ever took part in occult activities. Nor is there any proof that the girls, at her instigation, took part in occult rituals or danced in the woods or drank blood or stuck pins in dolls. But those allegations and the sensationalist nature of the trials have overwhelmed the importance of Tituba's background and her status as a symbol of Puritan fears.

There is good reason for Tituba's low profile in the history books. It stems from the dearth of useful, direct information about her. Historians need reliable written, artifactual, or statistical evidence with which they can detail events or on which to base their conclusions. The absence of reliable sources often means that a particular potentially significant element has to be omitted from a study. Such has been the case for most of the underclass in history, particularly women, Africans, and American Indians, who leave few useful trails for others to follow and are, therefore, easy to ignore in the historical record.

As expected, the biographical information about Tituba in the Salem documents is very thin. Nevertheless, some important information can be extracted from these meager sources. It is clearly evident from all references in those written records that Tituba was an American Indian and *not* African as later writers have assumed, and that she and her husband, John, also an American Indian, were slaves living in the household of the Reverend Samuel Parris. There is no reference anywhere in the seventeenth-century documents to Tituba as an African or as someone of African background. Like the mythology of Tituba as a voodoo priestess, there is no indication in the extant records that either Tituba or her husband had African ancestry. None of her contemporaries saw her as an African or even someone of mixed ancestry. She was never described as black or as a Negro. Nowhere in the seventeenth-century records is there so much as a hint that she was of even partial African descent.

Thus there should be no question of her ancestry. All of her contemporaries, without exception, describe Tituba as an Indian woman or as Parris's Indian servant. Her husband John's racial-ethnic background is just as clearly delineated in those records. He is always identified as Indian John or John Indian, or simply as the Indian man. The gradual metamorphosis of Tituba from an Indian to an African since the nineteenth century is an unfortunate mistake based on embellishment, imagination, and a tinge of racial bias, and has been a convenient way to fill in blanks left by the absence of more substantive information.

What is less clear from those seventeenth-century commentaries is where Tituba came from, how and when Parris acquired her, and what kind of intellectual and cultural baggage she brought with her to Massachusetts. The most reasonable theory for Tituba's origins was first put forward by Charles Upham, writing in the middle of the nineteenth century. Tituba and John "were spoken of," Upham said, "as having come from New Spain . . . that is, the Spanish West Indies, and the adjacent mainland." They were then sold in Barbados as slaves and subsequently brought to Massachusetts by Samuel Parris. Upham offered no direct evidence but because a good part of his narrative was based on Samuel Drake's work, he probably made use of Drake's edition of Samuel Fowler's 1866

"Account of the Life of Samuel Parris" in which Fowler claimed that Tituba and John were "Natives of South America called New Spain."

Unfortunately, Upham's likely suggestion has received some unlikely embellishments. Almost fifty years later, George Lincoln Burr asserted that Tituba and John were Carib Indians, probably from the mistaken association of all Caribbean natives with the Carib tribes. But there were other tribes resident in the Caribbean area, notably the Arawak-speaking peoples. Many of the Arawak tribes had migrated to the South American coast in the wake of the early Spanish conquests and, for reasons discussed in chapter 1, "Tituba's Roots," were of particular interest to slave catchers in Barbados. Nonetheless, Burr's mistaken assumption regarding Tituba's ancestry as a Carib continues to influence views of her cultural origins.

Barbados seemed to be a reasonable place to begin a search for Tituba's roots. Until 1989 no one had explored the documentary possibilities for searching out Tituba's background in West Indian colonial records or local sources on the island. Those records have finally yielded some tantalizing information that can permit a partial reconstruction of Tituba's early life. They provide evidence of Tituba's residence on the island and help to establish the most likely origins of an Amerindian slave in Barbados for that time.

The painstaking effort to look through the handwritten documents resulted in the discovery of the name "Tattuba" for a slave girl in a 1676 deed. The connection between Samuel Parris and that child are sufficient to make a case for Tituba's life on a Barbados plantation some four years before Parris left the island. The arguments for that association are discussed in detail in chapter 2, "My Own Country." The existence of such a unique name, which to date has not appeared in any other seventeenth-century slave list, certainly adds substantial support for Tituba's Barbados background. I also argue in that chapter that Tituba was not born on the island but was most likely a captive from South America who was brought to Barbados to be sold as a slave. This supposition again is based on substantial circumstantial evidence regarding the small Amerindian slave trade that prevailed during the thirty years before Parris left the island to return to Massachusetts.

Chapter 3 recreates the "Strange New World" of life on a Barbados sugar plantation by examining the sociofamilial environment that American Indians experienced during the decade prior to 1680 when Parris was known to be in Barbados. Amerindian slaves by that time were becoming integrated into the larger African-dominated culture. As early as the seventeenth century, Barbados was developing a syncretic culture that included elements of English, American Indian, and multicultural African lifestyles. That background lends support to the theory that Tituba was familiar with African folklore, but does not prove she was capable of practicing a witchcraft derived from African sources.

During her Barbados years Tituba lived in a society overwhelmingly African in population, one in which the African elements played a major role in shaping the development of a Creole culture. Indian culture probably had the least influence on that syncretic process, but it was not insignificant. Chapter 3 examines the relative effect of these various influences on the life of an Amerindian slave and speculates on how that Creole society, derived mainly from African customs and adaption to the conditions of slavery, would have shaped Tituba's life and the mental images she brought to Massachusetts.

Part II of this study focuses on life in Massachusetts. Chapter 4 examines New England life from the perspective of an American Indian slave, summarizing what is known about working conditions, legal status, health, religious influences, and other aspects of social-cultural life imposed on Indians and slaves by the Puritans. As we will see, Tituba successfully assimilated the outward appearance of selected aspects of Puritan culture and thus hid her identity as an Indian behind a servile camouflage that provided, at least until 1692, protection against abuse.

Chapter 5, "The Devil in Massachusetts: Accusations," examines the immediate events leading up to the witch-hunt that began in the spring of 1692. After a brief description of Puritan attitudes toward witchcraft and the fear of American Indians, this chapter traces the events early in 1692 that led to Tituba's arrest and subsequent confession. The Salem nightmare stripped away her servile facade, exposed her as a woman of imagination and will, and left Tituba vulnerable to persecution and possible execution.

Chapter 6, "The Reluctant Witch: Fueling Puritan Fantasies," provides a close analysis of Tituba's testimony and its multicultural dimensions and highlights its immediate effect on the community. That confession, given early in March, with its evidence of a diabolical conspiracy, initiated the legal process that led to the arrest of over one hundred fifty people and the hanging of nineteen before Governor William Phipps finally called a halt to the persecutions in October of 1692. It was Tituba who supplied the framework of, and the inspiration for the belief in, a diabolical conspiracy in Massachusetts.

Chapter 7 deals with the continuing subtle, but insidious, influence of Tituba's confession on the testimony of others and the creative use of her stories that both reinforced and reshaped traditional notions of the Devil. Confessors in particular reformulated Tituba's notion of evil to conform to their own preconception. This creative application of Indian-Creole ideas contributed to the convergence of folk and ministerial notions of witchcraft and eventually to the discrediting of witch-hunts themselves.

Why did the Puritans, folk and elite alike, believe Tituba's confession? Chapter 8 explores the Puritan perception of her behavior and how she was able to convince and captivate that audience. Tituba's acculturation made her testimony believable. That credibility was reinforced ironically by the continued association of native Americans with witchcraft and a refusal to fully integrate Indians into Puritan society.

In the absence of much hard evidence, the Epilogue draws some conclusions about Tituba's fate and that of her family after 1692. It also considers the long-term effect of Tituba's confession on the Puritan community. She participated in a process of cultural exchange that merged the world of print culture with that of the folk, activating change from the bottom up. This transformation was as much the result of the details of Tituba's fantasy as it was of the Puritan need to believe her story and accommodate the unfamiliar Indian ideas to their own notions of evil.

The analysis of Tituba's testimony and the reexamination of her role in the Salem events suggest a new type of approach to an understanding of early New England life, one that emphasizes the role of non-English influences on the shaping of colonial intellectual life. It assumes that interaction of people from various cultural mixes played a significant part in forming Puritan society in America. Scholars have demonstrated some interest in the impact of Africans on that developing society, but these works have only limited usefulness and make no case for cultural transmission. Studies of Indians in early America, on the other hand, stress the violent contacts between the native Americans and the English intruders, focusing on the reactive rather than the integrative aspects of cultural contact. Peaceful interaction, beyond the superficial borrowing of maize-based foods and hunting techniques from Indians, has not been an important factor in Puritan-Indian studies.

Tituba's prominence in Salem and the reaction of Puritans to her fantastic story suggest that there may have been other non-English ethnic influences on early New England history and that the process of cultural borrowing—the creation of a syncretic culture—did not stop at the edge of the Caribbean. New England too came under the influence of a dynamic exchange among red, white, and black peoples in early America. The effect may have been more subtle and thus more difficult to discern in New England, but the nuances of change were just as tenacious and imaginative.

Tituba's emergence as a major protagonist in the 1692 cataclysm allows us to glimpse one moment—albeit a powerful one—in the process of change in the New England mind brought on by multicultural contact. Was it, however, unique? To what extent was the Salem incident just another episode in the regular interaction of non-English oral or popular cultures with that of the literate, print-oriented population? How often, for instance, did New Englanders consult American Indians about sickness or misfortune? To what extent did those confrontations reshape old-world notions? Were Tituba's experience and the Salem events a culmination of years of intellectual interactions, or was that incident a one-time occurrence of cultural borrowing? Only more creative and speculative evaluations of the known sources can answer those questions.

There is no doubt that the Salem witch investigation enabled the Indian woman Tituba to emerge from obscurity. She was a slave who left an indelible mark on American history and no study of the Salem events can or should ignore her ill-fated contribution. Permitted to speak of things alien to English thought, she inspired a creative adaptation of ideas derived from West Indian slave society. It was Tituba's mental images that fueled Puritan fantasies of a devilish conspiracy and, tragically, launched the most gruesome but fascinating witchscare of early American history.

PART V

FICTION

The Salem witch trials have inspired a vast amount of fiction. Writers of modest talent and genius alike have been attracted by the themes of bigotry, superstition, persecution, and delusion, to say nothing of a ready-made cast of characters including heroes, villains, flamboyant personalities, and young girls. The outpouring of plays, novels, and poems began in the 1820s, when American writers were developing a sense of national identity and looking for American material. Little from the early period is remembered today apart from the works of true greatness, Nathaniel Hawthorne's novel *The House of the Seven Gables* and novella *Young Goodman Brown.* Sentimental, serialized fic tion with titles such as *The Salem Belle, a Tale of Love and Witchcraft in 1692* were the nineteenth-century equivalents of modern *True Romance* stories. Yet, among the forgotten works, there is some good, popular literature, still readable for those with a special interest in the subject.

The first novel, apart from an anonymous work called *Salem, an Eastern Tale,* published in 1820, was *Rachel Dyer* by John Neal. This uses the records of 1692 to show the helplessness of the accused witches facing trial, given that the judges' minds were already made up. J. W. Forest's *Witching Times,* serialized in Putnam's in 1856–1857, also emphasizes the trials' injustice and cruelty. Both novels show honesty and courage pitted against bigotry and cowardice. But, like almost every work on the subject to come, both weaken the mixture of ingredients with a love story.

John Greenleaf Whittier produced several poems using Salem material, all suggesting that fearless, free thought leads to truth and love, superstition to evil and hate. Both Henry Wadsworth Longfellow and Mary E. Wilkins wrote poetic plays dramatizing the particular plight of the by-that-time legendary character Giles Corey.

The flood of fictional writing on Salem lessened to a trickle in the twentieth century but produced two interesting novels, Esther Forbes's *Mirror for Witches* and Esther Hammand's *Road to Endor.* And, of course, one dramatic masterpiece, Arthur Miller's *The Crucible.*

7

Pulp to Masterpieces

From: John Neal, *Rachel Dyer* (1828), chapter 4

This work has an unusual structure, shifting in its first three chapters from history to fiction. It describes the founding of the Plymouth and Massachusetts Bay Colonies, the persecution of witches in the region, and the career of Sir William Phipps. Then it narrows its focus to the household of "Matthew" Parris in Salem Village. Fictional touches, such as that Parris's wife was dead before the witch-hunt started and John Indian was a "praying" warrior, lead into the "novel proper" in chapter 4. The influence of Cotton Mather's myth-making can be seen in a Tituba in league with local Indians in the practice of sorcery. After this, the main interest of the book lies in the depiction of the trials as travesties of justice, even by the standards of the day.

Confusingly, Dyer gives Parris's daughter in the book the name of his real-life niece, Abby.

Bridget Pope was of a thoughtful serious turn—the little Abby the veriest romp that ever breathed. Bridget was the elder, by about a year and a half, but she looked five years older than Abby, and was in every way a remarkable child. Her beauty was like her stature, and both were above her age; and her aptitude for learning was the talk of all that knew her. She was a favorite every where and with every body—she had such a sweet way with her, and was so unlike the other children of her age—so that when she appeared to merit reproof, as who will not in the heyday of innocent youth, it was quite impossible to reprove her, except with a mild voice, or a kind look, or a very affectionate word or two. She would keep away from her slate and book for whole days together, and sit for half an hour at a time without moving her eyes off the page, or turning away her head from the little window of their school-house (a log-hut plastered with blue clay in stripes and patches, and lighted with horn, oiled-paper and isinglass) which commanded a view of Naumkeag, or Salem village, with a part of the original woods of North America—huge trees that were found there on the first arrival of the white man, crowded together and covered with moss and dropping to pieces of old age; a meeting-house with a short wooden spire, and the figure of death on the top for a weather-cock, a multitude of cottages that appeared to be lost in the landscape, and a broad beautiful approach from the sea.

Speak softly to Bridget Pope at such a time, or look at her with a look of love, and her quiet eyes would fill, and her childish heart would run over—it would be impossible to say why. But if you spoke sharply to her, when her head was at the little window, and her thoughts were away, nobody knew where, the poor little thing would grow pale and serious, and look at you with such a look of sorrow—and then go away and do what she was bid with a gravity that would go to your heart. And it would require a whole day after such a rebuke to restore the dye of her sweet lips, or to persuade her that you were not half so angry as you might have appeared. At every sound of your voice, at every step that came near, she would catch her breath, and start and look up, as if she expected something dreadful to happen.

But as for Abigail Paris, the pretty little blue-eyed cousin of Bridget Pope, there was no dealing with her in that way. If you shook your finger at her, she would laugh in your face; and if you did it with a grave air, ten to one but she made you laugh too. If you scolded her, she would scold you in return, but always in such a way that you could not possibly be angry with her; she would mimic your step with her little naked feet, or the toss of your head, or the very curb of your mouth perhaps, while you were trying to terrify her. The little wretch!—everybody was tired to death of her in half an hour, and yet everybody was glad to see her again. Such was Abigail Paris, before Bridget Pope came to live in the house with her, but in the course of about half a year after that, she was so altered that her very play-fellows twitted her with being "afeard o' Bridgee Pope." She began to be tidy in her dress, to comb her bright hair, to speak low, to keep her shoes on her feet, and her stockings from about her heels, and before a twelve-month was over, she left off wading in the snow, and grew very fond of her book.

They were always together now, creeping about under the old beach-trees, or hunting for hazle nuts, or searching for sun-baked apples in the short thick grass, or feeding the fish in the smooth clear sea—Bridget poring over a story that she had picked up, nobody knows where, and Abigail, whatever the story might be, and although the water might stand in her eyes at the time, always ready for a roll in the wet grass, a dip in the salt wave, or a slide from the very top of the haymow. They rambled about in the great woods together on tip-toe, holding their breath and saying their prayers at every step; they lay down together and slept together on the very track of the wolf, or the she-bear; and if they heard a noise afar off, a howl or a war-whoop, they crept in among the flowers of the solitary spot and were safe, or hid themselves in the shadow of trees that were spread out over the whole sky, or of shrubbery that appeared to cover the whole earth—

Where the wild grape hangs dropping in the shade,
O'er unfledged minstrels that beneath are laid;

Where the scarlet barberry glittered among the sharp green leaves like threaded bunches of coral,—where at every step the more brilliant ivory-plumbs or clustered bunch-berries rattled among the withered herbage and rolled about their feet like a handful of beads,—where they delighted to go even while they were afraid to speak above a whisper, and kept fast hold of each other's hands, every step of the way. Such was their love, such their companionship, such their behaviour while oppressed with fear. They were never apart for a day, till the time of our story; they were together all day and all night, going to sleep together and waking up together, feeding out of the same cup, and sleeping in the same bed, year after year.

But just when the preacher was ready to believe that his Father above had not altogether deserted him—for he was ready to cry out with joy whenever he looked upon these dear children; they were so good and so beautiful, and they loved each other so entirely; just when there appeared to be no evil in his path, no shadow in his way to the grave, a most alarming change took place in their behavior to each other. He tried to find out the cause, but they avoided all inquiry. He talked with them together, he talked with them apart, he tried every means in his power to know the truth, but all to no purpose. They were afraid of each other, and that was all that either would say. Both were full of mischief and appeared to be possessed with a new temper. They were noisy and spiteful toward each other, and toward every body else. They were continually hiding away from each other in holes and corners, and if they were pursued and plucked forth to the light, they were always found occupied with mischief above their age. Instead of playing together as they were wont, or sitting together in peace, they would creep away under the tables and chairs and beds, and behave as if they were hunted by something which nobody else could see; and they would lie there by the hour, snapping and snarling at each other, and at everybody that passed near. They had no longer the look of health, or of childhood, or of innocence. They were meagre and pale, and their eyes were fiery, and their fingers were skinny and sharp, and they delighted in devilish tricks and in outcries yet more devilish. They would play by themselves in the dead of the night, and shriek with a preternatural voice, and wake everybody with strange laughter—a sort of smothered giggle, which would appear to issue from the garret, or from the top of the house, while they were asleep, or pretending to be dead asleep in the great room below. They would break out all over in a fine sweat like the dew on a rose bush, and fall down as if they were struck to the heart with a knife, while they were on the way to meeting or school, or when the elders of the church were talking to them and every eye was fixed on their faces with pity or terror. They would grow pale as death in a moment, and seem to hear voices in the wind, and shake as with an ague while standing before a great fire, and look about on every side with such a piteous look for children, whenever it thundered or lightened, or whenever the sea roared, that the eyes of all who saw them would fill with tears. They would creep away backwards from each other on their hands and feet, or hide their faces in the lap of the female Indian Tituba, and if the preacher spoke to them, they would fall into a stupor, and awake with fearful cries and appear instantly covered all over with marks and spots like those which are left by pinching or bruising the flesh. They would be struck dumb while repeating the Lord's prayer, and all their features would be distorted with a savage and hateful expression.

The heads of the church were now called together, and a day of general fasting, humiliation and prayer was appointed, and after that, the best medical men of the whole country were consulted, the pious and the gifted, the interpreters of dreams, the soothsayers, and the prophets of the Lord, every man of power, and every woman of power,—but no relief was had, no cure, no hope of cure.

Matthew Paris now began to be afraid of his own child. She was no longer the hope of his heart, the joy of his old age, the live miniature of his buried wife. She was an evil thing—she was what he had no courage to think of, as he covered his old face and tore his white hair with a grief that would not be rebuked nor appeased. A new fear fell upon him, and his knees smote together, and the hair of his flesh rose, and he saw a spirit, and the spirit said to him look! And he looked, and lo! the truth appeared to him; for he saw neighbour after neighbour flying from his path, and all the heads of the church keeping aloof and whispering together in a low voice. Then knew he that Bridget Pope and Abigail Paris were bewitched.

A week passed over, a whole week, and every day and every hour they grew worse and worse, and the solitude in which he lived, more dreadful to him; but just when there appeared to be no hope left, no chance for escape, just when he and the few that were still courageous enough to speak with him, were beginning to despair, and to wish for the speedy death of the little sufferers, dear as they had been but a few weeks before to everybody that knew them, a discovery was made which threw the whole country into a new paroxysm of terror. The savages who had been for a great while in the habit of going to the house of the preacher to eat and sleep "without money and without price," were now seen to keep aloof and to be more than usually grave; and yet when they were told of the children's behaviour, they showed no sort of surprise, but shook their heads with a smile, and went their way, very much as if they were prepared for it.

When the preacher heard this, he called up the two Indians before him, and spoke to Tituba and prayed to know why her people who for years had been in the habit of lying before his hearth, and eating at his table, and coming in and going out of his habitation at all hours of the day and night, were no longer seen to approach his door.

"Tituppa no say—Tituppa no know," she replied.

But *as* she replied, the preacher saw her make a sign to Peter Wawpee, her Sagamore, who began to show his teeth as if he knew something more than he chose to tell; but before the preacher could rebuke him as he deserved, or pursue the inquiry with Tituba, his daughter screamed out and fell upon her face and lay for a long while as if she were death-struck.

The preacher now bethought him of a new course, and after watching Tituba and Wawpee for several nights, became satisfied from what he saw, that she was a woman of diabolical power. A part of what he saw, he was afraid even to speak of; but he declared on oath before the judges, that he had seen sights, and heard noises that took away his bodily strength, his hearing and his breath for a time; that for nearly five weeks no one of her tribe, nor of Wawpee's tribe had slept upon his hearth, or eaten of his bread, or lifted the latch of his door either by night or by day; that notwithstanding this, the very night before, as he went by the grave-yard where his poor wife lay, he heard the whispering of a multitude; that having no fear in such a place, he made a search; and that after a long while he found his help Tituba concealed in the bushes, that he said nothing but went his way, satisfied in his own soul however that the voices he heard were the voices of her tribe; and that after the moon rose he saw her employed with a great black Shadow on the rock of death, where as every body knew, sacrifices had been offered up in other days by another people to the god of the Pagan—the deity of the savage—employed in a way that made him shiver with fright where he stood; for between her and the huge black shadow there lay what he knew to be the dead body of his own dear child stretched out under the awful trees—her image rather, for *she* was at home and abed and asleep at the time. He would have spoken to it if he could—for he saw what he believed to be the shape of his wife; he would have screamed for help if he could, but he could not get his breath, and that was the last he knew; for when he came to himself he was lying in his own bed, and Tituba was sitting by his side with a cup of broth in her hand which he took care to throw away the moment her back was turned; for she was a creature of extraordinary art, and would have persuaded him that he had never been out of his bed for the whole day.

The judges immediately issued a warrant for Tituba and Wawpee, both of whom were hurried off to jail, and after a few days of proper inquiry, by torture, she was put upon trial for witchcraft. Being sorely pressed by the word of the preacher and by the testimony of Bridget Pope and Abigail Paris, who with two more afflicted children (for the mischief had spread now in every quarter) charged her and Sarah Good with appearing to them at all hours, and in all places, by day and by night, when they were awake and when they were asleep, and with tormenting their flesh. Tituba pleaded guilty and confessed before the judges and the people that the poor children spoke true, that she was indeed a witch, and that, with several of her sister witches of great power—among whom was mother Good, a miserable woman who lived a great way off, nobody knew where—and passed the greater part of her time by the sea-side, nobody knew how, she had been persuaded by the black man to pursue and worry and vex them. But the words were hardly out of her mouth before she herself was taken with a fit, which lasted so long that the judges believed her to be dead. She was lifted up and carried out into the air; but though she recovered her speech and her strength in a little time, she was altered in her looks from that day to the day of her death.

From: Nathaniel Hawthorne, *Young Goodman Brown* (1835)

This novella brilliantly articulates the profound Puritan terror of evil as embodied by the devil but also rooted deep in the soul, perpetually threatening to destroy men's and women's feeble attempts to be godly. Hawthorne, a native of Salem and the great-great-grandson of John Hathorne, magistrate at the examinations of accused witches, knew the Puritan mentality to the core. His fascinated horror at its cruelty, inhumanity, hypocrisy, and greed was the inspiration for his best work, *The House of the Seven Gables, Young Goodman Brown,* and *The Scarlet Letter*, and his excellent early story, "Alice Doane's Appeal," a strange tale of incestuous love that makes direct reference to the witch trials.

Only two of the characters in *Young Goodman Brown*—Goody Cloyse and Goody Cory—are given the names of historical personages. But the setting is Salem Village and the period is established as 1692 by Goodman Brown's grandfather having "lashed the Quaker woman so smartly through the streets of Salem" (a historical incident of 1663) and his father having "set fire to an Indian village in King Philip's war" (the war was from 1675 to 1676). Hawthorne's mention of these incidents reminds us of the guilt he felt not just for the iniquities of his great-great-grandfather but for those of *his* father, William Hathorne, a chief persecutor of Quakers, and of William Hathorne Junior, John

Hathorne's brother, a military officer who befriended Indians, tricked them, and sold them into slavery.

At the deepest level, the novella shows the hell on earth human beings create when they search for wickedness in others and deny it in themselves.

Young Goodman Brown came forth at sunset into the street of Salem village; but put his head back, after crossing the threshold, to exchange a parting kiss with his young wife. And Faith, as the wife was aptly named, thrust her own pretty head into the street, letting the wind play with the pink ribbons of her cap while she called to Goodman Brown.

"Dearest heart," whispered she, softly and rather sadly, when her lips were close to his ear, "prithee put off your journey until sunrise and sleep in your own bed to-night. A lone woman is troubled with such dreams and such thoughts that she's afeared of herself sometimes. Pray tarry with me this night, dear husband, of all nights in the year."

"My love and my Faith," replied young Goodman Brown, "of all nights in the year, this one night must I tarry away from thee. My journey, as thou callest it, forth and back again, must needs be done 'twixt now and sunrise. What, my sweet, pretty wife, dost thou doubt me already, and we but three months married?"

"Then God bless you!" said Faith, with the pink ribbons; "and may you find all well when you come back."

"Amen!" cried Goodman Brown. "Say thy prayers, dear Faith, and go to bed at dusk, and no harm will come to thee."

So they parted; and the young man pursued his way until, being about to turn the corner by the meeting house, he looked back and saw the head of Faith still peeping after him with a melancholy air, in spite of her pink ribbons.

"Poor little Faith!" thought he, for his heart smote him, "What a wretch am I to leave her on such an errand! She talks of dreams, too. Methought as she spoke there was trouble in her face, as if a dream had warned her what work is to be done to-night. But no, no; 'twould kill her to think it. Well, she's a blessed angel on earth; and after this one night I'll cling to her skirts and follow her to heaven."

With this excellent resolve for the future, Goodman Brown felt himself justified in making more haste on his present evil purpose. He had taken a dreary road, darkened by all the gloomiest trees of the forest, which barely stood aside to let the narrow path creep through, and closed immediately behind. It was all as lonely as could be; and there is this peculiarity in such a solitude, that the traveller knows not who may be concealed by the innumerable trunks and the thick boughs overhead; so that with lonely footsteps he may yet be passing through an unseen multitude.

"There may be a devilish Indian behind every tree," said Goodman Brown to himself; and he glanced fearfully behind him as he added, "What if the devil himself should be at my very elbow!"

His head being turned back, he passed a crook of the road, and, looking forward again, beheld the figure of a man, in grave and decent attire, seated at the foot of an old tree. He arose at Goodman Brown's approach and walked onward side by side with him.

"You are late, Goodman Brown," said he. "The clock of the Old South was striking as I came through Boston; and that is full fifteen minutes agone."

"Faith kept me back a while," replied the young man, with a tremor in his voice, caused by the sudden appearance of his companion, though not wholly unexpected.

It was now deep dusk in the forest, and deepest in that part of it where these two were journeying. As nearly as could be discerned, the second traveller was about fifty years old, apparently in the same rank of life as Goodman Brown, and bearing a considerable resemblance to him, though perhaps more in expression than features. Still they might have been taken for father and son. And yet, though the elder person was as simply clad as the younger and as simple in manner too, he had an indescribable air of one who knew the world, and who would not have felt abashed at the governor's dinner table or in King William's court, were it possible that his affairs should call him thither. But the only thing about him that could be fixed upon as remarkable was his staff, which bore the likeness of a great black snake, so curiously wrought that it might almost be seen to twist and wriggle itself like a living serpent. This, of course, must have been an ocular deception, assisted by the uncertain light.

"Come, Goodman Brown," cried his fellow-traveller, "this is a dull pace for the beginning of a journey. Take my staff, if you are so soon weary."

"Friend," said the other, exchanging his slow pace for a full stop, "having kept covenant by meeting thee here, it is my purpose now to return whence I came. I have scruples touching the matter thou wot'st of."

"Sayest thou so?" replied he of the serpent, smiling apart. "Let us walk on, nevertheless, reasoning as we go; and if I convince thee not thou shalt turn back. We are but a little way in the forest yet."

"Too far! too far!" exclaimed the goodman, unconsciously resuming his walk. "My father never went into the woods on such an errand, nor his father before him. We have been a race of honest men and good Christians since the days of the martyrs; and shall I be the first of the name of Brown that ever took this path and kept—"

"Such company, thou wouldst say," observed the elder person, interpreting his pause. "Well said, Goodman Brown! I have been as well acquainted with your family as with ever a one among the Puritans; and that's no trifle to say. I helped your grandfather, the constable, when he lashed the Quaker woman so smartly through the streets of Salem; and it was I that brought your father a pitch-pine knot, kindled at my own hearth, to set fire to an Indian village, in King Philip's war. They were my good friends, both; and many a pleasant walk have we had along this path, and returned merrily after midnight. I would fain be friends with you for their sake."

"If it be as thou sayest," replied Goodman Brown, "I marvel they never spoke of these matters; or, verily, I marvel not, seeing that the least rumor of the sort would have driven them from New England. We are a people of prayer, and good works to boot, and abide no such wickedness."

"Wickedness or not," said the traveller with the twisted staff, "I have a very general acquaintance here in New England. The deacons of many a church have drunk the communion wine with me; the selectmen of divers towns make me their chairman; and a majority of the Great and General Court are firm supporters of my interest. The governor and I, too— But these are state secrets."

"Can this be so?" cried Goodman Brown, with a stare of amazement at his undisturbed companion. "Howbeit, I have nothing to do with the governor and council; they have their own ways, and are no rule for a simple husbandman like me. But, were I to go on with thee, how should I meet the eye of that good old man, our minister, at Salem village? Oh, his voice would make me tremble both Sabbath day and lecture day."

Thus far the elder traveller had listened with due gravity; but now burst into a fit of irrepressible mirth, shaking himself so violently that his snake-like staff actually seemed to wriggle in sympathy.

"Ha! ha! ha!" shouted he again and again; then composing himself "Well, go on, Goodman Brown, go on, but, prithee, don't kill me with laughing."

"Well, then, to end the matter at once," said Goodman Brown, considerably nettled, "there is my wife, Faith. It would break her dear little heart; and I'd rather break my own."

"Nay, if that be the case," answered the other, "e'en go thy ways, Goodman Brown. I would not for twenty old women like the one hobbling before us that Faith should come to any harm."

As he spoke, he pointed his staff at a female figure on the path, in whom Goodman Brown recognized a very pious and exemplary dame, who had taught him his catechism in youth, and was still his moral and spiritual adviser, jointly with the minister and Deacon Gookin.

"A marvel, truly, that Goody Cloyse should be so far in the wilderness at nightfall," said he. "But, with your leave, friend, I shall take a cut through the woods until we have left this Christian woman behind. Being a stranger to you, she might ask whom I was consorting with and whither I was going."

"Be it so," said his fellow-traveller. "Betake you to the woods, and let me keep the path."

Accordingly the young man turned aside, but took care to watch his companion, who advanced softly along the road until he had come within a staff's length of the old dame. She, meanwhile, was making the best of her way, with singular speed for so aged a woman, and mumbling some indistinct words—a prayer, doubtless—as she went. The traveller put forth his staff and touched her withered neck with what seemed the serpent's tail.

"The devil!" screamed the pious old lady.

"Then Goody Cloyse knows her old friend?" observed the traveller, confronting her and leaning on his writhing stick.

"Ah, forsooth, and is it your worship indeed?" cried the good dame. "Yea, truly is it, and in the very image of my old gossip, Goodman Brown, the grandfather of the silly fellow that now is. But—would your worship believe it?—my broomstick hath strangely disappeared, stolen, as I suspect, by that unhanged witch, Goody Cory, and that, too, when I was all anointed with the juice of smallage, and cinquefoil, and wolf's bane—"

"Mingled with fine wheat and the fat of a new-born babe," said the shape of old Goodman Brown.

"Ah, your worship knows the recipe," cried the old lady, cackling aloud. "So, as I was saying, being all ready for the meeting, and no horse to ride on, I made up my mind to foot it; for they tell me there is a nice young man to be taken into communion to-night. But now your good worship will lend me your arm, and we shall be there in a twinkling."

"That can hardly be," answered her friend. "I may not spare you my arm, Goody Cloyse; but here is my staff, if you will."

So saying, he threw it down at her feet, where, perhaps, it assumed life, being one of the rods which its owner had formerly lent to the Egyptian magi. Of this fact, however, Goodman Brown could not take cognizance. He had cast up his eyes in astonishment, and, looking down again, beheld neither Goody Cloyse nor the serpentine staff, but his fellow-traveller alone, who waited for him as calmly as if nothing had happened.

"That old woman taught me my catechism," said the young man; and there was a world of meaning in this simple comment.

They continued to walk onward, while the elder traveller exhorted this companion to make good speed and persevere in the path, discoursing so aptly that his arguments seemed rather to spring up in the bosom of his auditor than to be suggested by himself. As they went, he plucked a branch of maple to serve for a walking stick, and began to strip it of the twigs and little boughs, which were wet with evening dew. The moment his fingers touched them they became strangely withered and dried up as with a week's sunshine. Thus the pair proceeded, at a good free pace, until suddenly, in a gloomy hollow of the road,

Goodman Brown sat himself down on the stump of a tree and refused to go any farther.

"Friend," said he, stubbornly, "my mind is made up. Not another step will I budge on this errand. What if a wretched old woman do choose to go to the devil when I thought she was going to heaven: is that any reason why I should quit my dear Faith and go after her?"

"You will think better of this by and by," said his acquaintance, composedly. "Sit here and rest yourself a while; and when you feel like moving again, there is my staff to help you along."

Without more words, he threw his companion the maple stick, and was as speedily out of sight as if he had vanished into the deepening gloom. The young man sat a few moments by the roadside, applauding himself greatly, and thinking with how clear a conscience he should meet the minister in his morning walk, nor shrink from the eye of good old Deacon Gookin. And what calm sleep would be his that very night, which was to have been spent so wickedly, but so purely and sweetly now, in the arms of Faith! Amidst these pleasant and praiseworthy meditations, Goodman Brown heard the tramp of horses along the road, and deemed it advisable to conceal himself within the verge of the forest, conscious of the guilty purpose that had brought him thither, though now so happily turned from it.

On came the hoof tramps and the voices of the riders, two grave old voices, conversing soberly as they drew near. These mingled sounds appeared to pass along the road, within a few yards of the young man's hiding-place; but, owing doubtless to the depth of the gloom at that particular spot, neither the travellers nor their steeds were visible. Though their figures brushed the small boughs by the wayside, it could not be seen that they intercepted, even for a moment, the faint gleam from the strip of bright sky athwart which they must have passed. Goodman Brown alternately crouched and stood on tiptoe, pulling aside the branches and thrusting forth his head as far as he durst without discerning so much as a shadow. It vexed him the more, because he could have sworn, were such a thing possible, that he recognized the voices of the minister and Deacon Gookin, jogging along quietly, as they were wont to do, when bound to some ordination or ecclesiastical council. While yet within hearing, one of the riders stopped to pluck a switch.

"Of the two, reverend sir," said the voice like the deacon's, "I had rather miss an ordination dinner than to-night's meeting. They tell me that some of our community are to be here from Falmouth and beyond, and others from Connecticut and Rhode Island, besides several of the Indian powwows, who, after their fashion, know almost as much deviltry as the best of us. Moreover, there is a goodly young woman to be taken into communion."

Mighty well, Deacon Gookin!" replied the solemn old tones of the minister. "Spur up, or we shall be late. Nothing can be done, you know, until we get on the ground."

The hoofs clattered again; and the voices, talking so strangely in the empty air, passed on through the forest, where no church had ever been gathered or solitary Christian prayed. Whither, then, could these holy men be journeying so deep into the heathen wilderness? Young Goodman Brown caught hold of a tree for support, being ready to sink down on the ground, faint and overburdened with the heavy sickness of his heart. He looked up to the sky, doubting whether there really was a heaven above him. Yet there was the blue arch, and the stars brightening in it.

"With heaven above and Faith below, I will yet stand firm against the evil!" cried Goodman Brown.

While he still gazed upward into the deep arch of the firmament and had lifted his hands to pray, a cloud, though no wind was stirring, hurried across the zenith and hid the brightening stars. The blue sky was still visible, except directly overhead, where this black mass of cloud was sweeping swiftly northward. Aloft in the air, as if from the depths of the cloud, came a confused and doubtful sound of voices. Once the listener fancied that he could distinguish the accents of townspeople of his own, men and women, both pious and ungodly, many of whom he had met at the communion table, and had seen others rioting at the tavern. The next moment, so indistinct were the sounds, he doubted whether he had heard aught but the murmur of the old forest, whispering without a wind. Then came a stronger swell of those familiar tones, heard daily in the sunshine at Salem village, but never until now from a cloud of night. There was one voice, of a young woman, uttering lamentations, yet with an uncertain sorrow, and entreating for some favor, which, perhaps, it would grieve her to obtain; and all the unseen multitude, both saints and sinners, seemed to encourage her onward.

"Faith!" shouted Goodman Brown, in a voice of agony and desperation; and the echoes of the forest mocked him, crying, "Faith! Faith!" as if bewildered wretches were seeking her all through the wilderness.

The cry of grief, rage, and terror was yet piercing the night, when the unhappy husband held his breath for a response. There was a scream, drowned immediately in a louder murmur of voices, fading into far-off laughter, as the dark cloud swept away, leaving the clear and silent sky above Goodman Brown. But something fluttered lightly down through the air and caught on the branch of a tree. The young man seized it, and beheld a pink ribbon.

"My Faith is gone!" cried he, after one stupefied moment. "There is no good on earth; and sin is but a name. Come, devil; for to thee is this world given."

And, maddened with despair, so that he laughed loud and long, did Goodman Brown grasp his staff and set forth again, at such a rate that he seemed to fly along the forest path rather than to walk or run. The road grew wilder and drearier and more faintly traced, and vanished at length, leaving him in the heart of the dark wilderness, still rushing onward with the instinct that guides mortal man to evil. The whole forest was peopled with frightful sounds—the creaking of the trees, the howling of wild beasts, and the yell of Indians; while sometimes the wind tolled like a distant church bell, and sometimes gave a broad roar around the traveller, as if all Nature were laughing him to scorn. But he was himself the chief horror of the scene, and shrank not from its other horrors.

"Ha! ha! ha!" roared Goodman Brown when the wind laughed at him. "Let us hear which will laugh loudest. Think not to frighten me with your deviltry. Come witch, come wizard, come Indian powwow, come devil himself, and here comes Goodman Brown. You may as well fear him as he fear you."

In truth, all through the haunted forest there could be nothing more frightful than the figure of Goodman Brown. On he flew among the black pines, brandishing his staff with frenzied gestures, now giving vent to an inspiration of horrid blasphemy, and now shouting forth such laughter as set all the echoes of the forest laughing like demons around him. The fiend in his own shape is less hideous than when he rages in the breast of man. Thus sped the demoniac on his course, until, quivering among the trees, he saw a red light before him, as when the felled trunks and branches of a clearing have been set on fire, and throw up their lurid blaze against the sky, at the hour of midnight. He paused, in a lull of the tempest that had driven him onward, and heard the swell of what seemed a hymn, rolling solemnly from a distance with the weight of many voices. He knew the tune; it was a familiar one in the choir of the village meeting house. The verse died heavily away, and was lengthened by a chorus, not of human voices, but of all the sounds of the benighted wilderness pealing in awful harmony together. Goodman Brown cried out; and his cry was lost to his own ear by its unison with the cry of the desert.

In the interval of silence he stole forward until the light glared full upon his eyes. At one extremity of an open space, hemmed in by the dark wall of the forest, arose a rock, bearing some rude, natural resemblance either to an altar or a pulpit, and surrounded by four blazing pines, their tops aflame, their stems untouched, like candles at an evening meeting. The mass of foliage that had overgrown the summit of the rock was all on fire, blazing high into the night and fitfully illuminating the whole field. Each pendent twig and leafy festoon was in a blaze. As the red light arose and fell, a numerous congregation alternately shone forth, then disappeared in shadow, and again grew, as it were, out of the darkness, peopling the heart of the solitary woods at once.

"A grave and dark-clad company," quoth Goodman Brown.

In truth they were such. Among them, quivering to and fro between gloom and splendor, appeared faces that would be seen next day at the council board of the province, and others which, Sabbath after Sabbath, looked devoutly heavenward, and benignantly over the crowded pews, from the holiest pulpits in the land. Some affirm that the lady of the governor was there. At least there were high dames well known to her, and wives of honored husbands, and widows, a great multitude, and ancient maidens, all of excellent repute, and fair young girls, who trembled lest their mothers should espy them. Either the sudden gleams of light flashing over the obscure field bedazzled Goodman Brown, or he recognized a score of the church members of Salem village famous for their especial sanctity. Good old Deacon Gookin had arrived, and waited at the skirts of that venerable saint, his revered pastor. But, irreverently consorting with these grave, reputable, and pious people, these elders of the church, these chaste dames and dewy virgins, there were men of dissolute lives and women of spotted fame, wretches given over to all mean and filthy vice, and suspected even of horrid crimes. It was strange to see that the good shrank not from the wicked, nor were the sinners abashed by the saints. Scattered also among their palefaced enemies were the Indian priests, or powwows, who had often scared their native forest with more hideous incantations than any known to English witchcraft.

"But where is Faith?" thought Goodman Brown; and, as hope came into his heart, he trembled.

Another verse of the hymn arose, a slow and mournful strain, such as the pious love, but joined to words which expressed all that our nature can conceive of sin, and darkly hinted at far more. Unfathomable to mere mortals is the lore of fiends. Verse after verse was sung; and still the chorus of the desert swelled between like the deepest tone of a mighty organ; and with the final peal of that dreadful anthem there came a sound, as if the roaring wind, the rushing streams, the howling beasts, and every other voice of the unconverted wilderness were mingling and according with the voice of guilty man in homage to the prince of all. The four blazing pines threw up a loftier flame, and obscurely discovered shapes and visages of horror on the smoke wreaths above the impious assembly. At the same moment the fire on the rock shot redly forth and formed a glowing arch above its base, where now appeared a figure. With reverence be it spoken, the figure bore no slight similitude, both in garb and manner, to some grave divine of the New England churches.

"Bring forth the converts!" cried a voice that echoed through the field and rolled into the forest.

At the word, Goodman Brown stepped forth from the shadow of the trees and approached the congregation, with whom he felt a loathful brotherhood by the sympathy of all that was wicked in his heart. He could have well nigh sworn that the shape of his own dead father beckoned him to advance, looking downward from a smoke wreath, while a woman, with dim features of despair, threw out her hand to warn him back. Was it his mother? But he had no power to retreat one step, nor to resist, even in thought, when the minister and good old Deacon Gookin seized his arms and led him to the blazing rock. Thither came also the slender form of a veiled female, led between Goody Cloyse, that pious teacher of the catechism, and Martha Carrier, who had received the devil's promise to be queen of hell. A rampant hag was she. And there stood the proselytes beneath the canopy of fire.

"Welcome, my children," said the dark figure, "to the communion of your race. Ye have found thus young your nature and your destiny. My children, look behind you!"

They turned; and flashing forth, as it were, in a sheet of flame, the fiend worshippers were seen; the smile of welcome gleamed darkly on every visage.

"There," resumed the sable form, "are all whom ye have reverenced from youth. Ye deemed them holier than yourselves, and shrank from your own sin, contrasting it with their lives of righteousness and prayerful aspirations heavenward. Yet here are they all in my worshipping assembly. This night it shall be granted you to know their secret deeds; how hoary-bearded elders of the church have whispered wanton words to the young maids of their households; how many a woman, eager for widows' weeds, has given her husband a drink at bedtime and let him sleep his last sleep in her bosom; how beardless youths have made haste to inherit their fathers' wealth; and how fair damsels—blush not, sweet ones—have dug little graves in the garden, and bidden me, the sole guest, to an infant's funeral. By the sympathy of your human hearts for sin ye shall scent out all the places—whether in church, bed chamber, street, field, or forest—where crime has been committed, and shall exult to behold the whole earth one stain of guilt, one mighty blood spot. Far more than this. It shall be yours to penetrate, in every bosom, the deep mystery of sin, the fountain of all wicked arts, and which inexhaustibly supplies more evil impulses than human power—than my power at its utmost—can make manifest in deeds. And now, my children, look upon each other."

They did so; and, by the blaze of the hell-kindled torches, the wretched man beheld his Faith, and the wife her husband, trembling before that unhallowed altar.

"Lo, there ye stand, my children," said the figure, in a deep and solemn tone, almost sad with its despairing awfulness, as if his once angelic nature could yet mourn for our miserable race. "Depending upon one another's hearts, ye had still hoped that virtue were not all a dream. Now are ye undeceived. Evil is the nature of mankind. Evil must be your only happiness. Welcome again, my children, to the communion of your race."

"Welcome," repeated the fiend worshippers, in one cry of despair and triumph.

And there they stood, the only pair, as it seemed, who were yet hesitating on the verge of wickedness in this dark world. A basin was hollowed, naturally, in the rock. Did it contain water, reddened by the lurid light? or was it blood? or, perchance, a liquid flame? Herein did the shape of evil dip his hand and prepare to lay the mark of baptism upon their foreheads, that they might be partakers of the mystery of sin, more conscious of the secret guilt of others, both in deed and thought, than they could now be of their own. The husband cast one look at his pale wife, and Faith at him. What polluted wretches would the next glance show them to each other, shuddering alike at what they disclosed and what they saw!

"Faith! Faith!" cried the husband, "look up to heaven, and resist the wicked one."

Whether Faith obeyed, he knew not. Hardly had he spoken when he found himself amid calm night and solitude, listening to a roar of the wind which died heavily away through the forest. He staggered against the rock, and felt it chill and damp; while a hanging twig, that had been all on fire, besprinkled his cheek with the coldest dew.

The next morning young Goodman Brown came slowly into the street of Salem village, staring around him like a bewildered man. The good old minister was taking a walk along the graveyard to get an appetite for breakfast and meditate his sermon, and bestowed a blessing, as he passed, on Goodman Brown. He shrank from the venerable saint as if to avoid an anathema. Old Deacon Gookin was at domestic worship, and the holy words of his prayer were heard through the open window. "What God doth the wizard pray to?" quoth Goodman Brown. Goody Cloyse, that excellent old Christian, stood in the early sunshine at her own lattice, catechizing a little girl who had brought her a pint of morning's milk. Goodman Brown snatched away the child as from the grasp of the fiend himself. Turning the corner by the meeting house, he spied the head of Faith, with the pink ribbons, gazing anxiously forth, and bursting into such joy at sight of him that she skipped along the street and almost kissed her husband before the whole village. But Goodman Brown looked sternly and sadly into her face, and passed on without a greeting.

Had Goodman Brown fallen asleep in the forest and only dreamed a wild dream of a witch meeting?

Be it so, if you will; but, alas! it was a dream of evil omen for young Goodman Brown. A stern, a sad, a darkly meditative, a distrustful, if not a desperate, man did he become from the night of that fearful dream. On the Sabbath day, when the congregation were singing a holy psalm, he could not listen, because an anthem of sin rushed loudly upon his ear and drowned all the blessed strain. When the minister spoke from the pulpit, with power and fervid eloquence and with his hand on the open Bible, of the sacred truths of our religion, and of saintlike lives and triumphant deaths, and of future bliss or misery unutterable, then did Goodman Brown turn pale, dreading lest the roof should thunder down upon the gray blasphemer and his hearers. Often, awaking suddenly at midnight, he shrank from the bosom of Faith; and at morning or eventide, when the family knelt down at prayer, he scowled, and muttered to himself, and gazed sternly at his wife, and turned away. And when he had lived long, and was borne to his grave a hoary corpse, followed by Faith, an aged woman, and children and grandchildren, a goodly procession, besides neighbors not a few, they carved no hopeful verse upon his tombstone; for his dying hour was gloom.

From: Nathaniel Hawthorne, *The House of the Seven Gables* (1851), chapter 1, "The Old Pyncheon Family"

The "rusty wooden house with seven acutely peaked gables" of this novel is almost certainly the building still standing in Turner Street in Salem, visited by Hawthorne as a boy. The character of Colonel Pyncheon, who dominates the book despite dying before the narrative starts, is based on Hawthorne's great-great-grandfather, John Hathorne. Nathaniel so desired to distance himself from the magistrate that he inserted a "w" in the family name.

Hawthorne used a living model for the character of Judge Pyncheon, the descendant who mirrors the colonel both in life and in death. Of all people, this was Charles W. Upham, historian of the witch trials. Upham was a politician as well as an author and had had Hawthorne sacked from his post in the Custom House in Salem. The two men had opposed political views; Upham was a Whig and Hawthorne a Democrat.

The legend of the curse of Maule, established in the first chapter but resonating through the book, is derived from Sarah Good's curse on Nicholas Noyes at her execution: "I am no more a witch than you are a wizard, and God will give you blood to drink." Noyes was said to have died some years later from an internal hemorrhage, bleeding from the mouth. The character of Maule may have been based on Samuel Wardwell, one of the hanged witches. There is some evidence for the existence of land disputes between Hathorne and Wardwell such as Hawthorne ascribes to Pyncheon and Maule. But there was also a historical Thomas Maule (1645–1724), a Quaker persecuted for his religion and later imprisoned for his indictment of the authorities' handling of the witch trials.

The novel uses material from 1692 in a direct way only in its first chapter. But the witch trials are a constant point of reference as Hawthorne shows the descendants of New England Puritanism struggling out of the darkness of bigotry, hatred, and greed to the sunlight of tolerance, generosity, and love.

Half-way down a by-street of one of our New England towns stands a rusty wooden house, with seven acutely peaked gables, facing towards various point of the compass, and a huge, clustered chimney in the midst. The street is Pyncheon

Street; the house is the old Pyncheon House; and an elm-tree, of wide circumference, rooted before the door, is familiar to every town-born child by the title of the Pyncheon Elm. On my occasional visits to the town aforesaid, I seldom failed to turn down Pyncheon Street, for the sake of passing through the shadow of these two antiquities,—the great elm-tree and the weather-beaten edifice.

The aspect of the venerable mansion has always affected me like a human countenance, bearing the traces not merely of outward storm and sunshine, but expressive, also, of the long lapse of mortal life, and accompanying vicissitudes that have passed within. Were these to be worthily recounted, they would form a narrative of no small interest and instruction, and possessing, moreover, a certain remarkably unity, which might almost seem the result of artistic arrangement. But the story would include a chain of events extending over the better part of two centuries, and, written out with reasonable amplitude, would fill a bigger folio volume, or a longer series of duodecimos, than could prudently be appropriated to the annals of all New England during a similar period. It consequently becomes imperative to make short work with most of the traditionary lore of which the old Pyncheon House, otherwise known as the House of the Seven Gables, has been the theme. With a brief sketch, therefore, of the circumstance amid which the foundation of the house was laid, and a rapid glimpse at its quaint exterior, as it grew black in the prevalent east wind,—pointing, too, here and there, at some spot of more verdant mossiness on its roof and walls,—we shall commence the real action of our tale at an epoch not very remote from the present day. Still, there will be a connection with the long past—a reference to forgotten events and personages, and to manners, feelings, and opinion, almost, or wholly obsolete—which, if adequately translated to the reader would serve to illustrate how much of old material goes to make up the freshest novelty of human life. Hence, too, might be drawn a weighty lesson from the little-regarded truth, that the act of the passing generation is the germ which may and must produce good or evil fruit in a far-distant time; that, together with the seed of the merely temporary crop, which mortals term expediency, they inevitably sow the acorns of a more enduring growth, which may darkly overshadow their posterity.

The House of the Seven Gables, antique as it now looks, was not the first habitation erected by civilized man on precisely the same spot of ground. Pyncheon Street formerly bore the humbler appellation of Maule's Lane, from the name of the original occupant of the soil, before whose cottage-door it was a cow-path. A natural spring of soft and pleasant water—a rare treasure on the sea-girt peninsula, where the Puritan settlement was made—had early induced Matthew Maule to build a hut, shaggy with thatch, at this point, although somewhat too remote from what was then the centre of the village. In the growth of the town, however, after some thirty or forty years, the site covered by this rude hovel had become exceedingly desirable in the eyes of a prominent and powerful personage, who asserted plausible claims to the proprietorship of this, and a large adjacent tract of land, on the strength of a grant from the legislature. Colonel Pyncheon, the claimant, as we gather from whatever traits of him are preserved, was characterized by an iron energy of purpose. Matthew Maule, on the other hand, though an obscure man, was stubborn in the defence of what he considered his right; and, for several years, he succeeded in protecting the acre or two of earth, which, with his own toil, he had hewn out of the primeval forest, to be his garden-ground and homestead. No written record of this dispute is known to be in existence. Our acquaintance with the whole subject is derived chiefly from tradition. It would be bold, therefore, and possibly unjust, to venture a decisive opinion as to its merits; although it appears to have been at least a matter of doubt, whether Colonel Pyncheon's claim were not unduly stretched, in order to make it cover the small metes and bounds of Matthew Maule. What greatly strengthens such a suspicion is the fact that this controversy between two ill-matched antagonists—at a period, moreover, laud it as we may, when personal influence had far more weight than now—remained for years undecided, and came to a close only with the death of the party occupying the disputed soil. The mode of his death, too, affects the mind differently, in our day, from what it did a century and a half ago. It was a death that blasted with strange horror the humble name of the dweller in the cottage, and made it seem almost a religious act to drive the plough over the little area of his habitation, and obliterate his place and memory from among men.

Old Matthew Maule, in a word, was executed for the crime of witchcraft. He was one of the martyrs to that terrible delusion, which should teach us, among its other morals, that the influential classes, and those who take upon themselves to be leaders of the people, are fully liable to all the passionate error that has ever characterized the maddest mob. Clergymen, judges, statesmen,—the wisest, calmest, holiest persons of their day,—stood in the inner circle round about the gallows, loudest to applaud the work of blood, latest to confess themselves miserably deceived. If any one part of their proceedings can be said to deserve less blame than another, it was the singular indiscrimination with which they persecuted, not merely the poor and aged, as in former judicial massacres, but people of all ranks; their own equals, brethren, and wives. Amid the disorder of such various ruin, it is not strange that a man of inconsiderable note, like Maule, should have trodden the martyr's path to the hill of execution almost unremarked in the throng of his fellow-sufferers. But, in after days, when the frenzy of that hideous epoch had subsided, it was remembered how loudly Colonel Pyncheon had joined in the general cry, to purge the land from witchcraft; nor did it fail to be whispered, that there was an invidious acrimony in the zeal with which he had sought the condemnation of Matthew Maule. It was well known that the victim had recognized the bitterness of personal enmity in his persecutor's conduct towards him, and that he declared himself hunted to death for his spoil. At the moment of execution—with the halter about his neck, and while Colonel Pyncheon sat on horseback, grimly gazing at the scene—Maule had addressed him from the scaffold, and uttered a prophecy, of which history, as well as fireside tradition, has preserved the very words. "God," said the dying man, pointing his finger, with a ghastly look, at the undismayed countenance of his enemy,—"God will give him blood to drink!"

After the reputed wizard's death, his humble homestead had fallen an easy spoil into Colonel Pyncheon's grasp. When it was understood, however, that the Colonel intended to erect a family mansion—spacious, ponderously framed of oaken timber, and calculated to endure for many generations of his posterity—over the spot first covered by the log-built hut of Matthew Maule, there was much shaking of the head among the village gossips. Without absolutely expressing a doubt whether the stalwart Puritan had acted as a man of conscience and integrity throughout the proceedings which have been sketched, they, nevertheless, hinted that he was about to build his house over an unquiet grave. His home would include the home of the dead and buried wizard, and would thus afford the ghost of the latter a kind of privilege to haunt its new apartments, and the chambers into which future bridegrooms were to lead their brides, and where children of the Pyncheon blood were to be born. The terror and ugliness of Maule's crime, and the wretchedness of his punishment, would darken the freshly plastered walls, and infect them early with the scent of an old and melancholy house. Why, then,—while so much of the soil around him was bestrewn with the virgin forest-leaves,—why should Colonel Pyncheon prefer a site that had already been accurst?

But the Puritan soldier and magistrate was not a man to be turned aside from his well-considered scheme, either by dread of the wizard's ghost, or by flimsy sentimentalities of any kind, however specious. Had he been told of a bad air, it might have moved him somewhat; but he was ready to encounter an evil spirit on his own ground. Endowed with commonsense, as massive and hard as blocks of granite, fastened together by stern rigidity of purpose, as with iron clamps, he followed out his original design, probably without so much as imagining an objection to it. On the score of delicacy, or any scrupulousness which a finer sensibility might have taught him, the Colonel, like most of his breed and generation, was impenetrable. He, therefore, dug his cellar, and laid the deep foundations of his mansion, on the square of earth whence Matthew Maule, forty years before, had first swept away the fallen leaves. It was a curious, and, as some people thought, an ominous fact, that, very soon after the workmen began their operations, the spring of water, above mentioned, entirely lost the deliciousness of its pristine quality. Whether its sources were disturbed by the depth of the new cellar, or whatever subtler cause might lurk at the bottom, it is certain that the water of Maule's Well, as it continued to be called, grew hard and brackish. Even such we find it now; and any old woman of the neighborhood will certify that it is productive of intestinal mischief to those who quench their thirst there.

The reader may deem it singular that the head carpenter of the new edifice was no other than the son of the very man from whose dead gripe the property of the soil had been wrested. Not improbably he was the best workman of his time; or, perhaps, the Colonel thought it expedient, or was impelled by some better feeling, thus openly to cast aside all animosity against the race of his fallen antagonist. Nor was it out of keeping with the general coarseness and matter-of-fact character of the age, that the son should be willing to earn an honest penny, or, rather, a weighty amount of sterling pounds, from the purse of his father's deadly enemy. At all events, Thomas Maule became the architect of the House of the Seven Gables, and performed his duty so faithfully that the timber framework fastened by his hands still holds together.

Thus the great house was built. Familiar as it stands in the writer's recollection,—for it has been an object of curiosity with him from boyhood, both as a specimen of the best and stateliest architecture of a long-past epoch, and as the scene of events more full of human interest, perhaps, than those of a gray feudal castle,—familiar as it stands, in its rusty old age, it is therefore only the more difficult to imagine the bright novelty with which it first caught the sunshine. The impression of its actual state, at this distance of a hundred and sixty years, darkens inevitably through the picture which we would fain give of its appearance on the morning when the Puritan magnate bade all the town to be his guests. A ceremony of consecration, festive as well as religious, was now to be performed. A prayer and discourse from the Rev. Mr. Higginson, and the outpouring of a psalm from the general throat of the community, was to be made acceptable to the grosser sense by ale, cider, wine, and brandy, in copious effusion, and, as some authorities aver, by an ox, roasted whole, or at least, by the weight and substance of an ox, in more manageable joints and sirloins. The carcass of a deer, shot within twenty miles, had supplied material for the vast circumference of a pasty. A codfish of sixty pounds, caught in the bay, had been dissolved into the rich liquid of a chowder. The chimney of the new house, in short, belching forth its kitchen-smoke, impregnated the whole air with the scent of meats, fowls, and fishes, spicily concocted with odoriferous herbs, and onions in abundance. The mere smell of such festivity, making its way to everybody's nostrils, was at once an invitation and an appetite.

Maule's Lane, or Pyncheon Street, as it were now more decorous to call it, was thronged, at the appointed hour, as with a congregation on its way to church. All, as they approached, looked upward at the imposing edifice, which was henceforth to assume its rank among the habitations of mankind. There it rose, a little withdrawn from the line of the street, but in pride, not modesty. Its whole visible exterior was ornamented with quaint figures, conceived in the grotesqueness of a Gothic fancy, and drawn or stamped in the glittering plaster, composed of lime, pebbles, and bits of glass, with which the woodwork of the walls was overspread. On every side the seven gables pointed sharply towards the sky, and presented the aspect of a whole sisterhood of edifices, breathing through the spiracles of one great chimney. The many lattices, with their small, diamond-shaped panes, admitted the sunlight into hall and chamber, while, nevertheless, the second story, projecting far over the base, and itself retiring beneath the third, threw a shadowy and thoughtful gloom into the lower rooms. Carved globes of wood were affixed under the jutting stories. Little spiral rods of iron beautified each of the seven peaks. On the triangular portion of the gable, that fronted next the street, was a dial, put up that very morning, and on which the sun was still marking the passage of the first bright hour in a history that was not destined to be all so bright. All around were scattered shavings, chips, shingles, and broken halves of bricks; these, together with the lately turned earth, on which the grass had not begun to grow, contributed to the impression of strangeness and novelty proper to a house that had yet its place to make among men's daily interests.

The principal entrance, which had almost the breadth of a church-door, was in the angle between the two front gables, and was covered by an open porch, with benches beneath its shelter. Under this arched doorway, scraping their feet on the unworn threshold, now trod the clergymen, the elders, the magistrates, the deacons, and whatever of aristocracy there was in town or county. Thither, too, thronged the plebeian classes as freely as their betters, and in larger number. Just within the entrance, however, stood two serving-men, pointing some of the guests to the neighborhood of the kitchen, and ushering others into the statelier rooms,—hospitable alike to all, but still with a scrutinizing regard to the high or low degree of each. Velvet garments, sombre but rich, stiffly plaited ruffs and bands, embroidered gloves, venerable beards, the mien and countenance of authority, made it easy to distinguish the gentleman of worship, at that period, from the tradesman, with his plodding air, or the laborer, in his leathern jerkin, stealing awe-stricken into the house which he had perhaps helped to build.

One inauspicious circumstance there was, which awakened a hardly concealed displeasure in the breasts of a few of the more punctilious visitors. The founder of this stately mansion—a gentleman noted for the square and ponderous courtesy of his demeanor—ought surely to have stood in his own hall, and to have offered the first welcome to so many eminent personages as here presented themselves in honor of his solemn festival. He was as yet invisible; the most favored of the guests had not beheld him. This sluggishness on Colonel Pyncheon's part became still more unaccountable, when the second dignitary of the province made his appearance, and found no more ceremonious a reception. The lieutenant-governor, although his visit was one of the anticipated glories of the day, had alighted from his horse, and assisted his lady from her side-saddle, and crossed the Colonel's threshold, without other greeting than that of the principal domestic.

This person—a gray-headed man, of quiet and most respectful deportment—found it necessary to explain that his master still remained in his study, or private apartment; on entering which, an hour before, he had expressed a wish on no account to be disturbed.

"Do not you see, fellow," said the high-sheriff of the county, taking the servant aside, "that this is no less a man than the lieutenant-governor? Summon Colonel Pyncheon at once! I know that he received letters from England this morning; and, in the perusal and consideration of them, an hour may have passed away without his noticing it. But he will be ill-pleased, I judge, if you suffer him to neglect the courtesy due to one of our chief rulers, and who may be said to represent King William, in the absence of the governor himself. Call your master instantly!"

"Nay, please your worship," answered the man, in much perplexity, but with a backwardness that strikingly indicated the hard and severe character of Colonel Pyncheon's domestic rule; "my master's orders were exceeding strict; and, as your worship knows, he permits of no discretion in the obedience of those who owe him service. Let who list open yonder door; I dare not, though the governor's own voice should bid me do it!"

"Pooh, pooh, master high-sheriff!" cried the lieutenant-governor, who had overheard the foregoing discussion, and felt himself high enough in station to play a little with his dignity. "I will take the matter into my own hands. It is time that the good Colonel came forth to greet his friends; else we shall be apt to suspect that he has taken a sip too much of his Canary wine, in his extreme deliberation which cask it were best to broach in honor of the day! But since he is so much behindhand, I will give him a remembrancer myself!"

Accordingly, with such a tramp of his ponderous riding-boots as might of itself have been audible in the remotest of the seven gables, he advanced to the door, which the servant pointed out, and made its new panels reëcho with a loud, free knock. Then, looking round, with a smile, to the spectators, he awaited a response. As none came, however, he knocked again, but with the same unsatisfactory result as at first. And now, being a trifle choleric in his temperament, the lieutenant-governor uplifted the heavy hilt of his sword, wherewith he so beat and banged upon the door, that, as some of the by-standers whispered, the racket might have disturbed the dead. Be that as it might, it seemed to produce no awakening effect on Colonel Pyncheon. When the sound subsided, the silence through the house was deep, dreary, and oppressive, notwithstanding that the tongues of many of the guests had already been loosened by a surreptitious cup or two of wine or spirits.

"Strange, forsooth!—very strange!" cried the lieutenant-governor, whose smile was changed to a frown. "But seeing that our host sets us the good example of forgetting ceremony, I shall likewise throw it aside, and make free to intrude on his privacy!"

He tried the door, which yielded to his hand, and was flung wide open by a sudden gust of wind that passed, as with a loud sigh, from the outermost portal through all the passages and apartments of the new house. It rustled the silken garments of the ladies, and waved the long curls of the gentlemen's wigs, and shook the window-hangings and the curtains of the bedchambers; causing everywhere a singular stir, which yet was more like a hush. A shadow of awe and half-fearful anticipation—nobody knew wherefore, nor of what—had all at once fallen over the company.

They thronged, however, to the now open door, pressing the lieutenant-governor, in the eagerness of their curiosity, into the room in advance of them. At the first glimpse they beheld nothing extraordinary: a handsomely furnished room, of moderate size, somewhat darkened by curtains; books arranged on shelves; a large map on the wall, and likewise a portrait of Colonel Pyncheon, beneath which sat the original Colonel himself, in an oaken elbow-chair, with a pen in his hand. Letters, parchments, and blank sheets of paper were on the table before him. He appeared to gaze at the curious crowd, in front of which stood the lieutenant-governor; and there was a frown on his dark and massive countenance, as if sternly resentful of the boldness that had impelled them into his private retirement.

A little boy—the Colonel's grandchild, and the only human being that ever dared to be familiar with him—now made his way among the guests, and ran towards the seated figure; then pausing half-way, he began to shriek with terror. The company, tremulous as the leaves of a tree, when all are shaking together, drew nearer, and perceived that there was an unnatural distortion in the fixedness of Colonel Pyncheon's stare; that there was blood on his ruff, and that his hoary beard was saturated with it. It was too late to give assistance. The iron-hearted Puritan, the relentless persecutor, the grasping and strong-willed man, was dead! Dead, in his new house! There is a tradition, only worth alluding to as lending a tinge of superstitious awe to a scene perhaps gloomy enough without it, that a voice spoke loudly among the guests, the tones of which were like those of old Matthew Maule, the executed wizard,—"God hath given him blood to drink!"

Thus early had that one guest,—the only guest who is certain, at one time or another, to find his way into every human dwelling,—thus early had Death stepped across the threshold of the House of the Seven Gables!

Colonel Pyncheon's sudden and mysterious end made a vast deal of noise in its day. There were many rumors, some of which have vaguely drifted down to the present time, how that appearances indicated violence; that there were the marks of fingers on his throat, and the print of a bloody hand on his plaited ruff; and that his peaked beard was dishevelled, as if it had been fiercely clutched and pulled. It was averred, likewise, that the lattice window, near the Colonel's chair, was open; and that, only a few minutes before the fatal occurrence, the figure of a man had been seen clambering over the garden-fence, in the rear of the house. But it were folly to lay any stress on stories of this kind, which are sure to spring up around such an event as that now related, and which, as in the present case, sometimes prolong themselves for ages afterwards, like the toadstools that indicate where the fallen and buried trunk of a tree has long since mouldered into the earth. For our own part, we allow them just as little credence as to that other fable of the skeleton hand which the lieutenant-governor was said to have seen at the Colonel's throat, but which vanished away, as he advanced farther into the room. Certain it is, however, that there was a great consultation and dispute of doctors over the dead body. One—John Swinnerton by name—who appears to have been a man of eminence, upheld it, if we have rightly understood his terms of art, to be a case of apoplexy. His professional brethren, each for himself, adopted various hypotheses, more or less plausible, but all dressed out in a perplexing mystery of phrase, which, if it do not show a bewilderment of mind in these erudite physicians, certainly causes it in the unlearned peruser of their opinions. The coroner's jury sat upon the corpse, and, like sensible men, returned an unassailable verdict of "Sudden Death!"

It is indeed difficult to imagine that there could have been a serious suspicion of murder, or the slightest grounds for implicating any particular individual as the perpetrator. The rank, wealth, and eminent character of the deceased must have insured the strictest scrutiny into every ambiguous circumstance. As none such is on record, it is safe to assume that none existed. Tradition,—which sometimes brings down truth that history has let slip, but is oftener the wild babble of the time, such as was formerly spoken at the fireside and now congeals in newspapers,—tradition is responsible for all contrary averments. In Colonel Pyncheon's funeral sermon, which was printed, and is still extant, the Rev. Mr. Higginson enumerates, among the many felicities of his distinguished parishioner's earthly career, the happy seasonableness of his death. His duties all performed,—the highest prosperity attained,—his race and future generations fixed on a stable basis, and with a stately roof to shelter them, for centuries to come,—what other upward step remained for this good man to take, save the final step from earth to the golden gate of heaven! The pious clergyman surely would not have uttered words like these had he in the least suspected that the Colonel had been thrust into the other world with the clutch of violence upon his throat.

The family of Colonel Pyncheon, at the epoch of his death, seemed destined to as fortunate a permanence as can anywise consist with the inherent instability of human affairs. It might fairly be anticipated that the progress of time would rather increase and ripen their prosperity, than wear away and destroy it. For, not only had his son and heir come into immediate enjoyment of a rich estate, but there was a claim through an Indian deed, confirmed by a subsequent grant of the General Court, to a vast and as yet unexplored and unmeasured tract of Eastern lands. These possessions—for as such they might almost certainly be reckoned—comprised the greater part of what is now known as Waldo County, in the State of Maine, and were more extensive than many a dukedom, or even a reigning prince's territory, on European soil. When the pathless forest that still covered this wild principality should give place—as it inevitably must, though perhaps not till ages hence—to the golden fertility of human culture, it would be the source of incalculable wealth to the Pyncheon blood. Had the Colonel survived only a few weeks longer, it is probable that his great political influence, and powerful connections at home and abroad, would have consummated all that was necessary to render the claim available. But, in spite of good Mr. Higginson's congratulatory eloquence, this appeared to be the one thing which Colonel Pyncheon, provident and sagacious as he was, had allowed to go at loose ends. So far as the prospective territory was concerned, he unquestionably died too soon. His son lacked not merely the father's eminent position, but the talent and force of character to achieve it: he could, therefore, effect nothing by dint of political interest; and the bare justice or legality of the claim was not so apparent, after the Colonel's decease, as it had been pronounced in his lifetime. Some connecting link had slipped out of the evidence, and could not anywhere be found.

Efforts, it is true, were made by the Pyncheons, not only then, but at various periods for nearly a hundred years afterwards, to obtain what they stubbornly persisted in deeming their right. But, in course of time, the territory was partly re-granted to more favored individuals, and partly cleared and occupied by actual settlers. These last, if they ever heard of the Pyncheon title, would have laughed at the idea of any man's asserting a right—on the strength of mouldy parchments, signed with the faded autographs of governors and legislators long dead and forgotten—to the lands which they or their fathers had wrested from the wild hand of nature by their own sturdy toil. This impalpable claim, therefore, resulted in nothing more solid than to cherish, from generation to generation, an absurd delusion of family importance, which all along characterized the Pyncheons. It caused the poorest member of the race to feel as if he inherited a kind of nobility, and might yet come into the possession of princely wealth to support it. In the better specimens of the breed, this peculiarity threw an ideal grace over the hard material of human life, without stealing away any truly valuable quality. In the baser sort, its effect was to increase the liability to sluggishness and dependence, and induce the victim of a shadowy hope to remit all self-effort, while awaiting the realization of his dreams. Years and years after their claim had passed out of the public memory, the Pyncheons were accustomed to consult the

Colonel's ancient map, which had been projected while Waldo County was still an unbroken wilderness. Where the old land-surveyor had put down woods, lakes, and rivers, they marked out the cleared spaces, and dotted the villages and towns, and calculated the progressively increasing value of the territory, as if there were yet a prospect of its ultimately forming a princedom for themselves.

In almost every generation, nevertheless, there happened to be some one descendant of the family gifted with a portion of the hard, keen sense, and practical energy, that had so remarkably distinguished the original founder. His character, indeed, might be traced all the way down, as distinctly as if the Colonel himself, a little diluted, had been gifted with a sort of intermittent immortality on earth. At two or three epochs, when the fortunes of the family were low, this representative of hereditary qualities had made his appearance, and caused the traditionary gossips of the town to whisper among themselves, "Here is the old Pyncheon come again! Now the Seven Gables will be new-shingled!" From father to son, they clung to the ancestral house with singular tenacity of home attachment. For various reasons, however, and from impressions often too vaguely founded to be put on paper, the writer cherishes the belief that many, if not most, of the successive proprietors of this estate were troubled with doubts as to their moral right to hold it. Of their legal tenure there could be no question; but old Matthew Maule, it is to be feared, trode downward from his own age to a far later one, planting a heavy footstep, all the way, on the conscience of a Pyncheon. If so, we are left to dispose of the awful query, whether each inheritor of the property—conscious of wrong, and failing to rectify it—did not commit anew the great guilt of his ancestor, and incur all its original responsibilities. And supposing such to be the case, would it not be a far truer mode of expression to say of the Pyncheon family, that they inherited a great misfortune, than the reverse?

We have already hinted that it is not our purpose to trace down the history of the Pyncheon family, in its unbroken connection with the House of the Seven Gables; nor to show, as in a magic picture, how the rustiness and infirmity of age gathered over the venerable house itself. As regards its interior life, a large, dim looking-glass used to hang in one of the rooms, and was fabled to contain within its depths all the shapes that had ever been reflected there,—the old Colonel himself, and his many descendants, some in the garb of antique babyhood, and others in the bloom of feminine beauty or manly prime, or saddened with the wrinkles of frosty age. Had we the secret of that mirror, we would gladly sit down before it, and transfer its revelations to our page. But there was a story, for which it is difficult to conceive any foundation, that the posterity of Matthew Maule had some connection with the mystery of the looking-glass, and that, by what appears to have been a sort of mesmeric process, they could make its inner region all alive with the departed Pyncheons; not as they had shown themselves to the world nor in their better and happier hours, but as doing over again some deed of sin, or in the crisis of life's bitterest sorrow. The popular imagination, indeed, long kept itself busy with the affair of the old Puritan Pyncheon and the wizard Maule; the curse, which the latter flung from his scaffold, was remembered, with the very important addition, that it had become a part of the Pyncheon inheritance. If one of the family did but gurgle in his throat, a bystander would be likely enough to whisper, between jest and earnest, "He has Maule's blood to drink!" The sudden death of a Pyncheon, about a hundred years ago, with circumstances very similar to what have been related of the Colonel's exit, was held as giving additional probability to the received opinion on this topic. It was considered, moreover, an ugly and ominous circumstance, that Colonel Pyncheon's picture—in obedience, it was said, to a provision of his will—remained affixed to the wall of the room in which he died. Those stern, immitigable features seemed to symbolize an evil influence, and so darkly to mingle the shadow of their presence with the sunshine of the passing hour, that no good thoughts or purposes could ever spring up and blossom there. To the thoughtful mind there will be no tinge of superstition in what we figuratively express, by affirming that the ghost of a dead progenitor—perhaps as a portion of his own punishment—is often doomed to become the Evil Genius of his family.

The Pyncheons, in brief, lived along, for the better part of two centuries, with perhaps less of outward vicissitude than has attended most other New England families during the same period of time. Possessing very distinctive traits of their own, they nevertheless took the general characteristics of the little community in which they dwelt; a town noted for its frugal, discreet, well-ordered, and home-loving inhabitants, as well as for the somewhat confined scope of its sympathies; but in which, be it said, there are odder individuals, and, now and then, stranger occurrences, than one meets with almost anywhere else. During the Revolution, the Pyncheon of that epoch, adopting the royal side, became a refugee; but repented, and made his reappearance, just at the point of time to preserve the House of the Seven Gables from confiscation. For the last seventy years the most noted event in the Pyncheon annals had been likewise the heaviest calamity that ever befell the race; no less than the violent death—for so it was adjudged—of one member of the family by the criminal act of another. Certain circumstances attending this fatal occurrence had brought the deed irresistibly home to a nephew of the deceased Pyncheon. The young man was tried and convicted of the crime; but either the circumstantial nature of the evidence, and possibly some lurking doubt in the breast of the executive, or, lastly,—an argument of greater weight in a republic than it could have been under a monarchy,—the high respectability and political influence of the criminal's connections, had availed to mitigate his doom from death to perpetual imprisonment. This sad affair had chanced about thirty years before the action of our story commences. Latterly, there were rumors (which few believed, and only one or two felt greatly interested in) that this long-buried man was likely, for some reason or other, to be summoned forth from his living tomb.

It is essential to say a few words respecting the victim of this now almost forgotten murder. He was an old bachelor, and possessed of great wealth, in addition to the house and real estate which constituted what remained of the ancient Pyncheon property. Being of an eccentric and melancholy turn of mind, and greatly given to rummaging old records and hearkening to old traditions, he had brought himself, it is averred, to the conclusion that Matthew Maule, the wizard, had been foully wronged out of his homestead, if not out of his life. Such being the case, and he, the old bachelor, in possession of the ill-gotten spoil,—with the black stain of blood sunken deep into it, and still to be scented by conscientious nostrils,—the question occurred, whether it were not imperative upon him, even at this late hour, to make restitution to Maule's posterity. To a man living so much in the past, and so little in the present, as the secluded and antiquarian old bachelor, a century and a half seemed not so vast a period as to obviate the propriety of substituting right for wrong. It was the belief of those who knew him best, that he would positively have taken the very singular step of giving up the House of the Seven Gables to the representative of Matthew Maule, but for the unspeakable tumult which a suspicion of the old gentleman's project awakened among his Pyncheon relatives. Their exertions had the effect of suspending his purpose; but it was feared that he would perform, after death, by the operation of his last will, what he had so hardly been prevented from doing in his proper lifetime. But there is no one thing which men so rarely do, whatever the provocation or inducement, as to bequeath patrimonial property away from their own blood. They may love other individuals far better than their relatives,—they may even cherish dislike, or positive hatred, to the latter; but yet, in view of death, the strong prejudice of propinquity revives, and impels the testator to send down his estate in the line marked out by custom so immemorial that it looks like nature. In all the Pyncheons, this feeling had the energy of disease. It was too powerful for the conscientious scruples of the old bachelor; at whose death, accordingly, the mansion-house, together with most of his other riches, passed into the possession of his next legal representative.

This was a nephew, the cousin of the miserable young man who had been convicted of the uncle's murder. The new heir, up to the period of his accession, was reckoned rather a dissipated youth, but had at once reformed, and made himself an exceedingly respectable member of society. In fact, he showed more of the Pyncheon quality, and had won higher eminence in the world than any of his race since the time of the original Puritan. Applying himself in earlier manhood to the study of the law, and having a natural tendency towards office, he had attained, many years ago, to a judicial situation in some inferior court, which gave him for life the very desirable and imposing title of judge. Later, he had engaged in politics, and served a part of two terms in Congress, besides making a considerable figure in both branches of the State legislature. Judge Pyncheon was unquestionably an honor to his race. He had built himself a country-seat within a few miles of his native town, and there spent such portions of his time as could be spared from public service in the display of every grace and virtue—as a newspaper phrased it, on the eve of an election—befitting the Christian, the good citizen, the horticulturist, and the gentleman.

There were few of the Pyncheons left to sun themselves in the glow of the Judge's prosperity. In respect to natural increase, the breed had not thriven; it appeared rather to be dying out. The only members of the family known to be extant were, first, the Judge himself, and a single surviving son, who was now travelling in Europe; next, the thirty years' prisoner, already alluded to, and a sister of the latter, who occupied, in an extremely retired manner, the House of the Seven Gables, in which she had a life-estate by the will of the old bachelor. She was understood to be wretchedly poor, and seemed to make it her choice to remain so; inasmuch as her affluent cousin, the Judge, had repeatedly offered her all the comforts of life, either in the old mansion or his own modern residence. The last and youngest Pyncheon was a little country-girl of seventeen, the daughter of another of the Judge's cousins, who had married a young woman of no family or property, and died early and in poor circumstances. His widow had recently taken another husband.

As for Matthew Maule's posterity, it was supposed now to be extinct. For a very long period after the witchcraft delusion, however, the Maules had continued to inhabit the town where their progenitor had suffered so unjust a death. To all appearance, they were a quiet, honest, well-meaning race of people, cherishing no malice against individuals or the public for the wrong which had been done them; or if, at their own fireside, they transmitted, from father to child, any hostile recollection of the wizard's fate and their lost patrimony, it was never acted upon, nor openly expressed. Nor would it have been singular had they ceased to remember that the House of the Seven Gables was resting its heavy framework on a foundation that was rightfully their own. There is something so massive, stable, and almost irresistibly imposing in the exterior presentment of established rank and great possessions, that their very existence seems to give them a right to exist; at least, so excellent a counterfeit of right, that few poor and humble men have moral force enough to question it, even in their secret minds. Such is the case now, after so many ancient prejudices have been overthrown; and it was far more so in ante-Revolutionary days, when the aristocracy could venture to be proud, and the low were content to be abased. Thus the Maules, at all events, kept their resentments within their own breasts. They were generally poverty-stricken; always plebeian and obscure; working with unsuccessful diligence at handicrafts; laboring on the wharves, or following the sea, as sailors before the mast; living here and there about the town, in hired tenements, and coming finally to the almshouse as the natural home of their old age. At last, after creeping as it were, for such a length of time, along the utmost verge of the opaque puddle of obscurity, they had taken that downright plunge, which, sooner or later, is the destiny of all families, whether princely or plebeian. For thirty years past, neither town-record, nor gravestone, nor the directory, nor the knowledge or memory of man, bore any trace of Matthew Maule's descendants. His blood might possibly exist elsewhere; here, where its lowly current could be traced so far back, it had ceased to keep an onward course.

So long as any of the race were to be found, they had been marked out from other men—not strikingly, nor as with a sharp line, but with an effect that was felt rather than spoken of—by an hereditary character of reserve. Their companions, or those who endeavored to become such, grew conscious of a circle round about the Maules, within the sanctity or the spell of which, in spite of an exterior of sufficient frankness and good-fellowship, it was impossible for any man to step. It was this indefinable peculiarity, perhaps, that, by insulating them from human aid, kept them always so unfortunate in life. It certainly operated to prolong in their case, and to confirm to them as their only inheritance, those feelings of repugnance and superstitious terror with which the people of the town, even after awakening from their frenzy, continued to regard the memory of the reputed witches. The mantle, or rather the ragged cloak, of old Matthew Maule, had fallen upon his children. They were half believed to inherit mysterious attributes; the family eye was said to possess strange power. Among other good-for-nothing properties and privileges, one was especially assigned them,—that of exercising an influence over people's dreams. The Pyncheons, if all stories were true, haughtily as they bore themselves in the noonday streets of their native town, were no better than bond-servants to these plebeian Maules, on entering the topsy-turvy commonwealth of sleep. Modern psychology, it may be, will endeavor to reduce these alleged necromancies within a system, instead of rejecting them as altogether fabulous.

A descriptive paragraph or two, treating of the seven-gabled mansion in its more recent aspect, will bring this preliminary chapter to a close. The street in which it upreared its venerable peaks has long ceased to be a fashionable quarter of the town; so that, though the old edifice was surrounded by habitations of modern date, they were mostly small, built entirely of wood, and typical of the most plodding uniformity of common life. Doubtless, however, the whole story of human existence may be latent in each of them, but with no picturesqueness, externally, that can attract the imagination or sympathy to seek it there. But as for the old structure of our story, its white-oak frame, and its boards, shingles, and crumbling plaster, and even the huge, clustered chimney in the midst, seemed to constitute only the least and meanest part of its reality. So much of mankind's varied experience had passed there,—so much had been suffered, and something, too, enjoyed,—that the very timbers were oozy, as with the moisture of a heart. It was itself like a great human heart, with a life of its own, and full of rich and sombre reminiscences.

The deep projection of the second story gave the house such a meditative look, that you could not pass it without the idea that it had secrets to keep, and an eventful history to moralize upon. In front, just on the edge of the unpaved sidewalk, grew the Pyncheon Elm, which, in reference to such trees as one usually meets with, might well be termed gigantic. It had been planted by a great-grandson of the first Pyncheon, and, though now fourscore years of age, or perhaps nearer a hundred, was still in its strong and broad maturity, throwing its shadow from side to side of the street, overtopping the seven gables, and sweeping the whole black roof with its pendent foliage. It gave beauty to the old edifice, and seemed to make it a part of nature. The street having been widened about forty years ago, the front gable was now precisely on a line with it. On either side extended a ruinous wooden fence of open lattice-work, through which could be seen a grassy yard, and, especially in the angles of the building, an enormous fertility of burdocks, with leaves, it is hardly an exaggeration to say, two or three feet long. Behind the house there appeared to be a garden, which undoubtedly had once been extensive, but was now infringed upon by other enclosures, or shut in by habitations and outbuildings that stood on another street. It would be an omission, trifling, indeed, but unpardonable, were we to forget the green moss that had long since gathered over the projections of the windows, and on the slopes of the roof; nor must we fail to direct the reader's eye to a crop, not of weeds, but flower-shrubs, which were growing aloft in the air, not a great way from the chimney, in the nook between two of the gables. They were called Alice's Posies. The tradition was, that a certain Alice Pyncheon had flung up the seeds, in sport, and that the dust of the street and the decay of the roof gradually formed a kind of soil for them, out of which they grew, when Alice had long been in her grave. However the flowers might have come there, it was both sad and sweet to observe how Nature adopted to herself this desolate, decaying, gusty, rusty old house of the Pyncheon family; and how the ever-returning summer did her best to gladden it with tender beauty, and grew melancholy in the effort.

There is one other feature, very essential to be noticed, but which, we greatly fear, may damage any picturesque and romantic impression which we have been willing to throw over our sketch of this respectable edifice. In the front gable, under the impending brow of the second story, and contiguous to the street, was a shop-door, divided horizontally in the midst, and with a window for its upper segment, such as is often seen in dwellings of a somewhat ancient date. This same shop-door had been a subject of no slight mortification to the present occupant of the august Pyncheon House, as well as to some of her predecessors. The matter is disagreeably delicate to handle; but, since the reader must needs be let into the secret, he will please to understand, that, about a century ago, the head of the Pyncheons found himself involved in serious financial difficulties. The fellow (gentleman, as he styled himself) can hardly have been other than a spurious interloper; for, instead of seeking office from the king or the royal governor, or urging his hereditary claim to Eastern lands, he bethought himself of no better avenue to wealth than by cutting a shop-door through the side of his ancestral residence. It was the custom of the time, indeed, for merchants to store their goods and transact business in their own dwellings. But there was something pitifully small in this old Pyncheon's mode of setting about his commercial operations; it was whispered, that, with his own hands, all beruffled as they were, he used to give change for a shilling, and would turn a half-penny twice over, to make sure that it was a good one. Beyond all question, he had the blood of a petty huckster in his veins, through whatever channel it may have found its way there.

Immediately on his death, the shop-door had been locked, bolted, and barred, and, down to the period of our story, had probably never once been opened. The old counter, shelves, and other fixtures of the little shop remained just as he had left them. It used to be affirmed, that the dead shop-keeper, in a white wig, a faded velvet coat, an apron at his waist, and his ruffles carefully turned back from his wrists, might be seen through the chinks of the shutters, any night of the year, ransacking his till, or poring over the dingy pages of his day-book. From the look of unutterable woe upon his face, it appeared to be his doom to spend eternity in a vain effort to make his accounts balance.

And now—in a very humble way, as will be seen—we proceed to open our narrative.

From: J. W. de Forest, *Witching Times* (1857), chapter 10

This novel gives the witch trials their most detailed treatment in fiction. The main characters are invented, but all the others are based on actual people. The action follows the course of events from September 1691 to September 1693, fully confronting the injustice and horror of the examinations, trials, and hangings. Despite uneven writing, a curiously sub-Dickensian Samuel Parris, and an at times cloying love story, the novel brings to imaginative life the forces that drove the Salem witch-hunt, including professional self-interest. The portrayal of Nicholas Noyes as a judge whose obsessive love for the heroine causes him to try to destroy her husband and father is done with considerable psychological subtlety.

This excerpt, describing the state of affairs in Salem Village as the witch-hunt got underway, shows de Forest's shaky writing style but firm grasp of his subject matter.

A ghastly and blinding mist, like that which Tennyson saw in "The Vision of Sin," now gathered and linked around almost every soul in Salem. Through its distorting medium men looked with altered eyes upon each other and shivered at ugly forms and deeds which could not be and were not. Faint and vague was the agony, now, compared with its frantic culmination; yet, already it pierced everywhere, tremulous with frightful forebodings.

From Salem center to Salem village, hideous tales flew and returned, like shuttles of superstition, weaving all things, matter and spirit, into a pall of horror which seemed to shroud the whole community. The wind by day was ominous; the owl by night was appalling. The cat might be an incarnation of Satan; the creak of the floor might be his footstep. People looked with pale faces into their mirrors, fearful lest they should see reflected behind them some grisly demon. From house to house crept the fiendish infection, seizing on children as instruments, on grave men as dupes, on women and old persons—ay, even on the young and vigorous—as victims.

The delusion was like one of those hundred-armed monsters of the sea, flinging its poisonous antennae around every limb, and shooting a numb, helpless agony through every vein. Every family throbbed with fear and distrust; no one knew who would be next overtaken by the monstrous fatality; no one knew but that his nearest relative had covenanted with the enemy of souls. Men became more credulous, suspicious, and cruel-hearted, just in proportion as they grew more frantic with terror and fanaticism. The excitement was of a nature to develop the worst traits of the Puritans and change even their virtues into vices. The real piety and kindness of the many was for a time paralyzed; and those now disgraced the Christian religion who would willingly have laid down their lives for its glory.

Every day there was an increase in the number of the afflicted, and, parallel with it, a still greater increase in the number of the accused. Under the pressure of imprisonment, examinations, exhortations, and threats, persons began to confess themselves witches and to bear testimony against others as partners in their sin. Several misguided husbands, acting with a cruel conscientiousness and a shocking sincerity, actually bullied their pious wives into these horrible avowals. The jail was soon overcrowded; the Boston prisons were put in large requisition; yet the evil steadily increased, overleaping all barriers and submerging all remedies. It began even to be feared that the church had awakened to its peril too late and that already the greater part of the community had signed the bond of Satan. So, no effectual refuge remaining but God, to Him did all men fly with unutterable groanings and wailings; in prayer, public and private; in appointed fasts and fervent attendance at the sanctuary. Never had the churches been so full, nor the attention of the people to their ministers so earnest. Nor were the pastors unmindful of improving the day of their power. They preached often and zealously; they ransacked the Bible for texts on witchcraft; they were particularly stern in rebuking unbelief. Few were those who dared oppose their mistaken energy; all resistance seemed to have been quelled by the mere uproar of the coming storm.

Shall we abuse these old Puritans as stupid and superstitious because they did and suffered these things? Let us remember that Melancthon was an interpreter of dreams; that Luther fought the devil with an inkstand; that Kepler was of the Rosicrucians; that Tycho Brahe was the prince of astrologers; that Bishop Jewell prayed before Queen Elizabeth against witchcraft; that Blackstone held sorcery to be a crime; that the Stuarts pretended to heal scrofula; that Sir Isaac Newton sought the philosopher's stone.

Perhaps there were not more than three men in Salem who dared openly and vigorously denounce the present course of the community. These three were our utopian More, young Stanton, and farmer Cory. All three had the stuff in them out of which to manufacture a tough opposition party. More and Cory were obstinate, excitable, a little violent, gifted with that magnanimity which will not strike a helpless man, and, in short, just the fellows to stand up for the weak against the strong. Neither of them belonged to the church; both were perhaps a little undevotional, if not skeptical, in disposition; they at all events pretended to a considerable incredulity as to the devil; and, in their present exasperation, they spoke with extreme unbelief and scorn of the doctrine of witchcraft. Without this native tendency to free thinking, they would hardly have opposed the movement, for sorcery was a point of orthodox faith in those days—a matter of creed, in fact, with nearly all men. I do not mean to say that More was an atheist; on the contrary, he believed in God most reverently. Nor did he reject or lightly esteem the Bible. He simply interpreted it after a mild and humane fashion. In short, he was only skeptical by contrast with the rigid, implacable orthodoxy of that period; and, were he living in the present day, he would be, at the worst, a Unitarian or a Transcendentalist. As for Mark, he enlisted in the opposition chiefly through the influence of More, but partly, also, from the impulses of his own kind, sensible nature. It was a small army, certainly; and it had a great fight to undertake—a fight such as our latitudinarian age can illy realize.

Goody Bishop was swinging from the gallows as a signal of no quarter, like the death's head blowing at the topmast of a pirate schooner. More accepted the challenge and commenced the struggle with his characteristic enthusiasm and energy, disputing boldly, obstinately, and angrily on every occasion with the equally stubborn and wrathful advocates of the delusion. Like all sanguine people, he thought his own arguments unanswerable, and was filled with contemptuous, indignant amazement at the prejudices and contumacy of his opponents. "Master Curwin," he said, "it is you who are mulish and not I. You are mulish against reason, sir. You are so blown upon here, in New England, by harsh and sour winds of doctrine, that it makes you stiff-necked, sir, and wry-necked into the bargain, sir."

He went to Elder Higginson, and begged him to preach a sermon in opposition to, at least, the rashness and recklessness of the witch prosecutions. "Sir," said he, "even if you believe in sorcery, you cannot believe that we are all sorcerers. If you think it wrong to oppose the courts altogether, you can at least urge them to calmness, caution, and mercy. This is a horrible thing, to see members of your own flock, children of your own prayers, singled out as worse than demons."

The old man said that he had been very much distressed by the events of the last month; and he even wept once or twice during the conversation. The very next Sunday he preached a sermon on the subject, which won the enthusiastic approbation of More but which raised toward him the grim frowns of nearly the whole congregation. Justice Hawthorne got up and walked out of church, followed by two or three other fiery advocates of the prosecuting movement, while Justice Curwin waylaid the elder after service, and urged him, with tears in his stern, gray eyes, yet with grave reproof in his strong features, to give up those pernicious errors altogether, to throw aside those utterly dangerous thoughts of weak mercy. Deacon Bowson and almost every one else severely condemned Higginson's latitudinarianism and began to express doubts whether they could conscientiously sit under the ministrations of a man who was little better than Sadduceeistic.

Nobody called for a repetition of the sermon, nor could even More ask the elder to preach such another. So the old gentleman exchanged for a fortnight with Mr. Hall, of Beverly, who fed out far other spiritual food to the people of Salem; and, thereafter, he preached on that forbidden subject only in deeds, cheering the imprisoned, laboring with the condemned, giving what he could to widows and orphans. We must not blame him for not making himself a martyr; we must remember that, like most men of the epoch, he believed in sorcery; that he was afraid many of those accused ones were really guilty of the sin laid to their charge; and that the only part his conscience really called upon him to play was that of the good Samaritan.

More had another plan in his head, which was to get himself elected member of the general court from Salem, and bring in some new, wise, philosophical laws on the subject of witchcraft, which should forever put an end to these abuses. But that assembly would not meet until some time in the autumn, and, in the absence of the royal charter, everything was decided by the governor and council, while the very court which conducted the trials was an informal one, cited on the plea of instant necessity. Accordingly, he was reduced for the present to the circulation of a petition in which the evils and irregularities of the prosecutions were set forth and the governor was prayed to check them in his great good sense and clemency.

Oh, what arguments, what wranglings, what solemn reproofs, what regular oldwife scoldings More raised in scores of households with that paper! Farmer Peabody had just lost one of his calves; and he knew that it was all of that old witch (hang 'er up directly, I say), Goody Giggles. John Parker's wife, Alice, was safe in prison, at last; and John had no mind she should get out again to plague him with any more of her diableries. Mistress Margaret Hawkes's Negro slave girl, Candy, had been rendered quite useless, yea, rather mischievous, by somebody's witchcraft; and Mistress Hawkes naturally wanted remuneration, or, if that could not be had, legal vengeance for the loss of her Abigail's services. "Look at that black creeter," cried the frugal housewife, with indignant sniffs and snorts; "cost me twelve pound; ain't worth a shillin' now; don't do a stroke of work; breaks things all day long; can't mend her by no kind of cuffing."

Poor Mistress Hawkes! The next thing heard of, she and Candy were in prison for sorcery together.

Mistress Beadle's children were all bewitched, the whole kit and posse of them; and how could Master More expect *her* to sign a petition for mercy toward witches? She wished the women could "take hold of the business; 'deed she did; a lot on 'em would be swung up afore night, now I tell ye." In another house, the girl was spitting pins and shrieking; the boy was breaking crockery and trying to roll into the fire. As More lectured over his paper, a brickbat would come in through the window and smash the shining face of some unlucky platter which glittered on the mantelpiece; or a heavy table would commence dancing at such a rate as to endanger the precious noddle of the innocent little urchin who sat under it; or the housemaid would rush downstairs with shrieks, declaring that the best bedroom was full of broomsticks, and of awful figures dressed up in master's clothes; or the goodwife would return from an afflicted neighbor's, running over with astonishing, incredible, hideous tales of ghastly apparitions and fiendish annoyances. Fancy a whole neighborhood filled with Rochester knockings, Stratford mysteries, Cocklane ghosts, table-turnings, and animal magnetism, all vivified to madness by a blazing credulity, and you will have some faint idea of the condition of Salem.

More was canvassing it with his hopeless petition. He got six names besides his own and in a rage threw the paper into the fire. The very reasons why he was not a believer in the delusion disabled him from offering any successful opposition to it. Had he been orthodox and devout, he might have been listened to; but, in that case, he would probably have sided with the orthodox and devout majority. He was latitudinarian and indifferent; and so almost all good men regarded him with coldness, while those who favored him were apt to be the worst characters—

people who neglected church, and hated the clergy; sneerers at the Bible as well as scoffers at witchcraft; heretics, godless strangers, and dissolute sailors.

Quite beat out one day with his fruitless electioneering against the Juggernaut of the time, he stopped on his way home to obtain some groceries at Deacon Bowson's shop. That excitable merchant met him in the doorway, grasped him by the hand, and exclaimed, in a choaking voice, "Brother More!" Then turning away his head, and covering his face (not exactly like Caesar), he burst into tears. "What devil's to pay now?" cried More, getting into a rage immediately at this whimpering. "Oh! sir," snuffled the plaintive deacon, "to think that you and I should have fallen upon such awful times! How dreadful for us—cold—'fessors!"

Here his voice became inaudible again, and he melted into another moist and copious overflow. "Dreadful? Not a mite of it!" shouted More, dancing about the room with wrath. "I like it. I want to see it. Just show me one of your afflicted children, and see how I'll cure it."

And he brought down his fist on the counter with such force as to make all the iron weights hop up like nervous people when suddenly slapped on the shoulder. "Come, shut up those floodgates," he continued, catching Bowson by the collar, and tightening it as if he thought the water reached that gentleman's eyes through his windpipe. "Oh, Master More, don't strangulate me!" gasped the deacon, with hands aloft, and a purple face.

The hunter seemed to recollect that his friend had lungs, and, letting go of the collar, he began to slap the broad back of that claret broadcloth waistcoat. "There," said he, "I never meant to choke you; one person throttled a week is quite sufficient for one small town. But you make me mad with your snivelings and your lachrymations. I can't abear such watery-souled fellows, when I see the colony in so great need of cool, brave men. Come, get about, and deal me out some salt and spice, and eight yards of white linen for Rachel; linen for a gown, mind you; the same she looked at yestereve. And don't cry in the salt, I pray."

"Where are you going?" asked Bowson, panting for breath.

"Into the house, to see Sister Ann," replied the hunter, as he disappeared through a side door.

We must not attribute entire childishness to our good deacon on account of this ready flow of his tears. He was one of those juicy men, furnished by nature with too much lachrymal gland, who, at the pressure of any strong emotion, give forth an immediate supply of moisture. Tears of compassion and affectionate sympathy came from his eyes as easily as tears of unmanly terror.

More found his sister packing up a noble chicken pie for the especial digestion of Elder Noyse. "Why, Ann, have you gone at it too!" he exclaimed. "You women are enough, sometimes, to drive all sensible men mad. All the goodwives of Salem are cooking for the ministers. Send this to some poor person now, Sister Ann;

come, that will be a better use of the chickens. To think of putting all pullets of the village down the throats of two or three elders!"

So, Sister Ann, easily persuaded, dispatched Teague with the pie to the cabin of a dilapidated old goodwife of the vicinity. "What is the matter with pussy?" presently asked More, as he started at an overfed cat which was shivering and crouching under the table. "Oh," said Mrs. Bowson, "it is going to have a fit; that comes of overeating; I must really charge Rachel with the poor thing's ill health."

"You will feed your elders into fits, in the same way," observed More. He flung the door open and was trying to drive the creature out, when the deacon entered and shut it after him. In the same instant that epileptic pussy commenced spinning round on two legs, and, presently, set off in headlong furious circles about the room, knocking her insane head against various harder objects, bouncing desperately at the windows, and finally disappearing, with a scrabble, up chimney. At the very first start, Bowson leaped into a chair, and thence watched the frantic revolutions of the animal with eyes of scared vigilance. As it vanished up the vast sooty orifice of the fireplace, he pointed after it with one trembling finger, and squeaked out, "Wife, a manifestation!"

More burst into contemptuous laughter, and Mrs. Bowson exclaimed, in a mortified tone, "John, do get down! What do you mean? This is not the first time you have seen the cat in a fit."

"No," said he, cautiously descending from his high place of refuge, "not the first time; but I hope and pray it may be the last. Who knows what Satan may have to do with those whirligigs?"

And forgetting, apparently, why he came into the room, he walked out without another word. "Alas!" said Sister Ann, "I am afraid my husband's nature is not strong enough to keep a clear mind in these awful excitements. Since the execution of that poor Bishop, he has been greatly exercised, and what adds to his disquietude is that his best-beloved pastor, Elder Noyse, has now fully entered into the work. Until the trial, Master Noyse seemed strangely heedless of the spiritual mysteries among us; but then he awoke suddenly to an emulation of Elder Parris's zeal and urgency. On the Sunday before Bishop's death he gave us a powerful discourse on the fate of Agag and made application of it to those children of Satan who are supposed to be among us. And since then he has publicly and privately warned us against sorcery, besides visiting the afflicted, questioning the accused, and exhorting the magistrates to their work. I only hope that so much zeal is not wasted, and had not better be employed in pointing out the path to heaven than in trying to choke up the broad way to hell."

"Sister Ann," said More, "you are the same sensible woman always. I only wish that you would cast out this devil of witchcraft altogether from your belief. But I see that we shall agree in all that is important; that we shall stand by each other in the end. Clear your husband's mind of these magical ideas, as much as ever you can. You can do something for the cause of good sense and mercy in that way."

"I will pray for heavenly counsel, Brother," she replied, "and what God seems to favor, that I will strive to do."

More walked back into the shop, took his purchases without quarreling any further with the deacon, and set out for home. What he had said concerning the opulent state of the clerical larders was not exaggerated. The quantity of pies, cakes, puddings, turkeys, and choice edibles of all kinds, which the Salem goodwives poured into the houses of their ministers at this time was something memorable. Some wanted the spiritual consolations of the pastors in this dark hour of Satan's triumph; others had been intensely gratified by the last pungent discourse against the principalities and powers of the air; others, again, were anxious to secure friends in high places who could shield them from any chance accusation of witchcraft. Elder Noyse, being unmarried and therefore an object of general pity, was as overrun with good things as ever the Egyptians with frogs, and so forth. Parris, too, was unusually blessed in his basket and his store, and gave promise of blooming out into a brilliant case of apoplexy. Elder Higginson alone had to depend chiefly on home supplies.

More trudged on homeward, sad and sullen, recapitulating to himself with great contempt the absurd arguments which had been advanced against his petition during the day, occasionally wondering, in spite of his incredulity, at the incomprehensible phenomena which he had witnessed; anon laughing outright at the recollection of some scene of absurd simplicity and terror. He had already entered the forest when he heard footsteps behind him, and a familiar voice bidding him good evening. It was the first time since Elder Noyse's rejection, a period of about a month, that the two men had met to engage in conversation. The first words that the minister uttered showed, by their steady intonation, how much he had regained his confidence. How could he help it, when the whole community was prostrate at the feet of himself and his order? More, on the other hand, saluted him with extreme civility, for he was courteous by habit to women and the clergy; besides that, he wished to apologize tacitly for the pain which he had given the minister at their last interview. The dialogue which followed is of little consequence to our story, and perhaps in itself uninteresting; yet, after all, it may be worth the expense of a little time and paper, inasmuch as it sketches More's philosophy of life and shows the nature and degree of his heterodoxy.

"With your good will, sir," observed the minister, "I will hold you company as far as your cottage. These are wearying times to the spirit, which, indeed, could never endure them were not the members kept in health by vigorous exercise."

"Very justly said, Elder Noyse," responded More, quite pleased with this approval of one of his own favorite maxims. "I am much gratified to hear you advance and see you practice upon such reasonable ideas of life. I have always said that many of our doctrinal errors and rancorous emotions arise from our dwelling in bodies weakened by vicious habits. Yes, reverend sir, the pains and sorrows of humanity, bodily and spiritual, are the consequence, very often, of its own faults and follies, its own imprudence, luxury, and laziness. And look at the result, sir; it detracts from the nobility of endurance; it puts us on the footing of criminals rather than of martyrs. It is noble to endure agonies which come upon us unjustly, but it is no honor at all to bear the lash of our own misdeeds. Yes, when we suffer because of our own sins, then suffering becomes a crime more than a misfortune."

Two months before, the elder would have listened to all this in respectful silence, if not with uttered assent. But he had grown bolder now; he felt inclined to play the master and teacher; he was willing to triumph a little over this man who had so tortured him. "Master More," said he, "you forget that we always suffer in consequence of sin: our natural, original sin. And the very fact that we all go in anguish through this vale of mortality proves how thoroughly and personally each one of us partook of the disobedience of Adam."

"Reverend sir," replied More, "you must permit me to express some small doubts on that score. You say that men are evidently great sinners because they suffer greatly. But I believe that what we consider our sufferings are more apparent than real. For instance, death, or the fear of it, is one of the greatest torments of our existence; is it not? But if we could see the more perfect state into which death leads us, we should not regard it as terrible. Pain, also, if we could distinctly perceive the mental and bodily benefits which arise from it, would not be considered so much a thing to be avoided. Thus our sufferings consist more in a misapprehension of our situation than in any reality of anguish. At the same time, it is necessary that we should fear both pain and death, otherwise, man would rush upon fate and the race be extinguished before it had fulfilled its time."

"Master More," responded the elder, with an effort at severity, "do you know that you are doing away with the idea of punishment for sin, and thus either denying the condemning justice of heaven or else affirming that man is not a supremely guilty being? Do you not believe that man was created, and for a time existed, sinless? Do you not believe that he fell from that pure state by his own act, and brought upon himself and his posterity a just punishment?"

"I will tell you what I think of the fall," answered the hunter. "You theologians affirm that the original state of Adam was one of moral perfection; I affirm that the obligatory state of Adam was one of moral perfection. I only change the statement of the problem by that one word. Thus, I believe that his fall was not a fall from any actual state of purity but only from an idea of purity which God had imprinted on his conscience. I do not believe that he lived a while in a state of sinlessness; I believe that he fell with his first action, and, perhaps, with his first desire. I further believe, that man will fulfill this idea of perfection by steps to be taken partly in this world, partly in that to come. One great step to this end was the gradual growth of civility and morality through the many centuries of pagan history. Another greater step was the just example and self-elected sacrifice of Christ. Another great step to each one of us and, finally to the race, will be death. By this philosophy the moral history of Adam is made similar to the moral history of each of his successors. By this theory, also, we escape that incredible doctrine of original sin, and are not called upon, in logical necessity, to damn our infants."

"Master More," exclaimed Noyse, in some real indignation at these sweeping heresies, "I have heard it said, by a worthier man than I, that hell is paved with the skulls of infants."

More lost his temper—an article that he was constantly losing now—at this tremendous affirmation. "They must be infant Calvinists, then," said he; "for I know of no other skulls that would be thick enough for such a purpose."

As soon as he had uttered this uncivil sarcasm, he regretted it; and, as soon as he regretted it, he tried to make amends for it by an act of courtesy. He disliked to invite Noyse into the cabin and into Rachel's presence; yet he did so with appearance of perfect cordiality. The minister's heart vibrated in one second through many acceptances and refusals; but he yielded to the temptation. We may guess that, however earnest was his zeal for orthodoxy, the shadow of that roof suspended at once in his mind every disputatious wind of doctrine. He thought but of Rachel: how he should look her in the face; how he should address her. As he crossed the threshold, she raised her eyes from her ironing and flushed to a crimson, which was the antipodes of his own paleness. She thought for a moment that her father had been won over to the side of Noyse and had come with him to present once more that hateful suit. Her self-command partially returned when More's first expressions hinted to her that the visit was the result of accident; and then, like an inexperienced young thing as she was, ignorant of the cruel rights of coquetry, she felt that she owed the elder some amends for having refused his respectable hand and heart. She put her iron on the hearth, with its hot face to the smouldering coals, and sat respectfully down, nearly as hot faced herself, with folded hands and a look of serious attention.

As Noyse marked her gentle though forced smile, and the soft, subdued tremor visible through her eyes, and the beauty which clothed her more exuberantly than he had ever seen it before, all the anger that he might have harbored against her died away as if forever. The confidence of more than magisterial authority perished from his spirit, and he felt as if he could bend, ay, descend wonderfully, to secure one loving look from that blushing girl. He had to make a violent effort before he could rally his scattered wits and get them to charge into the breach of conversation. He did talk, however, and with that feverish animation which often marks the discourse of men distracted by some strong excitement.

The master of the house had a pet plan for converting and civilizing the Indians: he proposed to conquer them and hive them by force in some pleasant island of Barataria; there he would govern them by a system of socialism, as Moses governed the Hebrews and Lycurgus the Spartans; they would quit those disagreeable ways of taking scalps, and so forth, to become industrious, peaceful, and philosophical. Noyse, on the contrary, thought that nothing could be done effectually for the savages, except in the missionary way; and he gave a rather confused account of the pious labors of Eliot and Mayhew, among the decayed aboriginal populations of Massachusetts. Rachel timidly remarked that it was a pity if the English could not show the Indians to a better world, since they had left them so little room in this. The absent-minded elder highly approved of this observation, and gravely congratulated Rachel that she could see what was most needful for those poor heathens.

The interview lasted for half an hour; but it was a stiff, disagreeable one, and all three were more or less glad when it terminated. Yet Noyse, however relieved for the moment to get out of doors, went away from the cabin more enslaved than he ever had been previously. From that day, too, he began cautiously to resume his visits, much to the annoyance of Rachel, the perplexity of More, and the anguish of Mark Stanton. By the way, it was none of Stanton's business, although he was at the cabin at every spare moment, running backwards and forwards between it and the village in the enchanted haze of summer calms, or the weirdest of wizard winds, sometimes even through the demoniac fury and sorrow of rushing, howling, sobbing rains, sweeping on lightning wings from clouds of lofty darkness.

From: John Greenleaf Whittier, *Calef in Boston* (1849)

The poet and short-story writer who made most use of the Salem witch-hunt is John Greenleaf Whittier. His first poem on the subject, "The Weird Gathering," published in his first collection of poetry and prose, *Legends of New England,* in 1831, is highly melodramatic, beginning with the stanza,

A trumpet in the darkness blown—
A peal upon the air—
The church-yard answers to its tone
With boding shriek and wail and groan—
The dead are gliding there!

The poem describes a witches' gathering to which a woman comes to seek vengeance on a man who has wronged her. She sells her soul to the devil and ends by being hanged. The prose piece in the same collection, "The Haunted House," is equally simple and lurid. But Whittier's later poems using Salem witchcraft material—"Calef in Boston," "Moll Pitcher," "The Witch of Wenham," "Mabel Martin," and "Margaret Smith"—are subtler. "Calef in Boston" treats of the battle for the moral high ground between Robert Calef and Cotton Mather, with Calef winning hands down.

In the solemn days of old,
Two men met in Boston town,
One a tradesman frank and bold,
One a preacher of renown.

Cried the last, in bitter tone,—
"Poisonor of the wells of truth!
Satan's hireling thou hast sown
With his tares the heart of youth!"

Spake the simple tradesman then,—
"God be judge 'twixt thou and I;
All thou knowest of truth hath been
Unto men like thee a lie.

"Falsehoods which we spurn to-day
Were the truths of long ago;
Let the dead boughs fall away,
Fresher shall the living grow.

"God is good and God is light,
In this faith I rest secure;
Evil can but serve the right,
Over all shall love endure.

"Of your spectral puppet play
I have traced the cunning wires;
Come what will, I needs must say,
God is true, and ye are liars."

When the thought of man is free,
Error fears its lightest tones;

So the priest cried, "Sadducee!"
And the people took up stones.

In the ancient burying-ground,
Side by side the twain now lie,—
One with humble grassy mound,
One with marbles pale and high.

But the Lord hath blest the seed
Which that tradesman scattered then,
And the preacher's spectral creed
Chills no more the blood of men.

Let us trust, to one is known
Perfect love which casts out fear,
While the other's joys atone
For the wrong he suffered here.

From: H. W. Longfellow, *Giles Corey of the Salem Farms* (1868), act 1

Longfellow starts his play by showing Tituba gathering ingredients for her cauldron. He embellishes the sorcery myth by having her dupe Mary Walcott into thinking Sarah Good is bewitching her. In a debate between Cotton Mather and John Hathorne, in the face of the witchcraft, Cotton Mather is the voice of reason. However, later in the drama, Longfellow shows how superstition, greed, and the desire for vengeance drove on the persecution, sending Giles and Martha Corey to their deaths.

SCENE I. *The woods near Salem Village. Enter* TITUBA, *with a basket of herbs.*

TITUBA. Here's monk's-hood, that breeds fever in the blood;
And deadly nightshade, that makes men see ghosts;
And henbane, that will shake them with convulsions;
And meadow-saffron and black hellebore,
That rack the nerves, and puff the skin with dropsy;
And bitter-sweet, and briony, and eye-bright,
That cause eruptions, nosebleed, rheumatisms:
I know them, and the places where they hide
In field and meadow; and I know their secrets

And gather them because they give me power
Over all men and women. Armed with these,
I, Tituba, an Indian and a slave,
Am stronger than the captain with his sword,
Am richer than the merchant with his money,
Am wiser than the scholar with his books,
Mightier than Ministers and Magistrates,
With all the fear and reverence that attend them!
For I can fill their bones with aches and pains,
Can make them cough with asthma, shake with palsy,
Can make their daughters see and talk with ghosts,
Or fall into delirium and convulsions.
I have the Evil Eye, the Evil Hand:
A touch from me, and they are weak with pain;
A look from me, and they consume and die.
The death of cattle and the blight of corn,
The shipwreck, the tornado, and the fire,—
These are my doings, and they know it not.
Thus I work vengeance on mine enemies,
Who, while they call me slave, are slaves to me!

Exit TITUBA.

Enter MATHER, *booted and spurred, with a riding-whip in his hand.*

MATHER. Methinks that I have come by paths unknown
Into the land and atmosphere of Witches;
For, meditating as I journeyed on,
Lo! I have lost my way! If I remember
Rightly, it is Scribonius the learned
That tells the story of a man who, praying
For one that was possessed by Evil Spirits,
Was struck by Evil Spirits in the face;
I, journeying to circumvent the Witches,
Surely by Witches have been led astray.
I am persuaded there are few affairs
In which the Devil doth not interfere.
We cannot undertake a journey even,
But Satan will be there to meddle with it
By hindering or by furthering. He hath led me

Into this thicket, struck me in the face
With branches of the trees, and so entangled
The fetlocks of my horse with vines and brambles,
That I must needs dismount, and search on foot
For the lost pathway leading to the village.
Re-enter TITUBA. What shape is this? What monstrous apparition,
Exceeding fierce, that none may pass that way?
Tell me, good woman, if you are a woman—

TITUBA. I am a woman, but I am not good.
I am a Witch!

MATHER. Then tell me, Witch and woman,
For you must know the pathways through this wood,
Where lieth Salem Village?

TITUBA. Reverend sir,
The village is near by. I'm going there
With these few herbs. I'll lead you. Follow me.

MATHER. First say, who are you? I am loth to follow
A stranger in this wilderness, for fear
Of being misled, and left in some morass.
Who are you?

TITUBA. I am Tituba the Witch,
Wife of John Indian.

MATHER. You are Tituba?
I know you then. You have renounced the Devil,
And have become a penitent confessor.
The Lord be praised! Go on, I'll follow you.
Wait only till I fetch my horse, that stands
Tethered among the trees, not far from here.

TITUBA. Let me get up behind you, reverend sir.

MATHER. The Lord forbid! What would the people think,
If they should see the Reverend Cotton Mather
Ride into Salem with a Witch behind him?
The Lord forbid!

TITUBA. I do not need a horse;
I can ride through the air upon a stick,
Above the tree-tops and above the houses,
And no one see me, no one overtake me!

[*Exeunt.*]

SCENE II.
A room at JUSTICE HATHORNE'S. *A clock in the corner. Enter* HATHORNE *and* MATHER.

HATHORNE. You are welcome, reverend sir, thrice welcome here
Beneath my humble roof.

MATHER. I thank your Worship.

HATHORNE. Pray you be seated. You must be fatigued
With your long ride through unfrequented woods.
[*They sit down.*]

MATHER. You know the purport of my visit here,—
To be advised by you, and counsel with you,
And with the Reverend Clergy of the village,
Touching these witchcrafts that so much afflict you;
And see with mine own eyes the wonders told
Of spectres and the shadows of the dead,
That come back from their graves to speak with men.

HATHORNE. Some men there are, I have known such, who think
That the two worlds—the seen and the unseen,
The world of matter and the world of spirit—
Are like the hemispheres upon our maps,
And touch each other only at a point.
But these two worlds are not divided thus,
Save for the purposes of common speech.
They form one globe, in which the parted seas
All flow together and are intermingled,
While the great continents remain distinct.

MATHER. I doubt it not. The spiritual world
Lies all about us, and its avenues

Are open to the unseen feet of phantoms
That come and go, and we perceive them not
Save by their influence, or when at times
A most mysterious Providence permits them
To manifest themselves to mortal eyes.

HATHORNE. You, who are always welcome here among us,
Are doubly welcome now. We need your wisdom,
Your learning in these things, to be our guide.
The Devil hath come down in wrath upon us,
And ravages the land with all his hosts.

MATHER. The Unclean Spirit said, "My name is Legion!"
Multitudes in the Valley of Destruction!
But when our fervent, well-directed prayers,
Which are the great artillery of Heaven,
Are brought into the field, I see them scattered
And driven like Autumn leaves before the wind.

HATHORNE. You, as a Minister of God, can meet them
With spiritual weapons; but, alas!
I, as a Magistrate, must combat them
With weapons from the armory of the flesh.

MATHER. These wonders of the world invisible,—
These spectral shapes that haunt our habitations,—
The multiplied and manifold afflictions
With which the aged and the dying saints
Have their death prefaced and their age embittered,—
Are but prophetic trumpets that proclaim
The Second Coming of our Lord on earth.
The evening wolves will be much more abroad,
When we are near the evening of the world.

HATHORNE. When you shall see, as I have hourly seen,
The sorceries and the witchcrafts that torment us,
See children tortured by invisible spirits,
And wasted and consumed by powers unseen,
You will confess the half has not been told you.

MATHER. It must be so. The death-pangs of the Devil

Will make him more a Devil than before,
And Nebuchadnezzar's furnace will be heated
Seven times more hot before its putting out.

HATHORNE. Advise me, reverend sir. I look to you
For counsel and for guidance in this matter.
What further shall we do?

MATHER. Remember this,
That as a sparrow falls not to the ground
Without the will of God, so not a Devil
Can come down from the air without his leave.
We must inquire.

HATHORNE. Dear sir, we have inquired;
Sifted the matter thoroughly through and through,
And then resifted it.

MATHER. If God permits
These Evil Spirits from the unseen regions
To visit us with surprising informations,
We must inquire what cause there is for this,
But not receive the testimony borne
By spectres as conclusive proof of guilt
In the accused.

HATHORNE. Upon such evidence
We do not rest our case. The ways are many
In which the guilty do betray themselves.

MATHER. Be careful. Carry the knife with such exactness,
That on one side no innocent blood be shed
By too excessive zeal, and, on the other,
No shelter given to any work of darkness.

HATHORNE. For one, I do not fear excess of zeal.
What do we gain by parleying with the Devil?
You reason, but you hesitate to act!
Ah, reverend sir! believe me, in such cases
The only safety is in acting promptly.
'Tis not the part of wisdom to delay

In things where not to do is still to do
A deed more fatal than the deed we shrink from.
You are a man of books and meditation,
But I am one who acts.

MATHER. God give us wisdom
In the directing of this thorny business,
And guide us, lest New England should become
Of an unsavory and sulphurous odor
In the opinion of the world abroad!

[*The clock strikes.*]

I never hear the striking of a clock
Without a warning and an admonition
That time is on the wing, and we must quicken
Our tardy pace in journeying Heavenward,
As Israel did in journeying Canaan-ward!

[*They rise*].

HATHORNE. Then let us make all haste; and I will show you
In what disguises and what fearful shapes
The Unclean Spirits haunt this neighborhood,
And you will pardon my excess of zeal.

MATHER. Ah, poor New England! He who hurricanoed
The house of Jacob is making now on thee
One last assault, more deadly and more snarled
With unintelligible circumstances
Than any thou hast hitherto encountered!

[*Exeunt.*]

SCENE III.
A room in WALCOT'S *house.* MARY WALCOT *seated in an arm-chair.* TITUBA *with a mirror.*

MARY. Tell me another story, Tituba.
A drowsiness is stealing over me
Which is not sleep; for, though I close mine eyes,

I am awake, and in another world.
Dim faces of the dead and of the absent
Come floating up before me,—floating, fading,
And disappearing.

TITUBA. Look into this glass.
What see you?

MARY. Nothing but a golden vapor.
Yes, something more. An island, with the sea
Breaking all round it, like a blooming hedge.
What land is this?

TITUBA. It is San Salvador,
Where Tituba was born. What see you now?

MARY. A man all black and fierce.

TITUBA. That is my father.
He was an Obi man, and taught me magic,—
Taught me the use of herbs and images.
What is he doing?

MARY. Holding in his hand
A waxen figure. He is melting it
Slowly before a fire.

TITUBA. And now what see you?

MARY. A woman lying on a bed of leaves,
Wasted and worn away. Ah she is dying!

TITUBA. That is the way the Obi men destroy
The people they dislike! That is the way
Some one is wasting and consuming you.

MARY. You terrify me, Tituba! Oh, save me
From those who make me pine and waste away!
Who are they? Tell me.

TITUBA. That I do not know.

But you will see them. They will come to you.

MARY. No, do not let them come! I cannot bear it!
I am too weak to bear it! I am dying!
[*Falls into a trance.*]

TITUBA. Hark! there is some one coming!
Enter HATHORNE, MATHER, *and* WALCOT.

WALCOT. There she lies,
Wasted and worn by devilish incantations!
O my poor sister!

MATHER. Is she always thus?

WALCOT. Nay, she is sometimes tortured by convulsions.

MATHER. Poor child! How thin she is! How wan and wasted!

HATHORNE. Observe her. She is troubled in her sleep.

MATHER. Some fearful vision haunts her.

HATHORNE. You now see
With your own eyes, and touch with your own hands,
The mysteries of this Witchcraft.

MATHER. One would need
The hands of Briareus and the eyes of Argus
To see and touch them all.

HATHORNE. You now have entered
The realm of ghosts and phantoms,—the vast realm
Of the unknown and the invisible,
Through whose wide-open gates there blows a wind
From the dark valley of the shadow of Death,
That freezes us with horror.

MARY (*starting*). Take her hence!
Take her away from me! I see her there!
She's coming to torment me!

WALCOT(*taking her hand*). O my sister!
What frightens you? She neither hears nor sees me.
She's in a trance.

MARY. Do you not see her there?

TITUBA. My child, who is it?

MARY. Ah, I do not know.
I cannot see her face.

TITUBA. How is she clad?

MARY. She wears a crimson bodice. In her hand
She holds an image, and is pinching it
Between her fingers. Ah, she tortures me;
I see her face now. It is Goodwife Bishop!
Why does she torture me? I never harmed her!
And now she strikes me with an iron rod!
Oh, I am beaten!

MATHER. This is wonderful!
I can see nothing! Is this apparition
Visibly there, and yet we cannot see it?

HATHORNE. It is. The spectre is invisible
Unto our grosser senses, but she sees it.

MARY. Look! look! there is another clad in gray!
She holds a spindle in her hand, and threatens
To stab me with it! It is Goodwife Corey!
Keep her away! Now she is coming at me!
Oh mercy! mercy!

WALCOT (*thrusting with his sword*). There is nothing there!

MATHER (*to* HATHORNE). Do you see anything?

HATHORNE. The laws that govern
The spiritual world prevent our seeing
Things palpable and visible to her.

These spectres are to us as if they were not.
Mark her; she wakes.
[TITUBA *touches her, and she awakes.*]

MARY. Who are these gentlemen?

WALCOT. They are our friends. Dear Mary, are you better?

MARY. Weak, very weak.
[*Taking a spindle from her lap, and holding it up.*]
How came this spindle here?

TITUBA. You wrenched it from the hand of Goodwife Corey
When she rushed at you.

HATHORNE. Mark that, reverend sir!

MATHER. It is most marvellous, most inexplicable!

TITUBA (*picking up a bit of gray cloth from the floor*). And here, too, is a bit of her gray dress,
That the sword cut away.

MATHER. Beholding this,
It were indeed by far more credulous
To be incredulous than to believe.
None but a Sadducee, who doubts of all
Pertaining to the spiritual world,
Could doubt such manifest and damning proofs!
HATHORNE.Are you convinced?

MATHER (*to* MARY). Dear child, be comforted!
Only by prayer and fasting can you drive
These Unclean Spirits from you. An old man
Gives you his blessing. God be with you, Mary!

END OF ACT I.

From: Mary E. Wilkins Freeman, *Giles Corey* (1893), act 3

Mary E. Wilkins Freeman anticipates Arthur Miller's plot device in *The Crucible* of a love motive for the first witchcraft accusations. Acts I and II have established that Ann Hutchinson is in love with Paul Bayley and jealous of Olive Corey, Giles and Martha's daughter. Act III, reproduced here, blends fact and fiction to show the train of events at Olive Corey's trial, which leads to Giles Corey's arrest and imprisonment.

The Meeting-house in Salem Village. Enter People of Salem Village *and take seats. The* Afflicted Girls, *among whom are* Ann Hutchins *and* Mercy Lewis, *occupy the front seats.* Nancy Fox *and* Phœbe. *Enter the magistrates* John Hathorne *and* Jonathan Corwin *with* Minister Parris, *escorted by the* Marshal, Aids, *and four* Constables. *They place themselves at a long table in front of the pulpit.*

Hathorne (*rising*).We are now prepared to enter upon the examination. We invoke the blessing of God upon our proceedings, and call upon the Marshal to produce the bodies of the accused.

[*Exeunt* Marshal *and* Constables. Afflicted Girls *twist about and groan. Great excitement among the people.*]

[*Enter* Marshal *and* Constables *leading* Martha *and* Olive Corey *in chains.* Giles *follows. The prisoners are placed facing the assembly, with the* Constables *holding their hands.* Giles *stands near. The* Afflicted Girls *make a great clamor.*]

Ann. Oh, they are tormenting! They will be the death of me! I will not! I will not!

Giles. Hush your noise, will ye, Ann Hutchins!

Parris. Peace, Goodman Corey!

Hathorne. Martha Corey, you are now in the hands of authority. Tell me now why you hurt these persons.

Martha. I do not. I pray your worships give me leave to go to prayer.

Hathorne. We have not sent for you to go to prayer, but to confess that you are a witch.

Martha. I am no witch. I am a gospel woman. There is no such thing as a witch. Shall I confess that I am what doth not exist? It were not only a lie, but a fool's lie.

Mercy. There is a black man whispering in her ears.

Hathorne. What saith the black man to you, goodwife?

Martha. I pray your worships to ask the maid. Perchance, since she sees him, she can also hear what he saith better than I.

Hathorne. Why do you not tell how the devil comes in your shape and hurts these maids?

Martha. How can I tell how? I was never acquaint with the ways of the devil. I leave it to those wise maids who are so well acquaint to tell how. Perchance he hath whispered it in their ears.

Afflicted Girls. Oh, there is a yellow bird! There is a yellow bird perched on her head!

Hathorne. What say you to that, Goodwife Corey?

Martha. What can I say to such folly?

Hathorne. Constables, let go the hands of Martha Corey.

[*The* Constables *let go her hands, and immediately there is a great outcry from the* Afflicted Girls.]

Afflicted Girls. She pinches us! Hold her hands! Hold her hands again! Oh! oh!

Ann. She is upon me again! She digs her fingers into my throat! Hold her hands! Hold her hands! She will be the death of me!

Giles. Devil take ye, ye lying trollop! 'Tis a pity somebody had not been the death of ye before this happened!

Hathorne. Constables, hold the hands of the accused.

[Constables *obey, and at once the afflicted are quiet.*]

Hathorne. Goodwife Corey, what do you say to this?

Martha. I see with whom we have to do. May the Lord have mercy upon us!

Hathorne. What say you to the charges that your husband, Giles Corey, hath many a time brought against you in the presence of witnesses—that you hindered him when he would go to prayer, causing the words to go from him strangely; that you were out after nightfall, and did ride home on a broomstick; and that you scoffed at these maids and their affliction, as if you were a witch yourself?

Giles. I said not so! Martha, I said it not so!

Hathorne. What say you to your husband's charge that you did afflict his ox and cat, causing his ox to fall in the yard, and the cat to be strangely sick?

Giles. Devil take the ox and the cat! I said not that she did afflict them.

Hathorne. Peace, Goodman Corey; you are now in court.

Martha. I say, if a gospel woman is to be hung as a witch for every stumbling ox and sick cat, 'tis setting a high value upon oxen and cats.

Giles. I would mine had all been knocked in the head, lass, and me too!

Hathorne. Peace! Ann Hutchins, what saw you when Goodwife Corey went home with you through the wood?

Ann. Hold fast her hands, I pray, or she will kill me. The trees were so full of yellow birds that it sounded as if a mighty wind passed over them, and the birds lit on Goody Corey's head. And black beasts ran alongside through the bushes, which did break and crackle, and they were at Goody Corey and me to go to the witch dance on the hill. And they said to bring Olive Corey and Paul Bayley. And Goody Corey told them how she and Olive would presently come, but not Paul, for he never would sign the book, not even though Olive trapped him by the arts they had taught her. And Goody Corey showed me the book then, and besought me to sign, and go with her to the dance. And when I would not, she and Olive also afflicted me so grievously that I thought I could not live, and have done so ever since.

Hathorne. What say you to this, Goodwife Corey?

Martha. I pray your worship believe not what she doth charge against my daughter.

Corwin. Mercy Lewis, do you say that you have seen both of the accused afflicting Ann Hutchins?

Mercy. Yes, your worship, many a time have I seen them pressing her to sign the book, and afflicting when she would not.

Corwin. How looked the book?

Mercy. 'Twas black, your worship, with blood-red clasps.

Corwin. Read you the names in it?

Mercy. I strove to, your worship, but I got not through the C's; there were too many of them.

Hathorne. Let the serving-woman, Nancy Fox, come hither.

[Nancy Fox *makes her way to the front.*]

Hathorne. Nancy, I have heard that your mistress afflicts you.

Nancy. That she doth.

Hathorne. In what manner?

Nancy. She sendeth me to bed at first candlelight as though I were a babe; she maketh me to wear a woollen petticoat in winter-time, though I was not brought up to't; and she will never let me drink more than one mug of cider at a sitting, and I nigh eighty, and needing on't to warm my bones.

Corwin. Hath she ever afflicted you? Your replies be not to the point, woman.

Nancy. Your worship, she hath never had any respect for my understanding, and that hath greatly afflicted me.

Hathorne. Hath she ever shown you a book to sign?

Nancy. Verily she hath; and when I would not, hath afflicted me with sore pains in all my bones, so I cried out, on getting up, when I had set awhile.

Hathorne. Hath your mistress a familiar?

Nancy. Hey?

Hathorne. Have you ever seen any strange thing with her?

Nancy. She hath a yellow bird which sits on her cap when she churns.

Hathorne. What else have you seen with her?

Nancy. A thing like a cat, only it went on two legs. It clawed up the chimbly, and the soot fell down, and Goody Corey set me to sweeping on't up on the Lord's day.

Giles. Out upon ye, ye lying old jade!

Hathorne. Silence! Nancy, you may go to your place. Phœbe Morse, come hither.

[Phœbe Morse *approaches with her apron over her face, sobbing. She has her doll under her arm.*]

Hathorne. Cease weeping, child. Tell me how your aunt Corey treats you. Hath she ever taught you otherwise than you have learned in your catechism?

Phœbe (*weeping*). I don't know. Oh, Aunt Corey, I didn't mean to! I took the pins out of my doll. I did. Don't whip me for it.

Hathorne. What doll? What mean you, child?

Phœbe. I don't know. I didn't stick them in so very deep, Aunt Corey! Don't let them hang me for it!

Hathorne. Did your aunt Corey teach you to stick pins into your doll to torment folk?

Phœbe (*sobbing convulsively*). I don't know! I don't know! Oh, Aunt Corey, don't let them hang me! Olive, you won't let them! Oh! oh!

Corwin. Methinks 'twere as well to make an end of this.

Hathorne. There seemeth to me important substance under this froth of tears. (*To* Phœbe.) Give me thy doll, child.

Phœbe (*clutching the doll*). Oh, my doll! my doll! Oh, Aunt Corey, don't let them have my doll!

Martha. Peace, dear child! Thou must not begrudge it. Their worships be in sore distress just now to play with dolls.

Parris. Give his worship the doll, child. Hast thou not been taught to respect them in authority?

[Phœbe *gives the doll to* Hathorne, *whimpering.* Hathorne, Corwin, *and* Parris *put their heads together over it.*]

Hathorne (*holding up the doll*). There be verily many pins in this image. Goodwife Corey, what know you of this?

Martha. Your worship, such a weighty matter is beyond my poor knowledge.

Hathorne. Know you whence the child got this image?

Martha. Yes, your worship. I myself made it out of a piece of an old homespun blanket for the child to play with. I stuffed it with lamb's wool, and sewed some green ravellings on its head for hair. I made it a coat out of my copperas-colored petticoat, and colored its lips and cheeks with pokeberries.

Hathorne. Did you teach the child to stick in these pins wherewith to torment folk?

Martha. It availeth me naught to say no, your worship.

Mercy (*screams*). Oh, a sharp pain shoots through me when I look at the image! 'Tis through my arms! Oh!

Hathorne (*examining the doll*). There is a pin in the arms.

Ann. I feel sharp pains, like pins, in my face; oh, 'tis dreadful!

Hathorne (*examining the doll*). There are pins in the face.

Phœbe (*sobbing*). No, no! Those are the pins I stuck in for Aunt Corey. Don't let them hang me, Aunt Corey.

Parris. That is sufficient. She has confessed.

Hathorne. Yes, methinks the child hath confessed whether she would or no. Goodwife Corey, Phœbe hath now plainly said that she did stick these pins in this image for you. What have you to say?

Martha (*courtesying*). Your worship, the matter is beyond my poor speech.

[Hathorne *tosses the doll on the table,* Phœbe *watching anxiously.*]

Hathorne. Go to your place, child.

Phœbe. I want my doll.

Parris. Go to thy place as his worship bids thee, and think on the precepts in thy catechism. [Phœbe *returns sobbing.*]

Afflicted Girls. Oh, Goody Corey turns her eyes upon us! Bid her turn her eyes away!

Ann. Oh, I see a black cat sitting on Goody Corey's shoulder, and his eyes are like coals. Now, now, he looks at me when Goody Corey does! Look away! look away! Oh, I am blind! I am blind! Sparks are coming into my eyes from Goody Corey's. Make her turn her eyes away, your worships; make her turn her eyes away!

Hathorne. Goody Corey, fix your eyes upon the floor, and look not at these poor children whom you so afflict.

Martha. May the Lord open the eyes of the magistrates and ministers, and give them sight to discover the guilty!

Parris. Why do you not confess that you are a witch?

Martha (*with sudden fervor*). I am no witch. There is no such thing as a witch. Oh, ye worshipful magistrates, ye ministers and good people of Salem Village, I pray ye hear me speak for a moment's space. Listen not to this testimony of distracted children, this raving of a poor lovesick, jealous maid, who should be treated softly, but not let to do this mischief. Ye, being in your fair wits and well acquaint with your own knowledge, must know, as I know, that there be no witches. Wherefore would God let Satan after such wise into a company of His elect? Hath He not guard over His own precinct? Can He not keep it from the power of the Adversary as well as we from the savages? Why keep ye the scouts out in the fields if the Lord God hath so forsaken us? Call in the scouts! If we believe in witches, we believe not only great wickedness, but great folly of the Lord God. Think ye in good faith that I verily stand here with a black cat on my shoulder and a yellow bird on my head? Why do ye not see them as well as these maids? I would that ye might if they be there. Black cat, yellow bird, if ye be upon my shoulder and my head, as these maids say, I command ye to appear to these magistrates! Otherwise, if I have signed the book, as these maids say, I swear unto ye that I will cross out my name, and will serve none but the God Almighty. Most worshipful magistrates, see ye the black cat? See ye any yellow bird? Why are ye not afflicted as well as these maids, when I turn my eyes upon ye? I pray you to consider that. I am no saint; I wot well that I have but poorly done the will of the Lord who made me, but I am a gospel woman and keep to the faith according to my poor measure. Can I be a gospel woman and a witch too? I have never that I know of done aught of harm whether to man or beast. I have spared not myself nor minded mine own infirmities in tasks for them that belonged to me, nor for any neighbor that had need. I say not this to set myself up, but to prove to you that I can be no witch, and my daughter can be no witch. Have I not watched nights without number with the sick? Have I not washed and dressed new-born babes? Have I not helped to make the dead ready for burial, and sat by them until the cock crew? Have I ever held back when there was need of me? But I say not this to set myself up. Have I not been in the meeting-house every Lord's day? Have I ever stayed away from the sacrament? Have I not gone in sober apparel, nor wasted my husband's substance? Have I not been diligent in my household, and spun and wove great store of linen? Are not my floors scoured, my brasses bright, and my cheese-room well filled? Look at me! Can I be a witch?

Ann. A black man hath been whispering in her ear, telling her what to say.

Hathorne. What say you to that, Goody?

Martha. I say if that be so, he told me not to his own advantage. I see with whom I have to do. I pray you give me leave to go to prayer.

Hathorne. You are not here to go to prayer. I much fear that your many prayers have been to your master, the devil. Constables, bring forward the body of the accused.

[Afflicted Girls *shriek.* Constables *lead* Olive *forward.* Martha *is led to one side.*]

Martha. Be of good cheer, dear child.
Giles. Yes, be not afraid of them, lass; thy father is here.
Hathorne. Silence! Olive Corey, why do you so afflict these other maids?
Olive. I do not, your worship.
Ann. She is looking at me. Oh, bid her look away, or she will kill me!
Olive. Oh, Ann, I do not! What mean you, dear Ann?
Hathorne. I charge you, Olive Corey, keep your eyes upon the floor.
Giles. Look where you please, lass, and thy old father will uphold thee in it; and I only wish your blue eyes could shoot pins into the lying hussies.
Hathorne. Goodman, an ye disturb the peace again, ye shall be removed from court. Ann Hutchins, you have seen this maid hurt you?
Ann. Many a time she hath hurt me nigh to death.
Olive. Oh, Ann, I hurt thee?
Ann. There is a flock of yellow birds around her head.

[Olive *moves her head involuntarily, and looks up.*]

Afflicted Girls. See her look at them!
Hathorne. What say you to that, Olive?
Olive. I did not see them.
Hathorne. Ann Hutchins, did you see this maid walking in the wood with a black man last week?
Ann. Yes, your worship.
Hathorne. How did he go?
Ann. In black clothes, and he had white hair.
Hathorne. How went the accused?
Ann. She went in her flowered petticoat, and the flowers stood out, and smelt like real ones; her kerchief shone like a cobweb in the grass in the morning, and gold sparks flew out of her hair. Goody Corey fixed her up so with her devilish arts to trap Paul Bayley.
Hathorne. What mean you?
Ann. To trap the black man, your worship. I knew not what I said, I was in such torment.
Hathorne. Olive Corey, did your mother ever so change your appearance by her arts?

Olive. My mother hath no arts, your worship.

Ann. Her cheeks were redder than was common, and her eyes shone like stars.

Hathorne. Olive, did your mother so change your looks.

Olive. No, your worship; I do not know what Ann may mean. I fear she be ill.

Hathorne. Mercy Lewis, did you see Olive Corey with the black man?

Mercy. Yes, your worship; and she called out to me to go with them to the dance, and I should have the black man for a partner; and when I would not she afflicted me, pulling my hair and pinching me.

Hathorne. How appeared she to you?

Mercy. She was dressed like a puppet, finer than I had ever seen her.

Hathorne. Olive, what did you wear when you walked with the black man?

Olive. Your worship, I walked with no black man.

Ann. There he is now, standing behind her, looking over her shoulder.

Hathorne. What say you to that, Olive?

Olive (*looking in terror over her shoulder*). I see no one. I pray you, let my father stand near me.

Parris. Nay: the black man is enough for you.

Giles (*forcing his way to his daughter*). Here I be, lass; and it will go hard if the hussies can see the black man and old Giles in one place. Where be the black man now, jades?

Hathorne (*angrily*). Marshal!

Corwin (*interposing*). Nay, good Master Hathorne, let Goodman Corey keep his standing. The maid looks near swooning, and albeit his manner be rude, yet his argument hath somewhat of force. In truth, he and the black man cannot occupy one place. Mercy Lewis, see you now this black man anywhere?

Mercy. Yes, your worship.

Corwin. Where?

Mercy. Whispering in your worship's ear.

Parris. May the Lord protect his magistrates from the wiles of Satan, and maintain them in safety for the weal of his afflicted people!

Hathorne. This be going too far. This be presumption! Who of you now see the black man whispering to the worshipful esquire Jonathan Corwin?

Mercy. He is gone now out of the meeting-house. 'Twas but for a moment I saw him.

Corwin. Speak up, children. Did any other of ye see the black man whispering to me?

Afflicted Girls. No! no! no!

Corwin. Mercy Lewis, you say of a truth you saw him?

Mercy. Your worship, it may have been Minister Parris's shadow falling across the platform.

Corwin. This is but levity, and hath naught to do with the trial.

Hathorne. We will proceed with the examination. Widow Eunice Hutchins produce the cape.

[Widow Hutchins *comes forward, holding the cape by a corner.*]

Hathorne. Put it over your daughter's shoulders.
Hutchins. Oh, your worships, I pray you not! It will kill her!
Ann. Oh, do not! do not! It will kill me! Oh, mother, do not! Oh, your worships! Oh, Minister Parris!
Parris. Why put the maid to this needless agony?
Corwin. Put the cape over her shoulders.

[Widow Hutchins *approaches* Ann *hesitatingly, and throws the cape over her shoulders.* Ann *sinks upon the floor, shrieking.*]

Ann. Take it off! Take it off! It burns! It burns! Take it off! Have mercy! I shall die! I shall die!
Hathorne. Take off the cape; that is enough. Olive Corey, what say you to this? This is the cape you gave Ann Hutchins.
Olive. Oh, mother! mother!
Martha (*pushing forward*). Nay, I will speak again. Ye shall not keep me from it; ye shall not send me out of the meeting-house! (*The afflicted cry out.*) Peace, or I will afflict ye in earnest! I *will* speak! If I be a witch, as ye say, then ye have some reason to fear me, even ye most worshipful magistrates and ministers. It might happen to ye even to fall upon the floor in torment, and it would ill accord with your offices. Ye shall hear me. I speak no more for myself—ye may go hang me—I speak for my child. Ye shall not hang her, or judgment will come upon ye. Ye know there is no guile in her; it were monstrous to call her a witch. It were less blasphemy to call her an angel than a witch, and ye know it. Ye know it, all ye maids she hath played with and done her little kindnesses to, ye who would now go hang her. That cape—that cape, most worshipful magistrates, did the dear child earn with her own little hands, that she might give it to Ann, whom she loved so much. Knowing, as she did, that Ann was poor, and able to have but little bravery of apparel, it was often on her mind to give her somewhat of her own, albeit that was but scanty; and she hath toiled overtimes at her wheel all winter, and sold the yarn in Salem, and so gained a penny at a time wherewithal to buy that cape for Ann. And now will it hang her, the dear child?

Dear Ann, dost thou not remember how thou and my Olive have spent days together, and slept together many a night, and lain awake till dawn talking? Dost thou not remember how thou couldst go nowhere without Olive, nor she without thee, and how no little junketing were complete to the one were the other not there? Dost thou not remember how Olive wept when thy father died? Mercy Lewis, dost thou not remember how my Olive came over and helped thee in thy work that time thou wert ailing, and how she lent thee her shoes to walk to Salem?

Oh, dear children, oh, maids, who have been playmates and friends with my dear child, ye will not do her this harm! Do ye not know that she hath never harmed ye, and would die first? Think of the time when this sickness, that is nigh to madness, shall have passed over, and all is quiet again. Then will ye sit in the meeting-house of a Lord's day, and look over at the place where my poor child was wont to sit listening in her little Sabbath best, and ye will see her no more, but will say to yourselves that ye have murdered her. And then of a week-day ye will see her no more spinning at her wheel in the doorway, nor tending the flowers in her garden. She will come smiling in at your doors no more, nor walk the village street, and ye will always see where she is not, and know that ye have murdered her. Oh, poor children, ye are in truth young, and your minds, I doubt not, sore bewildered! If I have spoken harshly to ye, I pray ye heed it not, except as concerns me. I wot well that I am now done with this world, and I feel already the wind that bloweth over Gallows Hill in my face. But consider well ere ye do any harm to my dear child, else verily the day will come when ye will be more to be pitied than she. Oh, ye will not harm her! Ye will take back your accusation! Oh, worshipful magistrates, oh, Minister Parris, I pray you have mercy upon this child! I pray you mercy as you will need mercy!

[*Falls upon her knees.*]

Hathorne. Rise, woman; it is not now mercy, but justice that has to be considered.

Parris. In straits like this there is no mercy in the divine will. Shall mercy be shown Satan?

Corwin. Mercy Lewis, is it in truth Olive Corey who afflicts you?

Mercy (*hesitating*). I am not so sure as I was.

Other Afflicted Girls. Nor I! nor I! nor I!

Mercy. Last time I was somewhat blinded and could not see her face. Methinks she was something taller than Olive.

Ann (*shrieks*). Oh, Olive is upon me! The sun shines on her face! I see her, she is choking me! Oh! oh!

Mercy (*to* Ann). Hush! If she be put away you'll not get Paul Bayley; I'll tell you that for a certainty, Ann Hutchins.

Ann. Oh! oh! she is killing me!

Mercy. I see her naught; 'tis a taller person who is afflicting Ann. (*To* Ann.) Leave your outcries or I will confess to the magistrates. [Ann *becomes quiet.*]

Corwin. Ann Hutchins, saw you in truth Olive Corey afflicting you?

Ann (sullenly). It might have been Goody Corey.

Corwin. Mercy Lewis, saw you of a certainty Olive Corey walking in the wood with a black man?

Mercy. It was the wane of the moon; I might have been mistaken. It might have been Goody Corey; their carriage is somewhat the same.

Corwin. Give me the cape, Widow Hutchins. (Widow Hutchins *hands him the cape; he puts it over his shoulders.*) Verily I perceive no great inconvenience from the cape, except it is an ill fit.

[*Takes it off and lays it on the table. The two magistrates and* Minister Parris *whisper together.*]

Hathorne. Having now received the testimony of the afflicted and the witnesses, and duly weighted the same according to our judgment, being aided to a decision, as we believe, by the divine wisdom which we have invoked, we declare the damsel Olive Corey free and quit of the charges against her. And Martha Corey, the wife of Giles Corey, of Salem Village, we commit unto the jail in Salem until—

Giles. Send Martha to Salem jail! Out upon ye! Why, ye be gone clean mad, magistrates and ministers and all! Send Martha to jail! Why, she must home with me this night and get supper! How think ye I am going to live and keep my house? Load Martha down with chains in jail! Martha a witch! Then, by the Lord, she keeps His company overmuch for one of her trade, for she goes to prayer forty times a day. Martha a witch! Think ye Goodwife Martha Corey gallops a broomstick to the hill of a night, with her decent petticoats flapping? Who says so? I would I had my musket, and he'd not say so twice to Giles Corey. And let him say so twice as 'tis, and meet my fist, an he dares. I be an old man, but I could hold my own in my day, and there be some of me left yet. Who says so twice to old Giles Corey? Martha a witch! Verily she could not stop praying long enough to dance a jig through with the devil. Martha! Out upon ye, ye lying devil's tool of a parson, that seasons murder with prayer! Out upon ye, ye magistrates! your hands be redder than your fine trappings! Martha a witch! Ye yourselves be witches, and serving Satan, and he a-tickling in his sleeve at ye. Send Martha in chains to Salem jail, ye will, will ye? (*Forces his way to* Martha, *and throws his arm around her.*) Be not afraid, good lass, thy man will save thee. Thou shalt not go to jail! I say thou shalt not! I'll cut my way through a whole king's army ere thou shalt. I'll raise the devil myself ere thou shalt, and set him tooth and claw on the whole brood of them. I'll—(*One of the afflicted shrieks.* Giles *turns upon them.*) Why, devil take ye, ye lying hussies, ye have done this! Ye should be whipped through the town at the tail of a cart, every one of ye. Ye ill-favored little jades, puling because no man will have ye, and putting each other up to this d—— mischief for lack of something better. Out upon ye, ye little—

Mercy (*jumping up and screaming in agony*). Oh, Giles Corey is upon me! He is afflicting me grievously! Oh, I will not! Chain him! chain him! chain him!

Ann. Oh, this is worse than the others! This is dreadful! He's strangling me! I—Oh—your—worships! Oh—help!—help! *[Falls upon the floor.]*

Afflicted Girls. Chain him! chain him!

Hathorne. Marshal, take Giles Corey into custody and chain him.

[Marshal *and* Constables *advance.*
Tableau—Curtain falls.]

From: Esther Forbes, *Mirror for Witches* (1928)

This strange, rather compelling historical novel makes use of the witchcraft trial records but otherwise bears no relationship to historical events. The orphaned daughter of a witch and warlock, Doll Bilby, who witnessed her parents' horrible deaths, is brought to Salem from England in 1633 by a doting foster father. After making a compact with the devil, she is tried for witchcraft in 1672 and found guilty.

Insofar as the novel deals with the ripple effects of traumatic harm done to one individual, so that in time the whole of society is affected, it addresses a central aspect of the Salem witch-hunt, and all witch-hunts.

This excerpt is from the last section of the book, after the pregnant Doll Bilby has been sent to jail.

6. *The Labors of a Witch and the Prayers of the Godly.*

The year was nine days old and no more. Then was Doll Bilby taken in labor and brought prematurely to bed.

The Salem midwife—ancient Nan Hackett—would have none of her, and it seemed that, whatever it was she must bear, she should bear alone. Nor did she ask for mortal aid. She was content with that phantom which stood night and day (as many saw) at her bed's head. Mr. Zelley remembered that Goody Goochey, when first she came to Cowman Corners, had served the beginning as well as the end of life—that is, she had been a midwife as well as a layer-out of the dead. He went to the woman and begged her, in pity's name and partly commanded her in the name of the General Court, to get herself to Salem jail and there give such service as might be.

She was afraid. She did not wish to be midwife to a witch and the first to welcome a black imp into the world. She drank three piggins of ale and took a leather bottle of brandy with her. She set upon her thumbs and fingers those iron rings with which she was accustomed to guard herself against the ghosts of the dead. She thought, after all, is not a live imp of greater danger to a good Christian's soul than the body of a dead church elder? Mr. Zelley went with her to the jail.

The witch at the moment was not in pain. She lay with eyes black as the pits of Hell. Her white mouth was open. She roused herself a little and made Mr. Zelley a brief speech in which she said that she had, as he knew, sought God and spiritual peace, and now, let him look into her face and say that she had failed to find either. It was true, said Mr. Zelley. Her face was fulfilled of heavenly peace. He left her without a word.

Outside he found a conclave of idle men and women who laughed and joked coarsely. One big ruddy wench (who had already borne, to the embarrassment of the community, three fatherless children) was crying out loudly that God knew it was enough for woman to give birth to human child, which is round and sleek as a melon. God help the witch now in labour with an imp, for it would come into the world with spiked tail and horns. Such a thing would be the death of any mortal woman. All were afraid. Some believed a clap of thunder would come down from Heaven and destroy the woman. Others that a fiend would rise up from Hell to succour her. Some said that the witches and warlocks for an hundred miles had gathered together and now, mounting broomsticks, were about to charge down upon Salem. One said, "Have you not heard? Judge Bride has suffered an apoplexy. Judge Lollimour is at death's door." This was not so.

Another said Captain Tom Buzzey's hands (those hands that had held the witch) had withered. They had shrivelled to the size of a child's. This was not so.

All said the witch is in labour. She's with child by the Devil. God will burn her soul in Hell. This was so.

The day wore on. The sun, as sometimes may be in the midst of winter, was so warm the snow melted and water dripped from the eaves of the jail. It was tender as a day in spring. Planks and rugs were laid in the slush, for certain clergymen came to pray and must have dry land to kneel upon. They prayed that God recollect the number of good, pious Christian people there were at Salem and not destroy all, for they feared His wrath might blast the whole village. God made no sign, but the water dripped from the eaves and a sweet spring fragrance rose from the melting snow.

The multitude gaped and feared. Sometimes they smelt sulphur, saltpeter, brimstone, and the stench as of a sloughing serpent. They heard the crying of a phantom voice and the swishing of a thousand brooms. So they waited through the day expecting every moment to see crabbed Goody Goochey hobble out with a black imp upon a blanket to show them.

There was no sound from the cell. Not one cry nor moan from the witch, not one word from Goochey. The jailors would open the door. It stuck. Their keys would not fit it. They could not open the door, and believed devils were holding it fast. They dared not peek in the chink because of their pink-eye.

By sundown most went home.

7. *Mr. Zelley opens a Dungeon Door, and what came of it.*

The next day dawned cold and grey over an icy sea, and the gulls and terns came in from the harbour crying and lamenting. There was now no tenderness in the air, and the water that had but yesterday melted under the rays of a genial sun froze to glassy ice. A wind sharp as needles came in off the sea and few if any watched the night out on their knees beside the dungeon walls. As soon as it was possible to see six feet ahead, the multitude again began to assemble, but this time they came without laughter or conversation. They were shrouded in hoods, shawls, etc., for warmth, and seemed a spectral band. Now and then one or another of them would raise a pious voice in prayer, lamentation, or thanksgiving, but for the most part they stood bowed and mute. All night there had been no sound from the witch's cell—never a sound. Who was there so bold as to enter in to her and bring back a report, for John Ackes's hand shook so he could not manage the key? Some said Mr. Zelley would go—he had no normal, wholesome fear of witches or demons. Others said, "Where does he lie tonight?" Others, "Go, run and fetch him"; and a boy (it was Widow Hannah's bonded boy Jake Tulley) said the man lay at the Black Moon and that he would run and fetch him. This he did.

Mr. Zelley came in a steeple hat and a greatcoat. He spoke to no one. No one spoke to him. He entered the jail and took the cell key from Ackes, and, after some shaking and effort, he turned the lock and pushed hard on the door, which swung in so suddenly he almost fell on his knees beside that straw bed where he had sat so many wicked hours with the witch-girl. A hundred had crowded down the passage and into the doorway after Mr. Zelley. All stopped at the threshold of the cell. They stood agape, some filled with curiosity, some with fear, others with pious ejaculations and elevated thoughts.

Goody Goochey (who indeed proved to be no woman, but a man) lay in a drunken fit in a corner. His face was purple and his throat twisted and bruised as though he had been half strangled—which he always averred to his dying day was the truth, for he had seen the scaly black demon come at him with great hands outstretched to his throat, and that was the last he could really remember until certain ones tumbled him out into the snow. He was sure, however, that, as he lay thus almost unconscious in a corner, a great concourse of spectrals and infernals had filled the cell. They had danced, sung, and made much of the witch, praising her, encouraging her, etc. Because the man was known to be an impostor (he had for many years made all think him a woman) and because of his swinish, drunken ways, many did not believe what he said.

All could see that Bilby's Doll was dead. She lay with her round eyes open to the ceiling, and her expression was one of peace and content. Whatever she might have borne was dead within her.

8. *Without* HELL *where is* HEAVEN? *And without a Devil where is* GOD? *Also the last of Doll Bilby and an end to these instructions.*

There are court records, affidavits, etc.; there are diaries, letters, and such; there is the memory of old gaffers and goodies to prove that once Doll Bilby flourished. But of physical, inanimate objects nothing that was associated with her evil life and awful end now exists. The house she lived in mysteriously rotted and fell into the cellar hole. The grave they dug her is now lost under a ploughed field (a sterile field that yields little). Where the dungeon was now is a brick house, a fine big house of red bricks had out from England. No one will live there. Yet any gamin, for a copper penny, and any courting couple, for wanton pleasure, will show you the very spot in the white birch thicket where Doll met her demon lover night after night under the moonlight, in that world of witchery which none today will ever see. For in those days there were sights and wonders that will not come again. In those days God was nearer to man than He is today, and where God is there also must be His Evil Opponent—the Prince of Lies, for show me Paradise, and there, around a corner, I will show you Hell.

From: Esther Hammand, *The Road to Endor* (1940), chapter 34, "Hobgoblins"

This fictionalized biography of Samuel Parris, culminating in the events of 1692, sheds more light on seventeenth-century London, Barbados, and Massachusetts than on the historical character of Parris or his part in the witch-hunt. Hammand is a tireless researcher and the book brings to life events such as the Great Fire of London, the restoration of King Charles II, and the return of Increase Mather to Boston with the new charter for the colony. But she is not a good enough writer to create three-dimensional characters or offer profound insights into motives or causes. The chapter included here shows the "circle" practicing sorcery under the tutelage of Tituba. Later in the book Parris almost disappears as a character, not surprisingly, since Hammand had made him a hero and there cannot be anything heroic about driving on a witch-hunt.

Who would believe what strange bugbears
Mankind creates itself, of fears, . . .
For fear does things so like a witch,
'Tis hard t' unriddle which is which.
—Butler, Hudibras, 1678

Things were going very badly in the ministry house in the winter of 1691. The shortage of firewood had driven the minister out of the sacred quiet of his study into the living room, where the various activities of the household were carried on and Bettie and Nabbie whispered and giggled under Elizabeth's admonitions to be good and quiet.

Samuel's patience was worn thin, and as soon as supper was well out of the way he would pack the girls off to bed to be rid of them. There they would be out of the way and safe, he told himself, and their foolish chatter would not drive him distracted.

At bedtime Elizabeth would tiptoe in to see that they were asleep and warmly tucked in. Then the household would settle down to darkness and dreams. But little maids with enterprising minds cannot sleep all evening and all night, too. And all unbeknown, after their elders were asleep, the children's adventure began.

It was Mary Walcott who thought of it. She had hung around and watched while the ministry house was building, and she knew a *secret* that nobody else but the carpenter and Mr. Burroughs knew. There was a secret staircase and a secret room, snug and warm, in the heart of the great chimney cluster. There they could sit as late as they pleased, with Tituba telling ghost tales and old Goody Good calling up "sperrits"—nobody would know.

There were many houses in New England which had such hiding places to afford protection from Indian attacks when a house might almost any day have to be a fortress. People knew about some of them; but the ministry house had kept its secret well. Mr. Burroughs, who planned the chamber, had left the village in bad temper; the carpenter had moved away; and Mary had almost forgotten about the place until the Circle meetings began—then she remembered. Sometimes they met at Good's, but her poor shack was too cold. Sometimes they went to Mistress Putnam's, but there was always the danger of neighbors dropping in. So, in the nick of time, Mary remembered; and with finger on her lips, she extorted solemn promises never to tell a living soul, and revealed her secret to Nabbie and Bettie—and Tituba.

The way to the secret chamber was an adventure in itself. One first went into the black room back of the chimney: a big windowless closet with doors opening into each of the upstairs chambers and a cubbyhole into the lean-to storeroom where the slaves slept. There were broken chairs and trundle beds in it, and quilting frames hobnobbed with garlands of dried apples and corn hung by the husks to dry. The thrill of feeling around for the secret spring which let one into the holy of holies was an ecstatic one to the girls. It was like a bottomless black hole with a winding stair leading down down down into depths of darkness and finally landed one in the cellar in a snug warm chamber in the center of the chimney stack, with stone walls and a tiny fireplace in one corner.

Here on many a winter night, the Circle met, huddling about a tiny blaze of charcoal or faggots while Tituba told the eight girls weird tales of the Caribbees. Elizabeth complained of the noise and said that there must be bats in the chimney, but John Indian could never find any. Samuel was too wrapped up in his own troubles to pay heed to trifles.

The Circle meetings were more and more exciting. Tituba could read your palm and tell what kind of girl you were and when you would be wed. Old Good could hold her hands tight against your forehead and mumble an outlandish lingo and put you to sleep—and when you woke up everybody would laugh and tell you the funny things you did while you were asleep. Old Good was a poor woman who often came during the day to beg food from Elizabeth. Elizabeth was kind, but Bettie and Nabbie knew that most of the neighbors were suspicious and disdainful of her. So when she came to the ministry house for food, they never by word or expression let on what went on in the secret chamber by nights. Mary Walcott could see pictures in the water in a black kettle—sometimes pictures of things that had happened and sometimes things that were going to happen. And after the meetings were over, the girls would go to bed and dream the strangest things—and sometimes the dreams would come true.

It was very mysterious and sometimes very frightening. Most of the girls were almost grown up and said: Pooh, they weren't scared! But Nabbie and Bettie would scurry up the crooked little stairs and through the black room and jump into bed with the covers pulled up over their heads and hug each other tight—tight—tight—so that the black man wouldn't get them. Tituba had known of folkses (even big folkses) that were carried off to nobody knew where by goblins—and never seen again. She would shake her turbaned head and say solemnly:

"An effen yuh evah tells yuh pappies er yo' mammies any of de secret signs—wo-be-yuntuh-yuh!"

The time came when Nabbie couldn't stand the excitement any longer; and in the middle of a dark January night she began to scream and scream. Samuel and Elizabeth came running in, in their long white nightgowns. At the sight of them

Bettie began to shriek too: and both of them kicked the covers off and hid themselves under the bed babbling strange words that Samuel said were neither Latin nor Greek nor Hebrew nor any other tongue he ever heard of.

Elizabeth tried to soothe them, but they were out of their heads completely and screeched when she came near them, not knowing who she was. Tituba heated water in big kettles to bathe them and put hot stones at their feet, but nothing did any good.

Then Samuel sent John Indian posthaste through the snow for Dr. Griggs, the new doctor who had come occasionally to Salem Village after Dr. Swinnerton had died in December. Dr. Griggs was a grandfatherly old man with big wooden-rimmed spectacles and a long white beard. He made the children drink a medicine made of powdered peony seeds dissolved in wine which restored their wits and comforted their senses and made them forget the nightmare. He left a tiny package of root of the male peony to be given them with all their drinks and broths. He was very kind and told them of the ancient physician who first took knowledge of the herb which took its name from that good old man: Paeon. The medicine seemed to help the children at first. They became still and quiet before the good doctor had finished his story about Paeon and his herbs. But almost as soon as the doctor was gone they began to have fits again; and Elizabeth had to lie with them in their bed till morning patting and comforting them.

When daylight came, their fears left them, but a night or two later the fits came on again. That time Dr. Griggs was sorely troubled and said he feared the children were under an evil hand.

Only then did Samuel mention the tales which had been told about the former occupants of the ministry house: the two wives of Mr. Burroughs, Mrs. Lawson and her child, the slave boy, Corythus. At that Dr. Griggs looked very grave indeed. Being newly come to the village, he had heard naught of the trouble, he said, but the matter looked bad. It might be as in the time of our Lord: This kind goeth not out but by prayer and fasting.

Parris, badly frightened, and having kept a fast by himself without success, sent for Mr. Hale and Mr. Noyes and Mr. Lawson to join him in a day of fasting and prayer; requesting that they come privately and make no mention to anyone of the curse that had once more fallen on the ministry house.

He had thought of sending to Mr. Cotton Mather for aid, but Dr. Griggs advised against it, pursing up his lips and puffing out his cheeks in his best professional manner.

"Mr. Cotton Mather is a busy man and his zeal is not always according to knowledge," he said. "Not that I am in any way belittling Mr. Cotton Mather, you understand, but confidentially I may say that I think him too young a man to handle a case of this kind with discretion."

"But the Goodwin girl was healed and restored," Samuel protested, his jealousy of Mather put aside in his emergency.

The doctor puffed his cheeks again. "Aye! And so also, if my memory serves me, were her brother and sisters who were not under Mr. Mather's care.

"But there is a man in Boston, Deacon Sanderson, who is so fortunate as to possess a copy of Perkins's *Discourse of the Damned Art of Witchcraft.* That book is the best authority in England. I believe the deacon would be willing to lend it to you in your necessity. Meanwhile we will continue constant in prayer, putting our faith in the Great Physician."

The news of the trouble at the parsonage spread and the villagers hastened to offer consolation and help. Everybody had a different remedy which had given relief to someone similarly afflicted.

Samuel shut himself up in his study to fast and pray, and between the visitors and the children Elizabeth was almost distracted.

In one way, however, the affliction brought a blessing. Parishioners whose rates were long overdue brought in contributions in country pay: a bushel of turnips; a sack of ground corn; a side of hog meat; a steer's hindquarter; and countless wild pigeons and rabbits and a turkey or two. The most welcome of all was a huge sledload of oak wood from an unexpected source: Giles Corey.

He saved his face by explaining to Elizabeth that the wood was to pay his wife's obligations; but it was plain to be seen that he was fairly eaten up by curiosity in regard to the bewitchment. He told of cases he had known in his native Yorkshire long ago. His gaunt frame was tense with emotion and his pale-blue eyes were fierce as a hawk's as he denounced the devil and his agents. His wonder tales frightened Elizabeth almost to death, so that she cried after he was gone.

Later the same day Goodwife Corey came. "Giles telled me he'd ben to see you," she said, "an' I jest had to ride over an' tell you not to take to heart anything he said. Giles is an old fool about bewitchments. He sees Old Horny in every bush, seems like." She patted Elizabeth's shoulder. "Jest put your trust in the Lord Jesus, dearie. He healed the sick and cast out demons when He was on earth, and His power is just the same today. Satan has no power beyond what the Blessed Lord gives him, dearie, and the Lord never telled him he could torment His little ones. Suffer the little ones to come unto me, he says, dearie. An' He'll guard 'em, never you fear.

"I don't hold with them as sees witches in ev'ry untoward hap'nin'. I'm past threescore an' I never yet did see a witch, an' never expect to—not in a Christian land. Mebbe they have 'em in heathendom—but not in the Lord's own Zion. Never fear, dearie. The Lord is mindful of His own."

Elizabeth, being a minister's daughter and a minister's wife, knew well enough that such a philosophy was heresy, for if one disbelieved in witches 'twas only a step to disbelieving in the devil, and the next thing one knew one wouldn't put faith in God either. But she found comfort in it. And she could not but feel that Martha was a woman of faith, for before she left she dropped on her knees before the hearth and went to prayer, with a simple assurance that seemed to bring the Lord Jesus right into the room, with His hand outstretched to heal and save.

From: Arthur Miller, "Why I Wrote *The Crucible*," *The New Yorker* (Oct. 21 & 28, 1996)

Arther Miller's *The Crucible* (1953) is far too well known to reproduce here. It is one of the greatest plays of the twentieth century. From the point of view of the historian, it is unfortunate that it is also most people's main source of knowledge of the Salem witch-hunt, since it perpetuates the myth of Tituba as a West Indian sorceress and suggests an imaginary love motive as the persecution's starting point. In real life the play's lovers, Abigail Williams and John Proctor, were aged eleven and sixty, and probably never met except in court. But, more satisfactorily, still from the point of view of the historian, the play shows the fear, self-delusion, and dedication to personal agendas that drove on the witch-hunt.

As he explains in the following essay, written at the time *The Crucible* was filmed, Miller conceived the play in response to the insanity of the McCarthy persecution of alleged Communists. Yet *The Crucible* has proved of enduring relevance. Perhaps the reason, he says, is that it deals with the subject of "human sacrifice to the furies of fanaticism and paranoia that goes on repeating itself for ever."

No question.

As I watched *The Crucible* taking shape as a movie over much of the past year, the sheer depth of time that it represents for me kept returning to mind. As those powerful actors blossomed on the screen, and the children and the horses, the crowds and the wagons, I thought again about how I came to cook all this up nearly fifty years ago, in an America almost nobody I know seems to remember clearly. In a way, there is a biting irony in this film's having been made by a Hollywood studio, something unimaginable in the fifties. But there they are—Daniel Day-Lewis (John Proctor) scything his sea-bordered field, Jean Allen (Elizabeth) lying pregnant in the frigid jail, Winona Ryder (Abigail) stealing her minister-uncle's money, majestic Paul Scofield (Judge Danforth) and his righteous empathy with the Devil-possessed children, and all of them looking as inevitable as rain.

I remember those years—they formed *The Crucible*'s skeleton—but I have lost the dead weight of the fear I had then. Fear doesn't travel well, just as it can warp judgment, its absence can diminish memory's truth. What terrifies one generation is likely to bring only a puzzled smile to the next. I remember how in 1964, only twenty years after the war, Harold Clurman, the director of *Incident at Vichy,* showed the cast a film of a Hitler speech, hoping to give them a sense of the Nazi period in which my play took place. They watched as Hitler, facing a vast stadium full of adoring people, went up on his toes in ecstasy, hands clasped under his chin, a sublimely self-gratified grin on his face, his body swivelling rather cutely, and they giggled at his overacting.

Likewise, films of Senator Joseph McCarthy are rather unsettling—if you remember the fear he once spread. Buzzing his truculent sidewalk brawler's snarl through the hairs in his nose, squinting through his cat's eyes and sneering like a villain, he comes across now as nearly comical, a self-aware performer keeping a straight face as he does his juicy threat-schtick.

McCarthy's power to stir fears of creeping Communism was not entirely based on illusion, of course; the paranoid, real or pretended, always secretes its pearl around a grain of fact. From being our wartime ally, the Soviet Union rapidly became an expanding empire. In 1949, Mao Zedong took power in China. Western Europe also seemed ready to become Red, especially Italy, where the Communist Party was the largest outside Russia, and was growing. Capitalism, in the opinion of many, myself included, had nothing more to say, its final poisoned bloom having been Italian and German Fascism. McCarthy—brash and ill-mannered but to many authentic and true—boiled it all down to what anyone could understand: we had "lost China" and would soon lose Europe as well because the State Department—staffed, of course, under Democratic Presidents—was full of treasonous pro-Soviet intellectuals. It was as simple as that.

If our losing China seemed the equivalent of a flea's losing an elephant, it was still a phrase—and a conviction—that one did not dare to question; to do so was a risk drawing suspicion on oneself. Indeed, the State Department proceeded to hound and fire the officers who knew China, its language, and its opaque culture—a move that suggested the practitioners of sympathetic magic who wring the neck of a doll in order to make a distant enemy's head drop off. There was magic all around; the politics of alien conspiracy soon dominated political discourse and bid fair to wipe out any other issue. How could one deal with such enormities in a play?

The Crucible was an act of desperation. Much of my desperation branched out, I suppose, from a typical Depression-era trauma—the blow struck on the mind by the rise of European Fascism and the brutal anti-Semitism it had brought to power. But by 1950, when I began to think of writing about the hunt for Reds in America, I was motivated in some great part by the paralysis that had set in among many liberals who, despite their discomfort with the inquisitors' violations of civil rights, were fearful, and with good reason, of being identified as covert Communists if they should protest too strongly.

In any play, however trivial, there has to be a still point of moral reference against which to gauge the action. In our lives, in the late nineteen-forties and early nineteen-fifties, no such point existed anymore. The left could not look straight at the Soviet Union's abrogations of human rights. The anti-Communist liberals could not acknowledge the violations of those rights by congressional committees. The far right, meanwhile, was licking up all the cream. The days of "J'accuse" were gone, for anyone needs to feel right to declare someone else wrong. Gradually, all the old political and moral reality had melted like a Dali watch. Nobody but a fanatic, it seemed, could really say all that he believed.

President Truman was among the first to have to deal with the dilemma, and his way of resolving it—of having to trim his sails before the howling gale on the right—turned out to be momentous. At first, he was outraged at the allegation of widespread Communist infiltration of the government and called the charge of "coddling Communists" a red herring dragged in by the Republicans to bring down the Democrats. But such was the gathering power of raw belief in the great Soviet plot that Truman soon felt it necessary to institute loyalty boards of his own.

The Red hunt, led by the House Committee on Un-American Activities and by McCarthy, was becoming the dominating fixation of the American psyche. It reached Hollywood when the studios, after first resisting, agreed to submit artists' names to the House Committee for "clearing" before employing them. This unleashed a veritable holy terror among actors, directors, and others, from Party members to those who had had the merest brush with a front organization.

The Soviet plot was the hub of a great wheel of causation; the plot justified the crushing of all nuance, all the shadings that a realistic judgment of reality requires. Even worse was the feeling that our sensitivity to this onslaught on our liberties was passing from us—indeed, from me. In *Timebends*, my autobiography, I recalled the time I'd written a screenplay ("The Hook") about union corruption on the Brooklyn waterfront. Harry Cohn, the head of Columbia Pictures, did something that would once have been considered unthinkable: he showed my script to the F.B.I. Cohn then asked me to take the gangsters in my script, who were threatening and murdering their opponents, and simply change them to Communists. When I declined to commit this idiocy (Joe Ryan, the head of the longshoremen's union, was soon to go to Sing Sing for racketeering), I got a wire from Cohn saying, "The minute we try to make the script pro-American you pull out." By then—it was 1951—I had come to accept this terribly serious insanity as routine, but there was an element of the marvellous in it which I longed to put on the stage.

In those years, our thought processes were becoming so magical, so paranoid, that to imagine writing a play about this environment was like trying to pick one's teeth with a ball of wool: I lacked the tools to illuminate miasma. Yet I kept being drawn back to it.

I had read about the witchcraft trials in college, but it was not until I read a book published in 1867—a two-volume, thousand page study by Charles W. Upham, who was then the mayor of Salem—that I knew I had to write about the period. Upham had not only written a broad and thorough investigation of what was even then an almost lost chapter of Salem's past but opened up to me the details of personal relationships among many participants in the tragedy.

I visited Salem for the first time on a dismal spring day in 1952; it was a side-tracked town then, with abandoned factories and vacant stores. In the gloomy courthouse there I read the transcripts of the witchcraft trials of 1692, as taken down in a primitive shorthand by ministers who were spelling each other. But there was one entry in Upham in which the thousands of pieces I had come across were jogged into place. It was from a report written by the Reverend Samuel Parris, who was one of the chief instigators of the witch-hunt. "During the examination of Elizabeth Proctor, Abigail Williams and Ann Putnam"—the two were "afflicted" teen-age accusers, and Abigail was Parris's niece—"both made offer to strike at said Procter; but when Abigail's hand came near, it opened, whereas it was made up, into a fist before, and came down exceeding lightly as it drew near to said Procter, and at length, with open and extended fingers, touched Procter's hood very lightly. Immediately Abigail cried out her fingers, her fingers, her fingers burned . . . "

In this remarkably observed gesture of a troubled young girl, I believed, a play became possible. Elizabeth Proctor had been the orphaned Abigail's mistress, and they had lived together in the same small house until Elizabeth fired the girl. By this time, I was sure, John Proctor had bedded Abigail, who had to be dismissed most likely to appease Elizabeth. There was bad blood between the two women now. That Abigail started, in effect, to condemn Elizabeth to death with her touch, then stopped her hand, then went through with it, was quite suddenly human center of all this turmoil.

All this I understood. I had not approached the witchcraft out of nowhere or from purely social and political considerations. My own marriage of twelve years was teetering and I knew more than I wished to know about where the blame lay. That John Proctor the sinner might overturn his paralyzing personal guilt and become the most forthright voice against the madness around him was a reassurance to me, and, I suppose, an inspiration; it demonstrated that a clear moral outcry could still spring even from an ambiguously unblemished soul. Moving crabwise across the profusion of evidence, I sensed that I had at last found something of myself in it, and a play began to accumulate around this man.

But as the dramatic form became visible, one problem remained unyielding: so many practices of the Salem trials were similar to those employed by the congressional committees that I could easily be accused of skewing history for a mere partisan purpose. Inevitably, it was no sooner known that my new play was about Salem than I had to confront the charge that such an analogy was specious—that there never were any witches but there certainly are Communists. In the seventeenth century, however, the existence of witches was never questioned by the loftiest minds in Europe and America; and even lawyers of the highest eminence, like Sir Edward Coke, a veritable hero of liberty for defending the common law against the king's arbitrary power, believed that witches had to be prosecuted mercilessly. Of course, there were no Communists in 1692, but it was literally worth your life to deny witches or their powers, given the exhortation in the Bible, "Thou shalt not suffer a witch to live." There had to be witches in the world or the Bible lied. Indeed, the very structure of evil depended on Lucifer's plotting against God. (And the irony is that klatches of Luciferians exist all over the country today, there may even be more of them now than there are Communists.)

As with most humans, panic sleeps in one unlighted corner of my soul. When I walked at night along the empty, wet streets of Salem in the week that I spent there, I could easily work myself into imagining my terror before a gaggle of young girls flying down the road screaming that somebody's "familiar spirit" was chasing them. This anxiety-laden leap backward over nearly three centuries may have been helped along by a particular Upham footnote. At a certain point, the high court of the province made the fatal decision to admit, for the first time, the use of "spectral evidence" as proof of guilt. Spectral evidence, so aptly named, meant that if I swore that you had sent out your "familiar spirit" to choke, tickle, poison me or my cattle, or to control thoughts and actions, I could get you hanged unless you confessed to having had contact with the Devil. After all, only the Devil could lend such powers of visible transport to confederates, in his everlasting plot to bring down Christianity.

Naturally, the best proof of the sincerity of your confession was your naming others whom you had seen in the Devil's company—an invitation to private vengeance, but made official by the seal of the theocratic state. It was as though the court had grown tired of thinking and had invited in the instincts: spectral evidence—that poisoned cloud of paranoid fantasy—made a kind of lunatic sense to them, as it did in plot-ridden 1952, when so often the question was not the acts of an accused but the thoughts and intentions in his alienated mind.

The breathtaking circularity of the process had a kind of poetic tightness. Not everybody was accused, after all, so there must be *some reason why you were.* By denying that there is any reason whatsoever for you to be accused, you are implying, by virtue of a surprisingly small logical leap, that mere chance picked you out, which in turn implies that the Devil might not really be at work in the village or, God forbid, even exist. Therefore, the investigation itself is either mistaken or a fraud. You would have to be a crypto-Luciferian to say that—not a great idea if you wanted to go back to your farm.

The more I read into the Salem panic, the more it touched off corresponding ages of common experiences in the fifties: the old friend of a blacklisted person crossing the street to avoid being seen talking to him; the overnight conversions of former leftists into born-again patriots; and so on. Apparently, certain processes are universal. When Gentiles in Hitler's Germany, for example, saw their Jewish neighbors being trucked off, or farmers in Soviet Ukraine saw the Kulaks sing before their eyes, the common reaction, even among those unsympathetic to Nazism or Communism, was quite naturally to turn away in fear of being identified with the condemned. As I learned from non-Jewish refugees, however, there was often a despairing pity mixed with "Well, they must have done *something.*" Few of us can easily surrender our belief that society must somehow make sense. The thought that the state has lost its mind and is punishing so many innocent people is intolerable. And so the evidence has to be internally denied.

I was also drawn into writing *The Crucible* by the chance it gave me to use a new language, that of seventeenth-century New England. That plain, craggy English was liberating in a strangely sensuous way, with its swings from an almost legalistic precision to a wonderful metaphoric richness. "The Lord doth terrible things amongst us, by lengthening the chain of the roaring lion in an extraordinary manner, so that the Devil is come down in great wrath," Deodat Lawson, one of the great witch-hunting preachers, said in a sermon. Lawson rallied his congregation for what was to be nothing less than a religious war against the Evil One—"Arm, arm, arm!"—and his concealed anti-Christian accomplices.

But it was not yet my language, and among other strategies to make it mine I enlisted the help of a former University of Michigan classmate, the Greek-American scholar and poet Kimon Friar. (He later translated Kazantzakis.) The problem was not to imitate the archaic speech but to try to create a new echo of it which would flow freely off American actors' tongues. As in the film, nearly fifty years later, the actors in the first production grabbed the language and ran with it as happily as if it were their customary speech.

The Crucible took me about a year to write. With its five sets and a cast of twenty-one, it never occurred to me that it would take a brave man to produce it on Broadway, especially given the prevailing climate, but Kermit Bloomgarden never faltered. Well before the play opened, a strange tension had begun to build. Only two years earlier, the *Death of a Salesman* touring company had played to a thin crowd in Peoria, Illinois, having been boycotted nearly to death by the American Legion and the Jaycees. Before that, the Catholic War Veterans had prevailed upon the Army not to allow its theatrical groups to perform, first, *All My Sons,* and then any play of mine, in occupied Europe. The Dramatists Guild refused to protest attacks on a new play by Sean O'Casey, a self-declared Communist, which forced its producer to cancel his option. I knew of two suicides by actors depressed by upcoming investigation, and every day seemed to bring news of people exiling themselves to Europe: Charlie Chaplin, the director Joseph Losey, Jules Dassin, the harmonica virtuoso Larry Adler, Donald Ogden Stewart, one of the most sought-after screenwriters in Hollywood, and Sam Wanamaker, who would lead the successful campaign to rebuild the Old Globe Theatre on the Thames.

On opening night, January 22, 1953, I knew that the atmosphere would be pretty hostile. The coldness of the crowd was not a surprise; Broadway audiences were not famous for loving history lessons, which is what they made of the play. It seems to me entirely appropriate that on the day the play opened, a newspaper headline read "ALL 13 REDS GUILTY"—a story about American Communists who faced prison for "conspiring to teach and advocate the duty and necessity of forcible overthrow of government." Meanwhile, the remoteness of the production was guaranteed by the director, Jed Harris, who insisted that this was a classic requiring the actors to face front, never each other. The critics were not swept away. "Arthur Miller is a problem playwright in both senses of the word," wrote Walter Kerr of the *Herald Tribune*, who called the play "a step backward into mechanical parable." The *Times* was not much kinder, saying, "There is too much excitement and not enough emotion in *The Crucible*." But the play's future would turn out quite differently.

About a year later, a new production, one with younger, less accomplished actors, working in the Martinique Hotel ballroom, played with the fervor that the script and the times required, and *The Crucible* became a hit. The play stumbled into history, and today, I am told, it is one of the most heavily demanded trade-fiction paperbacks in this country; the Bantam and Penguin editions have sold more than six million copies. I don't think there has been a week in the past forty-odd years when it hasn't been on a stage somewhere in the world. Nor is the new screen version the first. Jean-Paul Sartre, in his Marxist phase, wrote a French film adaptation that blamed the tragedy on the rich landowners conspiring to persecute the poor. (In truth, most of those who were hanged in Salem were people of substance, and two or three were very large landowners.)

It is only a slight exaggeration to say that, especially in Latin America, *The Crucible* starts getting produced wherever a political coup appears imminent, or a dictatorial regime has just been over-thrown. From Argentina to Chile to Greece, Czechoslovakia, China, and a dozen other places, the play seems to present the same primeval structure of human sacrifice to the furies of fanaticism and paranoia that goes on repeating itself forever as though imbedded in the brain of social man.

I am not sure what *The Crucible* is telling people now, but I know that its paranoid center is still pumping out the same darkly attractive warning that it did in the fifties. For some, the play seems to be about the dilemma of relying on the testimony of small children accusing adults of sexual abuse, something I'd not have dreamed of forty years ago. For others, it may simply be a fascination with the outbreak of paranoia that suffuses the play—the blind panic that, in our age, often seems to sit at the dim edges of consciousness. Certainly its political implications are the central issue for many people; the Salem interrogations turn out to be eerily exact models of those yet to come in Stalin's Russia, Pinochet's Chile, Mao's China, and other regimes. (Nien Cheng, the author of *Life and Death in Shanghai,* has told me that she could hardly believe that a non-Chinese—someone who had not experienced the Cultural Revolution—had written the play.) But below its concerns with justice the play evokes a lethal brew of illicit sexuality, fear of the supernatural, and political manipulation, a combination not unfamiliar these days. The film, by reaching the broad American audience as no play ever can, may well unearth still other connections to those buried public terrors that Salem first announced on this continent.

One thing more—something wonderful in the old sense of that word. I recall the weeks I spent reading testimony by the tome, commentaries, broadsides, confessions, and accusations. And always the crucial damning event was the signing of one's name in "the Devil's book." This Faustian agreement to hand over one's soul to the dreaded Lord of Darkness was the ultimate insult to God. But what were these new inductees supposed to have *done* once they'd signed on? Nobody seems even to have thought to ask. But, of course, actions are as irrelevant during cultural and religious wars as they are in nightmares. The thing at issue is buried intentions—the secret allegiances of the alienated heart always the main threat to the theocratic mind, as well as its immemorial quarry.

NOTES

Introduction

An excellent Hitler biography is *Adolf Hitler,* John Toland.

For Slobodan Milosevic's career, see *Milosevic: Portrait of a Tyrant,* Dusho Doder and Louise Branson.

A summation of Joe McCarthy's career can be found in *The Reader's Companion to American History,* ed. Eric Foner and John A. Garraty, pp. 709–710.

The McMartin day care sex abuse scandal is fully reported in *Satan's Silence,* Debbie Nathan & Michael Snedeker, pp. 67–92.

Part I: The Background

For the dates of the great European witch-hunt and estimate of numbers who died, see *Europe's Inner Demons,* Norman Cohn, pp. 231–232.

Chapter 1: Witchcraft

On the influence of the *Malleus Maleficarum,* see *Witches and Neighbours,* Robin Briggs, p. 382.

The importance of William Perkins is mentioned in *The History of the Colony of Massachusetts Bay,* Thomas Hutchinson, vol. 2, chapter 1.

The most recent edition of *Mein Kampf* is translated by Ralph Manheim with an introduction by Konrad Heiden.

The Turner Diaries: A Novel is by Andrew McDonald.

Chapter 2: The Massachusetts Bay Colony

Saint Augustine lived from 354 to 430, and his most famous work was his *Confessions.*

The experiences of Mary Fisher, Mary Dyer, and other Quaker women in New England is most illuminatingly put into a wider feminist context in Stevie Davies's *Unbridled Spirits.*

The complete *Narrative* of Mary Rowlandson can be found in *Puritans among the Indians,* edited by Alden T. Vaughan and Edward W. Clark.

The best account of the Salem Village conflicts is in *Salem Possessed* by Boyer and Nissenbaum, *passim* but particularly pp. 80–132.

Part II: The Witch-hunt

The records of the examinations of accused witches, depositions, petitions, formal examinations, and arrest warrants are gathered together in *The Salem Witchcraft Papers,* edited by Paul Boyer and Stephen Nissenbaum.

Samuel Parris's sermons are in his manuscript sermon notebook in the Connecticut Historical Society in Hartford, Connecticut, and have been published in *The Sermon Notebook of Samuel Parris, 1689–1694,* edited by James F. Cooper, Jr., and Kenneth P. Minkema.

The Salem Village Book of Record and the Salem Village Church Book of Record are in the Danvers Archival Center, First Church Collection, in Danvers, Massachusetts, and are included in *Salem-Village Witchcraft,* edited by Paul Boyer and Stephen Nissenbaum.

The Confession of Ann Putnam can be found in *Salem Witchcraft,* by Charles Upham, vol. II, p. 510.

Part III: The Hunter and the Hunted

Biographies of Samuel Parris and George Burroughs are: *A Quest for Security: The Life of Samuel Parris, 1653–1720* by Larry Gragg and *The Devil and George Burroughs* by Gilbert Upton.

Chapter 4: Samuel Parris

Parris's response to the Salem villagers' offer is in *Salem Witchcraft* by Charles Upham, vol. II, p. 289.

The record of the meeting of June 18, from the Salem Village Book of Record, is reproduced in *Salem Witchcraft,* vol. I, pp. 291–292.

The record of the meeting of 10th October, in the Salem Village Book of Record, is reproduced in *Salem-Village Witchcraft,* Boyer and Nissenbaum, p. 349.

The excerpt from Calef's *More Wonders of the Invisible World* can be found in Burr, *Narratives,* pp. 341–342.

The record of the meeting of October 16 from the Salem Village Book of Record, can be found in *Salem-Village Witchcraft,* p. 356. The entries from the Salem Village Church Book of Record, November 1689 to October 1696, are reproduced in *Salem-Village Witchcraft,* pp. 270–312. The sermon preached on March 27, 1692, is in Samuel Parris's Sermon Notebook, reproduced in *The Sermon Notebook of Samuel Parris, 1689–1694,* pp. 194–198. The sermon preached on September 11, 1692, is in Samuel Parris's Sermon Notebook, reproduced in *The Sermon Notebook of Samuel Parris, 1689–1694,* pp. 204–206. The petition of John Tarbell et al., the deed of Samuel Parris, and the vote of Salem Village inhabitants, are reproduced in *Salem-Village Witchcraft,* pp. 265–268.

Chapter 5: George Burroughs

The letter from Bryan Pendleton appears in *Portland in the Past* by William Goold, pp. 119–120, reproduced in *The Devil and George Burroughs,* by Gilbert Upton, p. 29.

A full account of the financial transactions between Burroughs and John Putnam can be found in *Salem Witchcraft,* vol. I, pp. 256–263.

The deposition of Nathaniel Ingersoll and Samuel Sibley is in *Salem Witchcraft,* vol. I, pp. 258–259.

The testimony of Thomas Haynes is in *Salem Witchcraft,* vol. I, pp. 260–261.

The statement of Henry Skerry and the bond signed by George Burroughs and others is in *Salem Witchcraft,* vol. I, p. 262.

For Burroughs's return to Casco, see *The Devil and George Burroughs,* by Gilbert Upton, p. 43.

Burroughs's letters are in *The History of Wells and Kennebunk,* by Edward E. Bourne, pp. 208–210, reproduced in *The Devil and George Burroughs,* pp. 46–47.

The letter from Thomas Putnam is in *Salem Witchcraft,* vol. II, pp. 139–140, reproduced in *The Salem Witchcraft Papers,* Boyer and Nissenbaum, vol. I, pp. 165–166. The complaint against George Burroughs et al. is in the *Essex Institute Fowler Papers* vol. 16, p. 11, reproduced in *The Salem Witchcraft Papers,* vol. I, p. 151.

The letter of Elisha Hutchinson is in *Bowditch Mss,* Massachusetts. Historical Society, reproduced in *The Salem Witchcraft Papers,* vol. I, p. 152.

The arrest warrant is in the Massachusetts Historical Society, reproduced in *The Salem Witchcraft Papers,* vol. I, p. 152.

The minutes of the examination of George Burroughs are in the Essex County Archives, reproduced in *The Salem Witchcraft Papers,* vol. I, pp. 153–154.

Indictments 1 and 2 are in the Massachusetts Historical Society, reproduced in *The Salem Witchcraft Papers,* pp. 154–156. Indictment no. 3 is in the Peabody-Essex Museum Mss. Collection, reproduced in *The Salem Witchcraft Papers,* vol. I, pp. 156–157. Indictment no. 4 is in the Massachusetts Historical Society, reproduced in *The Salem Witchcraft Papers,* vol. I, pp. 157–158.

The summons for Jonathan, Elizabeth, Thomas, and Samuel Ruck is in the Essex County Archives and reproduced in *The Salem Witchcraft Papers,* vol. I, p. 158.

The summons for James Greenslit is in the Essex County Archives and reproduced in *Salem Witchcraft Papers,* vol. I, p. 159.

The account of the physical examinations of George Burroughs and George Jacobs, Jr., are in the Essex County Archives and reproduced in *The Salem Witchcraft Papers,* vol. I, p. 160.

The deposition of Thomas Greenslit is in the Massachusetts Historical Society, reproduced in *The Salem Witchcraft Papers,* vol. I, pp. 160–161.

The deposition of Simon Willard and William Wormall is in the Essex County Archives, reproduced in *The Salem Witchcraft Papers,* vol. I, p. 161.

The deposition of Simon Willard is in the Essex County Archives, reproduced in *The Salem Witchcraft Papers,* vol. I, p. 162.

The deposition of Mary Webber is in the Massachusetts Historical Society, reproduced in *The Salem Witchcraft Papers,* vol. I, p. 162–163.

The deposition of Hannah Harris is in Essex County Archives and reproduced in *The Salem Witchcraft Papers,* vol. I, p. 163.

The deposition of Ann Putnam, Jr., is in the Essex County Archives, reproduced in *The Salem Witchcraft Papers,* vol. I, p. 164.

The deposition of Thomas Putnam et al. is in the Essex County Archives, reproduced in *The Salem Witchcraft Papers,* vol. I, pp. 164–165.

The deposition of Ann Putnam, Jr., is in the Essex County Archives, reproduced in *The Salem Witchcraft Papers,* vol. I, pp. 166–167.

The deposition of Edward Putnam and Thomas Putnam is in the Essex County Archives, reproduced in *The Salem Witchcraft Papers,* vol. I, p. 167.

The deposition of Sarah Bibber is in the Essex County Archives, reproduced in *The Salem Witchcraft Papers,* vol. I, p. 168.

The deposition of Mercy Lewis is in the Essex County Archives, reproduced in *The Salem Witchcraft Papers,* vol. I, pp. 168–169.

The deposition of Thomas Putnam and Edward Putnam is in the Essex County Archives, reproduced in *The Salem Witchcraft Papers,* vol. I, p. 169.

The deposition of Elizabeth Hubbard is in the Essex County Archives, reproduced in *The Salem Witchcraft Papers,* vol. I, p. 170.

The deposition of Susannah Sheldon is in the Essex County Archives, reproduced in *The Salem Witchcraft Papers,* vol. I, p. 171.

The deposition of Benjamin Hutchinson is in the Essex County Archives, reproduced in *The Salem Witchcraft Papers,* p. 172.

The deposition of Abigail Hobbs and Mary Warren is in the Massachusetts Historical Society, reproduced in *The Salem Witchcraft Papers,* vol. I, pp. 172–173.

The deposition of Mary Warren is in the Massachusetts Historical Society, reproduced in *The Salem Witchcraft Papers,* vol. I, pp. 173–174.

The deposition of Mary Walcott is in the Bowditch Mss., Massachusetts Historical Society, reproduced in *The Salem Witchcraft Papers,* vol. I, p. 174.

The deposition of Thomas Putnam and Edward Putnam is in the Massachusetts Historical Society, reproduced in *The Salem Witchcraft Papers,* vol. I, pp. 175–176.

The deposition of John Putnam, Sr. and Rebecca Putnam is in the Peabody Essex Museum Mss. Collection, reproduced in *The Salem Witchcraft Papers,* vol. I, p. 176.

The deposition of Elizar Keysar is in the New York Public Library—Manuscripts and Archives Division, reproduced in *The Salem Witchcraft Papers,* vol. I, pp. 176–177.

The memorandum is in the Essex County Archives, *The Witchcraft Papers,* vol. 2, vol. I, p. 177.

For Mather's request to Samuel Sewall, see Burr, *Narratives,* p. 206.

Part IV: The Historians

Mather's statement about the Indians appears in *Magnalia Christi Americana,* book II, p. 60. It reads in full, "The story of the prodigious war, made by the spirits of the invisible world upon the people of New England, in the year 1692, hath entertained a great part of the English world with a just astonishment: and I have met with some strange things, not here to be mentioned, which have made me often think, that this inexplicable war might have some of its original among the Indians, whose chief sagamores are well known unto some of our captives to have been horrid sorcerers, and hellish conjurers, and such as conversed with demons."

Part V: Fiction

For the lashing of Quaker women through the streets of Salem, see Bishop, *New England Judged,* pp. 279–280.

For the betrayal of Indians by William Hathorne, Jr., see Robinson, *The Devil Discovered,* p. 89.

For Hawthorne's using Charles Upham as a model for Judge Pyncheon, see ed. Gross, *The House of the Seven Gables,* p. 24n.

For the character of Maule being based on Samuel Wardwell, see Robinson, *Salem Witchcraft,* pp. 207–209.

For details of the historical Thomas Maule, a fascinating character who managed to survive in Puritan Massachusetts despite being a Quaker and writing two short books highly critical of the regime, see M. Bushnell Jones, *Thomas Maule.*

Bibliography

Alford, C. Fred. *Reparation and Civilisation: A Kleinian Account of the Large Group.* Free Associations 19. London, 1990.

Andrews, Charles M. *Colonial Period of American History.* 4 vols. New Haven, 1934.

Anon. *The Wonderful Discoverie of the Witchcrafts of Margaret and Phillip Flower.* London, 1619.

Axtell, James. *The European and the Indian: Essays in the Ethnohistory of Colonial North America.* New York, 1981.

Bailyn, Bernard. *The New England Merchants in the Seventeenth Century.* Cambridge, Mass., 1995.

Beck, Aaron T. *Cognitive Therapy of Personality Disorders.* New York, 1990.

Bishop, George. *New England Judged.* London, 1667.

Bourne, Edward E. *The History of Wells and Kennebunk.* Portland, Maine, 1875.

———. Boyer, Paul, and Stephen Nissenbaum. *Salem Possessed: The Social Origins of Witchcraft.* Cambridge, Mass., 1974.

———. *Salem-Village Witchcraft: A Documentary Record of Local Conflict in Colonial New England.* Belmont, Calif., 1972.

———. *The Salem Witchcraft Papers: Verbatim Transcripts of the Legal Documents of the Salem Witchcraft Outbreak of 1692.* New York, 1977.

Brattle, Thomas. "The Letters of Thomas Brattle, F.R.S., 1692." In Burr, *Narratives.*

Briggs, Robin. *Witches & Neighbours.* London, 1996

Burr, George Lincoln. *Narratives of the Witchcraft Cases, 1648–1706.* New York, 1914.

Bushnell Jones, M. *Thomas Maule, the Salem Quaker, and Free Speech in Massachusetts Bay.* Salem, Mass., 1936.

Cahill, Robert Ellis. *Horrors of Salem's Witch Dungeon.* Collectible Classics No. 9. Peabody, Mass., 1986.

Calef, Robert. *More Wonders of the Invisible World; or, The Wonders of the Invisible World Display'd in Five Parts.* London, 1700. In Burr, *Narratives.*

Clark, Charles E. *The Eastern Frontier: The Settlement of Northern New England, 1610–1763.* New York, 1970.

Cohn, Norman. *Europe's Inner Demons: The Daemonizations of Christians in Mediaeval Christendom.* Rev. ed. London, 1993.

Cooper, James F., Jr., and Kenneth P. Minkema. *The Sermon Notebook of Samuel Parris, 1689–1694.* Boston, 1993.

Craven, Wesley Frank. *The Colonies in Transition, 1660–1713.* New York, 1968.

Crews, Frederick, et al. *The Memory Wars.* New York, 1995.

Davies, Stevie. *Unbridled Spirits. Women of the English Revolution: 1640–1660.* London. 1998.

Demos, John Putnam. *Entertaining Satan: Witchcraft and the Culture of Early New England.* New York, 1982.

———. *A Little Commonwealth: Family Life in Plymouth Colony.* New York, 1970.

Doder, Dusho, and Louise Branson. *Milosevic: Portrait of a Tyrant.* New York, 1999.

Earle, Alice Morse. *Child Life in Colonial Days.* New York, 1899.

———.*Home Life in Colonial Days.* New York, 1899.

———.*The Sabbath in Puritan New England.* New York, 1892.

Fleming, Sandford. *Children and Puritanism.* New Haven, Conn., 1933.

Foner, Eric, and John A. Garraty, eds. *The Reader's Companion to American History.* Boston, 1991.

Forbes, Esther. *Mirror for Witches.* 1928.

Forest, J. W. *Witching Times.* 1857.

Friedman, Lawrence M. *Crime and Punishment in American History.* New York, 1993.

Gay, Peter. *A Loss of Mastery.* Berkeley, Calif., 1966.

Goold, William. *Portland in the Past.* Portland, Maine, 1886.

Gragg, Larry. *A Quest for Security: The Life of Samuel Parris, 1653–1720.* New York, 1990.

Hale, John. *A Modest Inquiry into the Nature of Witchcraft.* In Burr, *Narratives.*

Hammand, Esther. *The Road to Endor.* 1940.

Hansen, Chadwick. *Witchcraft at Salem.* New York, 1969.

Harris, M. L., M. F. Harris, E. Spiller, and M. Carr, eds. *John Hale: A Man Beset by Witches; His Book, a Modest Inquiry into the Nature of Witchcraft.* Beverly, Mass., 1992.

Hawthorne, Nathaniel. *Alice Doane's Appeal.* 1835. In *Short Stories,* 1946.

———.*The House of the Seven Gables,* 1851; reprint, ed. Seymour L. Gross. New York, 1967.

———.*The Scarlet Letter.* 1850; reprint, New York: Penguin, 1986.

———.*Young Goodman Brown.* 1835. In *Short Stories,* ed. Newton Arvin, New York, 1946.

Heimart, Alan, and Andrew Delbanco. *The Puritans in America: A Narrative Anthology,* Cambridge, Mass., 1985.

Hitler. *Mein Kampf.* Trans. Ralph Manheim. New York, 1999.

Hutchinson, Thomas. *The History of the Colony of Massachusetts Bay.* London, 1765.

Kences, James E. *Some Unexplored Relationships of Essex County Witchcraft to the Indian Wars of 1675 and 1689.* Essex Institute Historical Collections. Vol. 120. July 1984.

Kittridge, George Lyman. *Witchcraft in Old and New England.* New York, 1920.

Kramer, Heinrich, and James Sprenger. *Malleus Maleficarum,* 1484. Trans. Montague Summers, 1928.

Lawson, Deodat. *A Brief and True Narrative of Some Remarkable Passages Relating to Sundry Persons Afflicted by Witchcraft, at Salem Village Which Happened from the Nineteenth of March to the Fifth of April 1692.* Boston, 1692. In Burr, *Narratives.*

Levin, David, ed. *What Happened in Salem.* New York, 1960.

Longfellow, Henry Wadsworth. *Giles Corey of the Salem Farms.* 1868.

McDonald, Andrew. *The Turner Diaries: A Novel.* New York, 1996.

Macfarlane, Alan. *Witchcraft in Tudor and Stuart England: A Regional and Comparative Study.* London, 1970.

Mather, Cotton. *The Life of His Excellency, Sir William Phips, Knt., Late Captain General and Governor in Chief of the Province of the Massachusetts Bay, New England.* Boston, 1697; resissued, New York, 1929.

———.*Magnalia Christi Americana, or The Ecclesiastical History of New England, from Its First Planting in the Year 1620, until the year of Our Lord 1608, in Seven Books.* London, 1702.

———.*Memorable Providences Relating to Witchcrafts and Possessions: A Faithful Account of many Wonderful and Surprising Things, That Have Befallen Several Bewitched and Possessed Persons in New England, Particularly a Narrative of the Marvellous Trouble and Relief Experienced by a Pious Family in Boston, Very Lately and Sadly Molested with Evil Spirits.* Boston, 1689. Reproduced in full in Burr, *Narratives.*

———.*The Return of Several Ministers Consulted.* In Levin, *What Happened in Salem.*

———.*The Wonders of the Invisible World.* Boston, 1693. Excerpted in Burr, *Narratives.*

Mather, Increase. *Cases of Conscience Concerning Evil Spirits Personating Men.* In Levin, *What Happened in Salem.*

———.*An Essay for the Recording of Illustrious Providences, Wherein an Account is Given of Many Remarkable and Very Memorable Events, Which Have Happened in this Last Age, Especially in New-England.* Boston, 1684. Excerpted in Burr, *Narratives.* Known as *Remarkable Providences.*

Maule, Thomas, *New England Persecutors Mauled with their own Weapons,* 1697.

———.*Truth Held Forth and Maintained.* New York, 1695.

Miller, Arthur. *The Crucible.* New York, 1953.

———."*Why I Wrote* The Crucible." *The New Yorker* (October 21 & 28, 1996).

Miller, Perry. *The New England Mind: The Seventeenth Century.* New York, 1939.

Morgan, Edmund S. *The Puritan Family: Essays on Religious and Domestic Relations in Seventeenth Century New England.* Boston, 1944.

———.*Visible Saints: The History of a Puritan Idea.* New York, 1963.

Morison, Samuel Eliot. *The Puritan Pronaos: Studies in the Intellectual Life of New England in the Seventeenth Century.* New York, 1936.

Nathan, Debbie, and Michael Snedeker. *Satan's Silence: Ritual Abuse and the Making of a Modern American Witchhunt.* New York, 1995.

Neal, John. *Rachel Dyer.* 1820.

Nevins, Winfield S. *Witchcraft in Salem Village in 1692.* New York, 1916.

Pendergrast, Mark. *Victims of Memory: Incest Accusations and Shattered Lives.* Hinesburg, Vermont, 1995.

Penrose, L. S. *On the Objective Study of Crowd Behaviour.* London, 1952.

Perley, Sidney. *The History of Salem, Massachusetts.* 3 vols. Salem, Mass., 1924–1928.

Phipps, Governor. *Letters to the Home Government 1692, 1693.* In Burr, *Narratives.*

"Records and Files of the Quarterly Courts of Essex County, Mass."

Robinson, Enders A. *The Devil Discovered: Salem Witchcraft, 1692.* New York, 1991.

———.*Salem Witchcraft and Hawthorne's House of the Seven Gables.* Bowie, Md., 1992.

Rosen, Barbara, ed. *Witchcraft.* London, 1969.

Saint Augustine. *Confessions of Saint Augustine.* Trans. John K. Ryan. New York, 1960.

"Salem Village Book of Record." In Boyer and Nissenbaum, *Salem-Village Witchcraft.*

"Salem Village Church Book of Record." In Boyer and Nissenbaum, *Salem-Village Witchcraft.*

Salem Witchcraft Papers. See Boyer and Nissenbaum.

Sargant, William. *Battle for the Mind.* London, 1957.

Starkey, Marion. *The Devil in Massachusetts.* New York, 1949.

Thomas, Keith. *Religion and the Decline of Magic.* New York, 1971.

Toland, John. *Hitler;* reissue, New York, 1992.

Trask, Richard B. *The Devil Hath Been Raised.* Danvers, Mass., 1992.

———. *The Meetinghouse at Salem Village.* Danvers, Mass., 1992.

Upton, Charles W. *Salem Witchcraft, with an Account of Salem Village and a History of Opinions on Witchcraft and Kindred Subjects.* Boston, 1867.

Vaughan, Alden T. *New England Frontier: Puritans and Indians, 1620–1675.* Boston, 1965.

Vaughan, Alden T., and Edward W. Clark, eds. *Puritans among the Indians: Accounts of Captivity and Redemption, 1676–1724.* Cambridge, Mass., 1981.

Whittier, John Greenleaf. *Complete Poetical Works;* reprint, Bell-PS American Literature Series, 1992.

———. *Legends of New England.* 1831; reprint, Gainesville, Fl., 1965.

Wigglesworth, Michael. *The Day of Doom; or a Poetical Description of the Great and Last Judgement with Other Poems.* Ed. Kenneth B. Murdock. New York, 1929.

Wilkins Freeman, Mary E. *Giles Corey.* 1893.

Winthrop, John. *Winthrop Papers. Vols. 1–5.* Boston, 1929.

Wright, Lawrence. *Remembering Satan.* New York, 1994.

Ziff, Larzer. *Puritanism in America.* New York, 1963.

INDEX